THE LIFESPAN DEVELOPMENT OF WRITING

The Lifespan Development of Writing

CHARLES BAZERMAN
University of California,
Santa Barbara

ARTHUR N. APPLEBEE
University at Albany, State
University of New York

VIRGINIA W. BERNINGER
University of Washington

DEBORAH BRANDT
University of
Wisconsin–Madison

STEVE GRAHAM
Arizona State University

JILL V. JEFFERY
Leiden University

PAUL KEI MATSUDA
Arizona State University

SANDRA MURPHY
University of California, Davis

DEBORAH WELLS ROWE
Vanderbilt University

MARY SCHLEPPEGRELL
University of Michigan

KRISTEN CAMPBELL WILCOX
University at Albany,
State University of New York

National Council of Teachers of English
1111 W. Kenyon Road, Urbana, Illinois 61801-1096

Staff Editor: Bonny Graham
Interior Design: Jenny Jensen Greenleaf
Cover Design: Pat Mayer
Cover Images: monkeybusinessimages/iStock/Thinkstock,
Liderina/iStock/Thinkstock, and sv_sunny/iStock/Thinkstock

NCTE Stock Number: 28169; eStock Number: 28176
ISBN 978-0-8141-2816-9; eISBN 978-0-8141-2817-6

©2018 by the National Council of Teachers of English.

It is the policy of NCTE in its journals and other publications to provide a forum for the open discussion of ideas concerning the content and the teaching of English and the language arts. Publicity accorded to any particular point of view does not imply endorsement by the Executive Committee, the Board of Directors, or the membership at large, except in announcements of policy, where such endorsement is clearly specified.

NCTE provides equal employment opportunity (EEO) to all staff members and applicants for employment without regard to race, color, religion, sex, national origin, age, physical, mental or perceived handicap/disability, sexual orientation including gender identity or expression, ancestry, genetic information, marital status, military status, unfavorable discharge from military service, pregnancy, citizenship status, personal appearance, matriculation or political affiliation, or any other protected status under applicable federal, state, and local laws.

Every effort has been made to provide current URLs and email addresses, but because of the rapidly changing nature of the Web, some sites and addresses may no longer be accessible.

Library of Congress Cataloging-in-Publication Data

A catalog record of this book has been requested.

To the memory of Arthur N. Applebee

CONTENTS

III Final Thoughts

ACKNOWLEDGMENTS

It is far too rare for scholars from different disciplines and methodological camps to have a chance to talk and write together in search of common ground. Specialization, departmentalization, professional demands—all make such experiences impractical and unlikely. Yet the authors of this volume were given such an opportunity. For this opportunity, we must thank Charles Bazerman. In a series of in-person retreats and virtual conferences over the course of four years, we were able to pursue our joint interest in lifespan writing development. Chuck brought this group together, kept us together, challenged us, encouraged us, and in his gentle way never for a minute let us off the hook. We worked hard because we saw him working even harder—making sure everyone had a say, keeping us on task, articulating our commonalities, respecting our differences, and insisting on productive understandings. He also made sure that after each long, intense day of work at the University of California, Santa Barbara campus, we would be refreshed by visits to the beach, tours of the mountains, and convivial and healthful meals. We are grateful to Chuck for his vision, leadership, and selflessness.

The Spencer Foundation provided a conference grant that paid for logistics and staff support for our meetings over several years. We are grateful to Spencer for the trust they put in our interdisciplinary effort and their commitment to improving research and teaching in writing across the lifespan. Thanks also to the Gevirtz Graduate School of Education at UC Santa Barbara for providing meeting space and additional support.

Our work was made easier, livelier, and better organized by the contributions of Ryan Dippre and Erika I-Tremblay, who served at different times as assistants to this project. They each did a remarkably patient job of transcribing hours of recorded discussion and offered timely observations and aid.

Thanks to Kurt Austin, publications director at the National Council of Teachers of English, for his encouragement and attention during the review and production process. We are especially grateful to Kurt for his willingness to work with so many coauthors. Thanks also to the anonymous reviewers who helped us in our final push to completion.

During the course of our work, our incomparable colleague Arthur Applebee fell ill, and he died before this volume was completed. When he was with us, we could count on Arthur to bring the discussions back from the brink of confusion or triviality. He kept our sights on the big picture, and he had a remarkable ability to synthesize and restate our disparate thoughts in a way that would end an impasse and take our work to higher ground. Those familiar with Arthur's scholarship are likely to hear his voice most directly in the second chapter, but his voice continues to resonate in all of us who had the privilege and luck to be in his sphere of influence. Thanks to Arthur's colleagues, Kristen Wilcox and Jill Jeffery, for joining the research team and helping to bring the book to fruition. Thanks also to Judith Langer for her assistance. *The Lifespan Development of Writing* is dedicated to the memory of Arthur Applebee.

I

THE PROJECT

CHAPTER ONE

Introduction

Every school year teachers greet new classes of learners assigned by age or stage or special need. We become experienced with the populations we teach and may learn to imagine the world through their eyes. The kindergartner, the English language learner, the prepubescent, the first-year college student, the adult basic learner: students we come to know well but whose pasts we have had no hand in and whose futures are as yet unmade. Educational researchers too tend to set up their inquiries around particular, recurring populations who drive the questions that the researchers ask and the understandings that they reach. We may readily grant that learning and development are lifelong, yet we stay focused—as we must—on the immediacies of our academic locations.

But the cyclical demands and institutional segmentations that mark the professional work of educators bring drawbacks. For one thing, they may lead to uncertainty as we try to mediate standards, curricula, or assessments that typically carry more abstract or less coherent assumptions about our students than those we bring from experience. Segmentation also may lead to unwarranted certainties about the decisions we do make—certainties that may inadvertently underestimate students' capabilities or misidentify their accomplishments. Likewise, we may be deprived of a full appreciation of our own teaching efforts as those efforts come to fruition—or sputter out—beyond the confines of a semester or an academic year. We also risk forgetting that learners experience their lives as a whole, in and out of school, with a past, a present, and an aspirational future. They take the long view even when we don't. Finally, segmented conditions lead to a professional knowledge base that is fragmented and pocked with unknowns.

Nowhere are these drawbacks more visible than in the realm of writing. Writing emerges early in life but can develop well into adulthood. Writing is a productive and performative capacity, akin to craft. It requires an integration of muscle, mind, knowledge, language(s), tools, and social worlds that are themselves in dynamic change across time. Writing is effortful and remains effortful at all ages. It takes time to learn and time to do. Learners may need to backtrack before moving on. Yet there is currently no adequate accepted theory of writing development that might inform the design of the school curriculum or motivate appropriate assessment practices across the years of formal education. We know too little about how writing develops before, during, and after schooling; too little about how a person's writing experiences relate to each other developmentally across the lifespan. Lifespan perspectives could go a long way in helping teachers and researchers across locations better pull together on behalf of writing literacy. The challenges are acute. Writing is at least as difficult to teach as to do. Yet, compared to reading, writing has been given short shrift in the professional preparation of most teachers, and writing instruction struggles for time in a crowded pedagogical agenda. It does not help that research on writing remains scattered across disciplines and that longitudinal writing studies in any discipline are rare. Still we know that students face a world where writing grows ever more integral to collective practices of learning, working, participating, and interacting with others—as well as to the systems of access and reward associated with each. The challenge is to more wholly democratize a complex, slow-growing human capacity that no longer belongs in the hands of the few.

This book grows out of a four-year collaboration among a small group of writing scholars who emerged from our academic silos to share what we knew and thought about writing and writing development. Housed in university schools of education or departments of English, we were versed in different fields including cognitive psychology, educational psychology, disability studies, and neuroscience; emergent literacy; linguistic theory; second language learning; curriculum and assessment design; teacher professional development; urban education; and composition and rhetoric. The populations we studied included preschool children; elementary and adolescent writers; special needs learners; college students; multilingual writers of various ages; workplace writers; scientific and scholarly authors; and teachers of writing. We were diverse by training, method, philosophy, and focus. Some built models; some conducted ethnographies; some employed discourse analysis; some did meta-analyses. Some focused primarily on instruction, others on theory building, or policy, or assessment, or educational equity, or teacher professional development. Our classroom teaching backgrounds were equally varied. While no doubt major perspectives were not represented in our team and in the book, we tried to be as inclusive as we could. At several points we asked ourselves whether an area or perspective were missing, and as we spotted gaps we added people to the group to broaden our vision. The brief biographies of the authors in the back matter of this book indicate the range of our experiences and interests. Yet, despite our many differences, we shared curiosity about the phenomenon of writing in its many forms and functions and a belief, strengthened by this collaboration, that multitheoretical, multidisciplinary, and multiage perspectives can enrich our work and the work of others.

Our goals were ambitious. Could we build a description of writing development that was realistic and rich, useful to researchers, teachers, and policymakers, and based on principles broad enough to capture understandings across fields, populations, and perspectives? Might these principles serve as heuristics that could be returned to different age groups or contexts in order to stimulate future research and help instructors see better the developmental possibilities alive in their classrooms? We knew these principles would be provisional. We knew they would not be prescriptive. But we hoped to show how taking long views on writing development—including recognizing the long investments it requires—could strengthen curriculum, teaching, assessment, research, and policy.

It turns out there was much we could indeed agree on, and the points of agreement became the substance of the collaboratively authored framing chapters (Parts I and III). Yet we still had our distinctive views and ways of proceeding, though grown and modified by the intense negotiations of our meetings. These distinctive views are embodied in the separately authored chapters of Part II.

We ultimately focused on eight principles. They appear in Chapter 2. However, reaching consensus on those principles involved dialogue and debate that often took us to the limits of our knowledge and did not always end in resolution. As will be elaborated below, we grappled from beginning to end with the freighted nature of our key terms, trying to differentiate *development* from norms or idealizations that too often mask, mischaracterize, or punish human variation. *Writing*, too, we recognized, manifests itself only through particular acts of language and embodied effort; in particular practices, genres, contexts, and occasions; and as part of shifting relationships with other systems of communication and meaning making. In fact, it was in the group's collaborative search for a definition of *writing development* that our disciplinary differences came most clearly to the fore. These differences did not necessarily dictate the particular definitions that each of us sought. Rather, more subtly, they affected where each of us chose to begin the search. We found ourselves gazing in different directions. It did not take long to realize, however, that these differences should not be resolved away. Rather they served as object lessons in the complexity of this task. Writing development takes its character from many sources; happens in many planes of existence; and registers in many inward and outward forms. Our four years of dialogue and debate taught us that the more places and ways one can look for writing development, the more fully it might be seen.

In the following sections of this chapter, then, we provide a kind of backstory to the book that follows, elaborating on key challenges, interchanges, and decision points that took place in three multiday retreats held at the University of California, Santa Barbara between 2013 and 2016 and in several video conferences interspersed throughout that time. Over that time we also wrote informally and formally, alone and in teams, and sometimes in response to one another. Our aim throughout was to build a capacity for developmental thinking inclusive of multiple perspectives.

Defining Terms: What Do We Mean by Development?

It was important throughout our deliberations to keep our working definitions flexible, accommodating, and critical, and this was especially true for the central term *development*. We generally agreed on associating development with a reorganization or realignment of previous experience that registers through writing or in a changed relationship to writing. We resisted strongly teleological or linear conceptions of writing development and debated the extent to which such development requires intentionality or self-perception. We worried about an ability to distinguish between self-actualized development and resignation to externally imposed expectations. We sought to locate development not merely in an achievement of change but also in actions or efforts toward change. Some argued for particular thresholds, for instance reserving for development forms of growth that can be carried into new contexts or that increase the range of resources one can call upon going forward. Still others advocated for less individualistic and more ecological criteria, taking a view of development as a mutual achievement between self and others that is sustained in shared contexts. We all recognized that writing development occurred in inextricable relationship to other forms of development—biological, cognitive, social, cultural, historical, technological—making development dynamic and not once and for all. As with so much of our deliberation, our aim in sharing these contested definitions was not to wrestle one another into agreement. Rather it was a means for remaining accountable to one another's definitions, as best we could, as the work proceeded.

Writing Development: Where and How to Look?

Several basic questions wove themselves through our deliberations. What drives writing development? What is developing and how? Where can evidence of writing development be detected? Given the multiple disciplinary and methodological perspectives we brought to the discussion, it was not surprising that we had different starting points for addressing these questions, although these starting points sometimes cut across, overlapped with, and combined different disciplinary and theoretical orientations. When differences in emphasis arose, they did not necessarily result in disagreement or contention; rather they led to a sharper sense of the multiple dimensions along which writing develops, its multiple sources, and the multiple ways and places it can manifest itself. In other words, we came to treat our different approaches to this inquiry not only as a potential strength in theory building but as a reminder of the scope and complexity of writing development itself.

Look to the embodied act of writing. For some of us, questions of writing development began with a close-in focus on the experience of composing. Understand what a writer must do mentally to carry off an act of writing and you will find hot spots for development. Through this perspective, the focus is on inner resources (skills, knowledge, experience) that an individual gathers and individuates over time to engage in productive literacy. Writing development is associated with training of the mind for writing, including cultivating dispositions and cognitive strategies for handling the challenging work it requires. The brain as a developing organ matters to an embodied perspective on writing. A maturing brain can support automaticity, extended attention, complexity, and abstraction in handling the demands of writing. At the same time, injuries to the brain or developmental neural irregularities due to genetic influences may interfere with writing and writing development. A focus on embodiment foregrounds individuals' own contributions to their writing development, as each new writing experience potentially can be used to confirm, deepen, reorganize, discard, or refine strategies for writing going forward. From this perspective, development will manifest itself as changes in acts of writing, individual or collaborative. It will be seen in increasing self-regulation of writing processes and expanding understanding of what a writing act entails, as well as in levels of motivation to persist.

Look to the medium of written language(s). Language is the medium through which writers make meaning for themselves and others. So exploring how language and language development matter to writing and writing development was an important starting point for some project members. From this perspective the focus is on processes by which developing writers gain access to and control over a range of linguistic resources that their surrounding societies have developed for carrying out written meaning making. Appropriating these socially shared textual resources requires figuring out how they are related to particular contexts of use and communities of practice, including academic disciplines. It requires figuring out how textual language works to address the separation in time and distance between writers and their readers and the ways that genres, vocabularies, and grammatical constructions in particular languages are geared for carrying out the sometimes specialized work of written communication in various domains. From this perspective, development can be detected in written texts. Development will register as changes in textual features over time, as writers gather and creatively employ more options for written meaning making and learn to take them into an expanding number of contexts. When approached analytically from a developmental perspective, written texts can be a window into relationships between language growth and writing growth.

Look to contexts of participation. For some of us, defining writing development began by gazing outward toward the social worlds of writers and the ways writing works as a medium of social participation in those worlds. From this perspective writing and its development appear as social achievements that are made and sustained through human relationships. Other people—parents, caregivers, teachers, siblings, friends, colleagues, interested readers—become important figures from this perspective as they serve as co-participants in social practices that involve writing. Writers' development at any age or stage proceeds through opportunities to engage with responsive others who bestow meaning and value on their efforts. From this angle, development appears as collaborative and mutual. Local contexts are the hot spots for development as they manifest organized practices through which the activity of writing takes its meanings. This perspective illuminates how cultural and ideological variation, group identities, and socioeconomic and political forces all bear on the human experience of writing development. Development from this angle will be detected in the changing ways by which a person participates with others in writing environments and events—new and recurring—across the life course. This perspective brings a deeply relational approach to understandings of writing development.

Look to the historical and cultural catalysts of writing development. To the question of what drives writing development, some of us looked first to the large-scale forces that pull people into the technologies of writing at different times and places. Here the gaze turns toward the historical and cultural processes as well as the institutional and material infrastructures that generate writing literacy and condition its character. These include tools, technologies, and circulatory systems that stimulate and regulate writing across local contexts. If individual writers change themselves from within, catalysts of writing development change them from without. This perspective brings emphasis to the contingency of writing development, how it is not a universal, invariable, natural, or inevitable process. The cultural, political, and economic development of writing as a technology has its own history that precedes and will succeed individuals in time. Where, when, and how one enters that stream of history matters to developmental experience and outcomes. The course of a generation's literacy development can be changed, sometimes radically, by innovations or disruptions—as the arrival of digital media can attest. The educational system to which one is exposed also is a major catalyst and conditioner of writing development. As a technology for teaching and learning, school curriculum sets horizons and expectations that will have formative bearing. From this perspective, writing development registers as a potentiality of time, place, and position.

Out of the pluralistic backgrounds we brought to the project we were able to conceptualize multiple dimensions of writing development. Writing is an embodied process of mental assertion *and* a language act *and* a participatory event with others in context *and* an encounter with cultural-historical potentials of writing as a technology. These dimensions interact with one another, all from within the biosocial life of the writer. Writing requires attention to and orchestration of these multiple dimensions. Yet they may be in different discrete states of development at any age or stage of the life course. Further, by choice or necessity, individual writers will give these dimensions more or less conscious attention during a particular writing event.

Even as we conceptualized multiple dimensions of development we realized how much more needs to be understood about their interactions across the lifespan. How might growth in one dimension pull along another? How might struggles in one dimension deter or spur growth in others? How do achieved integrations of these developmental dimensions fare when writers enter a new context or encounter a new demand or seek to deepen or expand their repertoires of writing skills? What travels, what falls away, and why? How do life transitions (biological and social) relate to the experience of writing development? What happens to writing development in the migration to a different language environment or when society-wide changes scramble the relationship of writing to other systems of communication and meaning making? Is it possible to identify developmental processes that remain relevant across contexts and ages? While chapters to come offer partial answers to some of these questions, we confronted limitations in our knowledge at nearly every turn in our deliberations. We were confronted with the fact that research on lifespan writing development is itself underdeveloped, even as it is key to arriving at more insightful approaches to theory, policy, pedagogy, and assessment.

Problems of Norms and Normativity

Throughout our discussions, we struggled with questions of norms and normativity. Social norms exert a strong influence on writing and writing development. In literacy-reliant societies, expectations for writing accompany the roles that people play across the life course (as students, breadwinners, etc.). The need and desire to participate with others, make contributions, build identity, succeed in school, earn a living, and seek knowledge, pleasure, or expression—all of these can pull people toward writing and build up their experiences with it over time. Social norms also figure prominently in educational curricula, standards, and assessments, all of which carry assumptions about students' maturity, experience, and proficiency by grade level. Indeed, social norms are expressed in the very conventions of written language itself as those conventions embody what is expected or demanded of textual communication in particular contexts or on particular occasions.

But it is important to remember that norms are not synonymous with what is normal in writing development. At best, norms are incomplete descriptions of development. As abstract milestones, they do not often account for the heterogeneous processes and timing by which writers reach them. They often obscure aspects of writing development (biological, linguistic, intellectual, social) that, as we said, are in shifting configurations with one another over the course of a writing life, making a developmental journey fitful and uneven but no less normal. Most troublesome, norms are laden with values and assumptions that overlook the cultural and linguistic differences, variations in circumstances, and social inequities that characterize life as people experience it. In the unexamined gap between what is ideal and what is real, between what is expected and what is enabled, it is possible for deficit thinking to creep in. It is also possible to develop models of writing development with glaring blind spots.

Problems of norms and normativity arose at several points in our work, for instance, in discussions of monolingual and multilingual writing development. In most situations, children are exposed to reading and writing after the fundamental functions of language capacity have been developed through talk. Monolinguals learn to speak and write in the same language, and some multilingual students who start developing their second or third language early in their lives will have somewhat similar experiences. The latter individuals may experience speech delay or a "silent period" in their first language acquisition but will soon have more robust and well-developed language both in L1 and L2 that can be taken into encounters with literacy. However, when individuals acquire a second language for the first time in adolescence or adulthood, this sequence is not in place. L2 language and literacy will be developing simultaneously. Limited language resources may restrict what can be expressed and how writing can be facilitated. In some cases, in fact, literacy experiences will scaffold oral language development. As another example, congenitally deaf learners will have a different path to written literacy than hearing learners, as there is no written version of sign language. Deaf learners have to learn to write in the spoken languages of their contexts and so they begin writing in an L2. These cases illustrate that paths to writing development defy generalizations and might be interrupted and facilitated in different ways.

Balancing the powerful pull of social norms against the dangers of normativity remained a recurring tension in our work. It ultimately turned us away from attempting a general, typified, age- or stage-based account of writing development across the lifespan. Age and life stage do matter to the experience of writing development—as later chapters will explore. But how they matter will be a function of their relationship to many other factors.

Cross Talk

We spent large portions of our meeting time together sharing research from our multiple fields and focal populations. These listening sessions helped to sensitize us to a longer view of writing development as well as to a more inclusive view of the world of writing research. We swapped articles and papers, wrote research summaries, asked one another questions, traded citations, argued and quibbled at times, and developed lists of convergence points. Sometimes we found ourselves translating findings or perspectives from one area into another as a way to forge new connections. We sought to treat writing and development in ways that related to all the populations with which we were collectively familiar. If one of us offered a too-narrow characterization or assertion, it was identified and reworked. We searched for principles of writing development that, while perhaps associated with a particular research base or methodology, held relevance and heuristic value across populations, contexts, and theoretical orientations. This search required all of us to revisit the knowledge bases of our particular disciplines through the perspectives of our colleagues (as we were coming to understand them) either to identify candidate concepts for the group to consider or to fact-check someone else's candidate concept against the scholarship we knew best.

The aim in this endeavor was not to downplay our differences but to identify concepts robust enough to address them. The overall aim was to stimulate fuller developmental vision.

Two examples will illustrate this process. As Chapter 2 elaborates, *variability* is a central feature of writing development. Variability is often associated with individual differences in personalities, dispositions, genetic makeup, or life experiences—differences that make no two students, no two writers, no two texts exactly the same. This kind of individual variability is well observed (if not always well accommodated) in classrooms. But the term also has salience from linguistic and sociocultural perspectives as variability in writing development relates to more macro, structural considerations, including the diverse social worlds people inhabit, their identities and positions in those worlds, and the range of languages and dialects they embrace. Further, variability can be an outcome of unequal flows of power and access and differential treatment that condition experience with literacy in and out of classrooms. Approaching variabilities in writing development from such a multidimensional perspective forces deeper understandings of their origins and better ways to sort them out. *Variability* will have developmental significance but that significance will deserve further analysis. Is it the kind that dissipates under conditions of fair and equal instruction? Is it the kind that flourishes under conditions of fair and equal instruction? After a sometimes heated debate on the topic, we collected into one principle the many meanings of *variability*— including its value and validity in a heterogeneous society and its more disabling association with differential or discriminatory treatment. We made this decision with the hope of stimulating more nuanced and critical attention to variability in writing development where it occurs.

As another example, we took up an insight from cognitive science that writing develops through the borrowing and redirection of general cognitive processes for the more specific demands of writing. General capacities of perception or planning, for instance, are "hijacked" into writing processes and, with experience, become more elaborated and specified as writing-based skills. During this discussion, we noticed that a move from general to specific is a pattern that also shows up in textual representations by children, as initially they may use only a mark to stand for entire narratives or messages (and may even use the same mark on another occasion to stand for different ones). Later they will elaborate mark making as they specify meanings more discursively. Likewise, the move from the general to the specific has been noted in the processes by which college students are initiated into disciplinary writing practices. Schematic versions of arguing or knowledge making become increasingly elaborated and specialized as students become more socialized into their fields and can knowledgably take on more aspects of the work. This pattern of general to specific is an example of the kind of cross-cutting developmental process for which we searched and sought to raise up for further exploration: Whether in cognitive processes, texts, or social practices, in any language and at any age or stage, where we can see the general being made into the more specific, where we can observe "hijacking" being attempted, development, we think, will be close by.

We offer these brief examples (developed further in Chapter 2) to demonstrate how a diverse group of scholars proceeded to identify principles of writing development drawn from specific research bases but with broad generative potential. In the chapter that follows, eight principles are developed, focusing on the research bases from which they originated (i.e., cognitive psychology, linguistics, sociocultural ethnography) but pulling them across populations and contexts as much as possible. Then we offer individual chapters, some coauthored with additional scholars, that develop one or more of these principles using the research bases that we know best. In the final two individual chapters, Steve Graham demonstrates how one scholar can stretch beyond his research base to develop a more inclusive theoretical orientation to writing and writing development, and Charles Bazerman envisions a future agenda for longitudinal writing studies.

For all of our differences in this cross-disciplinary experiment, certain driving commonalities prevailed. Chief among them was the certainty that writing develops through writing. Guided opportunities for writing can and should begin early in life and, with continual relevance and engagement, development of productive literacy will continue throughout a lifetime. We also all recognize that many of the developmental principles that we offer here pose extreme challenges to current educational policy and practice. The complexity of writing development, its slow growth, its context sensitivity and variability, its interanimation with other processes of human development, and its susceptibility to fast-moving technological and communicative change all defy many of the usual routines by which teaching, learning, and assessment are organized. But for writing to take its rightful and needed position in the educational experience, we all must confront and even potentially relish these challenges.

Chapter Overview

Chapter 2 presents a synthesized framework for understanding writing development across the lifespan. The framework is a culmination of four years of interaction among the authors of this book. The chapter begins by pointing out how studies on writing development have in recent decades grown in diversity and depth but remain fragmented along lines of theory, method, and age ranges or populations studied. We emphasize that meaningful, competent writing performances that meet the demands of the moment rely on many kinds of well-practiced and deeply understood capacities working together; however, these capacities can vary in their realization and developmental trajectories from one individual to another. Without an integrated framework to understand lifespan development of writing abilities in its variation, high-stakes decisions about curriculum, instruction, and assessment are often made in unsystematic ways that may fail to support the development they are intended to facilitate; further, research may not consider the range of issues at stake in studying writing in any particular moment. Based on research drawn from different disciplinary perspectives, the chapter proposes eight principles upon which an account of writing development consistent with research findings could be founded. These principles are proposed as a basis for further lines of inquiry into how writing develops across the lifespan.

Chapter 3 explores the beginnings of writing in early childhood. Using longitudinal and cross-sectional data from 2½- to 6-year-olds, Deborah Rowe re-examines the common portrayal of early writing development as progress toward convention, finding children's writing marked as much by variability as by ordered progress. She proposes that early childhood writing might be more profitably conceptualized as overlapping waves of development in which children simultaneously add more advanced writing strategies to their repertoires, reduce the use of less sophisticated ones, and simultaneously draw on both to participate as writers. The chapter discusses ways that our developmental storylines affect assessment and instruction and argues against the use of single age-related norms to assess young children's writing progress.

In Chapter 4, Mary Schleppegrell and Frances Christie describe a linguistic trajectory of writing development across the years of schooling, drawing on research on the writing development of first and second language writers. Using theory and constructs from systemic functional linguistics, they illustrate how a meaning-oriented perspective can be used to track growth in writing across genres and disciplines. The authors connect this functional description to findings of writing research from other traditions and draw implications for assessment and pedagogy.

In Chapter 5, Virginia W. Berninger, Kira Geselowitz, and Peter Wallis explore how students' definitions of writing change across early childhood, middle childhood, and early adolescence. Comparisons from grade 1 to grade 5 or from grade 3 to grade 7 show an early focus on transcription, writing tools, and medium to later focus on meaning making, translation across multiple levels of language, communication with others, multiple cognitive processes, and integration of multiple writing components. These perspectives are then compared to those of writing researchers and students in grades 4 to 9 with persisting writing disabilities to identify commonalities and contrasts. Overall, the findings are consistent with the overall theme of this book that the complexities of writing development at target times and across the lifespan are best understood from multiple perspectives.

In Chapter 6, Kristen Wilcox and Jill Jeffery highlight the role of agency in adolescents' writing development. They draw upon the National Study of Writing Instruction to illustrate through a diverse array of adolescents' own voices how they experience the affordances and constraints for the development of their writing in their secondary school English, mathematics, science, and social studies classes. Wilcox and Jeffery assert that middle and high school teachers play a crucial role in inviting adolescents who come to school with a variety of prior writing experiences and language backgrounds to see writing as a way to be part of important and increasingly complex disciplinary conversations.

In Chapter 7, Sandra Murphy and Mary Ann Smith challenge the idea of a uniform or standardized curriculum. They argue instead that highly skilled teachers are best positioned to intentionally and purposefully fashion a curriculum that takes their students into account. Drawing on data collected during their work with exemplary teachers of writing, Murphy and Smith illustrate how knowledgeable teachers adapt curricula to address their students' individual strengths, needs, abilities, and interests.

In Chapter 8, Deborah Brandt draws on the interdisciplinary field of life-course human development to explore sources of diversity, stability, and unevenness in the writing development of working adults. The chapter is based on a qualitative analysis of in-depth interviews conducted between 2005 and 2012 with a diverse, multiaged group of sixty adults whose occupations engage them in daily writing at work. As individuals discussed the writing they do, how they learned to do it, and what effect it has on them and others, they illuminated contingent, sometimes fragile relationships between their personal efforts at writing development and their working conditions over time. The chapter concludes by arguing for the generative role that the life-course perspective can play in writing studies and its analytic relevance in other contexts, including schools.

In Chapter 9, Steve Graham presents a writer(s)-within-community model that situates writing within the context of multiple writing communities. It is proposed that the writing conducted within a specific writing community is driven, shaped, and constrained by the characteristics of said community and the cognitive resources and dispositions of the members of the community involved in the writing task. Graham further specifies factors that shape the development of the writing community as well as the development of individual writers. This model of writing encompasses both social contextual and cognitive motivational views of writing.

In Chapter 10, Charles Bazerman proposes, as a thought experiment, considerations that would go into designing a true longitudinal study of writing across the lifespan, drawing on principles and practices of longitudinal studies in other domains. Such a study would need to collect rich multidimensional data including linguistic, textual, social, interactional, psychological, economic, cultural, and even neurological data in order to look at all dimensions potentially relevant to writing development. Despite the difficulties, commitments, and massive resources associated with such a study, thinking through its designs can give guidance and perspective to less ambitious and more practicable studies.

A final collaborative chapter sums up themes and issues of writing development to be investigated in future research, in particular the multiple interacting developmental dimensions of writing, how they may be related to other aspects of development, and how they emerge under varying life conditions and participations to form individualized trajectories for each developing writer. We then draw out the implications of this complex and variable view of writing for policy.

CHAPTER TWO

Toward an Understanding of Writing Development across the Lifespan

Writing is an integral part of schooling, work, and social life (National Commission on Writing, 2003, 2004, 2005, 2006). Full participation in contemporary society calls for learning to communicate in writing for work, personal life, and citizenship. Through writing, people gain voice, express their interests, and act within the literate world and its institutions. Being able to write in ways expected in different disciplinary contexts is now recognized as an integral part of subject-matter learning for children in schools (Common Core State Standards Initiative, 2010). In addition, as writing continues to evolve as a technology and resource in our society, students need to learn to participate in new writing practices and new social situations made possible by emerging technologies (Brandt, 2015; Selfe & Hawisher, 2004). However, children come to school with varied life experiences that position them in different ways as they learn to engage in disciplinary literacies and use new technologies. For these reasons, we need a better understanding of how to support writing development. This calls for a description of writing development that is realistic and rich, based on broad principles, and useful to researchers, teachers, and policymakers. In developing such a description, we need to recognize the roles of both early and continuing life experiences and of individual variation.

Despite extensive research in recent decades on many aspects of writing and writing instruction at different ages and in different situations, now aggregated in several handbooks (e.g., Bazerman, 2008; MacArthur, Graham, & Fitzgerald, 2006; Smagorinsky, 2006; Beard, Myhill, Riley, & Nystrand, 2009; Leki, 2010), we still lack a coherent framework for understanding the complexities of writing development, curriculum design, and assessment over the lifespan. Because we lack an integrated framework, high-stakes decisions about curriculum, instruction, and assessment are often made in unsystematic ways that may fail to support the development they are intended to facilitate. Current expectations and practices may also limit conceptions about what learners can accomplish in writing at different ages, whether writing is done in school settings or out. While attempts to make writing development appear regular and predictable may reflect a desire to make assessment easier and instruction better regulated, the cost is a mismeasure of student writing skill and instruction that stunts rather than supports writing growth.

The statement presented here was collaboratively written by a group of scholars who came together to address the need for a vision of writing development that incorporates its complexities and many dimensions, and that accounts for the individuality of trajectories that can lead to distinctive voices and expressions. We, as the participants in this panel, treat writing as a form of inscribed meaning making that expands the potential for verbal communication and expression across time and distance. Writing develops as an ongoing struggle to control and integrate meanings that are socially relevant and individually generated through the technologies of writing and its practices in the context of one's lifeworld. Development entails change across time, as part of growing up and growing older biologically, cognitively, linguistically, and socially. Change occurs with experience with writing, within evolving technologies, language, genres, social uses, and educational expectations. Development will register as a growing potential to use writing in a broadening array of significant situations and to reap its benefits and rewards.

Articulating a model of development requires us to become more explicit about all the dimensions of writing development, and therefore all the areas in which experience, knowledge, and motivation for writing must develop. Below we articulate eight principles that we agree on and that can inform a model of development.

1. Writing can develop across the lifespan as part of changing contexts.

Each individual's lived history influences writing development from earliest childhood through adulthood in the context of accumulating yet changing forms of engagement in families, communities, schools, and workplaces (Brandt, 2001), in different language communities and in multiple languages (Leki, Cumming, & Silva, 2008). The writing children encounter in their early years occurs within the communicative cultures of family and community. As young writers develop, their social worlds expand and so do the worlds in which their writing occurs. The earliest observations of others' writing from which the child may develop concepts of writing as a desirable and purposive activity often occur at home or in other intimate settings, through media made available in those local settings, or through adult-supervised forays into local social worlds. Early writing activities are likely to be in play settings, and early audiences are likely to be family, teachers, friends, or other community members who are predisposed to attribute meaning and intent to texts (Dyson, 1997, 2013; Heath, 1983; Moll, Amanti, Neff, & Gonzalez, 1992; Valdés, 1996).

At the most basic level, beginning writers learn that marks on the page can be intentional, and can represent meanings they or others wish to record. They learn how print can mediate their own activities and those of others in the current time and place as well as in future times and distant places. With experience, writers form understandings about the processes used to record written messages, including the ways writing is linked to their spoken language(s). Writers also form understandings of the purposes for which writing is used in different social situations, learning that social purposes shape writing forms and content and are expressed in an evolving set of written genres.

For those children who enter formal schooling, the institutional atmosphere, the teacher as primary audience, and the expectations for performance often become a primary context for writing development. As schooling continues, depending on the writing curriculum, socially diminished environments of examination by distant examiners may become influential social contexts for writing development, constraining more local and more engaging writing activities. At the same time, the young writer may develop expanding writing experiences within the family, special interests, or the community. Each of these experiences provides specialized pathways for engaging with and practicing new genres, for confronting different kinds of cognitive, linguistic, motivational, and social demands, and for developing new forms of communicative relationships. For some writers, as their adolescent and adult social worlds expand into new professional, commercial, civic, and other affiliational contexts, so do the possibilities and exigencies for their writing development.

Through participating in varied social activities through writing, writers may develop multiple voices and identities that enable further participation in more specialized contexts (Compton-Lilly, 2014). Writing makes the writer visible within a group attentive to his or her texts, giving the writer an identity as part of the group, but also as an individual within the group, making a particular contribution from a particular standpoint (Royster, 2000). Effective writing makes what one wants to communicate visible, meaningful, and consequential to audiences, potentially affecting what happens within social groups and organizations and the actions they may take. In this way effective writing influences social processes. But social processes also influence writing development (Herrington & Curtis, 2000). As social groups change through the lifespan, the roles and identities the writer takes on through writing develop, along with the accompanying skills and stances. Writing to be perceived as a good student or as a budding intellectual or as a popular peer-group member in high school may be superseded by roles as creative writer, emerging professional, or political activist.

While schooling often highlights individual authorship and responsibility as part of the monitoring of each student's growth, even if collaborative projects are part of the pedagogy, once graduates enter professional or corporate worlds, writers' identity can become subsumed or even made anonymous within the groups' work. But even without specific authorial attribution, writers can reflexively come to understand their identities and roles by looking at what they have written, what they have contributed to group goals, and how others have responded to or been influenced by their contribution. Writers can then use that knowledge to guide their further participation in the group, to build even stronger and more influential identities. Even in corporate settings where texts are not necessarily identified as coming from a particular author or group, still the perception of the contribution of each participant by co-workers and supervisors is important for the writer's future opportunities (Beaufort, 1999, 2007; Spinuzzi, 2008).

The growing body of texts that becomes part of each social grouping's resources and understandings forms the context of each new piece of writing, whether these are sacred texts and commentaries within religious communities, the research literature in an academic discipline, the regulations of a government agency, or the records of a school (Bazerman, 1999, 2013). These texts become part of an ongoing discussion, establishing an immediate rhetorical situation that any new piece of writing must address in order to influence the group's attitudes and actions. As writing develops within higher education and then career, the skills of intertextual representation and position become more intricate and more specialized by domain (Haas & Flower, 1988).

2. Writing development is complex because writing is complex.

When we appreciate all the "moving parts" that must be activated and orchestrated during acts of writing, we can understand why writing development is such a complex and multidimensional process. These moving parts include brains, muscles, intentions, language, and a range of intersubjective understandings, social coordinations, and cultural practices that must be integrated into an ongoing, meaning-making whole. Written texts embody the writer's goals and meanings in choices of language and other representational modalities. Readers, in turn, experience and make sense of a piece of writing through their own interpretive processes, filtered through their own knowledge, skills, dispositions, and purposes. Developing writers learn to anticipate and speak to the readers' interpretive processes in order to evoke the meanings they wish to communicate and the effects they wish to have. Over time developing writers build up a repertoire of language knowledge and resources as well as other representational tools, and use those resources intentionally to achieve personal, social, or institutional ends, within specific situations and in response to circumstances. Each act of writing, whether individual or collaborative, is a unique performance, creating locally relevant meanings fitting the situation to achieve the writer's needs and purposes at an intersection of all these dimensions. This means that writing and learning to write are no simple things.

Writing is a complex achievement that involves brains interacting with social and physical environments (Berninger & Chanquoy, 2012). Writing develops as a result of nature-nurture interactions; brains do not cause writing development independent of environmental input, which in turn changes brain processing during writing. Multiple brain systems support writing development. These include (a) cognition and memory (short-term, working, and long-term); (b) multileveled language (subword, word, syntax, and text); (c) sensory and motor (eye, ear, hand, and mouth) capacities; (d) social, emotional, and motivational factors; and (f) attention and executive functions. These systems are engaged in different ways depending on the task at hand and the writer's individual and developmental differences; writing develops easily when the systems work together in concert, but when they do not writers may benefit from individually tailored, developmentally appropriate instruction (Berninger, 2015). Brain research is beginning to generate findings that are educationally relevant to writing instruction across development. For a recent review of brain research in early childhood, middle childhood, and adolescence, and instructionally relevant lessons from brain research, see James, Jao, and Berninger (2016).

Writing occurs in relation to experiences writers may think about and report on, whether they are part of daily life or the result of specialized investigations. Much of this work occurs in the mind of the writer, drawing on prior experiences with texts and meaning making, social relations, and communicative interaction, as well as on knowledge of the world, the topic, the purposes for writing, the different ways text can be structured, strategies and processes for regulating the writing process (including planning, monitoring, evaluating, and revising), and various motivational dispositions and skills for translating and transcribing ideas into text. Often this mental work occurs in interaction with other people, with technologies used in composition, and with other texts seen as relevant to the current situation.

Written interactions communicate information, coordinate actions, share experiences and feelings, and form and enact relationships, though often at a temporal and spatial distance that makes it difficult to envision the people one is communicating with. The writer must understand, address, and align the reader to a common communicative situation. Because the social circumstances and social exigencies are less immediately visible in writing, the developing writer must understand them more fully in order to communicate appropriately and effectively. Using socially recognizable forms associated with particular social relationships and actions (that is, genres) helps orient both reader and writer to shared understandings and helps them make sense of the communication. Thus a developing writer needs not only to be familiar with a range of genres, but also must understand the associated social situations and goals; even more, the writer needs to make the genre relevantly meet specific needs in specific circumstances in a unique individual communication. Through this process writers are constantly changing genres, even calling on multiple genres to bring understandings of the interaction and communication to bear. These complex uses of genres require even greater understanding of them and their social structuring of events and purposes.

Writing is a complex semiotic achievement. While discussions of writing sometimes focus narrowly on print processes, writing almost always involves other modes of meaning making as well. Young writers often transgress boundaries between writing and other sign systems in unconventional ways, creating written texts that weave together print, talk, drama, gesture, art, and handling of objects. While in the past, the movement to print-only products was typically seen as a sign of increasing sophistication in writing (despite many examples of works that effectively mixed words and art), digital texts make more evident the potential of multimodality.

Writing is a culturally mediated achievement (Vygotsky, 1978, 1989), reflecting the interwoven effects of history, people, linguistic resources, and material contexts. Writing skill is often treated as adhering solely (and stably) in the individual and the performance of writing is often treated as emanating solely from the individual. But such a view obscures the vital and lively constitutive power that contexts play in conditioning, stabilizing, amplifying, or interfering with individual writing efforts. In actuality, writing is dynamic, a synergistic process engaging self and world.

To acknowledge writing as dynamic and distributed is to remember that it is a relational and cooperative achievement, constituted and sustained through inner and outer resources that depend on one another for success. The writing developments of the people born before us circulate in the form of tools, practices, artifacts, conventions, and dissemination systems—as what Cole (1998, p. 129) might call "partial solutions to frequently encountered problems," there for appropriation, exploration, and innovation by new generations. As a cultural production, writing is a shared need and responsibility carried by a society and its members. Individual writing development will always bear the marks of larger arrangements by which the powers of writing are being harnessed as economic, political, and cultural assets (Duffy, 2007; Lorimer Leonard, 2013; Pritchard, 2016). Especially now, as writing is being pulled into economic productivity and global competition and as writing has become a predominant form of labor, many people's writing development takes shape as an aspect of work, as a byproduct of the development of goods and services (Brandt, 2001, 2015).

Writing and writing development emerge, then, within the material, political, and social worlds that nurture, actualize, and exploit them. This dependency is what can make writing development fragile and contingent, linking it to patterns of educational, economic, and political inequality. Where a society is not cooperative with and generous toward a learner, development will be made more difficult.

3. Writing development is variable; there is no single path and no single endpoint.

Writing development is variable within all age cohorts, children through adults. Rather than following a lockstep series of stages in which one writing accomplishment gives way to the next, more sophisticated one, writers simultaneously use more and less sophisticated writing strategies as they respond to the needs of the task of the moment. This is due to the variability people experience in the social worlds they engage with, their different experiences of language development, the unequal distribution of power and status in society, and individual differences (Sternglass, 1997).

Variability in writing development arises in part from variability in our social worlds. People write in order to participate in socially organized activities in which they use literacy to assert their presence, needs, desires, or interests. Writers communicate with intimates at a distance, share stories, create aesthetic texts for their own pleasure, keep business records of production and sales, enter into contractual agreements, fulfill accountability obligations for government bureaucracies, argue for political ideals and actions, or engage in scientific inquiry (Dias, Freedman, Medway, & Paré, 1999; Dias & Paré, 2000). Even writing directed toward oneself, whether a shopping list or personal journal, uses social tools of communication. While in contemporary society there are some professions or social roles, such as creative writers or journalists, that are associated more prominently with writing, demands and opportunities for writing are both varied and widely distributed. Developmental trajectories for learning writing purposes, forms, and strategies are shaped by locally valued forms of writing and the variety of occasions for their use in the writer's social worlds. People are socially positioned in different ways to engage in these varied practices, contributing to varied trajectories of writing development (Beaufort, 1999).

The languages and language varieties used in social life across and within communities also vary. Some children grow up in households where they speak the same language and dialect used in schooling in the region, and their home language and literacy practices may enable them to move seamlessly into the literacy practices of the school. However, many children speak dialects or languages that are not used for writing in school contexts, requiring that they learn a new language or language variety as they learn to write. In addition, they may engage in home and community literacy practices that are not made relevant by the school.

Because of the complex linguistic situations in many regions, the mobility of learners across linguistic borders, and the globalization of professional communication, learning to write at all levels through higher education and professional practice may be infused with the complexities, challenges, and advantages of multilingualism and multiliteracy. Bilingual, bidialectal, and multilingual learners bring a wider range of linguistic resources to the development of writing ability, and these resources can be recruited to support their writing development in a new language or variety. Experiences in multiple languages engender a more self-conscious awareness of language that can support a reflective attitude toward language and foster thoughtful writing choices. School systems may also foster the advantages of bidialectalism and bilingualism in the development of writing.

However, features of writing that present the writer's linguistic, ethnic, national, gender, and socioeconomic backgrounds can affect the writer's standing in literate communities. For some readers, these differences expressed through writing are recognized as points of connection, while for other readers, the same set of differences is alienating or stigmatizing. Writer identities are constructed in both personal writing genres and in less personal genres, such as manuscripts for academic journals. When features that construe identities are met with negative responses, writers are often pressed into difficult choices in their use of language resources that in turn may affect their standing in the various communities they belong to (Matsuda & Tardy, 2007; Tardy & Matsuda, 2009).

Variation in social processes and linguistic development results in differences in access to statuses and roles, in the authority of one's voice, and in the resources one has to participate, as these are often unequally distributed. Power to present one's interests, views, and knowledge through writing to various social groups depends on one's standing within the group. For example, a writer must hold an official position or be formally invited to enter into a bureaucracy's policy discussion. Different participants will have different areas of credibility and will have different influences on the outcome. Wealth, credentials, and affiliations also influence the authority and range of one's credible statements, depending on attitudes in the ambient culture and institutions. Opportunities to have written voice in consequential social groups can motivate and provide direction for writing development, and ongoing success at being heard recursively provides further motivation. Inversely, the lack of consequential opportunity to be heard can dampen motivation and developmental processes. Poverty and other marginalizing social factors, although they may be overcome by individuals, may limit resources and developmental opportunities as well as create stigmatizing social attributions that affect writing development.

As any teacher can attest, writers bring different skills, interests, and approaches to writing tasks. While people share many common attributes, no two people are exactly alike. People vary biologically, genetically, and psychologically, and these differences are shaped, and sometimes accentuated, by variability in our social worlds. This variability is clearly reflected among and within writers (Rijlaarsdam et al., 2012). To illustrate, developing writers at a particular age differ in terms of their knowledge about writing, how they approach the task of writing, their views about their writing capabilities, the value they place on writing, and their facility with skills such as spelling, typing, handwriting, and sentence construction (Graham, 2006). Further, children who value writing and view themselves as capable are more likely to seek opportunities to write, whereas children who do not value it or are less positive about their capabilities are more likely to avoid writing. The amount of writing that children engage in affects the quality of what they write (Graham, McKeown, Kiuhara, & Harris, 2012). Individuals' developmental trajectories are also marked by normal variation in pacing and sequence of learning, and by both forward movement and "backward transitions" when writers use less sophisticated strategies in more difficult tasks or unfamiliar social situations (Rowe & Wilson, 2015).

Biological conditions such as congenital blindness or deafness change one's way of approaching language learning and one's orientation toward written language (Berent, 1996; Albertini, 2008). Genetic and neurological differences, which underlie autism or specific learning disabilities such as dysgraphia (impaired handwriting), dyslexia (impaired word spelling), and oral and written language learning disability (OWL LD, impaired written syntax) (see Berninger, 2015), also affect developmental pathways in learning to write. Nevertheless, students who exhibit biologically based developmental or individual differences do respond to individually tailored instruction, especially if environmental variables due to socioeconomic, language, and cultural diversity are also taken into account.

There is also considerable variation within each writer. Just because a writer is particularly adept at writing within one genre (e.g., story writing) does not mean that he or she is equally adept at writing in another genre (Graham, Hebert, Sandbank, & Harris, 2016). Moreover, writers evidence considerable variability when writing within the same genre (Gearhart, Herman, Novak, & Wolf, 1995).

4. Writers develop in relation to the changing social needs, opportunities, resources, and technologies of their time and place.

Changes in the historical conditions of writing change what a writer needs to understand and make choices about. Writing from the beginning has been located within social practices and has evolved as society and its needs have changed. For example, one of the earlier uses of writing was to distribute laws widely throughout extended kingdoms, on stone-incised columns developed for that purpose. These public postings of the laws facilitated creation of large jurisdictions with common laws, which then in turn supported both the extension of empires and the rise of legal professionals to interpret the laws and argue for clients, leading to the invention of new genres, archives, and socially organized activities based on these documents (Goody, 1986). While writing in its earliest forms served limited social needs through a small number of genres, today writing is part of participating in wide ranges of social practices and organized social activities from corporations to journalism, from science to social media, from civic participation to private trauma support groups (Bazerman, 2006).

The changing roles of writing in changing social configurations have used and fostered new communicative technologies, which then have made possible new social arrangements. Papyrus and parchment made easier the production of larger and more extended documents than ones incised on stone or clay; they also facilitated the collection and circulation of large numbers of documents. These material and symbolic advances fostered cultures of erudition as well as the rise of bureaucracies. The extended circulation and collection of more complex documents also required new symbolic devices for organizing texts and making them more intelligible, such as spacing between words and punctuation. Print and cheaper paper brought other changes to the social and symbolic aspects of writing (including book, chapter, and subheading titles), and the digital revolution is now creating new social arrangements and symbolic inventions for the writer to make sense of and act with, not only in the prominent emergence of social media with its new symbols of hashtags and emoticons, but in the way business, education, and even government and politics are transacted.

Writing tools also affect writers' composing processes. While in the past inscription most often involved writing by hand, today writers have access to a variety of text-entry tools. Writers type their texts using keyboards, swipe and pinch text on touchscreens, or orally dictate messages using voice-recognition software. Revision occurs differently using digital word-processing tools versus paper, pencil, and eraser (MacArthur & Graham, 1987; Hawisher, 1987). Technologies also facilitate interactive collaborative processes in composing, feedback, revision, and audience response, as well as change to temporalities of interaction and response. Technologies also are changing access to information in and around composing. Because technologies also facilitate new social arrangements and activities, mediated by new genres and use of multimedia, these provide new possibilities for meaningful and engaging composition.

5. The development of writing depends on the development, redirection, and specialized reconfiguring of general functions, processes, and tools.

Since writing systems were developed late in human history, writing makes use of cognitive, linguistic, social, and cultural capacities and conventions that evolved independently of writing. One implication of this is that many of the functions, processes, and tools relevant to writing are not specific to writing, but call for development, redirection, and specialized reconfiguration to be put into the service of writing.

To illustrate, writing development depends on the application of a broad array of cognitive capacities and processes that are applied to writing (Graham & Harris, 2011). These include attention, perception (vision, hearing), motoric systems, memory systems, learning, language, thinking, and executive functioning. Writing depends on learning how to apply and reshape these more basic systems so that they can be used to create text. For instance, writers learn how to transcribe ideas onto the page by developing and reconfiguring motoric skills into handwriting and keyboarding. Likewise, writers must learn to apply and redirect the process of executive functioning, so that they are able to deftly coordinate and regulate their goals and intentions and the constraints imposed by the writing topic, as well as the processes, knowledge, and skills involved in composing.

Similarly, language is reconfigured to facilitate writing and its development. Oral language is the foundation on which writing developed historically over time and on which writing develops in the individual, but the language of writing draws on different structures than speech to accomplish the purposes of writing across genres as learners engage with increasingly abstract knowledge. A simple example illustrates how oral language is reconfigured in the service of writing. While every speaker of a language uses nouns to talk about the world, as writers develop they learn to construct new kinds of noun structures, packing more information into nominal groups with embedded clauses and phrases (e.g., *he → the character in the story → the character who best represents the theme of friendship that the author de-velops throughout the novel).* They also learn to repackage whole clauses as nominalizations that distill what has been written into a nominal group that enables the discourse to move forward. For example:

> *The researchers observed that students who had not participated in the intervention were less able to accomplish the task. This observation neglects to account for . . .*

By distilling the prior clause into *this observation,* the writer is then able to evaluate the point. Writers also develop in their control of abstract nouns and expressions that enable them to represent experience as less contextualized and more general or universal, supporting the presentation of theoretical knowledge.

Growth in writing also calls for developing specialized cognitive skills, processes, and knowledge. Writers must master basic foundational skills such as spelling, punctuation/capitalization, and sentence construction, if their writing is to proceed fluidly and be fully accessible to their audiences. Additionally, they must refine general thinking skills so that these skills can be used for planning, monitoring, evaluating, and revising when writing (Graham, 2006), as well as developing specialized knowledge about different genres of writing (Donovan & Smolkin, 2006).

Writing is further influenced by the development, redirection, and reconfiguration of a variety of motivational dispositions (e.g., efficacy, values, and attributions). As writers develop, for example, they establish specific attitudes about their efficacy as writers, the value of writing in their own lives, and the reasons for their perceived writing successes and missteps. These writing-specific dispositions influence how they view themselves as writers, their effort and persistence when writing, and the quality of what they compose (Graham 2006).

It is notable that redirection and specialization pertain not only to syntax and cognition but to the social practices of writing as well. Just as an infant's hand gestures and coos will eventually differentiate into verbal greetings and adieus, a child's social engagements with family, friends, teachers, and others will be redirected and refined upon entry to written communication. Dyson

(1997) has demonstrated, for instance, how early grade school children can latch on to narrative writing as a "ticket to play" with classmates, as writing extends and refines their social drive for expression, aesthetic pleasure, recognition, and communion. Similarly, a young child's one-word text or one-word label on a piece of artwork will later emerge as more elaborated forms of description and exposition (Chapman, 1994). In other words, the general human urges to express, to seek response, to mark and label—all basic functions of social life—will be reorganized and refined as children gain participatory experience in particular domains where writing serves a meaningful function. In fact, socialization models have been widely used to explain the growth of writing in the young adult college student, as he or she gains a deepening understanding of particular writing practices associated with disciplines or professions. In this research, attention is paid to how general strategies or approaches to argument or analysis become more rhetorically refined and specialized as experience builds on experience (e.g., Carroll, 2002). Others have observed how general academic writing practices learned in the classroom can be retooled and elaborated for more particularized projects of personal growth (e.g., Herrington & Curtis, 2000).

6. Writing and other forms of development have a reciprocal relation and mutual supporting relationships.

Writing development does not occur in a vacuum. It influences and is influenced by development in a variety of dimensions including speech, reading, learning, emotions, identity, politics, sense of efficacy, and collective actions, to provide a few examples.

Take for instance writing's influence on learning and learning's influence on writing. Writing about content material enhances learning (see meta-analyses by Bangert-Drowns, Hurley, & Wilkinson, 2004; Graham & Perin, 2007), and can do so in multiple ways (Klein, 1999). First, writers produce new knowledge and learning as they generate content by converting ideas to written texts and through that process develop new meanings and understandings. Second, as writers record ideas in text, they revisit and review them, building on their ideas, making new connections, and constructing new inferences. Third, writing prompts students to recall genre schemata as they search for relevant knowledge and make new connections between ideas. Fourth, writers create new knowledge by setting rhetorical goals for their texts. As writers address those goals, they retrieve and organize their knowledge, leading to more elaborated understandings and ideas. Reciprocally, as students acquire more knowledge, this can be applied as they write. For example, writers generally produce better text when they know more about the topics they are writing about (Langer, 1986; Olinghouse, Graham, & Gillespie, 2015).

Similarly, writing and instruction in writing can improve how well one reads. To illustrate, when developing writers are taught about how texts are structured, how to write more complicated sentences, or how to spell words, there are corresponding improvements in their word reading, reading fluency, and reading-comprehension skills (Graham & Hebert, 2011). Similar kinds of gains have been observed in writing when reading is taught. This is not surprising, as reading and writing rely on common knowledge, skills, and processes. While writing facilitates reading development and reading facilitates writing development, the transfer is not strong enough to ensure that developing writers and readers learn all they need to know to become skilled writers and readers (Shanahan, 2016).

7. To understand how writing develops across the lifespan, educators need to recognize the different ways language resources can be used to present meaning in written text.

Language is the primary meaning-making resource we draw on to construe our experiences, enact social relationships, and structure texts, often with the assistance of other multimodal resources. Writing development calls for learning to use new language resources and to draw on familiar resources from spoken language in new and more conscious ways.

Oral language is the foundation on which writing developed historically and is also the foundation on which writing develops in the individual. Children learn the language(s) of their communities in interaction with others in the contexts of living everyday life. The particular languages and facilities with language that a child develops are dependent on the experiences and social relations that the child has opportunities to engage in. Development of facility with spoken language is highly consequential for participation in social activities throughout our lives, including through writing. But because people are socially positioned in different ways, and have different life experiences, not all members of every speech community develop the same facility with all forms of spoken discourse. This is also true of written discourse.

Writing development is seldom unconscious and embedded in engaging in the activities of everyday life in the ways spoken language is. Instead, in learning to write, it is necessary for the learner to develop a more self-conscious perspective on language and new ways of drawing on language as a resource for meaning making. This is obvious in the learning of letter-sound correspondences and the formation of letters, but it is also true in other aspects of writing. Writing has a more limited set of modalities to draw on than does spoken language. It has no phonological realization, for example, with the rich set of intonational and rhythmic resources that speech offers, and a written text typically has no shared context of understanding, with the potential for gestures and joint attention to contribute to meaning. Instead, in the evolution of writing over time, other resources of language have been developed and elaborated to enable the functions that written text performs in a culture (Halliday & Martin, 1993).

The grammar of the written texts children encounter and need to learn to write in school differs in significant ways from the grammar of informal spoken interaction (Chafe, 1985; Halliday, 1987; Schleppegrell, 2001). We described above how the noun, as a linguistic resource, develops in its structure and potential for meaning as it is used in written language to construe more elaborated and abstract expression. Other language resources that developing writers learn to draw on in new ways include conjunctions that are uncommon in everyday speech (e.g., concessive *although*; consequential *therefore*) (Schleppegrell, 1996). Writers also need to develop ever-more-nuanced language resources for making judgments in authoritative ways. In responding to literature in the later grades and through college writing, for example, students need to do more than present the affective responses of early childhood, learning to draw on language that enables them to evaluate the themes of a story or the craft of an author (Christie, 2012; MacDonald, 1994). Writing about the statements of others also requires new linguistic skills to represent their words and ideas efficiently, ethically, and purposefully to express nuanced evaluation and stance, and to synthesize and build on prior statements.

It is engagement in new practices that supports the development and use of new language resources in writing. For that reason, apprenticing students to new ways of writing and new genres requires that they become part of new communities where their participation has the potential to further contribute to shaping the ways language is used and new knowledge is developed. But research is also increasingly suggesting that explicit attention to language itself, drawing on a metalanguage for talking about language and meaning, can support writing development (Macken-Horarik & Morgan, 2011).

For most children learning to write in their mother tongues, writing can be a frustrating experience, as for many years their spoken language fluency runs far ahead of what they are able to do in writing. For people learning to write in a language that is learned later in life—as an adolescent or even as an adult—the new spoken language may be developing concurrently with writing. Developing a new language as adolescent or adult is not always spontaneous and effortless, and learning to write in an unfamiliar language presents additional challenges. Those who are literate in their first language can often transfer aspects of writing knowledge to writing in additional languages, but they also need to cope with differences in vocabulary and word usage, sentence structures, idiomatic phrases, and communicative norms and expectations. They also have to contend with different audience expectations regarding how ideas are organized, what counts as viable evidence, and how much information needs to be provided (Schleppegrell, 2002). Adults learning to write in a new language may also be under pressure to develop a high level of writing knowledge in academic and professional contexts while also coping with the challenge of learning and using the language in less formal interaction. While writing in new languages can be stimulating and exciting for some, many second language writers also experience a sense of frustration because they are not always able to express their ideas as easily and as expertly as they can in the language repertoire they developed earlier in life.

8. Curriculum plays a significant formative role in writing development.

The technological, social, cognitive, and linguistic dimensions we have presented suggest that writing development is very much a function of the situations, practices, and communities one is exposed to and engages within, with very different trajectories of development depending on experiences. Since schooling forms such an important part of the literacy experiences within which one develops writing skills, it is important to understand the role of curriculum in writing development. Students will learn those genres, skills, and strategies with which they are given experience through their school, and are much less likely to learn those that the schools ignore, reject, or simply postpone for attention in later years. When differences in curriculum are large, it may even be impossible to map writing development in a uniform way that is valid across contexts: At least that was the conclusion that Alan Purves (1992) reached after ten years of involvement in the IEA cross-national study of writing achievement. Finding wide differences in topics, instructional emphases, time devoted to otherwise seemingly comparable tasks, and "taste" in evaluating final products, the IEA assessment was unable to make cross-national comparisons of writing achievement, as even the concept of achievement varied.

Within the United States, curriculum variations influence the writing skills that students develop. States differ, for example, in the specific writing genres included on high-stakes assessments (e.g., "critical lens" essay for English in New York State, "transactional" writing across subjects in Kentucky), in their emphasis on writing that requires analysis and synthesis across multiple texts, in their emphasis on writing about literature as opposed to writing about other subjects, and finally in whether they require extended writing at all or rely instead on multiple-choice assessments (Applebee & Langer, 2013). What is assessed on state tests is likely to reflect what is taught and how, especially when high stakes are attached to assessment results, as they are in the present accountability environment (Hillocks, 2002; Jones, Jones, & Hargrove, 2003; Murphy, 2003; O'Neill, Murphy, Huot, & Williamson, 2006).

While curricula may vary widely, it is clear that writing in school subjects plays a central and critical role in students' writing development. Participating in the genres and discourses of disciplinary areas of schooling socializes students into a more formal, planned, authoritative, and technical "written mode" of language. In the Australian context, research on the writing children do in schools has led to contextualized linguistic descriptions of the ways children's spoken and written language develops over the years of schooling as they move from commonsense, everyday knowledge and familiar topics to less familiar and more abstract knowledge and topics in the disciplines they study in school. Christie (2012) has described this development in relation to age and the curriculum contexts in which children participate, and Christie and Derewianka (2008) have elaborated this understanding to describe writing development in different subject areas across the years of schooling. Such descriptions of writing development can usefully inform curriculum and assessment, as they provide trajectories of linguistic growth that are related to the genres with which students are expected to engage in school.

This statement has developed a view of writing as involving socially constituted tools, cognitive resources, motivational dispositions, and sets of language practices necessary to participate effectively in communities of practice, including those of the school. This enables us to see writing development as the ability to participate more effectively in the written genres of a wider range of communities of practice. Growth in writing, then, means access to more genres and more effective participation in a range of genres. This view of development calls for operationalizing writing development in new ways and developing new kinds of assessments.

If writing development is dependent on the curriculum that students encounter, the writing curriculum needs to support learning in specific disciplines and for specific purposes. The best starting points for writing instruction, then, are in the communities of practice that children engage with as they learn school subjects across the grades. These communities of practice involve content knowledge as well as knowledge about audience and purpose. Even very young children need to learn to write through activities that support their learning more generally. Authentic curricular activities that build knowledge toward learning give substance and meaning to what students are writing, providing both a focus to write about and the contextual frames (textual, interpersonal, and ideational) that are necessary for successful writing in these contexts.

But if writing development is at least to some extent dependent on the curriculum that students encounter, it is also dependent on the students a curriculum encounters. A curriculum ignorant of the students it is encountering will be counterdevelopmental. As discussed above, students come to school with different experiences of the social interaction, strategic practices, and language forms relevant to the writing they are expected to do. Students who have been educated in different educational systems may bring different views of writing and of ways to develop writing knowledge. Each child brings experiences that can contribute to and shape new learning, and a writing curriculum needs to enable the participation of all voices and sharing of all experiences to contribute to the learning context.

Since writers develop in relation to the changing social needs, opportunities, resources, and technologies of their time and place, effective curricula will also require close attention to the changing cultural, social, and technological environments in which students live. Rapidly changing information and communication technologies and the new discourses and social practices they generate demand their own appropriate space in the curriculum. Curriculum for the development of new skills and strategies (new literacies or multiliteracies) is needed if students are to live engaged lives in today's online age of information and communication and take full advantage of the information resources and opportunities available (Leu, Kinzer, Coiro, Castek, & Henry, 2013).

Final Comments

The picture of lifespan development of writing abilities presented here is closely tied to the situations, technologies, opportunities, and experiences each person has. As individuals, from their own perspectives, goals, experiences, repertoires of practices, and skills, actively engage with new situations, they repurpose their cognitive resources, expand their processes of composing and revision, engage their prior histories of literate interactions, and develop task-specific language skills. Their relations with others grow and change along with their identities and thinking, as writing experiences develop along person-specific trajectories within socially organized activities. Because school is the place young people often engage writing most extensively and intensively, from early childhood through late adolescence and even early adulthood, the school curriculum will be influential on their texts, attitudes toward writing, language skills, social roles, and conceptions of writing. Beyond the regularities (and different patterns) in schooling, constraints on experience and development that might bring some similarity or regularity may come from neurological and motor development. Common social experiences, relations, and roles (including relations with caregivers) that people have an opportunity to engage in at different points in their lives may also bring some degree of regularity. The complexity of writing tasks, such that some accomplishments rest on other more basic ones, which once automatized allow the writer to engage larger issues and to exercise more complex executive control over more extensive and strategic processes, may also suggest some developmental sequences. But atypicality (whether neurological, psychological, social, or linguistic) can foster different patterns of development, amplified by different kinds of engagement with the other factors that might otherwise predict regularity.

The complex, multidimensional portrait of writing development presented here strongly suggests that writing education needs to be built on meaning making and effective communication, while addressing social, linguistic, cognitive, motivational, and technological dimensions of writing development. Each dimension requires time to mature and develop sophistication across many experiences, but each writing experience brings all the dimensions together in a unified communicative event. This means that while teaching moments may direct focus to some specific aspect of one of the dimensions, all dimensions are always present, and students may find challenges coming from any of them at any time. Thus, for example, a difficulty in meeting a linguistic demand in a class activity may have its source in working memory or social understanding of the communication. A difficulty in developing a meaning may arise from lack of relevant linguistic resources, a lack of subject knowledge, anxieties about audience response, a difficulty in manipulating a new technology, or something else. Further, overall growth in writing abilities relies on development in each of the dimensions that are brought together in writing.

Because each of the dimensions takes time to develop, and then must be brought together in complex writing performances, learning to write takes many years. Every level of schooling makes new demands and requires new learning, so we should expect that students will not always immediately perform to the expectations within the new situation of each school level. We should not be too quick to blame prior teaching and learning, when the real issue is time to develop and unfamiliarity with new expectations. On the other hand, repeated negative educational experience with writing may preclude students' engagement in necessary developmental experiences and may create dispositions that interfere with later developmental opportunities. This makes good instruction and good understanding about writing development on the part of teachers of great importance.

Because of the complexity of writing and its long learning over many experiences, within the same classroom students may show varying strengths and weaknesses in different aspects of writing, varying control of different genres, different repertoires of expressive resources from varying language experiences, different motivations and purposes for writing, and unique meanings to express through writing. Because different individuals bring such variety to the task of learning to write, they may have very different trajectories of development across their lifespans.

For curriculum this calls for flexibility in design, so that the needs of individual students can be met. A lock-step, scripted approach in curriculum serves no one well. For assessment this means there is a need to develop fair and authentic writing assessments that display the full range and variation of student writing development. A single test cannot show the range of a student's work nor his or her development as a writer. For teacher preparation and professional development programs this means there is a need to prepare teachers who know their subjects deeply, who know how to assess the spectrum of their students' abilities, and who know how to tailor appropriate instruction. This calls for specialized linguistic, rhetorical, and writing-process knowledge as well as pedagogical knowledge for apprenticing students into new discursive practices.

While there is research in some dimensions of writing at all the age levels, there is not adequate research in all the dimensions at all the levels. Further, at any age level, it is rare that all the dimensions are studied simultaneously within a writer's performance and development. Even more, there is very little research that moves across age levels. The dimensions of writing we have attempted to synthesize here draw on our current patchwork of research. We hope this statement will serve as a spur to further much-needed understanding and inquiry as well as provide guidance for policy and practice.

References

Albertini, J. (2008). Teaching of writing and diversity: Access, identity, and achievement. In C. Bazerman (Ed.), *Handbook of research on writing: History, society, school, individual, text* (pp. 387–98). New York: Erlbaum.

Applebee, A. N., & Langer, J. A. (2013). *Writing instruction that works: Proven methods for middle and high school classrooms.* Berkeley, CA: National Writing Project; New York: Teachers College Press.

Bangert-Drowns, R. L., Hurley, M. M., & Wilkinson, B. (2004). The effects of school-based Writing-to-Learn interventions on academic achievement: A meta-analysis. *Review of Educational Research, 74*(1), 29–58.

Bazerman, C. (1999). *The languages of Edison's light.* Cambridge, MA: MIT Press.

Bazerman, C. (2006). The writing of social organization and the literate situating of cognition: Extending Goody's social implications of writing. In D. R. Olson and M. Cole (Eds.), *Technology, literacy and the evolution of society: Implications of the work of Jack Goody* (pp. 215–39). Mahwah, NJ: Erlbaum.

Bazerman, C. (2008). *Handbook of research on writing: History, society, school, individual, text.* New York: Erlbaum.

Bazerman, C. (2013). *Literate action: Vol. 2. A theory of literate action.* Fort Collins, CO: WAC Clearinghouse. Retrieved from http://wac .colostate.edu/books/literateaction/v2

Beard, R., Myhill, D., Riley, J., & Nystrand, M. *(2009). The SAGE handbook of writing development.* London, UK: SAGE.

Beaufort, A., (1999). *Writing in the real world: Making the transition from school to work.* New York: Teachers College Press.

Beaufort, A., (2007). *College writing and beyond: A new framework for university writing instruction.* Logan: Utah State University Press.

Berent, G. P. (1996). The acquisition of English syntax by deaf learners. In W. C. Ritchie & T. K. Bhatia (Eds.), *Handbook of second language acquisition* (pp. 469–506). San Diego: Academic Press.

Berninger, V. W. (2015). *Interdisciplinary frameworks for schools: Best professional practices for serving the needs of all students.* Washington, DC: American Psychological Association.

Berninger, V. W., & Chanquoy, L. (2012). What writing is and how it changes across early and middle childhood development: A multidisciplinary perspective. In E. L. Grigorenko, E. Mambrino, & D. D. Preiss (Eds.), *Writing: A mosaic of new perspectives* (pp. 65–84). New York: Psychology Press.

Brandt, D. (2001). *Literacy in American lives.* New York: Cambridge University Press.

Brandt, D. (2015). *The rise of writing: Redefining mass literacy.* New York: Cambridge University Press.

Carroll, L. A. (2002). *Rehearsing new roles: How college students develop as writers.* Carbondale: Southern Illinois University Press.

Chafe, W. L. (1985). Linguistic differences produced by differences between speaking and writing. In D. R. Olson, N. Torrance, & A. Hildyard (Eds.), *Literacy, language, and learning: The nature and consequences of reading and writing* (pp. 105–23). Cambridge, UK: Cambridge University Press.

Chapman, M. L. (1994). The emergence of genres: Some findings from an examination of first-grade writing. *Written Communication 11*(3), 348–80. doi:101177/0741088394011003003

Christie, F. (2012). *Language education throughout the school years: A functional perspective.* Malden, MA: Wiley-Blackwell.

Christie, F., & Derewianka, B. (2008). *School discourse: Learning to write across the years of schooling.* London, UK: Continuum.

Cole, M. (1998). *Cultural psychology: A once and future discipline.* Cambridge, MA: Harvard University Press.

Common Core State Standards Initiative. (2010). *Common core state standards for English language arts and literacy in history/social studies, science, and technical subjects.* Washington, DC: National Governors Association Center for Best Practices and the Council of Chief State School Officers. Retrieved from http://www.core standards.org/

Compton-Lilly, C. (2014). The development of writing habitus: A ten-year case study of a young writer. *Written Communication, 31*(4), 371–403. doi:10.1177/0741088314549539

Dias, P., Freedman, A., Medway, P., & Paré, A. (1999). *Worlds apart: Acting and writing in academic and workplace contexts.* Mahwah, NJ: Lawrence Erlbaum.

Dias, P., & Paré, A. (Eds.) (2000). *Transitions: Writing in academic and workplace settings.* Cresskill, NJ: Hampton Press.

Donovan, C. A., & Smolkin, L. B. (2006). Children's understanding of genre and writing development. In C. A. MacArthur, S. Graham, & J. Fitzgerald (Eds.), *Handbook of writing research* (pp. 13–43). New York: Guilford Press.

Duffy, J. (2007). *Writing from these roots: Literacy in a Hmong-American community.* Honolulu: University of Hawaii Press.

Dyson, A. H. (1997). *Writing superheroes: Contemporary childhood, popular culture, and classroom literacy.* New York: Teachers College Press.

Dyson, A. H. (2013). *Rewriting the basics: Literacy learning in children's cultures.* New York: Teachers College Press.

Gearhart, M., Herman, J. L., Novak, J. R., & Wolf, S. A. (1995). Toward the instructional utility of large-scale writing assessment: Validation of a new narrative rubric. *Assessing Writing*, 2(2), 207–42. doi:10.1016/1075-2935(95)90013-6

Goody, J. (1986). *The logic of writing and the organization of society.* Cambridge, UK: Cambridge University Press.

Graham, S. (2006). Writing. In P. A. Alexander & P. H. Winne (Eds.), *Handbook of educational psychology* (2nd ed., pp. 457–78). Mahwah, NJ: Erlbaum.

Graham, S., & Harris, K. R. (2011). Writing and students with disabilities. In J. M. Kauffman & D. P. Hallahan (Eds.), *Handbook of special education* (pp. 422–33). London, UK: Routledge.

Graham, S., & Hebert, M. (2011). Writing to read: A meta-analysis of the impact of writing and writing instruction on reading. *Harvard Educational Review*, 81(4), 710–44, 784–85.

Graham, S., Hebert, M., Sandbank, M. P., & Harris, K. R. (2016). Assessing the writing achievement of young struggling writers: Application of generalizability theory. *Learning Disability Quarterly*, 39(2), 72–82. doi:10.1177/0731948714555019

Graham, S., McKeown, D., Kiuhara, S., & Harris, K. R. (2012). A meta-analysis of writing instruction for students in the elementary grades. *Journal of Educational Psychology*, 104(4), 879–96. doi:10.1037/a0029185

Graham, S., & Perin, D. (2007). *Writing next: Effective strategies to improve writing of adolescents in middle and high schools.* Washington, DC: Alliance for Excellent Education.

Haas, C., & Flower, L. (1988). Rhetorical reading strategies and the construction of meaning. *College Composition and Communication*, 39(2), 167–83. doi:10.2307/358026

Halliday, M. A. K. (1987). Spoken and written modes of meaning. In R. Horowitz & S. J. Samuels (Eds.), *Comprehending oral and written language* (pp. 55–82). San Diego: Academic Press.

Halliday, M. A. K., & Martin, J. R. (1993). *Writing science: Literacy and discursive power.* London, UK: Falmer Press.

Hawisher, G. (1987). The effects of word processing on the revision strategies of college freshmen. *Research in the Teaching of English*, 21(2), 145–59.

Heath, S. B. (1983). *Ways with words: Language, life, and work in communities and classrooms.* New York: Cambridge University Press.

Herrington, A. J., & Curtis, M. (2000). *Persons in process: Four stories of writing and personal development in college.* Urbana, IL: National Council of Teachers of English.

Hillocks, G., Jr. (2002). *The testing trap: How state writing assessments control learning.* New York: Teachers College Press.

James, K. H., Jao, R. J., & Berninger, V. (2016). The development of multileveled writing systems of the brain: Brain lessons for writing instruction. In C. A. MacArthur, S. Graham, & J. Fitzgerald (Eds.), *Handbook of writing research* (2nd ed., pp. 116–29). New York: Guilford Press.

Jones, M. G., Jones, B. D., & Hargrove, T. (2003). *The unintended consequences of high-stakes testing.* New York: Rowman & Littlefield.

Klein, P. D. (1999). Reopening inquiry into cognitive processes in writing-to-learn. *Educational Psychology Review, 11*(3), 203–70.

Langer, J. A. (1986). *Children reading and writing: Structures and strategies.* Norwood, NJ: Ablex.

Leki, I.. (2010). Second language writing in English. In R. B. Kaplan (Ed.), *The Oxford handbook of applied linguistics* (2nd ed., pp. 100–09). Oxford, United Kingdom: Oxford University Press. doi:10.1093/oxfordhb/9780195384253.013.0007

Leki, I., Cumming, A. H., & Silva, T. (2008). *A synthesis of research on second language writing in English.* New York: Routledge.

Leu, D. J., Kinzer, C. K., Coiro, J., Castek, J., & Henry, L. A. (2013). New literacies: A dual-level theory of the changing nature of literacy, instruction, and assessment. In D. E. Alvermann, N. J. Unrau, & R. B. Ruddell (Eds.), *Theoretical models and processes of reading* (6th ed., pp. 1150–76). Newark, DE: International Reading Association.

Lorimer Leonard, R. (2013). Traveling literacies: Multilingual writing on the move. *Research in the Teaching of English, 48*(1), 1, 13–39.

MacArthur, C. A., & Graham, S. (1987). Learning disabled students' composing under three methods of text production: Handwriting, word processing, and dictation. *Journal of Special Education, 21*(3), 22–42. doi:10.1177/002246698702100304

MacArthur, C. A., Graham, S., & Fitzgerald, J. (2006). *Handbook of writing research.* New York: Guilford Press.

MacDonald, S. P. (1994). *Professional academic writing in the humanities and social sciences.* Carbondale: Southern Illinois University Press.

Macken-Horarik, M., & Morgan, W. (2011). Towards a metalanguage adequate to linguistic achievement in post-structuralism and English: Reflections on voicing in the writing of secondary students. *Linguistics and Education, 22*(2), 133–49. doi:10.1016/j.linged.2010.11.003

Matsuda, P. K., & Tardy, C. M. (2007). Voice in academic writing: The rhetorical construction of author identity in blind manuscript review. *English for Specific Purposes 26*(2), 235–49. doi:10.1016/j.esp.2006.10.001

Moll, L. C., Amanti, C., Neff, D., & Gonzalez, N. (1992). Funds of knowledge for teaching: Using a qualitative approach to connect homes and classrooms. *Theory Into Practice, 31*(2), 132–41.

Murphy, S. (2003). That was then, this is now: The impact of changing assessment policies on teachers and the teaching of writing in California. *Journal of Writing Assessment, 1*(1), 23–45.

National Commission on Writing for America's Families, Schools, and Colleges. (2004). *Writing: A ticket to work . . . or a ticket out: A survey of business leaders.* New York: College Board.

National Commission on Writing for America's Families, Schools, and Colleges. (2005). *Writing: A powerful message from state government.* New York: College Board.

National Commission on Writing for America's Families, Schools, and Colleges. (2006). *Writing and school reform: Including the neglected "r": The need for a writing revolution.* New York: College Board.

National Commission on Writing in America's Schools and Colleges. (2003). *The neglected "r": The need for a writing revolution.* New York: College Board.

Olinghouse, N. G., Graham, S., & Gillespie, A. (2015). The relationship of discourse and topic knowledge to fifth graders' writing performance. *Journal of Educational Psychology, 107*(2), 391–406. doi:10.1037/a0037549

O'Neill, P., Murphy, S., Huot, B., & Williamson, M. M. (2006). What teachers say about different kinds of mandated state writing tests. *Journal of Writing Assessment, 2*(2), 81–108.

Pritchard, E. D. (2016). *Fashioning lives: Black queers and the politics of literacy.* Carbondale: Southern Illinois University Press.

Purves, A. C. (1992). *The IEA study of written composition II.* Oxford, UK: Pergamon Press.

Rijlaarsdam, G., Van den Bergh, H., Couzijn, M., Janssen, T., Braaksma, M., Tillema, M., Van Steendam, E., & Raedts, M. (2012). Writing. In K. R. Harris, S. Graham, & T. Urdan (Eds.), *APA educational psychology handbook: Vol. 3. Application to learning and teaching* (pp. 189–227). Washington, DC: American Psychological Association. doi:10.1037/13275-009

Rowe, D. W., & Wilson, S. J. (2015). The development of a descriptive measure of early childhood writing: Results from the Write Start! Writing Assessment. *Journal of Literacy Research, 47*(2), 245–92. doi:10.1177/1086296X15619723

Royster, J. J. (2000). *Traces of a stream: Literacy and social change among African American women.* Pittsburgh, PA: University of Pittsburgh Press.

Schleppegrell, M. J. (1996). Conjunction in spoken English and ESL writing. *Applied Linguistics, 17*(3), 271–85. doi:10.1093/applin/17.3.271

Schleppegrell, M. J. (2001). Linguistic features of the language of schooling. *Linguistics and Education, 12*(4), 431–59. doi:10.1016/S0898-5898(01)00073-0

Schleppegrell, M. J. (2002). Challenges of the science register for ESL students: Errors and meaning-making. In M. J. Schleppegrell & M. C. Colombi (Eds), *Developing advanced literacy in first and second languages: Meaning with power* (pp. 119–42). Mahwah, NJ: Erlbaum.

Selfe, C. L., & Hawisher, G. E. (Eds.). (2004). *Literate lives in the information age: Narratives of literacy from the United States.* Mahwah, NJ: Erlbaum.

Shanahan, T. (2016). Relationships between reading and writing development. In C. A. MacArthur, S. Graham, & J. Fitzgerald (Eds.), *Handbook of writing research* (2nd ed., pp. 194–207). New York: Guilford Press.

Smagorinsky, P. (Ed.). (2006). *Research on composition: Multiple perspectives on two decades of change.* New York: Teachers College Press.

Spinuzzi, C. (2008). *Network: Theorizing knowledge work in telecommunications.* New York: Cambridge University Press.

Sternglass, M. S. (1997). *Time to know them: A longitudinal study of writing and learning at the college level.* Mahwah, NJ: Erlbaum.

Tardy, C. M., & Matsuda, P. K. (2009). The construction of author voice by editorial board members. *Written Communication, 26*(1), 32–52. doi:10.1177/0741088308327269

Valdés, G. (1996). *Con respeto: Bridging the distances between culturally diverse families and schools: An ethnographic portrait.* New York: Teachers College Press.

Vygotsky, L. S. (1978). *Mind in society: The development of higher psychological processes.* Cambridge, MA: Harvard University Press.

Vygotsky, L. S. (1989). *Thought and language.* Rev. and ed. Alex Kozulin. Cambridge, MA: MIT Press.

II

PERSPECTIVES ON LIFESPAN
WRITING DEVELOPMENT

CHAPTER THREE

Writing Development in
Early Childhood

DEBORAH WELLS ROWE
Vanderbilt University

This chapter is about the beginnings of writing in early childhood. It describes what writing looked like and how it developed for one group of children between the ages of 2½ and
6 years of age. The portrait of young writers presented in this
chapter is built on the foundation provided by emergent-literacy
research, but also expanded and reframed using sociocultural
perspectives on writing development.

Until recently, most of what we know about writing in early
childhood was shaped by the emergent-literacy perspective (Teale
& Sulzby, 1986b). Prior to the 1960s, researchers working from
a readiness perspective assumed that young children began to
learn literacy through school instruction, and further assumed
that learning to read preceded learning to write (see Teale &
Sulzby, 1986a). From this vantage point, there was little reason
to take note of children's mark-making activities prior to the start
of formal schooling.

Early childhood writing became an important focus for researchers and educators only when the beginnings of reading and
writing were retheorized from an "emergent literacy" perspective
(Teale & Sulzby, 1986b). Emergent-literacy researchers provided
evidence that young children began to learn about literacy very
early in life through informal interactions with parents, siblings,
peers, and teachers. Whereas readiness perspectives focused primarily on reading as the precursor to writing, this new perspective
broadened the focus to "literacy" and argued that reading and
writing were interrelated and learned concurrently. Emergent-

literacy researchers broadened the focus further by documenting children's flexible interweaving of semiotic systems, especially art and language, leading them to recognize the multimodal nature of early childhood composing (e.g., Dyson, 1989; Harste, Woodward, & Burke, 1984).

Whereas readiness perspectives had assumed that adults transmitted literacy knowledge to children through planned instruction, emergent-literacy researchers proposed the metaphor of hypothesis testing. They suggested that much as they do in oral language learning, children constructed and tested hypotheses about writing and reading as part of their everyday activities at home and at school.

Whereas the readiness perspective had tied the beginnings of reading and writing to the start of conventional decoding and spelling, emergent-literacy researchers took a radically different stance. They proposed that *intention* rather than *convention* was the defining feature of writing (Harste et al., 1984; Sulzby, 1985b). They acknowledged that young children approached writing with different print hypotheses, but suggested that their processes were not fundamentally different from those of older writers. From this perspective, writing began when children showed intentionality—the understanding that their marks could represent meaning. In her work on the "roots of literacy," Yetta Goodman (1986) defined reading and writing as "human interaction with print when the reader and writer *believe* [emphasis added] that they are making sense of and through written language" (p. 6). From an emergent-literacy perspective, young children's characteristically unconventional marks were not "prewriting" but instead were the beginning of the real thing. As Teale and Sulzby (1986b) wrote in their seminal volume, *Emergent Literacy,* "[T]he first years of the child's life represent a period when legitimate reading and writing development are taking place. These behaviors and knowledges are not *pre-* anything, as the term *prereading* suggests. . . . At whatever point we look, we see children *in the process of becoming* literate, as the term *emergent* indicates" (italics in original, p. xix). They described writing development as a process in which children constructed and refined their print hypotheses and strategies. The emergent-literacy perspective provided a new storyline for explaining the development of writing in early childhood.

This work has forever changed what I and other early literacy educators can see when we look at young children's writing. Products I threw away as meaningless scribbles when I was teaching kindergarten in the late 1970s I now analyze and understand using the categories generated by this line of research. Despite the continuing importance of these understandings for my everyday work with young children and for my research, I have found that the emergent-literacy perspective's focus on individual learners and their writing intentions can also be limiting. In my own work, I have found that using intentionality as the litmus test for the beginnings of writing can constrain our understandings of young writers. Ironically, I found that the focus on children's individual textual intentions pushed children's earliest experiences with writing to the side. Some children were too limited in their oral language to verbalize their intentions. Others were too inexperienced with writing to make connections between their marks and linguistic messages on their own, though they participated actively with adults in writing events. The image of early writing as an individual, in-head phenomenon seemed to account for only part of the process through which children learned to write.

The need to better account for the very beginnings of writing development has encouraged me to consider how we might expand the developmental storyline to include what children learn as they participate with others in writing events. Researchers working from sociocultural perspectives (Bloome, Carter, Christian, Otto, & Shuart-Faris, 2005; Gee, 2003) have challenged views that focus attention only on writing as an individual mental act, suggesting instead that writing is a collaborative process occurring between people as they negotiate authoring processes, meanings, and textual forms during their everyday activities. When writing is viewed as a social practice shared with other members of children's writing communities, the defining feature of writing is *participation* in literacy events.

Applied to my own research, these perspectives have shaped the contexts in which I choose to observe young writers and how I have framed the developmental storyline presented in this

chapter. To illustrate, I introduce 2-year-old Javani, a participant in the Write Start! study (Rowe & Neitzel, 2010; Rowe &
Wilson, 2015). In the fall of the preschool year, I invited him to
write his name and a caption for a photo showing him playing
in his classroom. His photo page (Figure 3.1), along with those
authored by his classmates, was to be included in a coauthored
class book. This photo-caption task is the context in which
most of the data reported in this chapter were collected and was
purposefully designed as an opportunity to observe changes in
children's participation as writers over time. A portion of Javani's
composing event is presented in Example 3.1. In Figure 3.1, numerals have been superimposed on the image of his completed
product to indicate the beginning point for the marks described
in the transcript.

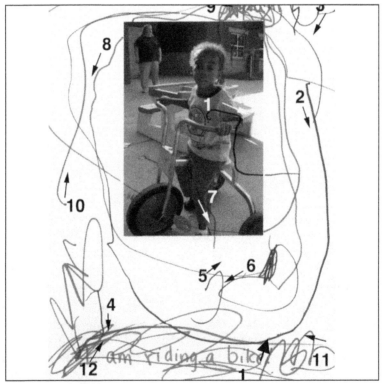

FIGURE 3.1. *Javani's photo page (age 2:11).*

EXAMPLE **3.1.** Javani writes his name and a photo caption.

Rowe	1. "What are you doing in the picture?"
Javani	2. "I'm riding."
Rowe	3. "You're riding the <u>bike</u>! You were outside riding the <u>bike</u>!" [touches the bike in the photo].
Rowe	4. "OK, take a marker" [points to marker basket], "and I want you to write your name at the top" [points, left to right, across top of page above the photo].
Javani	5. Javani picks up the marker and takes the cap off.
Rowe	6. ". . . and you can write what you're doing and we can put that in our book!"
Javani	7. Javani makes a mark on top of the photo at #1.
Rowe	8. [gently pushing his hand away]: "Write up here on your paper. Write up here on your paper," [taps three times on the page above the photo] "so we can see what you're doing!"
Javani	9. Javani begins marking at the right side of the photo at #2.
Rowe	10. [Spoken as Javani draws the line down beside the photo at #2]: "Good for you."
Javani	11. Javani completes a circle around the entire photo.
Rowe	12. "Oh, you drew a big circle around there. Yeah!" [taps the circle around the photo] "Tell me what that says?"
Javani	13. Javani looks at the page. He looks away from Rowe and gazes at the marker he is holding in his left hand. With his right hand, he uses his index and middle fingers together to make a small jabbing point at the bottom right corner of the page. He doesn't say anything.
Rowe	14. "Can you write Javani?" [runs her finger, left to right, above the photo several times.] "Write your name right up here."
Javani	15. Javani makes marks beginning in the upper right corner at #3.
Rowe	16. "Very good writing! Excellent!" [moves the page a bit, and points to the left side of the white space below picture]. "Now down here, write us something and tell us what you were doing."
Javani	17. Javani is already making the black mark seen at #4.
Rowe	18. "I am riding a bike" [offered as a suggestion for the message].
Javani	19. While Rowe talks, Javani continues marking in the center of the page at #5 and then #6 [moving to the right with scribble units, each in its own white space].

continued on next page

Example 3.1 continued

Rowe	20. Rowe reaches for a marker and pulls the page into her work-space, angling it toward her: "I'm gonna take a red marker and I'm gonna write in adult writing . . . I'm gonna write *J A V A N I*" [spells out the letters as she writes the letters in his name at the top of the page].
Rowe	21. Rowe moves her hand to the bottom left to touch the mark at #4: "And here's where you wrote" . . . [sweeps her hand across the marks to the right] "'I am riding a bike.'" [Rowe begins to write this message below, reading slowly, word by word, as she writes.] "I . .am . . . riding . . . a . . . bike."
Javani	22. As Rowe writes, Javani selects a thin red marker from the basket. He makes a red mark at #7 on the photo, then begins another photo circle in red at #8. When he completes the circle, he draws a scribble at #9, over the top of the print where Rowe has written his name.
Rowe	23. "Good for you!"
Javani	31. Javani starts to make marks at the left side of the space below the photo on top of Rowe's writing, but stops and revises his plan. He moves his marker to the right side of the page: "Look at me!"
Rowe	32. Rowe runs her hand across his #11 marks: "<u>Read</u> that to me."
Javani	33. Javani points at the left side of the marks, holding the marker in his right hand.
Rowe	34. "Tell me what that <u>says</u> . . . in <u>brown</u>."
Javani	35. Javani bends closer to the page and makes one brown mark at #12. He uses some force at the end of the mark and raises the marker from the page with a whole arm movement. He verbalizes one unintelligible word.
Rowe	36. "Yeah? Does it say, 'I am riding a bike'?"
Javani	37. Javani is adding brown scribbles at the right bottom of the page at #13. [He makes no verbal response. His marks are his response.]

Theory matters. It frames what we observe when working with young children and shapes the developmental storyline we derive from research observations. When this event is analyzed with a focus on Javani's individual writing intentions, there is relatively little to say, as he provides little understandable information about the meaning of his graphic activity. The marks have few, if any, printlike features that would allow the viewer to infer his hypotheses about print, and it is difficult to infer intentionality since he does not verbally assign meanings to his marks. Seen from a traditional emergent-literacy perspective, Javani is a literacy "have not." Since he does not provide evidence that he knows about conventional print features and he does not show evidence of intentionality, the emergent-literacy perspective provides little guidance for understanding this event as part of his development as a writer.

However, when the research lens is broadened to include the-child-engaged-in-practice as the unit of analysis (Rogoff, 2003), it is possible to see Javani as an active and responsive participant in writing. As expected by the adults in his classroom, he participates graphically, and uses both marking (e.g., turns 7, 9) and gesture (turn 13) as his turns in the ongoing adult-child interaction around the page. His bid for my attention at turn 31 ("Look at me!") shows he is socially engaged and wants to ensure we are establishing joint attention to his marks. I use talk and gesture to demonstrate key features of expected writing practices, including where the writing should be placed on the page (e.g., turns 4, 14) and a linguistic message appropriate for this writing task (turn 36). Though Javani is not yet orally assigning meaning to his marks, his participation in these writing events provides scaffolded opportunities to learn about writing processes, messages, and purposes.

If we assume learning to write begins as soon as children like Javani begin to participate, however peripherally, in the writing practices of their homes, schools, and communities (Lave & Wenger, 1991), it is possible to study writing development long before children independently form textual intentions. In this chapter, I adopt a sociocultural perspective on development (Lave & Wenger, 1991; Miller & Goodnow, 1995; Vygotsky, 1978) that assumes that "human development is a process of *people's changing participation in sociocultural activities of their communities*" [italics in original] (Rogoff, 2003, p. 52). Instead of viewing individual development as separate from cultural variables, a sociocultural perspective suggests that individual and cultural processes are mutually constituting: "[P]eople develop as they participate in and contribute to cultural activities that they themselves develop with the involvement of other people in successive generations" (Rogoff, 2003, p. 52). Individuals are not separate from the kinds of materials, activities, and institutions that make up the social practices in which they participate (Vygotsky, 1978).

When viewed through this theoretical lens, Javani's participation in Example 3.1 can be analyzed as part of the beginnings of his developmental trajectory as a writer—a path that is situated in and shaped by local writing practices in his classroom (and the photo-caption task) where adults encouraged collaborative and playful adult-child interactions and valued unconventional forms of writing. As Rogoff (2003) suggests, developmental research conducted from sociocultural perspectives necessarily foregrounds the child as the unit of analysis, but also interprets developmental patterns against the background of the particular social practices in which young children participate. The resulting storyline is one of situated development.

Writing Development in Early Childhood: Developmental Storylines and Unresolved Issues

Researchers working from a developmental perspective have been concerned with the ways that children's writing hypotheses (Ferreiro & Teberosky, 1982) and participation in writing events (Rowe, 2008b) change across time. A good deal of attention has been devoted to establishing that children's writing becomes more sophisticated and conventional across the preschool years, even without formal school lessons. Cross-sectional research has shown that group means for preschoolers' aggregate writing scores increase with age (Gombert & Fayol, 1992; Levin & Bus, 2003), and also that, as a group, older preschoolers use more sophisticated writing forms, directional patterns, and message content than younger children (Tolchinsky-Landsmann & Levin, 1985). Recent longitudinal work (Molfese et al., 2011) with 4- and 5-year-olds has shown progression in scores for name writing, letter writing, and letter formation across time. Overall, when measures of central tendency are used to describe age-group patterns in early writing, they have produced a developmental storyline that highlights progress toward convention during the preschool years.

At the same time, many researchers have presented data to show that there is wide variation in children's writing and related skills at any particular age (Dyson, 1985; Hildreth, 1936; Sulzby, 1985b). For example, taking a component skills approach, Molfese and her colleagues (Molfese et al., 2011) conducted a longitudinal study of relationships between children's alphabetic knowledge, name writing, and letter writing at three time points (i.e., fall and spring of preschool, fall of kindergarten). Descriptive data showed that almost the full range of possible scores was observed for each measure at each time point. Describing features of children's holistic writing performances, Clay (1975) also reported great variability in the writing of same-age peers. In her words: "[W]hat one child discovers about print at 4:11 another equally intelligent child may not learn until 6:0" (p. 7).

In addition to the interindividual variability reported at various age points, researchers have also described intraindividual differences of two types. First, children often concurrently use more and less sophisticated writing strategies (Gombert & Fayol, 1992). For example, Bus and her colleagues (2001) reported that even after children demonstrated the alphabetic principle, they continued to use less sophisticated writing strategies such as letter-like forms. Second, individuals' levels of development differ across writing features. For example, Dyson (1985) reported that some children wrote sophisticated stories and messages using unconventional marks, while others used conventional letters but expressed less conventional content.

Finally, still under debate is whether early writing development involves a linear sequence of phases and whether there is a developmental ordering of categories for writing forms, directional patterns, and other features of writing. Researchers observing young writers in the context of controlled tasks involving dictation of researcher-selected words have more often argued for an ordered sequence of phases through which children pass as they learn to write. An example of this perspective is Ferreiro and Teberosky's (1982) five successive levels of writing, each organized by a central hypothesis about orthography. Several studies contend that children's understandings of general features of print common to many languages (e.g., units, linearity) develop first, and then are followed by learning about language-specific features such as directional patterns and letter shapes (Puranik & Lonigan, 2011; Tolchinsky-Landsmann & Levin, 1985).

Alternately, researchers observing children's writing in more open-ended situations have often argued against a strict linear sequence of writing development. For example, Sulzby (1985b) reported individual variation in the sequence in which kindergartners tested hypotheses about writing. Similarly, Dyson (1985) described kindergartners writing as a recursive process involving the coordination of overlapping features of writing. Her longitudinal case studies showed that the sequence in which children noticed and explored various features of print was influenced by their personal interests, styles of approaching writing, willingness to take risks, and purposes for writing. Luria (1978/1929) described writing development as a dialectical process marked both by gradual improvement in the kinds of writing characterizing each stage, and by setbacks occurring as children transitioned to new writing techniques. These seeming regressions are also reflected in the concurrent use of more and less sophisticated strategies (Bus et al., 2001; Gombert & Fayol, 1992).

To sum up, regardless of research approach, it appears that there is general consensus that, when young children are viewed as a group, their writing becomes more conventional across the preschool years. However, beyond this general observation, researchers' views about other aspects of early writing development are less settled. Despite many observations of the wide variation in children's writing patterns, the role of variability is undertheorized in current models of early writing development. Similarly, researchers continue to debate whether learning to write involves a sequential progression through a set of ordered hypotheses, or whether children's learning paths are more recursive and individually ordered. In this chapter, I consider these developmental issues from the vantage points provided by two time scales and two analytic approaches. I describe one group of preschoolers' writing seen from the vantage point of six-month intervals, but also zoom in to describe their approaches to writing within individual writing events. I conduct cross-sectional analyses of the writing of larger groups of same-age peers, and then follow a smaller subgroup of children longitudinally from 2½ to 6 years of age. With this data, I first describe how writing performances changed across the preschool years for one group of children who had frequent opportunities to engage in emergent writing with adults. My goal is to consider how these data may contribute to a more nuanced storyline describing early childhood writing development.

Data Source: The Write Start! Study

This chapter examines age-related patterns in the writing of 139 children aged 2:6 to 5:11 who participated in the Write Start! study (Rowe & Wilson, 2015) for one to three years. Children attended two high-quality childcare centers serving mostly African American families living in a low-income urban area of a midsized city in the southern United States. In their childcare or prekindergarten classrooms, children were frequently asked by researchers and teachers to write their own messages and the resulting texts were valued, regardless of their conventional correctness. In addition to observing the children at their classroom's writing center, in the fall and spring of each year all children completed a researcher-developed, standard writing task—the Write Start! Writing Assessment (Rowe & Wilson, 2009)—for which we asked children to write a caption for a photograph of themselves playing at school, and then to write their names. The photo-caption genre was selected because it was both meaningful and manageable for 2-year-olds, but also open enough that older children could respond with longer texts if they chose. Further, the task was designed to reflect local purposes for writing and patterns of interaction in classroom writing events. Figure 3.1, seen earlier, shows an example of a child's completed photo page.

The categories used to describe children's writing responses were initially based on existing research and then expanded to describe the full range of variation seen in the Write Start! sample. Categories describing four features of the children's writing—form, directionality, intentionality, and message content (Tables 3.1–3.4)—were sequenced from least to most sophisticated. This sequence was determined based on the usual order in which the larger group of children displayed these writing performances in the Write Start! study. The ordering was subsequently confirmed with growth-curve analysis (Rowe & Wilson, 2015). Though children often used a variety of forms, directional patterns, and so on, in each writing event, for the purpose of most analyses reported in this chapter children's writing is described in terms of the most sophisticated feature used in each event. Scoring the most sophisticated writing features made it possible to track the introduction of "new," more advanced writing features over time, thereby providing a view of the growing edge of children's writing performances. To create a group profile of writing development, the children's Write Start! assessment data have been divided into six-month age bands and examined cross-sectionally. To explore children's individual developmental trajectories, I conducted a longitudinal analysis of the ten children who began the study in Year 1 and continued through Year 3. I refer to these students as the longitudinal sample. Children's participation in photo caption events is interpreted using ethnographic understandings of local writing practices formed through long-term participation and observation in the children's classrooms. In this chapter, children's ages are presented in the year:month format and I refer to the Write Start! categories by the numbers assigned in the left-hand columns of Tables 3.1–3.4. (For additional details about methods used in the Write Start! study, see Rowe and Wilson, 2015).

What Develops? Describing Early Writing Development

In the next sections, I present categories developed to describe the writing of the young children who participated in the Write Start! study. Though these categories reflect the writing of one group of children who had frequent opportunities to participate in emergent writing, many of the writing patterns described in the following sections have also been reported in other studies. The last column in Tables 3.1–3.4 reports the concordance between the Write Start! categories used in this chapter and those identified in previous studies of preschool writing (Rowe & Wilson, 2015).

Writing Form Categories

The unconventional graphic forms of preschool writing are the most thoroughly described features of early childhood writing. Research has shown that children speaking a variety of alphabetic languages explore visual features of print such as complexity of forms (Levin & Bus, 2003), linearity (Levin & Bus, 2003; Tolchinsky-Landsmann & Levin, 1985), units (Levin & Bus, 2003; Tolchinsky-Landsmann & Levin, 1985), small unit size (Tolchinsky-Landsmann & Levin, 1985), quantity of characters (Ferreiro & Teberosky, 1982; Levin & Bus, 2003; Tolchinsky-Landsmann & Levin, 1985), and variety of characters (Clay, 1975; Levin & Bus, 2003; Tolchinsky-Landsmann & Levin, 1985). The categories illustrated in Table 3.1 were built on previous research and then refined to account for the writing responses generated by the 2- to 6-year-olds in the Write Start! study.

The forms preschoolers use in their writing provide important clues to their understanding of foundational principles about written language including: print is visually composed of marks surrounded by white space; alphabet letters have conventionally determined shapes and names; writing involves attention to both the sounds in spoken language and the marks on the page; and letters represent the sounds of spoken language. When children put pen to paper, they leave visible traces from which we can infer their current understandings of these principles (Tolchinksy, 2003). Children's unconventional writing provides a window on their learning and application of graphic transcription strategies, alphabet knowledge, and the alphabetic principle—understandings widely seen as important targets for beginning literacy instruction (National Reading Panel, 2000).

As seen in Table 3.1, children in our study used distinctly different kinds of writing forms in response to the learning problems posed by writing a photo caption. To participate as writers, children had to construct understandings about what writing marks look like and how writers choose which kinds of marks to make. In our study, some children initially renegotiated the writing task by drawing a recognizable picture of an object or person (F-1). Our qualitative observations suggested that drawing was sometimes used as an informed refusal (Sulzby, 1990);

TABLE 3.1. Write Start! Writing Assessment: Writing Form Categories

Score	Category	Description	Example	Key Study Concordance[a]
F-0	No marks	Child makes no marks		
F-1	Drawing only	Child draws a picture instead of writing; marks are clearly identifiable as a picture.		
F-2	Uncontrolled motor activity with a pen	Marks are unintentional; accidental swipes at paper with marker		
F-3	Scribbles	Purposefully makes marks; large mass of undifferentiated scribbles; uses forearm movements to create large scribbles		1, 4, 5, 6, 7, 8, 9
F-4	Scribble units	Small patches of scribbles separated from one another with space; usually created with wrist and hand movements		
F-5	Individual stroke units	Many repeated lines, circles, or curve strokes, usually of the same type; only one type of stroke in each unit		1, 4, 6, 7, 9, 10, 11
F-6a OR	Personal manuscript	Letter-like forms; combinations of strokes within the same unit; no behavioral evidence that child intended to write as a conventional letter		1, 2, 3, 4, 5, 6, 7, 8, 12, 13
F-6b	Personal cursive	Horizontal runs of loops, or zig-zags		1, 2, 3, 4, 5, 6, 7, 8, 10, 12

continued on next page

Table 3.1 *continued*

F-7	Conventional letters plus inventions	Child writes at least one recognizable letter, but it may be upside down or backwards; the remaining marks may be letter-like forms, scribbles, etc.		1, 2, 3, 4, 5, 6, 7, 8, 12, 13
F-8	Conventional letters (no letter/sound correspondence)	Upper or lower case, may be mixed; reversals are OK; recognizable by others as letters; no letter/sound correspondence.	 *"I am happy."*	2, 4, 6, 9, 10, 11, 13
F-9	Conventional letters, memorized words	Child uses conventional letters and words, but writes something memorized like her name or "I love you."	Child writes name.	
F-10	Invented spelling: First letter sound	First letter sound of word or syllable is represented; may not use conventional letter: c for "seal"; may contain other random letters; must have evidence that child is intentionally generating a spelling with letter/sound correspondence	 I was sliding the slide.	2, 9, 12, 13, 15
F-11	Invented Spelling: First and last	First and last letter sounds of word or syllables; many sounds left out	"rainbow" 	

continued on next page

Table 3.1 continued

F-12	Invented spelling: Most sounds represented	Attempts to sound out most sounds in the syllable or word; Letter choices may not be correct	"ship" *Cep*	9, 13, 15

ᵃNote: Numbers indicate key studies reporting a similar type of writing behavior, though the category name used in the key study may differ from the category name used for the purposes of this study: 1 = (Clay, 1975); 2 = (Dyson, 1985); 3 = (Ferreiro & Teberosky, 1982); 4 = (Gombert & Fayol, 1992); 5 = (Harste, Woodward, & Burke, 1984); 6 = (Hildreth, 1936); 7 = (Kenner, 2000); 8 = (Levin, Both-de Vries, Aram, & Bus, 2005); 9 = (Levin & Bus, 2003); 10 = (Luria, 1978/1929); 11 = (Martlew & Sorsby, 1995); 12 = (Sulzby, 1985b); 13 = (Sulzby, 1990); 14 = (Tolchinsky-Landsmann & Levin, 1985); 15 = (Tolchinksy & Teberosky, 1998).

that is, children sometimes told us they could not write, and then shifted to drawing as a way of participating in the photo-caption event. Most children, however, did participate as writers, despite the relative difficulty of the task.

Briefly, most children producing undifferentiated scribbles (F-3) made marks without any of the features usually associated with print such as linearity or small, individual units. Though some of the same physical-motor schemes were used to produce scribble units (F-4), the smaller size of the scribble marks and their placement on the page surrounded by white space showed initial attention to individually bounded units of print. Other categories demonstrated increasingly fine-grained observations of the visual details of print including the kinds, variations, and combinations of strokes characteristic of English alphabet letters. When producing stroke units (F-5), children wrote with strings of small, individual lines, circles, and curves. In personal manuscript (F-6a), these strokes were combined within the same unit, creating marks with even more resemblance to alphabet letters. Children who wrote using long wavy lines of personal cursive (F-6b) demonstrated attention to the linearity of writing. Personal cursive usually appeared concurrently with personal manuscript in our sample and so both forms were assigned the same ordinal score. The appearance of alphabet letters (F-7, F-8, F-9) showed children's increasing recognition that writing required the use of a particular set of conventional notational elements (Tolchinksy, 2003). Finally, with the shift to invented spelling (F-10, F-11, F-12), children approached writing with an increasingly fine-grained ability to segment words into phonemes, and to use letter-sound correspondence as the basis for deciding which alphabet letters to write.

From these descriptive observations, we infer that, while children initially participated in writing events using their existing physical-motor and gestural schemes, with experience they also began to attend to the visual details of print, then to the specific configurations of alphabet letters, and finally to selecting letters based on letter-sound correspondence.

Directionality Categories

In the preschool years, children are also learning about the layout of print on the page, the left-to-right sequence, and return-down-and-left directional patterns used for English print. Table 3.2 presents the Write Start! categories describing directional patterns in young children's writing. Observation of the directional patterns in children's writing provided additional clues to their understandings about the visual/temporal sequence of print and how they organized the motor activities of writing, and may also give clues to the visual scanning patterns they used for reading. Like other features of writing, children's global hypotheses about page layout and directionality were eventually replaced by more specific ones.

Initially, some children understood that the expected location for marks was on paper rather than on the table, but placed their marks randomly on the page (D-1). Others made a more specific observation that marks were arranged in lines, but produced unconventional linear arrangements (D-2) moving from right to left, or from the top to bottom of the page. Reversals of the directional patterns often occurred when children used unconventional right-side-of-page starting points (see Clay, 1991). Once they chose this incorrect starting point, they not only placed marks on the page in right-to-left order, but often flipped the orientation of individual letters to a mirror image. (See Tanera's name writing above her photos at ages 4:0, 4:6, and 5:0 in Table 3.9.)

TABLE **3.2.** Write Start! Writing Assessment: Directionality Categories

Score	Category	Description	Example	Key Study Concordance[a]
D-0	No writing marks made or a single dot, scribble unit, letter unit, or large scribble. Or, if child makes a clearly identifiable picture or drawing.	If picture, must be clearly identifiable as a picture (strict). Only a dot counts here; any small mark that is bigger than a dot should be scored below.		
D-1	Random placement of multiple units, letter-like forms, or letters	Child places writing marks without discernable pattern. Assumes multiple units are present.	Wil-yhum	1, 2, 12
D-2	Unconventional placement: linear	Child places writing marks in linear pattern with unconventional directionality: Right to Left Top to Bottom Bottom to Top, Mixed directions within same line, etc. Marks may not be conventional letters.	Breontez	1, 2, 15
D-3	Conventional linear placement, first line; other lines unconventional	Line 1 marks are placed left to right; after line 1 an unconventional directional pattern is used; marks may not be conventional letters.		1, 2, 15
D-4	Conventional linear placement, all lines	All lines are produced left to right; marks may or may not be conventional letters.		1, 2

[a]*Note:* Numbers indicate key studies reporting a similar type of writing behavior, though the category names used in the key study may differ from the names used for the Write Start! categories: 1 = (Clay, 1975); 2 = (Dyson, 1985); 3 = (Ferreiro & Teberosky, 1982); 4 = (Gombert & Fayol, 1992); 5 = (Harste, Woodward, & Burke, 1984); 6 = (Hildreth, 1936); 7 = (Kenner, 2000); 8 = (Levin, Both-de Vries, Aram, & Bus, 2005); 9 = (Levin & Bus, 2003); 10 = (Luria, 1978/1929); 11 = (Martlew & Sorsby, 1995); 12 = (Sulzby, 1985b); 13 = (Sulzby, 1990); 14 = (Tolchinsky-Landsmann & Levin, 1985); 15 = (Tolchinksy & Teberosky, 1998).

With more experience, children began to use conventional left-to-right directional patterns some of the time (D-4). They often established the first part of the left-to-right directional pattern, but used random or unconventional linear patterns when they reached the end of the line or otherwise ran out of space. Karim's photo label in Figure 3.2 is a good example. As seen by the numbers superimposed on his page, his first line of print, starting with a large *P,* was arranged in a left-to-right pattern. However, when he ran out of space, he continued vertically up the right side of the page, extended a run of personal cursive from right to left across the top of the page, and then finished with a series of circular stroke units vertically placed from top to bottom down the left side of the photo. Finally, children begin to use conventional, left-to-right, return-down-left directional arrangements for all lines of print (D-4). (See Javani's caption [age 5:7]—*I love to eat jelly.*—in Table 3.9.)

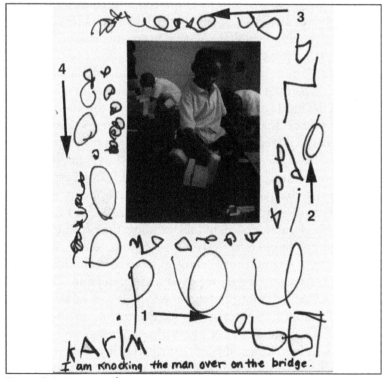

FIGURE **3.2.** *Karim's photo page.*

Intentionality Categories

Intentionality involves children's understandings that their marks can represent linguistic messages and their willingness to assign meaning to their marks (Harste, Woodward, and Burke, 1984). I have argued elsewhere (Rowe, 2008b) that when children demonstrate the message concept (Clay, 1975), the willingness to assign a linguistic message to their unconventional marks, they have reached a watershed point in early literacy learning. Once children see themselves as the kinds of persons who can express their meanings with marks, they have additional incentive to notice how print works in the demonstrations provided by people and texts in their environment. Observations of children's intentionality strategies provide cues to the ways they see themselves as writers and their understandings about how print represents meanings.

Intentionality does not come into being all at once. Like other understandings about writing, it is socially constructed through many moments of face-to-face participation in writing events (Rowe, 2008a). The Write Start! intentionality categories describe a developmental progression from global to more specific hypotheses for assigning meaning to marks.

In the Write Start! photo-labeling task, intentionality was observed by recording the messages children voiced during composing, and the messages they read in response to the adult request: "Read it to me." Initially, some children made marks, but did not read them (I-1). (See Table 3.3.) Some children responded to the request to read their marks with silence or by taking their turn with more writing, as Javani did in Example 3.1 at Turn 35. In a second nonverbal pattern, children responded by pointing to their marks, but offered no oral interpretation. In a third nonverbal pattern, children produced mumble reading; that is, children who otherwise conversed effectively with me purposefully responded with oral productions that were too quiet to be heard or that were mumbled so their messages were not understandable. These children appeared to understand that the request to read their marks required a linguistic response, but were unsure or uncomfortable in responding. Silence, making marks, pointing, and mumble reading were important ways of participating in emergent-writing events when no linguistic message was produced. In a fourth type

TABLE **3.3.** Write Start! Writing Assessment: Intentionality Categories

Score	Category	Description	Example	Key Study Concordance[a]
I-0	No marks	Child does not make marks		12
I-1	Marks/ no interpretation	Intentionally makes marks, but does not interpret them as a linguistic message	Refuses to read ("I can't; I don't know what it says") Gestures only (Points to marks, but does not provide oral reading) Mumble Reading (Child provides mumbled oral interpretation that is purposefully too quiet or is unintelligible)	12, 14
I-2	Sign concept	Writes/draws, hoping to create something, but without any idea of what the message might be	Writes, then asks assessor, "What did I write?"	1, 2
I-3	Intends message, no conventional correspondence	Reads message orally, but no correct letters are used; no speech/print match	No visible attempt at letter/sound correspondence. No evidence of matching speech units to marks.	10, 12, 13
I-4	Intends message/ global speech/print match; No letter/ sound correspondence	Reads message orally; must match voice or finger pointing to specific marks (usually syllables or words) to get credit. No evidence of letter/sound correspondence.	Uses voice pointing or finger pointing to show match between talk and specific marks. May match beginning/end of oral message to beginning/end of printed marks.	4, 7, 10, 13
I-5	Intends message/ some letter/sound correspondence	Reads message orally; at least one letter indicates attempt at letter/sound correspondence.	There is direct evidence (sounding out; child's verbal statement) that child has chosen at least one letter with a purposeful attempt to match speech to sound.	2, 9, 14, 15, 5

[a]*Note:* Numbers indicate key studies reporting a similar type of writing behavior, though the category name used in the key study may differ from the category name used for the Write Start! categories: 1 = (Clay, 1975); 2 = (Dyson, 1985); 3 = (Ferreiro & Teberosky, 1982); 4 = (Gombert & Fayol, 1992); 5 = (Harste, Woodward, & Burke, 1984); 6 = (Hildreth, 1936); 7 = (Kenner, 2000); 8 = (Levin, Both-de Vries, Aram, & Bus, 2005); 9 = (Levin & Bus, 2003); 10 = (Luria, 1978/1929); 11 = (Martlew & Sorsby, 1995); 12 = (Sulzby, 1985b); 13 = (Sulzby, 1990); 14 = (Tolchinsky-Landsmann & Levin, 1985); 15 = (Tolchinksy & Teberosky, 1998).

of nonverbal response, some children refused to read their marks, stating that they didn't know how to read. These informed refusals were most often made by older preschoolers unwilling to risk producing unconventional responses.

Beginning with category I-2, the sign concept (Clay, 1975), children demonstrated that they believed their marks represented meaning. Children displayed the sign concept when they asked an adult to read their marks. Clay has noted that children who make this request understand that their marks can represent a message, but do not believe they are capable of reading it. On the other hand, children who read their own marks demonstrated the message concept (I-3), showing both that they understood the semiotic potential of their marks and that they saw themselves as capable of taking up the roles of writer and reader (Rowe, 2008a). When children read their messages, some provided no indication of how the message was matched to the unconventional marks on the page (I-3). Others created a global link between marks and the oral message by pointing to print or by voice pointing (i.e., matching the cadence of their oral message to the cadence of writing) but without any attempt to use letter-sound correspondence (I-4). A final strategy for assigning meaning to marks involved reading the message based on some letter-sound correspondence (I-5).

Message Content Categories: Task-Message Match

Preschoolers are not only learning how the print system works, they are also learning about writing purposes, genres, and the style and content of messages expected in different social situations. When we asked children to write captions for their photos, they faced problems not only of writing form, directionality, and intentionality, but also of composing appropriate content for their written messages. Observing how children matched the content of their captions to the writing task allowed us to track their understandings about social purposes for writing. Because children composed their own messages, we were also able to observe the complexity of their messages.

The content of children's written messages is the least-studied aspect of early writing. For the Write Start! Writing Assessment's photo-labeling task, messages were described using categories that considered both the appropriateness of the message content and the complexity of the language used in the message (i.e., word, phrase, or sentence). (See Table 3.4.) Observations of task-message match were based on the content of the oral messages children read aloud during composing or in response to the adult's request to read their writing. Therefore, task-message match categories describe the oral message apart from judgments about the marks used to represent it.

Even when children began to demonstrate intentionality by assigning meaning to their marks, the content of their messages was sometimes related to neither the social event underway nor the image on the page (TM-1). For example, one child read the message, "I love my mommy and my brother," as the caption for a photo showing her playing with plastic alphabet letters in the classroom. Children appeared to understand that reading their marks meant saying something verbally, but they did not fully understand how to connect their messages to social and material cues present in the writing event. Some children showed a global understanding that texts should be matched to the larger social situation (i.e., school) by producing a conventional school literacy performance (TM-2: reciting the alphabet or counting). Reegan used this strategy when he read "One, two, three, four" for his marks below a photo showing him driving a toy car on the playground. Beginning with category TM-3, global relations to writing materials, functions, or processes, children showed awareness that the message should in some way relate to the writing event underway. These messages described the social function (e.g., "I'm gonna take it home.") or material features of the writing event (e.g., "It's blue.") or provided a global description of the writing process (e.g., "I went around and around."). The final four categories showed awareness that the caption should relate to the items pictured in the photo. Some children generated messages that globally described the photo (TM-4: "It's about my class."), often sounding more like oral comments to the adult than a written caption. Finally, children created conventional captions describing objects and actions pictured in the photos in the form of a word, phrase, or sentence (TM-5, TM-6, TM-7).

TABLE 3.4. Write Start! Writing Assessment: Task-Message Match (Message Content) Categories

Score	Category	Description	Example	Key Study Concordance[a]
TM-0	No under-standable oral or written message	No message assigned to marks		14
TM-1	Message unre-lated to photo labeling task	Child reads a message, but it is not related to photo content, or to the writing materials, processes, or functions of the photo-labeling task		2, 14
TM-2	Message unrelated to photo-labeling task/other conventional message	Child reads message not related to photo or task. Only "standard" messages like those in the example would score here; otherwise, score as 1.	"I Love You" "A, B, C, D" Names of family/ friends (not pictured)	1, 14, 13
TM-3a	Global rela-tion to writing materials OR	Child reads mes-sage that describes characteristics of writ-ing materials in use; often sounds like oral language directed at assessor rather than a written label.	"It's red." To describe marker.	14
TM-3b	Global rela-tion to writing functions OR	Child reads message that describes social function of writing product; often sounds like oral language directed at assessor rather than a written label.	"It's for you. I'm gonna take it home."	
TM-3c	Global rela-tion to writing processes	Child reads message that describes pro-cesses used in writing marks; often sounds like oral language directed at assessor rather than a written label.	"I went around and around." To describe use of pen.	14

Table 3.4 continued

TM-4	Global rela-tion to photo content	Child reads message that is related to items pictured in photo; often sounds like oral language directed at assessor rather than a written label.	"It's about dinosaurs."	2
TM-5	Photo label/ word	Child reads message as word that serves as a label for items or actions in photo	"Bike" (The child is on the playground riding a bike.)	1, 2
TM-6	Photo label/ phrase	Child reads message as phrase that serves as a label for items or actions in photo.	"My new shoes" (Photo shows child wearing new shoes.)	1, 2
TM-7	Photo label/ sentence	Child reads message as sentence that serves as a label for items or actions in photo.	"I am play-ing with Aran." (Photo shows child playing with Aran.)	1, 2

[a]Note: Numbers indicate key studies reporting a similar type of writing behavior, though the category names used in the key study may differ from the names used for the Write Start! categories: 1 = (Clay, 1975); 2 = (Dyson, 1985); 3 = (Ferreiro & Teberosky, 1982); 4 = (Gombert & Fayol, 1992); 5 = (Harste, Woodward, & Burke, 1984); 6 = (Hildreth, 1936); 7 = (Kenner, 2000); 8 = (Levin, Both-de Vries, Aram, & Bus, 2005); 9 = (Levin & Bus, 2003); 10 = (Luria, 1978/1929); 11 = (Martlew & Sorsby, 1995); 12 = (Sulzby, 1985b); 13 = (Sulzby, 1990); 14 = (Tolchinsky-Landsmann & Levin, 1985); 15 = (Tolchinksy & Teberosky, 1998).

Writing Development over Time: Age-Group Patterns in Writing

Cross-sectional analyses were used as a first approach to describing age-related developmental changes in writing between 2½ and 6 years of age. Children's Write Start! assessment scores, recording the most advanced category observed for each writing feature, were grouped into six-month age bands. To make cross-age comparisons easier, in this chapter, results are reported as relative frequencies—percentages of children receiving each score in the age band.

WRITING FORMS

Previous research has consistently shown that children's marks become more conventional with age (e.g., Gombert & Fayol, 1992; Levin & Bus, 2003; Tolchinsky-Landsmann & Levin, 1985)—a pattern that was also confirmed by cross-sectional analysis of the Write Start! data. Table 3.5 displays the relative frequency of writing forms used by each age group of Write Start! participants. The bolded entries are the most frequent (modal) writing forms used by children in each age band. The group's age-related progress toward convention is easily seen by the way boldfaced, typical performances are mostly arranged from left to right across the table's columns, mirroring the table's left-to-right ordering of categories from less to more sophisticated.

For the youngest age band, 2:6 to 2:11, scribbles (F-3) and scribble units (F-4) predominated. Three-year-olds most often produced personal manuscript (F-6). Four-year-olds typically

TABLE 3.5. Relative Frequency of Form Scores for the Photo-Caption Task

Age in years:months	No. of children	Drawing	Scribbles	Scribble units	Stroke units	Personal manuscript/cursive	Conventional letters + invention	Conventional letters	Memorized word	Invented spelling: First sound	Invented Spelling: First/last sounds
2:6-2:11	18	0.0	**27.8**	**27.8**	22.2	22.2	0.0	0.0	0.0	0.0	0.0
3:0-3:5	40	0.0	25.0	10.0	22.5	**30.0**	7.5	5.0	0.0	0.0	0.0
3:6-3:11	48	2.1	8.3	4.2	8.3	**41.7**	22.9	12.5	0.0	0.0	0.0
4:0-4:5	65	1.5	3.1	0.0	9.2	16.9	**41.5**	18.5	7.7	1.5	0.0
4:6-4:11	73	0.0	0.0	1.4	1.4	12.3	**39.7**	20.5	11.0	12.3	1.4
5:0-5:5	42	0.0	0.0	0.0	0.0	9.5	26.2	**31.0**	14.3	16.7	2.4
5:6-5:11	13	0.0	0.0	0.0	0.0	0.0	**30.8**	23.1	23.1	23.1	0.0

Note. Data are reported as a percentage of children in the age band receiving each score. Boldface entries are modal forms for each age band.

produced a mixture of conventional letters and invented forms (F-7). For young 5-year-olds, conventional letters chosen without letter-sound correspondence (F-8) were the most frequent writing form, while the smaller sample of 5½-year-olds most often combined conventional letters with invented forms (F-7).

While the progress-toward-convention narrative works well to describe the typical writing forms used by different age groups, it tells only part of the story. Table 3.5 also shows that, for each age band, there was also considerable variation in the forms children used when writing. Same-age peers wrote with many different forms. The range of normal writing variation is visible in the percentages scores arrayed to the left or right of modal responses for each age band. For example, for 2½-year-olds, though scribbles (F-3) and scribble units (F-4) were most common, the children's writing performances also showed attention to the visual details of letters. Nearly as many 2½-year-olds produced stroke units (F-5), or personal manuscript and personal cursive (F-6). Examination of forms used by 3-, 4-, and 5-year-olds shows similar variability within age bands.

To further explore these patterns of variability, we followed the age-related trajectories of *writing form categories*. Reading down the columns of Table 3.5, it is apparent that not all writing forms were used at every age. The use of some form categories increased with age, while others decreased. As new, more advanced writing forms were added to the group's repertoire, some less advanced forms ceased to be used as the most advanced category.

Forms used by the youngest children in our study were those that focused on physical-motor (F-3: scribbles) and visual details of writing (F-4: scribble units, F-5: stroke units). Though some of these forms continued to be used by a few children as old as four, the relative frequencies for each of these categories followed a rapidly declining trajectory and reached zero for the oldest age groups.

While the use of these less advanced forms was declining, new, more advanced writing forms were added to the group's writing repertoire. Writing forms containing conventional letters (F-7: conventional letters plus invented forms, F-8: conventional letters chosen without letter-sound correspondence) first appeared in low frequencies in the writing of children in the 3:0–3:5 age band and then followed a rapidly increasing trajectory. Writing forms produced with attention to letter-sound correspondence (F-10: invented spellings of first sounds) first appeared in low frequencies at age four, and then increased slowly for children in the 4:0–4:5 age band and beyond.

Not all categories followed simple increasing or decreasing trajectories, however. Personal manuscript and personal cursive (F-6) are such a case. Relative frequency increased sharply for 3- and 3½-year olds, for whom it was the most frequent category. However, as 4-year-olds began to more frequently use conventional letters, the use of personal manuscript decreased sharply, then continued a more gradual decrease thereafter.

To sum up, examination of age-related changes in modal writing forms showed a clear pattern of progress toward more conventional forms with increasing age. However, there was considerable variability in the writing forms used by same-age peers that was not captured in the modal analysis. Progress toward convention not only occurred as children in each age group added new and more advanced forms to their repertoires, but also in the decreasing frequency of less conventional forms.

DIRECTIONALITY

At least within the constraints of the photo-labeling task, group patterns showed that many children controlled conventional directional patterns relatively early, even before they were typically using conventional letters in their writing—a conclusion also supported by two recent studies (Puranik & Lonigan, 2011; Treiman, Mulqueeny, & Kessler, 2015). Two-and-a-half-year-olds and young 3-year-olds typically arranged marks randomly on the page. (See Table 3.6.) Beginning at 3½ years of age, children most frequently used conventional directional patterns for all lines of writing, though random arrangement continued to be used by some children from all age bands. The percentage of children using conventional directional patterns increased steadily across the age bands, reaching 76.9% for 5-year-olds.

Though analysis of modal patterns in directionality categories showed a bimodal distribution of either random or conventional

TABLE **3.6.** Relative Frequency of Directionality Scores for the Photo-Caption Task

Age in years:months	Number of children	Single mark, scribbles or drawing[a]	Random placement	Unconventional linear	Conventional Line 1, then unconventional	Conventional, all lines
2:6-2:11	18	27.8	**44.4**	11.1	16.7	0.0
3:0-3:5	40	10.0	**50.0**	15.0	5.0	20.0
3:6-3:11	48	10.4	29.2	18.8	6.3	**35.4**
4:0-4:5	65	6.2	16.9	18.5	12.3	**46.2**
4:6-4:11	73	1.4	12.3	6.8	13.7	**65.8**
5:0-5:5	42	0.0	9.5	2.4	11.9	**76.2**
5:6-5:11	13	0.0	15.4	0.0	7.7	**76.9**

Note. Data are reported as a percentage of children in the age band receiving each score. Bolded entries are modal patterns for the age band.
[a] Directional patterns could not be determined when children used a single mark or mass of scribbles, or when they drew a picture.

directional patterns, not all children moved so quickly to convention. Examination of the full range of variability in directionality scores showed that some children in most age groups used unconventional linear arrangements (D-2) and partially conventional arrangements (D-3), but at lower frequencies than the modal categories. The trajectories of change for these categories were relatively flat with small increases followed by small decreases. Our qualitative observations suggested that a small group of children used unconventional spatial arrangements for a longer period. Some children, who continued to reverse the directional principles, seemed to be influenced by individual factors such as persistent preference for an incorrect starting point on the right side of the page (Clay, 1991).

When compared to writing forms, these data showed, conventional directional principles began to be established earlier in the preschool years. It is possible that directional principles were easier to learn for two reasons. First, directional patterns were entirely visible in the actions of other writers, and adults frequently demonstrated left-to-right directionality as they touched marks on the child's page. (See Example 3.1, turns 4, 14, 21, and 32.) There were no unstated principles to be inferred, as in the case of understanding how letters are chosen to represent sounds. Second, the conventional directional principles for arranging print on the page were less complex than the many visual details and representational principles children had to consider when writing with alphabet letters.

INTENTIONALITY

Age-related patterns in the ways children assigned meaning to their marks showed that 2- and 3-year-olds typically were willing to read their marks, but did not indicate how the messages were linked to the marks (see Table 3.7). Still, for both the 2½- and young 3-year-olds, 27.8% to 22.5% of children did not read a message when asked. The percentage of children who were unwilling to read their marks declined to only 10.4% for the older

TABLE 3.7. Relative Frequency of Intentionality Scores for the Photo-Caption Task

Age in years:months	Number of children	Doesn't read	Sign concept	Reads, no conventional correspondence	Global match, voice point	Read with letter/sound correspondence
2:6-2:11	18	27.8	0.0	**61.1**	11.1	0.0
3:0-3:5	40	22.5	0.0	**60.0**	17.5	0.0
3:6-3:11	48	10.4	0.0	**66.7**	22.9	0.0
4:0-4:5	65	4.6	0.0	33.8	**55.4**	6.2
4:6-4:11	73	2.7	0.0	37.0	**43.8**	16.4
5:0-5:5	42	2.4	0.0	31.0	**38.1**	28.6
5:6-5:11	13	0.0	7.7	0.0	**53.8**	38.5

Note. Data are reported as a percentage of children in the age band receiving each score. Boldface entries are modal patterns for each age band.

3-year-olds. For 2½ - and 3-year-olds, the leading edge of development involved reading messages using finger or voice pointing to indicate a global match between speech and print. For 4- and 5-year-olds, almost all children were willing to assign a meaning to their marks, typically creating a global match between speech and print using finger or voice pointing.

Examination of age-related trajectories of intentionality categories provided a more nuanced understanding of the development of intentionality. Group data showed that substantial numbers of 2½- and 3-year-olds did not read a message when asked (I-1), but that this category declined rapidly in subsequent age groups and disappeared entirely for the 5½-year-olds. Reading messages with global speech-print match was part of the repertoire of even the youngest age group, and followed an increasing trajectory, becoming the modal response for 4- and 5-year-olds. A more advanced intentionality strategy, reading messages by matching speech to print with some letter-sound correspondence (I-5), was first seen in the 4:0–4:5 age band and increased across the next three age bands.

MESSAGE CONTENT (TASK-MESSAGE MATCH)

More than other writing features, children's scores tended to be widely distributed across message content categories, with the percentage of students composing a topically related sentence growing larger across the age bands. As seen in Table 3.8, the most frequent pattern for 2½-year-olds was "no message." Children in this age band also produced messages totally unrelated to the task at hand, unrelated conventional school performances such as reciting alphabet letters or numbers in sequence, and general comments about some aspect of the ongoing event (see Table 3.8). Altogether, 61.2% of 2-½-year-olds' responses were scored in categories where message content was unrelated to the photo. This pattern suggests that many children had yet to form conventional understandings of the meaning-based functions of their writing.

Young 3-year-olds produced equal numbers of refusals to read and sentence-length photo labels. Similar to those of the 2-½-year-olds, 57.5% of the responses produced by young

TABLE 3.8. Relative Frequency of Task-Message Match Scores for the Photo-Caption Task

Age in years:months	Number of children	No message	Message unrelated to task	Message unrelated/ conventional	Global relation to materials, process function	Global relation to photo content	Photo label/word	Photo label/phrase	Photo label/sentence
2:6-2:11	18	**27.8**	5.6	5.6	22.2	0.0	5.6	11.1	22.2
3:0-3:5	40	**22.5**	5.0	12.5	17.5	10.0	5.0	7.5	20.0
3:6-3:11	50	8.3	2.1	25.0	8.3	2.1	12.5	6.3	**35.4**
4:0-4:5	65	4.6	4.6	18.5	3.1	1.5	13.8	15.4	**38.5**
4:6-4:11	73	1.4	2.7	12.3	1.4	0.0	15.1	5.5	**61.6**
5:0-5:5	42	2.4	2.4	2.4	0.0	0.0	9.5	2.4	**81.0**
5:6-5:11	13	0.0	15.4	7.7	0.0	0.0	7.7	0.0	**69.2**

Note. Data are reported as a percentage of children in the age band receiving each score. Boldface entries are modal patterns for the age band.

3-year-olds were unrelated to the photo. For older 3s, this pattern reversed, with 43.7% of responses unrelated to photo content, and 56.3% globally or specifically related to the photos. By the time children reached 5 years of age, more than 80% of children composed sentence-length labels directly related to photo content.

Examination of the full range of variability for each age band showed children's message types tended to be widely distributed across many different content categories. Children between the ages of 2:6 and 4:11 produced almost the full range of message types in each age band. These message content categories had different trajectories of change. Viewing the data in this way confirmed the decreasing trajectory of the "no response" category (TM-0) and the increasing trajectory for photo-caption sentences (TM-7). However, it also provided a more complex view of children's approaches to message content. For example, in all age bands, children continued to produce messages unrelated to the task (TM-1), but the trajectory of change remained fairly flat. The relative frequency of messages globally related to writing materials, processes, and function (TM-3a, 3b, 3c) was fairly high for 2½- and 3-year-olds, and then declined as children began to more frequently produce captions with topically related words, phrases, and sentences. Another interesting pattern was seen in the increasing trajectory and then decline of conventional literacy performances unrelated to the task (TM-2). This trajectory showed that a good number of 3½- and 4-year-olds used well-learned literacy and numeracy routines to solve the problem of composing their own written messages.

STRENGTHS AND LIMITATIONS OF DEVELOPMENTAL STORYLINES
BASED ON MEASURES OF CENTRAL TENDENCY

Descriptions of early writing development built on measures of central tendency provide a picture of age-related patterns in writing that supports a progress narrative. When writing is measured at longer intervals, in this case four to six months, there appears to be a sequential ordering (from less to more sophisticated) in the *typical* ways children add new, more sophisticated writing strategies to their repertoires. Ordered categories of the type created for the Write Start! study can be helpful introductions for adults who work with groups of young children. However, models of early writing development based on measures of central tendency provide only a partial understanding of the ways that writing develops. When the developmental storyline is built on single indicators of age-typical writing, the result is often an idealized progress narrative that models children's learning as a steady progression toward more sophisticated understandings about all features of writing. My data suggest that children are making progress in their understandings about writing across the preschool years, but that progress is marked by variability between children and within individuals.

Individual Trajectories in Learning to Write

To create a more nuanced developmental storyline and to further explore children's individual developmental trajectories, I conducted a longitudinal analysis of the Write Start! photo-caption sessions of the ten children who continued as participants in the study from year 1 to year 3. As in the cross-sectional analysis, I tracked the children's developing understandings about writing forms, directional patterns, intentionality, and message content. My interpretations of the photo-caption sessions were supported by ethnographic data collected as I and my research assistants wrote with these children throughout each school year. Tracking individuals over time allowed me to compare their patterns to the typical profiles resulting from cross-case analysis and also to describe developmental patterns not visible in the group data. In this section, I focus on both progress and variability as seen in the writing of individual children over time. First, I describe how children's writing became more conventional between ages of 2:6 and 5:11. Second, I focus on variability between and within individuals.

To provide an anchor for this discussion, Table 3.9 presents the photo pages written by two children from the longitudinal sample. Javani's and Tanera's texts are arranged in columns reflecting the age bands used in the cross-sectional analysis. The messages they read for their marks are provided below each image, along with the child's age at the time of the assessment. Below each writing sample, I present the child's Write Start! scores for his or her photo caption (cf. Tables 3.1–3.4.). To facilitate discussion of the children's photo captions, arrows have been added to indicate the location where the child began writing his/her caption.

Progress toward Convention

Before turning to a discussion of variability, it is important to acknowledge that, as shown by cross-sectional analysis of group data, the progress narrative describes important patterns in the writing trajectories of individual children in the longitudinal sample. When looking at children's trajectories over time, it is clear that they moved from global to more specific and conventional understandings of all features of print. To illustrate this pattern, some of the children's individual learning trajectories for print forms are graphed in Figure 3.3. I have graphed the trajectories for only six of the children (Tanera, Javani, and four

TABLE **3.9.** Write Start! Scores for Four Writing Features: Multidimensional Profiles for Javani and Tanera

	Age Band		
	2:6-2:11	3:0-3:5	3:6-3:11
Javani	No understandable message		"It says my name."
Javani	**Age: 2:11** F-3: Scribble D-0: Scribble I-1: Doesn't read message TM-0: No understandable message		**Age: 3:7** F-3: Scribble D-1: Random placement I-3: Reads, no conventional correspondence TM-4: Global relation to photo content
Tanera		No understandable message	
Tanera		**Age 3:0** F-6b: Personal cursive D-2: Unconventional linear I-1: Doesn't read message TM-0: No understandable message	

continued on next page

Table 3.9 continued

	4:0-4:5	4:6-4:11	5:0-5:5	5:6-5:11
Javani	"A Y, like J Y"	"I am playing with animals."		"I love to eat jelly."
	Age 4:0 F-8: Conventional letters/no letter sound correspondence D-0: Single letter I-3: Reads, no conventional correspondence TM-2: Message unrelated to photo content/conventional	Age 4:6 F-8: Conventional letters/no letter sound correspondence D-4: Conventional, all lines I-3: Reads, no conventional correspondence TM-7: Photo caption/sentence		Age 5:7 F-10: Invented spelling/first sound D-4: Conventional, all lines I-5: Reads with some letter/sound correspondence TM-4: Global relation to photo content
Tanera	"I am doing picking up flowers"	"I'm is doing a puzzle."	"I write something."	"I was playing with markers at the table."
	Age 4:0 F-7: Conventional letters plus inventions D-2: Unconventional linear I-4: Reads with global match TM-7: Photo caption/sentence	Age 4:6 F-6a: Personal manuscript D-3: Conventional Line 1, then unconventional I-3: Reads, no conventional correspondence TM-7: Photo caption/sentence	Age 5:0 F-8: Conventional letters, no letter sound D-4: Conventional, all lines I-4: Reads with global match/points to print TM-7: Photo caption/sentence	Age 5:7 F-9: Conventional letters, memorized word D-4: Conventional, all lines I-5: Reads with some letter/sound correspondence TM-7: Photo caption/sentence

Note: Images show the photo pages produced by Javani and Tanera in response to the Write Start! photo-caption task. Black arrows show the starting point for the child's photo caption. Scores below the images correspond to Write Start! categories for writing form (F), directionality (D), intentionality (I), and task/message match (message content) (TM).

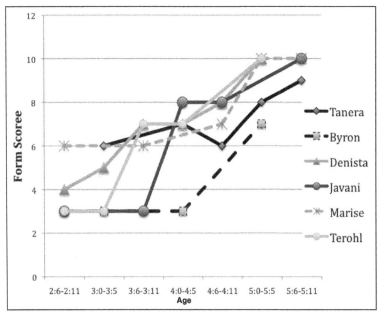

FIGURE **3.3.** *Individual trajectories in writing forms for six children in the longitudinal sample.*

of their peers) to increase the readability of the display. Though children's individual trajectories were clearly different, as seen by the differing paths of their line graphs, their trajectories show an overall trend toward higher scores.

Javani's and Tanera's photo pages, presented in Table 3.9, show overall patterns of progress in message content, form, directional patterns, and intentionality. For example, at ages 2:11 and 3:7, Javani wrote using scribbles. At ages 4:0 and 4:6 he transitioned to writing conventional letters without letter-sound correspondence, and at age 5:7 he used the alphabetic principle to invent spellings representing the first letter sounds of words. With regard to directional principles, he began with a single mass of scribbles at age 2:11, located several sets of scribbles randomly on the page at age 3:7, and again produced a single scribble at 4:0. By age 4:6 and 5:7, he used conventional directional patterns for multiple lines of print. With regard to intentionality strategies,

Javani did not read a message at age 2:11, but at 3:7, 4:0, and 4:6 read his message without any indication of matching speech to print. By 5:7, he read his message using some conventional letter-sound correspondence. The trajectory of Javani's messages is uneven, but over time he shifted from not reading his marks (age 2:11) to reading messages globally (ages 3:7, 5:7) or specifically related to the photo (age 4:6). Javani and Tanera's patterns are typical of the longitudinal sample in that most features show a clear trend toward more conventional understandings over time.

Interindividual Variabilty in Writing Development

While progress toward convention appeared to be an important part of writing development between 2½ and 6 years of age, variation among individuals' personal trajectories was also typical. Tracking individuals' writing over time provided additional insight into the variability seen within age groups in the cross-sectional analysis. Two patterns are especially evident when comparing the developmental trajectories of the children in the longitudinal sample. First, whether we discuss writing forms, directional patterns, intentionality strategies, or message content, children start from different points as 2½-year-olds. Second, the timing of children's transitions from one hypothesis to the next varies widely.

Differential Starting Points

As 2½-year-olds, the Write Start! children already approached writing quite differently. In Table 3.9, we see that Javani used scribbles as his most sophisticated writing form through the end of his third year. Tanera, on the other hand, was already producing personal cursive at age 3:0. Figure 3.3 illustrates the variable starting points for writing forms of six of the children in the longitudinal sample, reminding us that children in the same age band have varying levels of experience with writing, and that children's personal interests encourage them to focus on different facets of writing.

Differential Pacing

The pacing of children's learning also varies. For example, the differential timing of children's transitions to new print forms can be seen in Figure 3.3 in the differing slopes of the lines. For example, of the three children who were inventing spellings with first letter–sound correspondence by the end of the study (F-10), two (Javani and Terohl) continued to use scribbles (F-3) for an extended period into their third year. Denista, on the other hand, as a 3-year-old already produced forms with printlike features such as stroke units (F-5) and personal cursive (F-6). Children like Javani and Terohl scribbled for a longer time than some of their peers, but by age 5 they were using the alphabetic principle to invent spellings.

For each of the four features of writing discussed here, variability between children's individual trajectories was the norm. Children's developmental paths were characterized not only by different starting points, but also by different pacing. Differences between children were especially evident in the timing of transitions to new forms. Some children took longer than others to begin to use more conventional forms, but sometimes made large jumps in the conventionality of their writing forms in the four to six months elapsing between assessment points, allowing them to "catch up" with peers whose progress was more evenly distributed across the preschool years.

Intraindividual Variability in Early Writing Development

Describing the unique developmental paths of individual children also requires attention to variability *within* each child's learning. Viewed over time, young children's learning paths are characterized by seesaw trajectories, concurrent use of more and less sophisticated hypotheses, and unevenness in their learning about different features of writing.

SEESAW TRAJECTORIES

Though the general developmental trend for children in the longitudinal sample was toward more conventional understandings, many children seesawed back and forth between more and less sophisticated hypotheses for one or more features of writing. As seen in Table 3.9, Javani's writing showed a seesaw trajectory for message content. As a 4-year-old he composed a conventional message focusing on the specific actions pictured in the photo: "I am playing with animals" (TM-7). As a 5-year-old his message was only globally related to the photo (TM-4). He read, "I love to eat jelly" for a photo that showed him playing in the pretend kitchen of the dramatic play center. Tanera's writing showed a seesaw trajectory for writing forms and intentionality. At 4:0 years of age, she used a conventional letter T plus invented forms of personal cursive (F-7). However, at age 4:6, she used personal manuscript and no conventional letters (F-8). At 4:0 she read her message using the intentionality strategy of pointing globally to the print (I-4), while at the next assessment point she read her marks without indicating any speech-print correspondence (I-3).

For individuals, writing development does not appear to proceed as an even stepwise progression through a series of ordered hypotheses. Confirming previous research (e.g., Luria, 1978/1929), children who at a previous assessment point had displayed a more advanced writing feature sometimes used a less advanced feature six months later—a pattern also observed for all four writing features tracked in the Write Start! study.

DIFFERENCES ACROSS WRITING FEATURES

Children also displayed variability in their control of different features of writing. Confirming previous research (Dyson, 1985), the Write Start! children's understandings about writing forms, directionality, intentionality, and message content were not always equally well developed. While the conventionality of children's writing forms is often the basis on which adults judge their writing, data from this study suggest that this kind of one-dimensional judgment is not a good reflection of writing development. In particular, children who used the most conventional writing forms did not always produce the most sophisticated messages, and vice versa.

Take, for example, Jaron and Denista, two 4-year-olds whose photo-labeling pages are shown in Figures 3.4 and 3.5.

I am playing with blocks.

FIGURE 3.4. *Jaron's photo page.*

The numbers superimposed on Figure 3.4 show the sequence and direction for the child's writing. Visually, Jaron's writing is less sophisticated than Denista's. He has used personal cursive arranged in both conventional and unconventional directional patterns. Denista, on the other hand, has written her caption using randomly selected letters arranged in a conventional, horizontal, left-to-right sequence. Both children, however, created sentences with content that matched the photo, and both used voice pointing to indicate the match between marks and syllables in their messages. Jaron, for example, slowed and segmented his oral message into syllables, "I – am – play – ing – with – blocks," writing one up or down stroke of personal cursive for each syllable (Figure 3.4). Denista read her message, orally segmenting it into syllables and writing a letter below the photo as each syl-

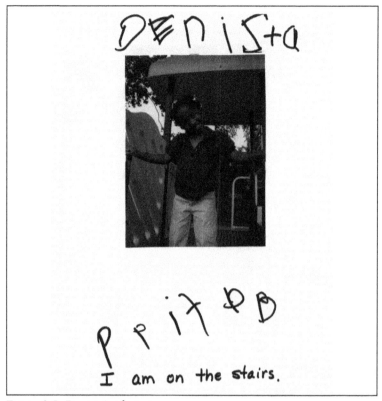

FIGURE 3.5. *Denista's photo page.*

lable was pronounced, breaking the last word into two syllables: " I – am – on – the – sta – irs." (See Figure 3.5.) While Denista's writing forms were clearly more sophisticated than Jaron's, both children displayed sophisticated understandings of expected message content and ways of assigning meaning to marks. Overall, examination of the individual children's writing showed that often their understandings were not equally sophisticated in all areas.

CONCURRENT HYPOTHESES

It is important to understand that the Write Start! scoring protocol produced a single score for each writing event reflecting the most sophisticated writing features used by the child. While this approach provided an indicator of children's changing approaches to writing, it did not capture their tendency to retain less mature forms in their repertoire and to continue to use them in combination with their more sophisticated forms—a pattern also observed in previous research (Dyson, 1985; Sulzby, 1985a).

To explore the question of whether Write Start! children concurrently used more and less sophisticated writing forms within a single writing event, I examined all of the photo-caption sessions of children in the longitudinal sample, recording all of the forms children used in each composing session. Forty-eight percent of the photo captions were constructed using multiple writing forms. Table 3.9 shows typical examples where, at age 3:0, Tanera uses both personal cursive (F-6) and scribble units (F-4) to produce her photo label, and at age 4:0 uses both conventional letters and personal cursive (F-7) to write her message below the photo. Overall, these findings are an important reminder that, for individuals, writing was not conducted with a single hypothesis about each feature of writing, but, instead, children often drew on a wider repertoire of more and less sophisticated hypotheses as they wrote.

Insights about Early Writing Development

In this chapter, my goal has been to describe age-related patterns in the writing of one group of children from 2:6 to 5:11 years of age. These patterns of participation were produced in a context where children had frequent opportunities to engage in emergent writing with adults who encouraged them to use their unconventional writing to compose their own messages. Given recent research (Gerde, Bingham, & Pendergast, 2015; Pelatti, Piasta, Justice, & O'Connell, 2014; Zhang, Hur, Diamond, & Powell, 2014) showing wide variation in the amount and types of writing experiences US children have in preschool classrooms, it is important to remember the situated nature of the developmental patterns reported in this chapter. While many of the writing patterns have previously been observed by researchers studying children learning to write in English and other alphabetic languages (see the key study concordances in Tables 3.1–3.4), more research is needed to understand how patterns of development are shaped by differing social practices and opportunities for young children's participation in writing. Nevertheless, this study provides data that are helpful in addressing the long-standing debate about whether early writing development is best characterized as sequenced and progressive (e.g., Ferreiro, 1990) or variable and individually patterned (e.g., Clay, 1991; Dyson, 1985; Sulzby, 1991). Results of the current study suggest it is both.

Sequences in Learning to Write

There is no evidence from this study to support a strictly invariant sequence in children's production of the forms, directional patterns, intentionality strategies, and types of messages described by the Write Start! categories. Instead, our data show that variability is a central characteristic of writing development for both individuals and groups. Nevertheless, when children's writing behaviors were observed at six-month intervals, as in the current analyses, the overall path of change for the group showed movement from less to more advanced writing categories. The Write Start! categories have been ordered to reflect the group trajectories observed in this study. Data supporting the match between the sequence of the Write Start! categories and children's trajectories over time included changes in modal writing categories with increasing age, the order in which the group added new, more advanced categories to their writing repertoires, and the changing relative frequencies of more and less advanced categories. Growth curve analyses showed that children's scores increased with age—a finding that could only be obtained if the order of categories was well matched to the actual trajectory of change (Rowe & Wilson, 2015).

Rethinking the Developmental Storyline for Writing in Early Childhood: Making a Place for Progress and Variability

Confirming previous research (e.g., Gombert & Fayol, 1992; Levin & Bus, 2003; Tolchinsky-Landsmann & Levin, 1985), all of the data examined here, whether cross-sectional comparisons of age-group patterns or longitudinal analyses of individuals, showed that, over time, children moved from global to more specific and conventional understandings of each of the print features studied. Though not a new observation, this finding underscores the importance of early writing experience as a venue for print learning (Levin, Share, & Shatil, 1996; Martlew & Sorsby, 1995; National Early Literacy Panel, 2008; Puranik & Lonigan, 2011).

Data patterns also showed that variability was the rule rather than the exception. Interindividual variability was seen in children's differential starting points and in the timing and pacing of transitions from one category to the next. Children of the same age exhibited a wide range of normal variation in their hypotheses about print, regardless of which of the four writing features was examined.

Intraindividual variability was also a key feature of the developmental paths of individual children in our study. Viewed over time, children's learning paths were characterized by back-and-forth movement where they seesawed between more and less sophisticated hypotheses for one or more features of writing. Variability also occurred as children concurrently used more and less sophisticated hypotheses in the same writing event. Writing was not accomplished with a single hypothesis about each feature of writing. Instead, children drew on a wider repertoire of more and less sophisticated hypotheses as they wrote.

Variability within individuals' personal developmental paths was particularly evident when looking at children's differential control of forms, intentionality strategies, directionality, and message content. Children's understandings of these features were not always equally well developed. The timing of children's learning about different writing features and their way of integrating them appeared to be more individually patterned than might be expected when looking at the ordered sequences of categories for each feature. While, for each feature, there remained a general progression toward more conventional understandings, all features were not attended to in the same way or at the same pace. Children pursued learning paths that our ethnographic observations suggested may have been influenced by their personal approaches to print, their interests, and their interactions with more experienced writers (Rowe & Neitzel, 2010).

The current study is not the first to find normal variability in young children's writing. As early as 1936, Hildreth reported wide variation in the writing of same-age peers:

> When the samples within any age level were arranged in order of excellence, considerable overlapping in the samples of any age group with the next was found. The least mature writers in the group 5.0 to 5.5, for example, were not so mature as the best writers in the age group 4.6 to 4.11. This was true for practically every age group for whom samples were collected. (p. 292)

However, after acknowledging the age-related variability in her participants' writing performances, Hildreth suggested that median writing performances should be viewed as age-group norms against which children's writing could be compared. In this way, she launched a developmental narrative that highlighted central tendencies and progress toward convention, and defined variable writing performances as outside the norm. This developmental storyline continues to guide current research and assessment of early writing.

Data from the current study have encouraged me to reconsider whether the simple version of the progress-toward-convention narrative, with its emphasis on representing age groups with typical (modal) performances, is the best fit for the writing development of the children in the Write Start! study. I have concluded that developmental narratives built primarily on measures of central tendency and the resulting descriptions of progress toward convention are useful as a general picture of learning to write. However, they are less useful for describing the expected learning paths of individual children because they obscure the great range of normal variation within and between children that is present in our data. Models of early writing built exclusively on measures of central tendency for groups tend to render the kinds of variability seen in this study invisible, and at worst define it as outside the norm. I argue, instead, that the field needs a more nuanced developmental storyline. Portraits of early writing that fail to capture both progress and variability run the risk of describing everyone in general and no one in particular.

Overlapping Waves of Writing Development

To account for the patterns reported here, a description of writing development in early childhood needs to forefront the normal variation in children's writing, while at the same time recognizing that young writers do, over time, form hypotheses that bring their personal understandings of writing in closer alignment with those of their communities. Siegler's (2000, 2006, 2007) overlapping-waves theory of cognitive development is a theoretical approach that is helpful for reconciling the role of progress and variability in the Write Start! data. Consistent with the findings presented in this chapter, Siegler (2000) has argued that, at any time point, children typically use a variety of ways of thinking, rather than a single one. Both more and less advanced strategies coexist in children's repertoires over long periods of time (Yaden & Tsai, 2012). Variability in development is seen in the changing relative frequencies with which children rely on particular strategies across time, and also in children's movement back and forth between more and less advanced strategies in their immediate attempts to solve problems. For Siegler, progress in development is visible as children construct new and increasingly more effective strategies over time, rely increasingly on relatively more advanced strategies, and decrease their use of less advanced ones. Though the trajectory of change involves a move toward more advanced ways of thinking, when viewed over longer timeframes the path of progress "reflects a back and forth competition, rather than a forward march" (Siegler, 2007, p. 105). He concludes that there is often a good deal of consistency in the order in which children construct new, more advanced strategies, with sequences most visible when measured at longer intervals and variability most clearly observed within events or between events recorded at close intervals.

Applied to the Write Start! data, Siegler's overlapping-waves theory (2000, 2006, 2007) supports our finding of a broad sequence with which children constructed new, more advanced writing performance. However, rather than stopping with a simple progress narrative, the overlapping-waves metaphor portrays early writing development as a complex process in which young literacy learners simultaneously add more advanced writing strategies to their repertoires, reduce the use of less sophisticated strategies, and draw on both more and less sophisticated strategies to participate in writing events. This metaphor of overlapping waves foregrounds variability, while at the same time recognizing that children's writing performances do on the whole become more sophisticated over time.

Implications for Early Education Policy and Assessment Practices

A major question addressed in this chapter is how writing changes with age and experience. Parents, teachers, and researchers are equally interested in understanding the kinds of writing they might expect to see from children of different ages—a question that is rooted in broader cultural models that recognize age as an important marker of development in early childhood (Rogoff, 2003).

In *The Cultural Nature of Human Development,* Rogoff (2003) points out that while many adults in Western industrialized cultures see time-since-birth as a central measure of child development, this is not the case in all cultures. The practice of dividing the human lifespan according to age is relatively new, fitting with industrial societies' goals for efficient management of schools and other institutions. One way this concern about age-related developmental progressions has been expressed is in questions about whether children are at, above, or below typical patterns for their same-aged peers. In the United States, this concern is at the forefront of current political discourse around educational standards that can be used to determine whether children's academic skills are "on grade level" (Common Core State Standards Initiative, 2010). In fact, Rogoff reports that age-related benchmarking is so associated with US cultural perspectives that it was called "the American question" when she studied at Piaget's Swiss institute.

In the United States, age takes on special importance in the early childhood years since it is a central criterion determining whether children are eligible to attend publicly funded educational programs, and for assigning age-eligible children to classes. While there are exceptions, many teachers find themselves working with

children in a fairly narrow age band. In this cultural and institutional context, where age is a central organizing construct for
cultural models of child development, adults need information
on age-related patterns in early childhood literacy.

Even so, the results reported in this chapter suggest that
age-related writing norms developed from measures of central
tendency must be interpreted with caution. Users of early writing assessments should avoid judging children's writing progress
based on its match to modal norms. Instead, educators need to
consider young children's writing performances in relation to the
wider array of normal variability seen within their age group.
Though there appear to be typical progressions in writing development, variations from these age-related progressions are as much
a part of the picture as are the progressions themselves. Educators
need both an understanding of typical paths and progressions,
and a keen eye for observing and supporting children's individual
paths of development.

Taking a Lifespan View of Early Writing Development

In this volume, we have collaboratively taken up the challenge of
examining writing development across the lifespan. In Chapter
2, we presented a set of principles intended to inform a model
of writing development across the lifespan, starting with preschoolers' unconventional scribbles and continuing through the
increasingly sophisticated texts produced by adolescents and
adults. Despite the great differences in the textual and life worlds
of writers across the lifespan, this chapter's portrait of the very
beginnings of writing underscores continuity in writing development that begins with children's earliest explorations of writing.

The Write Start! data provide a strong argument for our first
and eighth principles: the impact of *context* and *curriculum* on
the beginnings of children's writing development. The children
enrolled in Write Start! classrooms were surrounded by print at
home and at school, and had easy access to writing materials in
the classroom. Perhaps even more important, their development
was shaped by an emergent-literacy curriculum where adults

invited even the youngest children to write, and positioned them as persons capable of making meaning with marks—regardless of the conventionality of their texts. Emergent-literacy environments of this sort launch children on a developmental course framed by the social press to take up roles as writers (Rowe, 2008a). Development could look quite different in contexts where examples of writing were scarce or where adults equated good writing with conventional spellings.

Our second principle foregrounds the *complexity* of writing development in early childhood. Though writing a photo caption seems a simple task from an adult perspective, for preschoolers it required exploring and coordinating multiple facets of writing including their understandings of writing forms, intentionality strategies, directional patterns, and task-appropriate message content. Of course there are other kinds of understandings not analyzed here, as well. To participate appropriately as writers, children also needed to coordinate a complex set of interactive skills through which they negotiated access to space, materials, and attention and interaction with adults and peers. Like older writers, preschoolers are learning to coordinate many different facets of writing knowledge in order to take part in writing events.

Our third principle, *variability* in writing development, is a central pattern for the preschool writers in this study. While age is an organizing structure for many early childhood and elementary education programs, the Write Start! data suggest that educators and parents must expect and be prepared to respond to normal variability in the writing development of same-age peers. Young writers also display a good deal of intraindividual variability. Different facets of writing develop at different speeds, creating a complex pattern of overlapping waves of writing development. Though the source of variability in children's writing is not explored directly in this chapter, it is likely that children's interests and personal histories with writing, as well as their cognitive skills, are involved.

Our fourth principle foregrounds the impact of *writing resources and technologies*. The developmental trajectories described here were shaped by the page-based resources and technologies children used as they wrote at preschool. Children were exploring ways the small size and portability of the page facilitated certain types of mobility and social interaction around products. They were developing their skills in writing and drawing by hand. In the future, as children more often compose with touchscreen tablets and other digital tools, trajectories for writing development will also be shaped by the increased multimodality and mobility of these technologies.

Finally, the current study demonstrates how preschoolers were *reconfiguring general language functions and processes* in the service of writing—our fifth principle. Though these youngsters were still developing their oral language skills, they arrived at the writing table with considerable ability to express their ideas and interests through conversation and gesture. As they began to record their ideas in writing, their attention was turned to language as an object. Children formed increasingly more specific understandings of the ways speech is represented in writing—an understanding reflected in increased sophistication of their writing forms and intentionality strategies.

Overall, these principles of lifespan writing development serve to highlight what can and cannot be expected of a model of writing development in early childhood. Because writing development begins in early childhood with a highly contextualized trajectory, we cannot expect to have one simple set of benchmark accomplishments for young writers. We need to resist the urge to simplify the developmental picture by pushing contextual, curricular, and technological contexts to the background. Instead, we need to more fully describe local patterns of writing development as they occur in different social, curricular, and technological contexts.

Because writing development begins with a highly complex trajectory involving overlapping waves of learning about many different dimensions of writing, we cannot expect that a single facet of writing can be used as an indicator of the whole of a child's writing development. We need to resist the urge to simplify by tracing only the aspects of writing that are easiest to measure. Instead we need to continue to press for multidimensional portraits of children that can assist teachers in building from children's strengths, while recognizing where instructional nudges are needed to support learning of other facets of writing.

References

Bloome, D., Carter, S. P., Christian, B. M., Otto, S., & Shuart-Faris, N. (2005). *Discourse analysis and the study of classroom language and literacy events. A microethnographic perspective*. Mahwah, NJ: Erlbaum.

Bus, A. G., Both-de Vries, A., de Jong, M., Sulzby, E., de Jong, W., & de Jong, E. (2001). *Conceptualizations underlying emergent readers' story writing* (CIERA Report 2-015). Retrieved from University of Michigan, Center for Improvement of Early Reading website: http://www.ciera.org/library/reports/inquiry-2/2-015/2-015.pdf

Clay, M. M. (1975). *What did I write?* Auckland, NZ: Heinemann.

Clay, M. M. (1991). *Becoming literate: The construction of inner control*. Portsmouth, NH: Heinemann.

Common Core State Standards Initiative. (2010). *Common core state standards for English language arts & literacy in history/social studies, science, and technical subjects*. Washington, DC: National Governors Association Center for Best Practices and the Council of Chief State School Officers.

Dyson, A. H. (1985). Individual differences in emerging writing. In M. Farr (Ed.), *Advances in writing research: Vol. 1. Children's early writing development* (pp. 59–125). Norwood, NJ: Ablex.

Dyson, A. (1989). *Multiple worlds of child writers: Friends learning to write*. New York: Teachers College Press.

Ferreiro, E. (1990). Literacy development: Psychogenesis. In Y. Goodman (Ed.), *How children construct literacy: Piagetian perspectives* (pp. 12–25). Newark, DE: International Reading Association.

Ferreiro, E., & Teberosky, A. (1982). *Literacy before schooling*. Portsmouth, NH: Heinemann.

Gee, J. P. (2003). A sociocultural perspective on early literacy development. In S. B. Neuman & D. K. Dickinson (Eds.), *Handbook of early literacy research* (pp. 30–42). New York: Guilford Press.

Gerde, H. K., Bingham, G. E., & Pendergast, M. L. (2015). Reliability and validity of the Writing Resources and Interactions in Teaching Environments (WRITE) for preschool classrooms. *Early Childhood Research Quarterly, 31*, 34–46. doi:10.1016/j.ecresq.2014.12.008

Gombert, J. E., & Fayol, M. (1992). Writing in preliterate children. *Learning and Instruction,* 2(1), 23–41. doi:10.1016/0959-4752(92)90003-5

Goodman, Y. (1986). Children coming to know literacy. In W. H. Teale & E. Sulzby (Eds.), *Emergent literacy: Writing and reading* (pp. 1–14). Norwood, NJ: Ablex.

Harste, J. C., Woodward, V. A., & Burke, C. L. (1984). *Language stories and literacy lessons.* Portsmouth, NH: Heinemann.

Hildreth, G. (1936). Developmental sequences in name writing. *Child Development,* 7(4), 291–303.

Kenner, C. (2000). Symbols make text: A social semiotic analysis of writing in a multilingual nursery. *Written Language and Literacy,* 3(2), 235–66. doi:10.1075/wll.3.2.03ken

Lave, J., & Wenger, E. (1991). *Situated learning: Legitimate peripheral participation.* Cambridge, UK: Cambridge University Press.

Levin, I., Both-de Vries, A., Aram, D., & Bus, A. (2005). Writing starts with own name writing: From scribbling to conventional spelling in Israeli and Dutch children. *Applied Psycholinguistics,* 26(3), 463–77. doi:10.1017/S0142716405050253

Levin, I., & Bus, A. G. (2003). How is emergent writing based on drawing? Analyses of children's products and their sorting by children and mothers. *Developmental Psychology,* 39(5), 891–905. doi:10.1037/0012-1649.39.5.891

Levin, I., Share, D. L., & Shatil, E. (1996). A qualitative-quantitative study of preschool writing: Its development and contribution to school literacy. In C. M. Levy & S. Randsdell (Eds.), *The science of writing: Theories, methods, individual differences, and applications* (pp. 271–93). Mahwah, NJ: Erlbaum.

Luria, A. R. (1978). The development of writing in the child. In M. Cole (Ed.), *The selected writings of A. R. Luria* (pp. 145–94). White Plains, NY: M. E. Sharpe. (Original work published 1929)

Martlew, M., & Sorsby, A. (1995). The precursors of writing: Graphic representation in preschool children. *Learning and Instruction,* 5(1), 1–19. doi:10.1016/0959-4752(94)00014-G

Miller, P. J., & Goodnow, J. J. (1995). Cultural practices: Toward an integration of culture and development. In J. J. Goodnow, P. J. Miller, & F. Kessel (Eds.), *Cultural practices as contexts for development* (pp. 5–16). San Francisco: Jossey-Bass.

Molfese, V. J., Beswick, J. L., Jacobi-Vessels, J. L., Armstrong, N. E., Culver, B. L., White, J. M., . . . Molfese, D. L. (2011). Evidence of alphabetic knowledge in writing: Connections to letter and word identification skills in preschool and kindergarten. *Reading and Writing: An Interdisciplinary Journal, 24*(2), 133–50. doi:10.1007/s11145-010-9265-8

National Early Literacy Panel (2008). *Developing early literacy: Report of the National Early Literacy Panel: A scientific synthesis of early literacy development and implications for intervention.* Jessup, MD: National Institute for Literacy.

National Reading Panel. (2000). *Teaching children to read: An evidence-based assessment of the scientific research literature on reading and its implications for reading instruction.* Retrieved from https://www.nichd.nih.gov/publications/pubs/nrp/Documents/report.pdf

Pelatti, C. Y., Piasta, S. B., Justice, L. M., & O'Connell, A. (2014). Language- and literacy-learning opportunities in early childhood classrooms: Children's typical experiences and within-classroom variability. *Early Childhood Research Quarterly, 29*(4), 445–56. doi:10.1016/j.ecresq.2014.05.004

Puranik, C. S., & Lonigan, C. J. (2011). From scribbles to scrabble: Preschool children's developing knowledge of written language. *Reading and Writing: An Interdisciplinary Journal, 24*(5), 567–89. doi: 10.1007/s11145-009-9220-8

Rogoff, B. (2003). *The cultural nature of human development.* Oxford, UK: Oxford University Press.

Rowe, D. W. (2008a). The social construction of intentionality: Two-year-olds' and adults' participation at a preschool writing center. *Research in the Teaching of English, 42*(4), 387–434.

Rowe, D. W. (2008b). Social contracts for writing: Negotiating shared understandings about text in the preschool years. *Reading Research Quarterly, 43*(1), 66–95. doi:10.1598/RRQ.43.1.5

Rowe, D. W., & Neitzel, C. (2010). Interest and agency in two- and three-year-olds' participation in emergent writing. *Reading Research Quarterly, 45*(2), 169–95. doi:10.1598/RRQ.45.2.2

Rowe, D. W., & Wilson, S. (2009). *Write Start! writing assessment.* Writing assessment instrument. Vanderbilt University, Nashville, TN.

Rowe, D. W., & Wilson, S. J. (2015). The development of a descriptive measure of early childhood writing: Results from the Write Start!

writing assessment. *Journal of Literacy Research, 47*(2), 245–92. doi:10.1177/1086296X15619723

Siegler, R. S. (2000). The rebirth of children's learning. *Child Development, 71*(1), 26–35.

Siegler, R. S. (2006). Microgenetic analyses of learning. In D. Kuhn & R. S. Siegler (Eds.), *Handbook of child psychology* (6th ed.): Vol. 2. *Cognition, perception, and language* (pp. 464–510). Hoboken, NJ: Wiley.

Siegler, R. S. (2007). Cognitive variability. *Developmental Science, 10*(1), 104–09. doi:10.1111/j.1467-7687.2007.00571.x

Sulzby, E. (1985a). Children's emergent readings of favorite storybooks: A developmental study. *Reading Research Quarterly, 20*(4), 458–81.

Sulzby, E. (1985b). Kindergarteners as writers and readers. In M. Farr (Ed.), *Advances in writing research. Children's early writing* (Vol. 1, pp. 127–200). Norwood, NJ: Ablex.

Sulzby, E. (1990). Assessment of writing and children's language while writing. In L. M. Morrow & J. K. Smith (Eds.), *Assessment for instruction in early literacy.* Englewood Cliffs, NJ: Prentice Hall.

Teale, W. H., & Sulzby, E. (1986a). Introduction: Emergent literacy as a perspective for examining how young children become writers and readers. In W. H. Teale & E. Sulzby (Eds.), *Emergent literacy: Writing and reading* (pp. vii–xxv). Norwood, NJ: Ablex.

Teale, W. H., & Sulzby, E. (Eds.). (1986b). *Emergent literacy: Writing and reading.* Norwood, NJ: Ablex.

Tolchinksy, L. (2003). *The cradle of culture and what children know about writing and numbers before being taught.* Mahwah, NJ: Erlbaum.

Tolchinksy, L., & Teberosky, A. (1998). The development of word segmentation and writing in two scripts. *Cognitive Development, 13*(1), 1–24. doi:10.1016/S0885-2014(98)90018-1

Tolchinsky-Landsmann, L., & Levin, I. (1985). Writing in preschoolers: An age-related analysis. *Applied Psycholinguistics, 6*(3), 319–39. doi:10.1017/S0142716400006238

Treiman, R., Mulqueeny, K., & Kessler, B. (2015). Young children's knowledge about the spatial layout of writing. *Writing Systems Research, 7*(2), 235–44. doi:10.1080/17586801.2014.924386

Vygotsky, L. S. (1978). *Mind in society: The development of higher psychological processes*. Cambridge, MA: Harvard University Press.

Yaden, D., Jr., & Tsai, T. (2012). Learning how to write in English and Chinese: Young bilingual kindergarten and first grade children explore the similarities and differences between writing systems. In E. B. Bauer & M. Gort (Eds.), *Early biliteracy development: Exploring young learners' use of their linguistic resources* (pp. 55–83). New York: Routledge.

Zhang, C., Hur, J., Diamond, K. E., & Powell, D. (2014). Classroom writing environments and children's early writing skills: An observational study in Head Start classrooms. *Early Childhood Education Journal, 43*(4), 307–15. doi:10.1007/s10643-014-0655-4

CHAPTER FOUR

Linguistic Features of Writing Development: A Functional Perspective

MARY SCHLEPPEGRELL
University of Michigan

FRANCES CHRISTIE
University of Melbourne

This chapter describes how children's meaning-making capacities with written language emerge over the school years. Our account of the developmental progression is informed by systemic functional linguistics (SFL), Halliday's theory of language as social semiotic (Halliday, 1978, 2014). This linguistic theory proposes that we see language as a fundamental resource for making meaning, recognizing the social and cultural situatedness of language use. Every language offers a vast potential for acts of meaning, with its lexicogrammar[1] presenting a range of resources for sharing experience, enacting social relationships, and shaping meaningful messages. SFL sees *grammar* as a social resource that speakers/writers draw on for meaning making, rather than something internal to the individual, distinguishing it from other traditions of linguistic inquiry. The theory offers grammatical descriptions that can recognize linguistic progression in writing in at least two senses: first, in the sense that we can track developmental growth in children's writing as they move from childhood into adolescence and beyond; and second in the sense that we can explain how meanings unfold across a text. In both senses, we take account of the contexts, purposes, and genres of writing. From this broad perspective, development is recognized in the new meanings and ways of meaning that emerge as writers participate in new contexts of learning and text production. The notion of *choice* is fundamental to SFL, as writers have a range of options for meaning in different ways. Typically, the acts of meaning of writers and speakers differ, because writing and speech generally serve different purposes. The grammatical choices writers make therefore differ from those of speakers.

To illustrate the ways writers draw on language resources in new ways as they learn across the years of schooling, we present examples of texts from our own research and that of others. Christie and her colleagues in Australia describe trajectories of writing development differentiated by discipline and genre, based on their analysis of thousands of texts written by children in classroom contexts (see Christie, 1998, 2002b, 2010, 2012; Christie & Derewianka, 2008; Christie & Macken-Horarik, 2007, 2011; Rose & Martin, 2012). They identified new forms of expression that emerged in children's writing as they moved through the years of schooling, relating these developments to achievement of new purposes in writing to respond to the demands of different subject areas. Inspired by that work, Schleppegrell and her colleagues have promoted SFL-informed pedagogies for second language learners in K–12 classrooms. They have offered teachers linguistic metalanguage that describes the meanings writers present, enabling teachers both to support writing in different subject areas and to respond to children's texts with feedback that goes beyond a focus on errors (see Schleppegrell 1998, 2004b, 2006; Schleppegrell & Go, 2007; Schleppegrell et al., 2014). Many others have also used SFL tools to describe pathways of writing development in K–12 classrooms and beyond (e.g., Brisk, 2012, 2015; Byrnes, 2013; Coffin & Donohue, 2014; de Oliveira & Iddings, 2014; Derewianka, 2007; Gebhard, Chen, & Britton, 2014; Harman, 2013; Macken-Horarik, 2006).

The chapter characterizes the linguistic resources that enable the emergence of meaning making in the written mode in texts written by children in K–12 classrooms in the United States, Australia, and other countries. With learners from diverse backgrounds, the classrooms are typical of contemporary English-speaking contexts around the world, including children who speak English as a mother tongue and children who are learners of English. We thus recognize meaning making in the developing texts of L2 as well as L1 writers. We describe a developmental trajectory through which learners move as they grow in control of written English, with different individual pathways shaped by life experiences, including experiences of other languages, family background, and social positioning. We illustrate how learners develop along three dimensions: growing capacity to elaborate on their experience in writing; growth in ability to present their own views and perspectives; and control of the discourse patterns of written language as they learn to shape the flow of information in the texts they write. We then relate this trajectory to findings from research from other linguistic traditions to highlight the particular contributions of the SFL perspective. Finally, we suggest some implications of this understanding of writing development for research and instruction.

A Functional Approach to Writing Development across the School Years

All children initially encounter language as speech or signing, learned in intimate interaction with others, and used for the achievement of immediate goals as well as the expression of daily experience. Written language develops out of this foundation in oral/signed language,[2] and is another dimension of overall growth in meaning-making ability. Even when the language through which writing is learned is not the same language as the oral/signed language developed in early childhood, the experience of speaking/signing, of "languaging," is the basis on which the learning of writing can be negotiated.

By the time children come to school, they have good control of oral/signed registers[3] that they can build on as they learn to write, but still have more to learn about the lexicogrammatical choices they can draw on in written registers.[4] Spoken/signed language develops in interaction in the contexts of living. In contrast, writing calls for focused attention and effortful learning. Written language development typically occurs in contexts of schooling, where deliberate choices are made about the genres, topics, time commitments, and pedagogical activities through which writing is taught and learned. That makes the study of written language development inextricably linked with the ways learners' writing is shaped by those pedagogical contexts.

Learning to write K to 12 involves movement in control of language in increasingly abstract ways. In the early years, children develop an understanding that language can be represented on the page, with all the associated learning tasks to do with mastering spelling and writing systems, as well as the grammatical organization of written language. From the point of view of the young learner, a written passage is itself an abstraction, already a little removed from the immediacy of talk. All subsequent development takes the learner into further abstraction, for writing opens up many possibilities in creating, storing, and transmitting knowledge, information, and ideas across space and time. At the same time, writing also enables learners to express attitudes and judgments about experience in new ways that position them to participate in expanding social or disciplinary communities.

Entering these new contexts necessarily involves learning more abstract and technical knowledge, and children move from expressing "commonsense" experiences in early writing toward writing about increasingly abstract and "uncommonsense" experiences and knowledge in adolescence and adult life. The developmental shift should be understood in two senses. In the first and older sense, it reflects a movement from the oral to the written mode, where the grammatical shifts involved are a consequence of the history of written language as it evolved over the centuries to enable new ways of expression. In the second sense, the shift represents a developmental progression in control of written language from early childhood to adulthood, experienced by all successful students as they move up the years of schooling.

Figure 4.1 depicts the developmental progression we describe here in terms of movement from the spoken to the written mode. Reading from the bottom, a learner starts with the spoken mode, developed through experience with the immediate or "commonsense" world of much daily life. The grammar of early speech, characterized from the SFL perspective, is *congruent;* that is, it draws on grammatical forms for the functions those forms evolved to serve, and makes meaning in direct or overt ways. Thus, nouns express entities, things or persons (*the boys*), verbs express actions (*ran*), adverbs suggest how (*happily*), prepositional phrases create

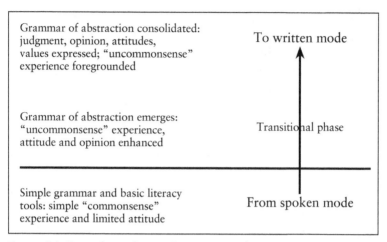

Grammar of abstraction consolidated: judgment, opinion, attitudes, values expressed; "uncommonsense" experience foregrounded	To written mode
Grammar of abstraction emerges: "uncommonsense" experience, attitude and opinion enhanced	Transitional phase
Simple grammar and basic literacy tools: simple "commonsense" experience and limited attitude	From spoken mode

FIGURE **4.1**. *From the spoken to the written mode.*

relevant contextual information (*in the park*), and these are all employed in patterned ways to make the message of a clause (*the boys ran happily in the park*). In addition, logical links between the messages of clauses are made with conjunctions (*and, then, but, when*) to create longer messages (*the boys ran happily in the park and then they went home for their dinner*).

Development of maturity in writing, expressed in mastery of the written mode, emerges by late childhood and early adolescence as writers gain control of the grammar of abstraction through which the "uncommonsense" experience learned through school subjects is most successfully presented. The grammar becomes *noncongruent* when the forms are used in grammatically metaphorical ways to shape meanings rather differently than do the congruent expressions. For example, actions are expressed as nouns, or more often noun groups, while the links between the meanings of separate clauses are buried in different verbal groups, as in *the boys' happy running in the park* (noun group) *was followed* (verbal group) by *their going home for their dinner* (noun group). The resulting expression is termed grammatically noncongruent, mainly because the actions of immediate experience (*ran, went*) have been turned into phenomena, things named by creating noun groups.

In addition, writers take up new relationships with the reader in the ways they appraise, evaluate, and judge, often expressing their perspectives in grammatical formulations that enable less subjective expression of those meanings. By late adolescence the successful writer controls discourses of the various subject areas with their different ways of expressing abstraction, interpretation, and evaluation, depending on the field and knowledge involved.

SFL's metalanguage of grammatical description offers constructs that enable us to characterize the ways meanings made in texts show progression across the school years.[5] The examples we use show writers responding to curricular contexts, writing genres that include recounts of experience, responses to and analyses of literature, science reports, historical explanations, and arguments. Writing a range of genres offers opportunities to engage in written expression for different purposes, calling on linguistic choices that are functional for achieving those purposes (Christie, 2012; Christie & Derewianka, 2008). For each example we present, we identify the genre being written and the age and country of the writer. As in most instances we are able only to excerpt these texts, we cite publications where more of the text and additional information about the context can be found. All of the texts were written in classrooms with diverse learners and several show evidence of second language backgrounds. As we are interested in characterizing development of meaning making in the written mode as learners engage with subject area learning, it is the texts and the language choices that are in focus, rather than the individual writers. We are not concerned here with grammatical accuracy, nor do we consider correctness as necessary evidence of development. We occasionally comment on word choice in the examples we offer, but generally treat vocabulary as an aspect of written language development that is integrated with the grammatical developments we describe. This intertwined relationship reveals itself most obviously in discussion of nominalization, grammatical metaphor, and the presentation of attitude and perspective, where choice of individual words and grammatical patterns are not separate.

While our descriptions often focus on the grammar of the clause and sentence, we show how the writer's choices are in service of crafting texts that serve their disciplinary and social purposes. The texts, mainly written in authentic instructional contexts, often call for the writers to draw on meanings in texts they have read, displaying new knowledge learned from reading. Overall, we offer a picture of typical development in instructed settings in a broad range of English-language classrooms in different parts of the world.

Into the Written Mode

In their early writing, children use simple vocabulary and grammar, typically write about "commonsense" experience, and express little attitude. They write clauses linked by additive or temporal conjunctions (e.g., *and, then*), as in this text (spelling corrected) from an Australian writer age 6:[6]

> Text 1:
> We went to see the lost dog's home // and I saw a cat // and I saw a dog.
> (Christie, 2012, p. 56)

An 11-year-old speaker of Chinese who had been in a US classroom for a little over a year, and who had had limited schooling before his immigration, also used clauses linked by additive conjunctions to write about a performance by a visitor to his classroom:

> Text 2:
> Mr. Lau relly like to play top // and he very good of this game // and he know how to origami.
> (Schleppegrell & Go, 2007, p. 532)

As these examples show, children can be in the same phase of writing development even at different ages; this older child, learning English as an additional language, is still developing an understanding of the ways ideas are linked together in writing.

In their early writing, children express attitude mainly in verbs that realize processes of affect[7] (e.g., *he liked it*); or through simple attributive processes (e.g., *he was very good*). Writers' comments and critique are often expressed in explicit reference to the cognitive processes involved (e.g., *I think...*), as in Text 3, the opening sentence in an American 7-year-old's written response to a question posed by the teacher about a character in a story (Was Jamaica happier receiving a gift or giving a gift?):

Text 3:
> I think // Jamaica is happier giving // because the Mayor put her name on the plaque.
>   (Schleppegrell, unpublished ms.)

In later years the reference to one's own *thinking* falls away as successful writers learn to represent their opinions and perspectives in other ways; for example, by writing, as a 14-year-old Australian girl did, "'To Kill a Mockingbird'" by Harper Lee contains believable characters which we can relate to and characters who hold our interest" (Christie & Derewianka 2008, p. 72). Below we illustrate development of the ability to infuse attitudinal meanings into texts in ways that respond to disciplinary expectations.

As writers develop, their written language is extended and elaborated, and they take up new discourse patterns that enable them to texture their writing, for example through flexible use of word order to present and develop information. One evidence of this is the writer's facility with *Theme*,[8] a construct of the SFL grammatical description that points to the different options writers choose to initiate the next clause as they develop a text.[9] Halliday refers to Theme as "the element (in the clause) that serves as the point of departure of the message; it is that which locates and orients the clause within its context" (2014, p. 89). A regular or unmarked Theme occurs when the Theme is conflated with the Subject of the clause (e.g., *We saw a lizard* or *The group of children climbed up the mountain*). A Theme is *marked* when it is something other than the Subject.

For example, Text 4, about a class trip, shows some developing facility in control of Theme by its 6-year-old Australian author. She understood, for example, the need to orient her readers to the details of her recount by using a marked Theme expressed in a prepositional phrase of time (*On Wednesday*) to open the text. Control of Theme is critical to emergent control of the grammar of written registers, for it helps shape the directions a text takes, sometimes foregrounding new information, sometimes pursuing and developing further aspects of established information.

In Text 4, the writer demonstrated how she could take information introduced in her first clause: *On Wednesday we went to Anakie Gorge,* and reintroduce it in Theme position in an *enclosed clause,* a clause that interrupts another clause without being a part of (embedded in) it:

> and <<when we went >>we went past Fairy Park.

Here *when we went* is a *marked Theme.* Such a marked Theme is a useful device, enabling the writer to compress the information introduced in the first clause (*we went to Anakie Gorge*) and make it the point of departure for the next clause.

The writer made considerable use of this device, helping to create a coherent, sustained written text, even though the consistent repetition of the additive conjunction (*and*) reveals that the text is like speech in other ways (spelling corrected; enclosed clauses are shown << >>).

> Text 4:
> On Wednesday we went to Anakie Gorge
> and <<when we went >> we went past Fairy Park
> and <<when we got there>> we walked down the path
> . . .
> and <<when everyone was down>> we had lunch
> and then we went for a walk to the creek
> . . .
> and <<when we were coming back >> Jeffrey fell in the creek
> and <<before we went>> we made fairy chains. The End.
> (Christie, 1998, p. 55)

Emergent control of Theme is one of the most important marks of overall developmental control of writing. Effective use of Theme is also related to control of *Reference,*[10] as we see in Text 5 by an Australian child, age 8, who was reviewing a novel she had read in class. In her introduction she identified the novel and went on, referring back to the book with the pronoun *it* to place the book in Theme position in her next sentences. We represent the thematic progression here, revealing the way in which the language choices help to build a coherent text, progressing it forward:

Text 5:
I read the book "Sister of the South" by Emily Rodda.

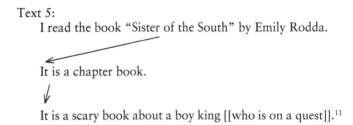

It is a chapter book.

It is a scary book about a boy king [[who is on a quest]].[11]

The writer then develops a description of the novel, where three main Themes (*He,* referring to the boy; *the quest;* and *They,* referring to Lief, Jasmine, and Barda) carry the discourse forward:

This is a story about a boy [[called Lief]].

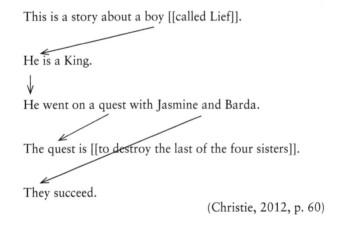

He is a King.

He went on a quest with Jasmine and Barda.

The quest is [[to destroy the last of the four sisters]].

They succeed.

(Christie, 2012, p. 60)

In fact, the last Theme choice (*they*) is confusing, since it would seem to refer to *the last of the four sisters,* though it was intended to refer to *Lief, Jasmine, and Barda.* Achieving control of Theme and Reference can be quite demanding for many students and takes some years.

Expanding Capacity

Another dimension of developing control of written language is movement into the capacity to expand noun-group structures in order to compress a great deal of information. In Text 6, a girl age 9, in an American classroom, showed emergent control of Theme, as well as a developing facility to compress information in expanded noun groups, as she retold and commented on a story read in class. She wrote in her opening paragraph:

> Text 6:
> On the days [[that Tomás is with Papa Grande in Iowa]], Papa Grande says some things [[that inspire him to become a storyteller]]. Tomás does some things [[that inspire him too]].

Here the writer compacted information in the noun groups by embedding clauses. In the first sentence, this contributes to a marked Theme as she expands *the days* to tell us which days (*that Tomás is with Papa Grande in Iowa*), orienting the reader to the timeframe of the events. The embedded clauses are also important for drawing on the abstractions necessary for interpreting literary texts, as in the first sentence of her second paragraph:

> One of the most important events in the story [[that show how Tomás felt and relates to him becoming a storyteller]] is Tomás with Papa Grande under a tree.
> (Schleppegrell et al., 2014, p. 32)

This sentence, with one "ranking" clause (*One of the most important events in the story is Tomás with Papa Grande under a tree*) and one "downranked" (embedded) clause, created an opening statement that presented a generalization about the story and its characters which the writer then went on to develop. The sentence was built using an *identifying process* (expressed in the verb *is*), and though the opening large noun group (*One of the most important events in the story*, occupying Theme position) is a little clumsy, it demonstrates that the writer was developing that capacity to express abstract experience that marks the transitional phase (see Figure 4.1). A sentence like this enabled her to write authoritatively about the story, presenting a thesis that was developed through analysis of Tomás's feelings to support her claims about how the events related to Tomás becoming a storyteller, the goal of the task. By identifying the events as *important*, she also engaged in early forms of the critique of literature that will be the focus of language arts development over the school years.

In the critical years of transition from late childhood to early adolescence, students need to write and read often dense written language, as they engage with more challenging subject matter and are expected to write in response to and bring evidence from texts they read. The greater density is marked by such things as elaborate noun groups, sometimes frequent use of prepositional phrases building circumstantial information of many kinds, and closely interwoven clauses, their thematic choices building information and interpretation of events, phenomena, or persons, depending on the disciplinary field at issue.

We see an early manifestation of this line of development in Text 7 below from an Australian girl, age 10, who wrote a science report showing density and a good sense of how to progress the information forward in an ordered way characteristic of much science writing. She opened with a general statement, and her Theme choices (underlined) developed the text while she also used technical language to build the field of knowledge:

Text 7:
Almost life in Antarctica is in the sea
and in the deep blue there is a food web.

She went on, signaling order in her next Theme, while the clause unfolded to introduce a range of technical terms:

First off there is plankton, phyto-plankton (two types of small microscopic life forms) and diatoms at the bottom of the food chain.

She characterized the creatures she has identified with a Theme that referred back to them as a group and introduced the technical term that categorizes them as a whole:

These small life forms are part of the class "Primary Producers."
(Christie & Derewianka, 2008, p.188)

The Theme of this final sentence enabled the writer to classify the technical terms she has introduced and develop a scientific taxonomy. This use of Reference and thematic progression shows the writer's emerging ability to write about "uncommonsense" knowledge in authoritative ways.

Comparison of the science report and the book review indicate some ways grammatical development will proceed differently in different subjects. For writing in science, the ability to pack information into the noun group will be crucial for presenting technicality and explanation, with little expression of affect or attitude (Halliday & Martin, 1993), while analysis of literary texts will call for elaboration through a range of clause types that enable the presentation of interpretation and perspective.

Developing Abstraction

By late childhood, successful writers are learning to present the knowledge they are developing in more abstract language. One resource for doing this is *nominalization,* representing in a noun group what might otherwise be expressed in a full clause. An example from an Australian boy, age 9, appeared in his story opening, in Text 8:

Text 8:
After an hour of trudging through the dark and depress-
ing forest . . .
(Christie & Derewianka, 2008, p. 35)

[A]n hour of trudging is a nominalization, representing a noncongruent expression; *trudging* is not functioning as a verb but as a noun, creating a phenomenon or thing. Presented as a process, the *trudging* would be expressed in a verb and a full clause with an actor:

"After they had *trudged* through the dark and depressing forest for an hour . . . "

The ability to represent the meaning of the full clause in the noun-group form *an hour of trudging* shows emergent control of noncongruent expression. This contrasts with the entirely congruent expression of meaning by younger writers, such as in Text 4 above, about a class visit. The emergence of the ability to represent meaning in such noncongruent ways is an important development.

We see its value in Text 9, an excerpt from a character analysis written by an American girl, age 9. She created a series of interconnected clauses that provided information about the character, using a series of Themes, unmarked and marked, to progress the text, while going on in the final clause to use an instance of nominalization (*speaking two languages*) to express evaluation of the character. A marked Theme introduced the text by naming the story:

> Text 9:
> In the story, "Pepita Talks Twice," Pepita was a girl [[who spoke two languages, English and Spanish]].

The writer then placed the character's name in Theme position to proceed:

> <u>Pepita</u> would help traslate for everyone,

while the next clause provided some important information about the character, with another marked Theme (*At first*) identifying this as early in the story:

> <u>At first</u> Pepita felt not very happy about speaking two lagages,

The next clause, introduced with a contrastive conjunction (*but*) used another marked Theme (*toward the end*), marking the passage of time:

> but <u>toward the end</u> Pepita felt relieved and glad,

while in the final clause, one of reason, the writer offered evaluation:

because speaking two languges saved her dog's life.
(Schleppegrell & Moore, 2018)

Expressed in congruent terms, she might have written:

> Pepita felt relieved and glad // because she could speak two
> languages // and that helped her save her dog's life.

The nominalization *speaking two languges* allowed the writer to create an abstraction, contributing to the overall force of her evaluation of the character, and adding to the sense of judgment.

While several of the writers whose work we have looked at above are multilingual or bilingual writers, we can get a clearer sense of the challenges for those learning English as an additional language from O'Dowd (2012). She used SFL to analyze the writing of middle school L2 learners (ages 11 to 13) in American classrooms who had been assessed as writing at different levels of English-language proficiency: *Beginning, Expanding,* and *Reaching.*[12] O'Dowd offered examples that involved interpretation of characters, and these show the learners moving from expansion of information through clause linking, as we saw in Texts 1 to 4, toward the nominalization we saw in Texts 8 to 9.

A learner O'Dowd characterized as at an intermediate or Expanding level wrote Text 10:

> Text 10:
> Marisa thinks // if she starts drawing horses like Euphemia
> // she would get respect.
> (O'Dowd, 2012, p. 12)

O'Dowd notes that the writer's use of clauses with an *if-then* relationship is evidence of capacity expanding beyond the beginning level. This adolescent writer is not just linking clauses with additive or temporal conjunctions, but has constructed a conditional relationship that is projected through the character's *thinking.*

O'Dowd also identified students who are more advanced, Reaching toward proficiency, as they attempted to use abstraction through nominalization, as in Text 11:

Text 11:
   So not able to draw a horse like Euphemia it really bothers her.
                                                (O'Dowd, 2012, p. 13)

O'Dowd pointed out that the writer is reaching toward structure
along these lines:

   So [[not being able to draw a horse like Euphemia]] really
   bothers her.

Here, *not able to draw a horse like Euphemia* presents an abstraction that shows movement toward development of the written
grammar, rather than drawing on the clause chaining of Text 10.
O'Dowd pointed out that the writer of Text 11 has attempted
something more advanced, creating a clause that both presents
how Marisa felt and why she felt that way, with the grammar of
abstraction emerging.
   The expression of attitude and evaluation is often seen in
children writing book reviews and other literary discussions in
the childhood to adolescence years. In Text 12, by an Australian
boy, age 12, the book being written about is thematized in a
sentence with two ranking clauses:

Text 12:
   "Sally's Story" by Sally Morgan is an autobiography
   about the life of an Aboriginal girl and her poor family,
   the Milroys,
   living in Perth in a suburb [[called Manning]] during the
   50's and 60's.

This is a dense opening sentence, compressing a great deal of
relevant information about the novel and its characters. It sets
the writer up to go on to introduce interpretation of characters
and events, below, where the opening Theme (*This*) refers back to
what has been said while signaling a progress forward in unfold-
ing details and interpretation, accomplished through a series of
embedded clauses that also create density in written expression:

This is the story of Sally [[growing up in a close-knit family [[and discovering her Aboriginal heritage [[and being
proud of her background //while living in a community
with racist attitudes.]]
(Christie & Derewianka, 2008, p. 68)

Here the student shows willingness to do much more than retell
the story, working toward attitudinal expression and interpretation (*close-knit family; proud of her heritage; racist attitudes*).
This ability to infuse attitudinal meanings into presentation of
events enables the expression of values in ways that are expected
in literary commentary.

Writing Authoritatively across School Subjects

Nominalization is one example of how, as successful children
move up the years of schooling, they learn to express understanding of more "uncommonsense" knowledge while they engage with
a range of school subjects. They learn to handle new registers,
requiring a grasp of changing disciplinary fields, often involving
technical language and often requiring an expanding range of
attitudinal and evaluative expression. By high school or mid-
adolescence, writers need to develop more specialized and technical language for learning across school subjects, and meanings,
ideas, attitudes, and values are often presented in dense language.
This phase in writing development is marked by further control of
noncongruent ways of expressing abstraction, involving, among
other things, an emergent control of grammatical metaphor. As
indicated above, an expression is said to be an example of grammatical metaphor when the most congruent grammatical form
is re-expressed in a less congruent way. We saw examples of
emerging grammatical metaphor in Text 9's *speaking two languages* and Text 11's *not able to draw a horse like Euphemia*. In
each case, the writer took a notion that is congruently expressed
in a full clause and presented it in a noun group, where it then
served as an abstraction that could be evaluated (e.g., *speaking
two languages saved her life*).

Grammatical metaphor often works in such a way that normally independent clauses are collapsed to re-express meaning

in different ways than would typically be used in speech. For example, a 14-year-old Australian boy studying history wrote Text 13, constituting one dense clause, characteristic of written language:

> Text 13:
> The Japanese surrender in August 1945 led to the declaration of independence of Indonesia and the appointment of Sukarno as the first president.
>
> (Christie, 2012, p. 111)

Expressed more congruently as speech, this would read, set out to show the number of clauses:

> After Japan surrendered in August 1945
> the leaders of Indonesia declared
> that Indonesia was independent
> and Sukarno was appointed president.

The congruent version presents events in their chronological order, while the noncongruent version enables the writer to fuse time and cause in ways characteristic of history discourse (Coffin, 2006). This shows that terms such as *surrender, declaration,* and *appointment* are not just advanced vocabulary items, but indicate capacity to draw on lexicogrammatical resources to put abstract concepts in relationship to each other in service of historical explanation. Control of grammatical metaphor and the expression of meanings in these grammatically noncongruent ways becomes increasingly important as writers engage with knowledge in secondary school subjects.

Whittaker (2010) (pp. 34–35) illustrated the development of grammatical metaphor in a classroom in Spain where students were learning history in English in a Content and Language Integrated Learning (CLIL) context. In texts written by the same student over three years, she showed how control of the written mode developed. In the first year of secondary schooling (age 11–12), the student wrote Text 14:

Text 14:
The civilizations were so important
because the most powerful people stood there
and because they were the main sources of work and
culture.

This is a congruent way of presenting causes, linking clauses with
the conjunction *because*. Two years later the same student, now
age 13–14, wrote Text 15:

Text 15:
At that time poor people didn't have resources [[to de-
velop]]
and rich people became richer with the rise of taxes and
prices during the Inflation after mercantilism.

Here the student presented cause in the prepositional phrase *with
the rise of taxes and prices during the Inflation after mercantilism,* fusing time and cause. Presenting the same ideas in clauses
linked with *because* as in Text 14 (e.g., *rich people became richer
// because taxes and prices rose // when there was Inflation after
mercantilism*) would not be wrong, but using *with* enabled the
writer to present the more authoritative stance and style valued
in academic written language. The following year the writer (now
age 15–16) wrote Text 16:

Text 16:
Another important cause was the differences of costums,
languages and traditions in the balcans (Balkans) [[that
led to many crisis]].

Here, the student presents the notion of *cause* in a noun group
(*another important cause*) that is the point of departure (Theme)
for a sentence that identifies *differences* of various sorts as *leading
to* crises. This developmental progression indicates that the writer
learned that causality is not just presented through *because*. In
fact, as students become more adept at the written mode, *cause,
condition, purpose,* etc. are more often infused into a clause
rather than coming between clauses. Here, these lexical and grammatical developments show the writer's increasing control of the

grammar of the genres of history. Sentence structure may become simpler as conjunctive meanings are expressed within rather than between clauses (as in Texts 13 and 16), and nominalization enables expression within a noun group of information that would otherwise be presented in a whole clause.

In writing science, along with the technical information the writer of Text 7 needed to handle, writers of more advanced texts need to explain complex processes and take an authoritative perspective. This calls for measured presentation using conditional, concessive, and causal expression in dense and complex clauses. In Text 17, an Australian boy, age 15, has written a report on hemophilia. This is a long report, and we excerpt here the final element:

> Text 17:
> Treatment and control
> So far, there is no *cure* for Hemophilia, though there are many treatments available. Gene replacement therapy is thought to one day be the cure, but at present, it is only being trialed. People [[who have tried gene replacement therapy]] have had promising results although some have had side effects, though for most, the occurrence of bleeds have dropped considerably. Injections of certain blood products are usually needed to prevent cases of internal bleeding; these infusions or injections can cure the clotting defect for a short period of time, though << if the same treatment is used over a long period>> the subject can develop an immunity to it. People with mild cases of hemophilia sometimes use desmopressin (also called DDAVP), which is a synthetic hormone [[that forces the production and release of certain factors in the blood // to aid clotting for a short period of time]].
> (Christie, 2012, p. 143)

The writer began with a marked Theme of time/extent (*So far*) that introduced the point developed in the rest of the paragraph. He used one other marked Theme to foreground some relevant information in an enclosed clause, showing some adeptness with resources for text structuring:

> though << if the same treatment is used over a long period>> the subject can develop an immunity

The text has many dense noun-group structures, some of which the student took from the sources he consulted, and many created using grammatical metaphor (e.g., *occurrence of bleeds, injections of certain blood products, the production and release of certain factors in the blood*). The writer uses objective forms of modality (e.g., *is thought to one day be the cure*) to present a distanced perspective on gene therapy, and the evaluative language that appears expresses judgments about features of the disease, its appearance, or its treatment (e.g., *promising results*). Achieving this voice in writing science is a challenge for many writers.

The challenges are apparent in Text 18, written by an undergraduate writer, age 19, to report on the results of a science experiment. In writing science, the ability to assess the merits of results from experimentation in authoritative yet measured ways is valued (e.g., Pollack, 2003). When a student does not control the language resources needed to accomplish this, the writing can seem tentative or uncertain, as Text 18 illustrates:

> Text 18:
> There were a lot of assumptions [[associated with this experiment]]
> which *could* cause some discrepancy in the final results.
> It was assumed [[that the temperature at the interface was the temperature of the liquid]]
> and this *may* not be the case.
> This assumption *could* have some effect on the final result because <<as stated earlier,>> the diffusion coefficient is a function of the temperature.
> (Schleppegrell, 2004b, p. 185)

In discussing results and commenting on the extent to which they can be trusted, the writer uses modal verbs (*could, may*) to suggest alternative possibilities operating in the experiment that might have affected her particular results. This presents these conclusions with a great deal of tentativeness, as conditions that she was not certain about. Other writers completing the same assignment drew on more distanced and objective forms of modality to accomplish the same discursive moves; for example, by presenting the uncertainty in nominalizations (e.g., *A great degree of uncertainty is attached to these results*).

Consider the different effect, for example, of presenting discrepancies in the results in this way, as another student in the class did:

> Perhaps the discrepancies in the final results were due to unexpected variations in temperature at the interface or in the air mixture.

Along with control of grammatical metaphor (e.g., *unexpected variations*), use of *perhaps* enables the writer to project the impersonal voice typical of science reporting.

Writing beyond the Classroom

As writers move into older adolescence and adulthood, their writing takes on value that goes beyond the classroom, as they engage with civic life and enter into public dialogue. At this time the ways they evaluate and show their perspectives develop as they learn to remove their personal selves and present their opinions as more general views. Text 19, from an excerpt to a letter to the editor of an Australian newspaper, was written by an Australian girl, age 16, to express concern about heavy advertising for a weight-loss program. After laying out the issues she wrote:

> Text 19:
> The pressure on many Australian teenagers, especially girls, due to this type of advertising is disturbing.
> It is of great concern [[that a reputable company such as Gloria Marshall is encouraging young women to conform to society's unreasonable and blatantly incorrect expectations]].
>
> (Christie, 2002b, p. 63)

Note the abstraction in identifying the problem as *the pressure due to this type of advertising*. This dense noun group with grammatical metaphor expressing cause in the phrase *due to* enables the writer to characterize the *pressure* as *disturbing*. Her opinion is further expressed in the generalized and impersonal *It is of great concern*, with her evaluation presented in the adjectives and adverbs *disturbing, unreasonable,* and *blatantly incorrect.* This is far beyond the simple expression of opinion of early childhood.

Summary

We have presented writing development as progressing in at least three dimensions: (1) in an emergent control of the discourse patterns of written language, (2) in the associated emergent capacity to elaborate on and expand experience in writing, and (3) in the growth in ability to express attitudes and judgments in nuanced ways. The trajectory identifies linguistic realizations of the increasing demands of knowledge development and presentation in school subjects across the years of schooling, including:

- ◆ the emergence of *marked Themes* and control of Reference and thematic progression that enables a writer to shape the flow of information in a text

- ◆ expansion of the noun group with embedded clauses and other resources for elaboration that enable a writer to compress information

- ◆ nominalization and other forms of grammatical metaphor that enable a writer to present abstractions and move beyond a clause-chaining style for writing in a range of disciplinary contexts

- ◆ attitudinally rich language to interpret and evaluate

- ◆ abstract processes of interpretation and relative absence of reference to self in expressing evaluation

Figure 4.2 offers another way of representing this trajectory, mapping growth in writing onto stages of development from early childhood to the late stages of adolescence, when, among successful students, the grammar of written registers is mastered and the abstract meanings characteristic of secondary school subjects and postsecondary learning are foregrounded.

The processes of learning bring significant challenges at all stages. The initial entry to literacy, with all the tasks involved in learning to spell, write, and construct even simple written language, takes some time in its mastery. Next comes movement

Grammar of abstraction consolidated: judgment, opinion, attitudes, values, and "uncommonsense" experience	Late adolescence
Grammar of abstraction emerges: "uncommonsense" experience, attitude and opinion extended	Midadolescence
Grammar of written language extended: "uncommonsense" experience elaborated, attitude enhanced	Late childhood to adolescence
Simple grammar and basic literacy tools: simple "commonsense" experience and limited attitude	Early childhood

FIGURE 4.2. *Growth in writing from early childhood to late adolescence.*

toward an emergent control of the denser lexicogrammatical patterns of written language that allow the writer to elaborate on and expand experience in writing. As the writer matures, capacity to express generalization and abstract ideas in written language further develops, along with growing confidence in expressing attitude and evaluation. A major challenge comes in the movement from the elementary to the middle and secondary school and from late childhood into adolescence, where the curriculum becomes more firmly differentiated into subject areas that bring their own disciplinary expectations. This is the point at which many children begin to fall behind in their school performance, as they fail to come to grips with the necessary discourse patterns in which increasingly abstract information and measured opinions and attitudes are expressed. Learners are challenged to infuse attitudinal expression into the texts they write in different ways according to disciplinary demands: for example, offering evaluation, judgment, and interpretation in the humanities and expressing likelihood, assessing significance, and acknowledging limitations in scientific fields. Looking at this developmental trajectory from both perspectives: as corresponding to the curriculum expectations of schooling, as in Figure 4.2, and as movement from speech to writing, as in Figure 4.1, describes writing development as progression in control of the discourse patterns of written language, in the capacity to elaborate on and expand experience in writing, and in ability to express attitudes and judgments in nuanced ways, offering a way of thinking about the linguistic challenges in relation to the social experiences children are having as they grow and participate in classroom learning.

Understanding written language development as movement from the oral to the written mode also helps us recognize various developmental trajectories of learners. L2 learners who have already learned to write in their mother tongues have experienced the transition to written language and may move quickly to adopt features of the written mode in the L2.[13] On the other hand, older second language learners who come to school without literacy skills in their mother tongues may find the transition into written language more challenging, but may proceed more rapidly than younger students, once they control the basic literacy tools, as they will bring greater social experience and maturity to the task. The same is likely the case for older learners of writing in their mother tongue.

Relating the Trajectory to Findings from Other Linguistic Traditions

Like us, other writing researchers have also characterized development as movement from patterns of speech into patterns of written language (e.g., Beers & Nagy, 2009; Bulté & Housen, 2014; Crossley & McNamara, 2014; Norris & Ortega, 2009; Ravid & Tolchinsky, 2002), many citing Halliday's (1987, 1998; Halliday & Martin, 1993) discussion of clause structuring differences in the two modes and describing the increasing complexity of the noun group (e.g., Ravid & Berman, 2010). Halliday (1987, p. 66) points out that "the categories of 'written' and 'spoken' are themselves highly indeterminate," but serve as convenient labels on a "continuum from most spontaneous to most self-monitored language: spontaneous discourse is usually spoken, self-monitored discourse is usually written" (p. 69). But his main point is that "[s]poken and written language do not differ in their systematicity: each is equally highly organized, regular, and productive of coherent discourse" (pp. 69–70). In other words, both speech and writing are complex, but in different ways: spoken language is grammatically intricate, with clause-chaining and interrupted constituents, but lexically sparse; while written language is lexically dense but grammatically more simple. As we have seen above, this is a result of the development of grammatical metaphor, which offers the possibility of distilling meaning, expressing what takes a whole clause in speech as a noun group or embedded clause in writing. This noncongruent expression enables writers to infuse evaluation into texts in authoritative ways that meet the demands and expectations of the disciplinary discourses they are learning to participate in.

Research on children's writing development agrees that they move from the clause-chaining patterns of oral language toward the more lexically dense patterns of written language as they progress through the years of schooling. However, the SFL perspective presented here clarifies some issues consistently raised by other studies. These contributions come from the functional, meaning-oriented constructs SFL offers to analyze texts in context. A text is not just a collection of clauses and sentences, but a larger unit of meaning that unfolds clause by clause and sentence by sentence, and so requires analysis of the text-forming resources of the language that enable that accumulation of meaning. In particular, the SFL constructs of grammatical metaphor and Theme put the focus on the ways writers build meaning from sentence to sentence and across a whole text. In addition, the way SFL identifies clauses of different types focuses on their functional roles in shaping meaning in a text. Here we show how the SFL constructs enable us to reinterpret findings from other research in ways that offer comprehensive explanations of accumulated research on writing development.

It is typical for research on writing development to characterize the trajectory as growth in lexical density and syntactic complexity (see Schleppegrell, 2008, for a review). While the pathway we have outlined demonstrates growth in lexical density, growth in *syntactic complexity* is less clear. As noted above, Halliday

(1987) does not characterize written language as more syntactically complex than spoken language; in fact, quite the opposite, as he recognizes the tremendous complexity of the grammar of informal spoken language. In the texts we present above, it is hard to argue that Text 14, with its several clauses, is less complex than Text 16, with its grammatical metaphor but simpler structure. SFL offers a means of recognizing different kinds of complexity and explaining some overall findings of research on writing development that are otherwise perplexing.

For example, research consistently shows that sentences become longer as learners move through the early years of schooling, but then become shorter. However, it has always been apparent that writing quality does not correlate with sentence length. Consider, for example, Text 20, a sentence written by an eleventh-grade writer who is developing an argument about a recall election in California in his history class (Schleppegrell, 2006). Here the student writes a sentence with five ranking clauses and three embeddings:

> Text 20:
> When people voted "yes" on the recall,
> I think
> they knew [[what they were doing,]]
> and since Governor Davis was recalled,
> that means [[that many people were not satisfied with the
> way [[he governed their state]]]].
> (Schleppegrell, 2006, p. 140)

For comparison, a representation of the same ideas, in a more "written-like" mode, might be something like Text 21:

> Text 21:
> People's *yes* votes in the recall election demonstrated their
> real dissatisfaction with Governor Davis's leadership of
> California.

Here the meanings are presented in one dense clause rather than in multiple clause structures. The structure is simpler, with two noun groups (*People's yes votes in the recall election; their real dissatisfaction with Governor Davis's leadership of California*) connected by the verb *demonstrated*. Verbs such as *demonstrate, show, indicate,* or *reveal* offer the writer resources for presenting and evaluating experience in abstractions. Here the sentence presents an interpretation of the voters' actions in a noun group (*their real dissatisfaction with Governor Davis's leadership of California*) that distills the meanings in *that means that many people were not satisfied with the way he governed their state.* Being able to reconstrue meanings presented in full clauses into noun groups, and to draw on a *showing* process to signify the meaning of one noun group in another is an important step in representing the symbolic meanings of school subjects (Christie & Cléirigh, 2008). This facility with grammatical metaphor is needed to engage in analysis and argumentation across disciplinary discourses. It is not just a matter of learning new vocabulary, although the word *demonstrated* is a useful resource for this sentence revision. Writing in this way calls for knowing and drawing on new patterns in constructing sentences that build theoretical knowledge and evaluation.

Researchers often measure the number of clauses in a sentence, using the construct *T-unit,* and compare results across age groups and text types (Schleppegrell, 2008). A T-unit analysis of Texts 20 and 21 shows that Text 20 has eight clauses in two T-units (separated by the *and*), compared to the one clause of Text 21. Recognizing the role of grammatical metaphor helps explain why Text 21 is a more sophisticated rendering of the same meaning as presented in Text 20. In her study of the development of adolescent writers, Myhill (2008) noted that subordination and clause complexity (thus, the number of clauses per T-unit) decreased as the writers used more sentence variety and expanded ideas within the clause—again, a result of developing grammatical metaphor. Ortega (2015, p. 86) called grammatical metaphor "[a] key lexico-grammatical resource, and a staple of mature and abstract linguistic expression." In studying second language writing development, Norris and Ortega (2009) called for indices of writing complexity that can account for trajectories in L2 writing development that move initially from additive conjunction to subordination, but then to clauses made dense in information through grammatical metaphor (see also Lambert & Kormos, 2014).

Beers and Nagy's (2009) exploration of the relationship between length of clause, length of T-unit, differences in genre, and
writing quality in grade 7 and 8 students' narrative and persuasive
writing also offers a useful example of findings that can be understood in new ways from the functional linguistics perspective.
They found that writing quality was correlated with *clauses per
T-unit* for narratives, but with *words per clause* in persuasive
essays. These findings resonate with the trajectory described
above, as narrative writing relies more on the use of a variety of
clause types to set events in relation to one another and to present characters' actions, saying, and feelings (thus, more clauses
per T-unit), while expository writing calls for nominalization
and other means of packing information into a clause to enable
the necessary explanation and evaluation (thus, more words per
clause). Beers and Nagy reported that higher-rated persuasive essays had more clause-internal elaboration through prepositional
phrases, conjoined phrases, attributive adjectives, and embedded
infinitive clauses, all features that extend and develop meaning
within a clause. On the other hand, they found that the use of
multiple-clause T-units led to higher ratings in narratives as they
represented "variation from the repetitive 'and then . . . and then
. . . and then' found in less sophisticated stories" (p. 197).

Beers and Nagy also reported that the lower-quality persuasive texts often had sentences "of the form 'I think X because
Y,'" (Beers & Nagy, 2009, p. 197). They refer to the *I think
X because Y* sentence as "awkward use of embedded clauses."
As noted above, the SFL approach reserves the term *embedded*
for those clauses that are down-ranked and functioning within
other clauses, contributing to clause density rather than discourse
structure. Distinguishing embedded clauses from other subordinate clauses helps better identify the language resources that
contribute to density of clause structure and differentiate them
from those used for creating intricate clause complexes. From
the SFL perspective, the clause *I think* "projects" another clause;
these are not in a relationship of embedding, for the clause that
projects is said to "throw out" the projected clause. We saw above
that the writers of Texts 3, 10, and 20 used *I think* to introduce
their perspectives, and identified this as a less sophisticated way
of presenting views that in more developed writers are typically

presented in other language choices (and in fact writing teachers often caution secondary school students not to use *I think* or *I believe*).

SFL could also inform other writing research in its analysis of Theme. As we saw above, the sentence constituent identified as Theme offers writers opportunities to structure their texts, linking back to something said previously, reorienting the text with information about time, place, cause, purpose, and other meanings, or continuing a previous focus of the text. Analysis of Theme helps researchers recognize how control of this texturing function contributes to progress in writing. Other studies approximate analysis of Theme by recognizing that variation in the ways sentences begin is consequential for achieving quality in writing. For example, McNamara, Crossley, and McCarthy (2010) use "mean number of words before the main verb" as one measure of "syntactic complexity" and Myhill (2008) uses a measure of "sentence variety" that is operationalized as the number of words that precede a finite verb. In the texts we have presented we can see that having more words before the main/finite verb indicates one of two possibilities: that the writer has used a marked Theme to shape the text and move it in a new direction, or that the writer has used a complex noun group as sentence subject. Both of these choices demonstrate increased control of the grammar of written language.

We have described how use of marked Theme and complex noun structures emerge in the transition years from late childhood to early adolescence. Typically, marked Themes first appear as prepositional phrases of time and place (as in Text 4), and later also function to take up material already presented and make it the point of departure for moving forward (as in Texts 5 and 7). We have also illustrated how compacting information in dense noun groups can result in long sentence subjects (as in Text 6). Myhill (2008) reported that the more effective young adolescent writers she studied used more varied sentence openings, drawing on a greater repertoire of options. Recognizing complex and marked Themes can contribute to a better understanding of dimensions of sentence variety. In addition, taking account of thematic structuring across a text can reveal the method of development a writer uses and the differences in thematic structure that are typical of different genres (see, e.g., Christie, 2012; North, 2005; Schleppegrell, 2004a). This makes Theme a relevant and important construct for studying writing development.

Finally, the study of interpersonal meaning and the development of the ability to infuse one's judgments and perspectives into texts in ways that vary by genre and discipline calls for much more attention from writing development researchers. Interpersonal meaning is a neglected area of research on writing development, and teachers often work with a reductionist perspective on *voice* that does not recognize the different language resources students need to achieve different goals (O'Hallaron & Schleppegrell, 2016). SFL offers an elaborated set of tools for analyzing interpersonal meaning through the Appraisal framework (Martin & White, 2005), and more research is needed to better understand how interpersonal meaning is presented in different genres and disciplinary discourses, and how resources for interpersonal meaning develop to enable judgment and evaluation.

Discussion and Implications

We have described writing development as expansion of meaning-making potential in the written mode, and as growth in capacity to participate in written discourses across disciplines. Detailed presentation of the increasing range of grammatical resources that writers draw on across the school years has provided evidence of the ways they are learning to respond to the demands of different subject areas. The development of the text and the development of the writer go hand in hand. This means that analysis of writing development is to a great extent a linguistic analysis.

Systemic functional linguistics offers a theory of language that is well-suited for describing growth in capacity to use written language for meaning making. Its conception of language as social semiotic brings focus on the rhetorical goals of writers, and its grammatical descriptions and constructs recognize the different ways writers present information, structure texts, and infuse those texts with their perspectives and attitudes. For research on writing development across the lifespan, SFL offers tools to describe the ways language choices enable writers to achieve their rhetorical goals, even while those goals shift as they engage in different discursive contexts and social experiences.

In the context of more challenging standards and high-stakes testing, SFL offers curriculum designers, teachers, and assessors descriptions of written language development that have theoretical grounding and validity. It details a developmental dimension for writing instruction with explicit criteria for shaping and assessing progress that are attuned to the different rhetorical purposes and goals of different subject areas. As the texts we have presented demonstrate, the developmental pathways available to individual learners are influenced by the curriculum offered. An effective writing curriculum will orient learners to features of the texts they read as models of written language attuned to disciplinary goals and genres (see, e.g., Christie, 2012; Fang & Schleppegrell, 2008). Through appropriate pedagogies and writing contexts, teachers can foster use of patterns of written language that enable growth toward elaboration and expansion of meaning as well as the abstraction, generalization, and evaluation that characterizes more advanced writing capacity. Writers can be oriented to the purposes and language features of new genres and learn how to draw on language resources that enable them to express ideas in ways that others will find interesting and provocative. In taking a lifespan perspective, such an approach means that instruction can develop writers' capacity in particular contexts of use, focused on the writer's goals and exploring the patterns of language that enable achievement of those goals. In this view, progress can be assessed in terms of the learners' expansion of language resources and accomplishment of the rhetorical purposes. In fact, it is important that assessment of writing development include authentic contexts and not only measure development in texts written to prompts that have no context and that expect students to write based only on prior knowledge and experience.

Writing does not occur in isolation from other activities, and emergence of writing along the trajectories we have described calls for development of disciplinary knowledge writers can draw on in meaningful ways. This means reading stimulating literature, engaging in scientific exploration, exploring historical artifacts, explaining mathematical phenomena, and learning across a range of fields. In addition, writers need to be positioned to have the authority to present their perspectives and express their attitudes. Achieving these goals calls for teachers who address the rhetorical demands of their disciplines, support students in drawing on the language resources that enable them to meet those demands, and respond to writers with respect for the perspectives they share. An effective writing curriculum will recognize the ways children's maturation enables them to adopt new ways of using language and will engage them in new disciplinary tasks that call for meaningful use of new language resources to meet new discursive demands.

An understanding of *genre* plays an important role in realizing this goal. The students whose writing we analyzed here were engaged in meaningful expression for particular discipline-related purposes, writing genres that their teachers presented as ways to get things done in the classroom. They learned to review the books they had read, report on the science they had learned, and argue for the points of view they had developed about historical events, among other things. Learning that different language choices are functional for achieving different goals supports students to write in ways that activate their own voices and creativity, drawing on ways of making meaning that they choose deliberately to achieve their own rhetorical purposes.

Written language has evolved over centuries in social contexts in which new meanings were developed through science, technology, historical inquiry, literary creativity, and philosophy. Knowledge and language develop together both historically and for each individual, and the years of schooling are opportunities for children to engage with a broad range of cultural knowledge, whether or not they will continue to engage with all of those areas as they move into adulthood. The schooling years are a period for exploring and developing flexibility in writing, so that as students move on into adulthood, they can participate in social life in the ways they choose. We have shown how language continues to develop into the years of older adolescence, recognizing the linguistic aspects of writing development. These linguistic aspects are central to understanding, supporting, and assessing children's growth in written expression across the years of schooling.

Notes

1. SFL theory treats grammar and vocabulary as two aspects of the same system of "lexicogrammar," with vocabulary realizing grammatical choice at the most "delicate" level (Halliday, 2014, pp. 58–90).

2. Our claim is that a foundation of meaning making in spoken/signed language is needed to negotiate the development of written language practices; we do not suggest that learners move from speech to writing in each language they use. Many children around the world learn to write in school in a language that is not their mother tongue, and learners in bi-/multilingual contexts may learn the written grammatical patterns of a language prior to or without learning the spoken. For those whose L1 is a signed language, learning to write always involves learning a new linguistic system.

3. Halliday, McIntosh, and Strevens (1964) originally proposed a notion of register to provide a principled way to describe shifts in language as speakers move from context to context. SFL register analysis identifies variation in language according to *field* (social activity), *tenor* (the relationship of participants), and *mode* (the manner of organizing the text; e.g., whether spoken or written), recognizing the range of linguistic repertoires all speakers/writers draw on as they engage in social life. The term has been reworked and developed (e.g., Halliday, 1991/2007), while more than one formulation has been proposed (e.g., Martin, 1985; Martin & Rose, 2003). Register remains a powerful tool for analysis of language, widely used in discussions of pedagogy and education more generally (e.g., Brisk, 2015; Christie, 2002a; Gibbons, 2006; Schleppegrell, 2004a.)

4. Some young children are better prepared than others, through literacy practices in the home, for their first experiences of learning to write. Those who do not have these experiences will need particular assistance in engaging with the grammar of written registers.

5. The SFL grammatical metalanguage sometimes differs from that of other linguistic descriptions because the focus is functional rather than formal, calling for additional terminology to identify key concepts.

6. Double slashes mark boundaries between ranking clauses (independent, paratactic, or hypotactic, but not embedded). As discussed below, SFL does not consider clauses projected through verbs of thinking or feeling to be "embedded."

7. SFL theory identifies a range of process types realized in verb choice (Halliday, 2014).

8. SFL uses capital letters for all functional terms (e.g., Subject, Theme).

9. Theme is a feature of all languages, and while it is realized in first position in the English clause, it is realized differently in other languages.

10. *Reference* is the technical term used to identify referring items such as pronouns or demonstratives, as well as synonyms and other items that create chains of reference in a text. Reference combines with Theme to help build texture and cohesion.

11. The squared brackets [[ ]] indicate an embedded or "downranked" clause, one that expands and is part of a noun group or other constituent. The emergence of embedded clauses is one measure of students' growth as writers.

12. These terms come from the WIDA proficiency standards: https://www.wida.us/

13. In their study of short-term growth in university L2 writers, Bulté and Housen (2014, p. 53) offered support for this, showing that the development writers experienced in an intensive ESL course relied on "mechanisms such as grammatical metaphor through nominalizations" and was "characterized by higher lexical density, longer NPs through the use of multiple modifiers, as well as by a reduced number of combined clauses."

References

Beers, S. F., & Nagy, W. E. (2009). Syntactic complexity as a predictor of adolescent writing quality: Which measures? Which genre? *Reading and Writing: An Interdisciplinary Journal, 22*(2), 185–200. doi:10.1007/s11145-007-9107-5

Brisk, M. E. (2012). Young bilingual writers' control of grammatical person in different genres. *Elementary School Journal, 112*(3), 445–68. doi:10.1086/663733

Brisk, M. E. (2015). *Engaging students in academic literacies: Genre-based pedagogy for K–5 classrooms.* New York: Routledge.

Bulté, B., & Housen, A. (2014). Conceptualizing and measuring short-term changes in L2 writing complexity. *Journal of Second Language Writing*, 26, 42–65. doi:10.1016/j.jslw.2014.09.005

Byrnes, H. (2013). Positioning writing as meaning-making in writing research: An introduction. *Journal of Second-Language Writing*, 22(2), 95–106. doi:10.1016/j.jslw.2013.03.004

Christie, F. (1998). Learning the literacies of primary and secondary schooling. In F. Christie & R. Misson (Eds.), *Literacy and schooling* (pp. 47–73). London, UK: Routledge.

Christie, F. (2002a). *Classroom discourse analysis: A functional perspective*. London, UK: Continuum.

Christie, F. (2002b). The development of abstraction in adolescence in subject English. In M. J. Schleppegrell & M. C. Colombi (Eds.), *Developing advanced literacy in first and second languages: Meaning with power* (pp. 45–66). Mahwah, NJ: Erlbaum.

Christie, F. (2010). The ontogenesis of writing in childhood and adolescence. In D. Wyse, R. Andrews, & J. Hoffman (Eds.), *The Routledge international handbook of English, language and literacy teaching* (pp. 146–57). London, UK: Routledge.

Christie, F. (2012). *Language education throughout the school years: A functional perspective*. Malden, MA: Wiley-Blackwell.

Christie, F., & Cléirigh, C. (2008). On the importance of "showing." In C. Wu, C. M. I. M. Matthiessen, & M. Herke (Eds.), *Proceedings of ISFC 35: Voices around the world*, (pp. 13–18). Sydney, AU: 35th ISFC Organizing Committee.

Christie, F., & Derewianka, B. (2008). *School discourse: Learning to write across the years of schooling*. London, UK: Continuum.

Christie, F., & Macken-Horarik, M. (2007). Building verticality in subject English. In F. Christie & J. R. Martin (Eds.), *Language, knowledge and pedagogy: Functional linguistic and sociological perspectives* (pp. 156–83). London, UK: Continuum.

Christie, F., & Macken-Horarik, M. (2011). Disciplinarity and school subject English. In F. Christie and K. Maton (Eds.), *Disciplinarity: Functional linguistic and sociological perspectives* (pp. 175–96). London, UK: Continuum.

Coffin, C. (2006). *Historical discourse: The language of time, cause, and evaluation*. London, UK: Continuum.

Coffin, C., & Donohue, J. (2014). *A language as social semiotic–based approach to teaching and learning in higher education.* Malden, MA: Wiley-Blackwell.

Crossley, S. A., & McNamara, D. S. (2014). Does writing development equal writing quality? A computational investigation of syntactic complexity in L2 learners. *Journal of Second Language Writing,* 26, 66–79. doi:10.1016/j.jslw.2014.09.006

de Oliveira, L. C., & Iddings, J. (Eds.). (2014). *Genre pedagogy across the curriculum: Theory and application in US classrooms and contexts.* Bristol, UK: Equinox.

Derewianka, B. (2007). Using appraisal theory to track interpersonal development in adolescent academic writing. In A. McCabe, M. O'Donnell, & R. Whittaker (Eds.), *Advances in language and education* (pp. 142–96). London, UK: Continuum.

Fang, Z., and Schleppegrell, M. J. (2008). *Reading in secondary content areas: A language-based pedagogy.* Ann Arbor: University of Michigan Press.

Gebhard, M., Chen, I.-A., & Britton, L. (2014). "Miss, nominalization is a nominalization": English language learners' use of SFL metalanguage and their literacy practices. *Linguistics and Education,* 26, 106–25. doi:10.1016/j.linged.2014.01.003

Gibbons, P. (2006). *Bridging discourses in the ESL classroom: Students, teachers and researchers.* London, UK: Continuum.

Halliday, M. A. K. (1978). *Language as social semiotic: The social interpretation of language and meaning.* London, UK: Edward Arnold.

Halliday, M. A. K. (1987). Spoken and written modes of meaning. In R. Horowitz & S. J. Samuels (Eds.), *Comprehending oral and written language* (pp. 55–82). San Diego: Academic Press.

Halliday, M. A. K. (1998). Things and relations: Regrammaticising experience as technical knowledge. In J. R. Martin & R. Veel (Eds.), *Reading science: Critical and functional perspectives on discourses of science* (pp. 185–235). London, UK: Routledge.

Halliday, M. A. K. (2007). The notion of "context" in language education. In. J. J. Webster (Ed.), *Language and education. The collected works of M. A. K. Halliday* (vol. 9, pp. 269–90). London, UK: Continuum. (Original work published in 1991.)

Halliday, M.A.K. (2014). *Halliday's introduction to functional grammar*. Revised by Christian M. I. M. Matthiessen. 4th Ed. New York: Routledge.

Halliday, M. A. K., & Martin, J. R. (1993). *Writing science: Literacy and discursive power*. Pittsburgh, PA: University of Pittsburgh Press.

Halliday, M.A.K., McIntosh, A., & Strevens, P. (1964). *The linguistic sciences and language teaching*. London, UK: Longman.

Harman, R. (2013). Literary intertextuality in genre-based pedagogies: Building lexical cohesion in fifth-grade L2 writing. *Journal of Second Language Writing, 22*(2), 125–40. doi:10.1016/j.jslw.2013.03.006

Lambert, C., & Kormos, J. (2014). Complexity, accuracy, and fluency in task-based L2 research: Toward more developmentally based measures of second language acquisition. *Applied Linguistics, 35*(5), 607–14. doi:10.1093/applin/amu047

Macken-Horarik, M. (2006). Recognizing and realizing "what counts" in examination English: Perspectives from systemic functional linguistics and code theory. *Functions of Language, 13*(1), 1–35.

Macken-Horarik, M., Sandiford, C., Love, K., & Unsworth, L. (2015). New ways of working "with grammar in mind" in school English: Insights from systemic functional grammatics. *Linguistics and Education, 31*, 145–58. doi:10.1016/j.linged.2015.07.004

Martin, J. R. (1985). Process and text: Two aspects of human semiosis. In J. D. Benson & W. S Greaves (Eds.), *Systemic perspectives on discourse: Vol. 1. Selected theoretical papers from the Ninth International Systemic Workshop* (pp. 248–74). *Advances in Discourse Processes: Vol. 15*. Norwood, NJ: Ablex.

Martin, J. R., & Rose, D. (2003). *Working with discourse: Meaning beyond the clause*. London, UK: Continuum.

Martin, J. R., & White, P. R. R. (2005). *The language of evaluation: Appraisal in English*. New York: Palgrave Macmillan.

McNamara, D. S., Crossley, S. A., & McCarthy, P. M. (2010). Linguistic features of writing quality. *Written Communication, 27*(1), 57–86. doi:10.1177/0741088309351547

Myhill, D. (2008). Towards a linguistic model of sentence development in writing. *Language and Education, 22*(5), 271–88. doi:10.2167/le775.0

Norris, J. M., & Ortega, L. (2009). Towards an organic approach to investigating CAF in instructed SLA: The case of complexity. *Applied Linguistics, 30*(4), 555–78. doi:10.1093/applin/amp044

North, S. (2005). Disciplinary variation in the use of theme in undergraduate essays. *Applied Linguistics 26*(3), 431–52. doi:10.1093/applin/ami023

O'Dowd, E. (2012). The development of linguistic complexity: A functional continuum. *Language Teaching, 45*(3), 329–46. doi:10.1017/S0261444810000510

O'Hallaron, C. L., & Schleppegrell, M. J. (2016). "Voice" in children's science arguments: Aligning assessment criteria with genre and discipline. *Assessing Writing, 30*, 63–73. doi:10.1016/j.asw.2016.06.004

Ortega, L. (2015). Syntactic complexity in L2 writing: Progress and expansion. *Journal of Second Language Writing, 29*, 82–94. doi:10.1016/j.jslw.2015.06.008

Pollack, H. N. (2003). *Uncertain science . . . uncertain world.* Cambridge, UK: Cambridge University Press.

Ravid, D., & Berman, R. A. (2010). Developing noun phrase complexity at school age: A text-embedded cross-linguistic analysis. *First Language, 30*(1), 3–26. doi:10.1177/0142723709350531

Ravid, D., & Tolchinsky, L. (2002). Developing linguistic literacy: a comprehensive model. *Journal of Child Language, 29*(2), 417–47. doi:10.1017/S0305000902005111

Rose, D., & Martin, J. R. (2012). *Learning to write, reading to learn: Genre, knowledge and pedagogy in the Sydney School.* Bristol, UK: Equinox.

Schleppegrell, M. (1998). Grammar as resource: Writing a description. *Research in the Teaching of English 32*(2), 182–211.

Schleppegrell, M. J. (2004a). *The language of schooling: A functional linguistics perspective.* Mahwah, NJ: Erlbaum.

Schleppegrell, M. J. (2004b). Technical writing in a second language: The role of grammatical metaphor. In L. J. Ravelli & R. A. Ellis (Eds.), *Analysing academic writing: Contextualized frameworks* (pp. 172–89). London, UK: Continuum.

Schleppegrell, M. J. (2006). The linguistic features of advanced language use: The grammar of exposition. In H. Byrnes (Ed.), *Advanced language learning: The contribution of Halliday and Vygotsky* (pp. 134–46). London, UK: Continuum.

Schleppegrell, M. J. (2008). Grammar, the sentence, and traditions of linguistic analysis. In C. Bazerman (Ed.), *Handbook of research on writing: History, society, school, individual, text* (pp. 549–64). New York: Erlbaum.

Schleppegrell, M. J., & Go, A. L. (2007). Analyzing the writing of English learners: A functional approach. *Language Arts 84*(6), 529–38.

Schleppegrell, M. J., & Moore, J. (2018). Linguistic tools for supporting emergent critical language awareness in the elementary school. In R. Harman (Ed.), *Bilingual learners and social equity: Critical approaches to Systemic Functional Linguistics* (pp. 23–43). New York: Springer.

Schleppegrell, M. J., Moore, J., Al-Adeimi, S., O'Hallaron, C. L., Palincsar, A. S., & Symons, C. (2014). Tackling a genre: Situating SFL genre pedagogy in a new context. In L. C. de Oliveira & J. Iddings (Eds.), *Genre pedagogy across the curriculum: Theory and application in US classrooms and contexts* (pp. 25–39). Sheffield, UK: Equinox.

Whittaker, R. (2010). Using systemic-functional linguistics in content and language integrated learning. *NALDIC Quarterly, 8*(1), 31–36.

CHAPTER FIVE

Multiple Perspectives on the Nature of Writing: Typically Developing Writers in Grades 1, 3, 5, and 7 and Students with Writing Disabilities in Grades 4 to 9

VIRGINIA W. BERNINGER, KIRA GESELOWITZ, AND PETER WALLIS
University of Washington

This chapter begins with a brief overview of research on writing development. It continues by making a case for investigating writing development from the multiple perspectives of writing researchers as well as of the developing writers themselves.

Research on assessing writing in developing writers (Jeffery, 2009; Rowe & Wilson, 2015; Saddler & Graham, 2007; Wilcox, Yagelski, & Yu, 2013) and effective instructional approaches for teaching writing to developing children and youths (Graham, Kiuhara, McKeown, & Harris, 2012; Murphy & Smith, 2015) has advanced knowledge of writing development (Jeffery & Wilcox, 2014; Schleppegrell, 2004; Wilcox & Jeffery, 2015). Much has been learned about how writing changes from preschool to early childhood (Rowe & Wilson, 2015), early childhood to middle childhood to early adolescence (Berninger & Chanquoy, 2012; Christie & Derewianka, 2008—see Table 8.1), early to middle adolescence (Wilcox & Jeffery, 2014), and even through adulthood (Brandt, 2001). Beginning in the preschool years, writing development appears to be dynamic and rarely linear (Rowe &

This chapter is dedicated to the memory of the late Arthur Applebee and his many contributions to the field of writing research and practice.

Wilson, 2015), as is also the case in grades 1 to 7 (Berninger & Hayes, 2012).

Moreover, as instructional practices in writing have changed so have the aspects of the writing development investigated. For example, in the United States only penmanship was emphasized in the nineteenth century, and in the mid-twentieth century composition was taught but not until the middle and upper grades (Applebee, 1981). Only recently, in the twenty-first century, has a balance emerged combining explicit teaching of specific writing skills and engaging children in the writing process from the beginning of schooling (see Applebee, 2000). Indeed, Applebee's vision for alternative models of writing is becoming reality in many schools and influencing the multiple aspects of writing that researchers consider: more emphasis on teaching different genres for a variety of specific writing purposes, integrating oral language with writing instruction, emphasizing writing at different levels of language (syntax, sentence combining, paragraph, and discourse), providing instruction in writing strategies, and viewing writing as participating in social action.

The populations of developing writers studied are also diverse. Both assessment and instructional research on writing have focused on English language learners (ELLs) as well as students for whom English is their first language (de Oliveira & Schleppegrell, 2015; Jeffery, Kieffer, & Matsuda, 2013; Wilcox, 2011; Wilcox & Jeffery, 2014, 2015). In addition, good writers and struggling writers (Lin, Monroe, & Troia, 2007) and students with specific learning disabilities (Graham, Schwartz, & MacArthur, 1993) have been studied.

The role of the self and of the other in writing development has been well recognized. Hayes and Flowers (1986) called attention to the role of the writer in the writing process. Although much writing research is focused on pedagogy (the role of the teacher in learning to write) or audience (writing for others), the developing writer, that is, the self that one brings to the task of learning and refining writing skill, also plays a role in writing development. Prior research has addressed the writer's affect toward the writing process (Jeffery & Wilcox, 2014), lifespan memory of the writing (and reading) acquisition process (Brandt, 2001), writers' perspectives on the role of literacy in their everyday lives and the sponsors of those literacy activities (Brandt, 1998), and theory of mind relevant to not only expressing one's own perspectives but also perceiving and understanding the perspectives of other (Davidson & Berninger, 2016).

However, research on writing development is also influenced by the diversity of the perspectives of writing researchers (Bazerman, 2013; Bazerman et al., 2010; contributors to this volume). Multiple, diverse perspectives have informed writing research and models specific to writing skills: cognitive (Hayes, 2009; Kellogg, 1994), linguistic (de Oliveira & Schleppegrell, 2015; Schleppegrell, 2004), sensorimotor (James & Li, 2017), social/emotional/motivational (Bazerman, this volume; Hamilton, Nolen, & Abbott, 2013; Nielsen et al., 2017), and attention/executive functions (e.g., for self-regulated writing, Harris, Graham, Mason, & Friedlander, 2008) as well as interdisciplinary (cognitive-linguistic-sensorimotor-social/emotional/motivational and attention/executive function domains) (Berninger, 2015).

Given the multiple perspectives of researchers, not surprisingly, prior research has used diverse methodological approaches to study developing writers' perspectives on writing: interviews of writers (Brandt, 2001; Graham et al., 1993; Wilcox & Jeffery, 2015); a combination of interviews and examination of writing samples (Saddler & Graham, 2007; Wilcox, 2011); a combination of interviews of teachers, student writers, and administrators; surveys; writing samples; and classroom observations (Wilcox, submitted); direct observation of children writing (forms and directional patterns), assessment of content, assignment of meaning to marks, and construction of message (Rowe & Wilson, 2015); and assessment of knowledge of writing by asking children questions about the purpose of writing, the attributes of good writing, and strategies for writing (Graham et al., 1993). Conversational language during the preschool years (Berninger & Garvey, 1981) differs from the formal academic register of writing during the school years (Silliman & Berninger, 2011). However, a longitudinal study from kindergarten to first grade showed that academic oral language as assessed by psychometric tests was related to writing acquisition (Berninger, Proctor, De Bruyn, & Smith, 1988). Also, typically developing writers exhibited normal variation in their writing and reading acquisition and individual differences in response to the same early literacy instruction (e.g., Berninger & Abbott, 1992). A cross-sectional study conducted with 900 children (50 boys and 50 girls at each grade level—first through ninth) selected to be representative of the US population at the time for ethnicity and mother's level of education added further understanding of the normal variation across writing development and processes involved. Results also documented interrelationships among writing, reading, and oral language at different levels (units of analysis—subword, word, and syntax), as well as cognitive (planning, translating, reviewing, and revising), sensorimotor (sequential finger movements), and working memory (supervisory attention and executive functions) processes within and across grade levels. Ability at one level of language (word, sentence, or text) did not predict ability at any of the other levels of language within an individual (see Berninger, 1994, 2009).

A series of instructional studies with at-risk students at the low end of normal variation showed that low-achieving writers in kindergarten, first, second, third, or fourth grades in school settings could be brought up to grade level in handwriting, spelling, and composing skills with grade-appropriate writing instruction (for review, see Berninger, 2009). Subsequently, six writing instruction studies conducted at the university provided one-to-one tutoring for participants with specific writing disabilities outside the normal range and were also effective in improving writing skills (see Berninger, 2009; Lessons 11, 13, and 14 in Berninger & Abbott, 2003; and Lesson Sets 2, 3, and 4 in Berninger & Wolf, 2009). Additional genetics and brain research on specific learning disabilities in written language (SLDs-WL) showed the following: (a) dyslexia is not just a reading disability—the persisting problem is spelling; (b) dysgraphia (impaired handwriting) may occur alone or co-occur with dyslexia; (c) oral language may be a strength in dysgraphia and dyslexia but is not in oral and written language learning disability (OWL LD) (impaired syntax in written and/or oral expression) (see Berninger & Richards, 2010).

However, in none of these studies had the perspectives of the developing writers been considered or examined. Therefore the approach applied to the two studies featured in this chapter was to elicit developing writers' perspectives on writing by asking them to explain to other developing writers what writing is. The goal was to analyze developing writers' explanations of what writing is to gain insight into the perspectives the developing writers themselves bring to the task of learning to write and how these perspectives may or may not change across time or be related to writing disabilities persisting beyond early childhood despite early intervention.

Both studies were informed by the first author's interdisciplinary training and experience as a research psychologist (developmental sociolinguistics, psycholinguistics, cognitive psychology, social cognition, and psychobiology) and a clinical psychologist in pediatric medical settings for children ages birth to three, three to six, grades 1 to 6 and 7 to 12, and adolescents and adults. The first study, a five-year longitudinal study with overlapping cohorts (grades 1 to 5 or 3 to 7), was therefore designed to elicit developing writers' perspectives on writing in the annual assessments. Research findings have supported the contribution of all five domains of development to typical writing development: the cognitive domain (Niedo, Abbott, & Berninger, 2014), the language domain by ear, mouth, eye, and hand at text level, syntax level, and morphophonemic word levels (Abbott, Berninger, & Fayol, 2010; Berninger, Nagy, & Beers, 2011), the sensorimotor domain (Richards et al., 2009), the attention/executive function domain (Berninger, Abbott, Cook, & Nagy, 2017), and the social/emotional domain (Hamilton et al., 2013; Nielsen et al., 2017). Research has also supported the role of these specific writing skills: transcription (Alstad et al., 2015) and translation (Niedo et al., 2014). Relevant to translation, the generative nature of multiple genres in composition has been demonstrated (Davidson & Berninger, 2015). See Berninger (2009, 2015, Chapters 4, 5, and 6 and companion website) for a review of other research on writing development during early childhood, middle childhood, and adolescence. However, the findings specific to the writers' perspectives are reported in this chapter for the first time.

The first study reported in the current chapter is based on the longitudinal study of typical writing development. We coded the themes in the children's explanations of what writing is; these explanations were conceptualized as one indicator of developing writers' metacognitions about writing, which may in turn influence how they respond to writing instruction, engage in independent writing at school or home or elsewhere in their daily lives, and perform on formal assessments of their writing. The frequency of occurrence of each of the coded themes was tallied and displayed for comparison with writing researchers' perspectives on what writing is. We tested the hypothesis that the developing writers' responses would reflect the five domains of development and specific writing skills, in keeping with what writing researchers have found, but might provide additional insights as well from the perspectives of developing writers. Also of interest was whether developing writers might exhibit the same kind of "motherese" observed for oral language, in which both adults and older children adapt their use of language when interacting with younger children to the younger children's individual developmental levels (Snow, 1972). Thus, we also asked the children to explain writing to both younger children and children in the same grade.

The second study reported in the current chapter is from the University of Washington Multidisciplinary Learning Disabilities Center. One research aim of this interdisciplinary research has been to validate differential diagnoses of persisting specific learning disabilities in written language (SLDs-WL) in grades 4 to 9 despite early intervention in students whose development is otherwise in the normal range (Berninger, Richards, & Abbott, 2015). Another research aim has been to evaluate response to computerized instruction by students with and without SLDs-WL: dysgraphia (impaired handwriting), dyslexia (impaired spelling), and oral and written language learning disability—OWL LD (impaired syntax in written expression). At completion of each session of computerized writing lessons, students were asked questions about their perspectives on writing assessment and instruction. Their responses were coded to analyze, interpret, and synthesize the multiple perspectives of developing writers with and without persisting SLDs-WL.

Study 1

Methods

Each year for five consecutive years participating children completed a half-day annual assessment of multiple writing and related developmental skills. They completed standardized measures, with national norms or researcher-generated norms, of all five domains of development and specific writing skills; engaged in learning activities some of which involved writing and/or other language skills; and took frequent snack, movement, and thinking breaks to rejuvenate and sustain attention and engagement during their once-a-year literacy trek to be university students. It was during the thinking break in years 1 and 5 that children in each cohort were asked to explain what writing is (in grade 1 and again in grade 5 for cohort 1 or in grade 3 and again in grade 7 for cohort 2). The children's explanations were coded to connect with the themes reflected in them about what writing is. See Appendix A for examples of what the children said or wrote for each of the coded themes.

Cohort 1 explanations of what writing is. In grade 1, 78 children (33 boys and 45 girls) explained orally to the graduate student assessor what writing is. After the session the graduate student transcribed the audio recording for coding. Then in grade 5, the 68 children (29 boys and 39 girls) who were still participating in the longitudinal study again explained what writing is—but this time the explanations were provided in writing.

Cohort 2 explanations of what writing is. In grade 3, 77 children (39 boys and 38 girls) explained orally what writing is and the graduate student assessor transcribed the explanation into writing after the session. In grade 7, 72 children (37 boys and 35 girls) who were still participating in the longitudinal study again explained what writing is—but this time the explanations were provided in writing.

Although the children were recruited from a large urban school district in the Pacific Rim where 83 languages are spoken and English was not the only language spoken in the homes of

|

some of the participating children, English was the first language of all participating children. In addition, parents completed annual questionnaires and annually shared writing samples of their children from school work along with information about the instructional program at school including teacher feedback (see Berninger & Hayes, 2012). Examining these showed that students were generally receiving the kind of balanced writing instruction Applebee (2000) described, which combines explicit instruction in writing skills and engagement in the writing process through varied activities to write across the curriculum. For more details about the longitudinal study, see Abbott et al. (2010).

Results

The coded themes are summarized in Table 5.1 to facilitate for typically developing writers both cross-sectional comparisons from grades 1 to 3 to 5 to 7 and longitudinal comparisons from grade 1 (year 1 cohort 1) to grade 5 (year 5 cohort 1) and from grade 3 (year 1 cohort 2) to grade 7 (year 5 cohort 2). Appendix A provides examples for each coded theme in their explanations.

Initial reading of the explanations of writing—whether transcribed oral transcripts in younger writers or written explanations in the older writers—for the most part did not show variation whether directed to grademates or to younger children (kindergarten in year 1 when students were in first or third grade) or older children (fifth or seventh grade in year 5 when students were asked to explain writing to a kindergartner, a third grader, or a student in the same grade—fifth or seventh) (see Figure 5.1). Thus, the coded themes are based mainly on the explanation of writing at the same grade level as the developing writer providing the explanation. However, two cases were identified in which seventh graders show evidence of adapting their explanations of writing to the grade level of the student for whom they were providing the explanation.

TABLE 5.1. Mixed Writing Development Model: Cross-Sectional Grades 1, 3, 5, and 7 and Longitudinal Grades 1 to 5 (Cohort 1) and Grades 3 to 7 (Cohort 2) for Themes in Typically Developing Writers' Responses to "Explain What Writing Is"

Coded Theme	Grade 1	Grade 3	Grade 5	Grade 7
I. Developmental Domains				
Sensorimotor Domain				
Tools used	49	19	0	6
Medium	12	2	0	9
Tool-medium (e.g., paper)	0	3	0	4
Tool-function	0	7	0	11
Medium-function	0	7	0	18
Tool-medium-function	0	7	12	10
Language Domain				
Levels of language	0	9	14	79
Cross-language systems relationships				
Writing-oral language	0	0	1	2
Reading-writing	0	2	1	16
Cognition Domain				
Meaning making	1	6	2	13
Flow	0	0	0	2
Creativity	0	0	0	5
Imagination	0	0	0	3
Art form	0	0	3	1
Social/Emotional/Motivational Domain				
Communication with others	7	10	21	38
Easy-difficult dimension	0	0	2	2
Affect toward writing	1	5	4	9
Avoidance versus persistence	0	0	0	4
Attention/Executive-Function Domain				
Planning	0	0	0	2
Setting goals	0	0	0	1
Brainstorming	0	0	0	3
Organizing	0	0	0	10
Reviewing/revising/editing	0	0	0	5
II. Writing Skills				
Transcription				
Likened to drawing	16	6	1	4
Handwriting	0	5	0	2
Spelling	0	0	4	2
Punctuation/capitalization	0	0	1	5
Translation Cognition-Language				
Idea expression	0	1	12	17
Self-expression—opinions and points of view	1	0	11	17
Expressing humor	0	0	0	1
Expressing theories, research, facts	0	0	0	3
Translation Emotion-Language				
Expressing affect/feeling	0	0	2	9

continued on next page

Table 5.1 continued

Metacognitions about Writing				
Could not define writing	16	2	0	1
Described functions of writing	62[a]	25	21	70[b]
Described forms of writing (genres)	0	3	3	51
Provided examples of writing	0	7	4	31
Integrated multiple writing components	0	0	16	14
III. Relationship between Writing and School				
Subject in curriculum	0	2	0	1
Pedagogy—what teachers do	0	1	0	9
School assignments—what students do	0	2	0	0
Supports learning	0	2	0	0
Tests	0	1	0	1
Homework	0	0	0	4

Notes: [a]Most examples about letter writing (*n*=29) or spelling words (*n*=16), that is, transcription.
[b]More diversity (21 functions), of which informing/describing and explaining were most frequent (*n*=14 each).

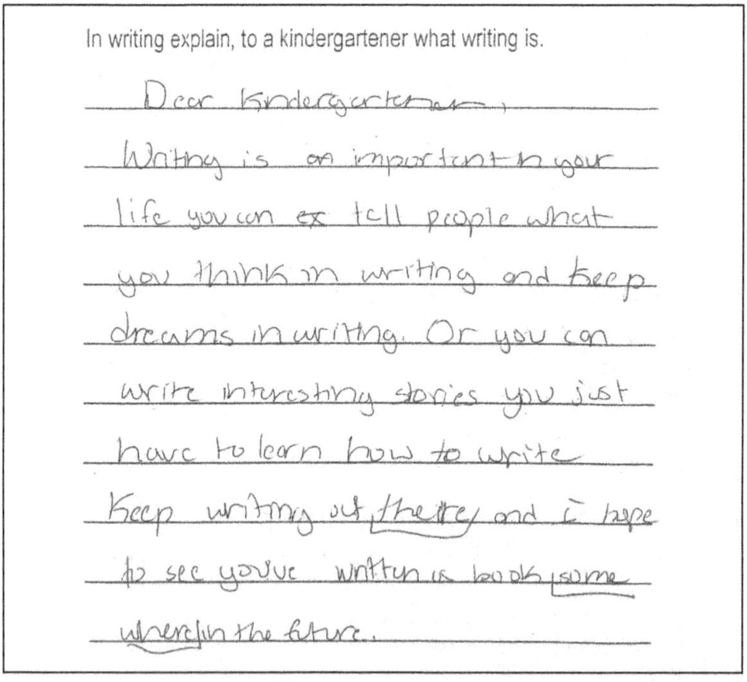

In writing explain, to a kindergartener what writing is.

Dear Kindergartener,
Writing is an important in your life you can ex tell people what you think in writing and keep dreams in writing. Or you can write interesting stories you just have to learn how to write. Keep writing out there and i hope to see youve written in books some where in the future.

FIGURE 5.1. *Six examples of cohort 1 and cohort 2 students' written explanations of what writing is, directed to grademates or to younger children.*

Figure 5.1 continued

In writing explain, to a third grader what writing is.

Dear third grader,

You've learned that the only thing writing is, is homework and work, but many people have discovered writing is wonderful and you should have find your passion some of yours may be writing. Don't When writing your writi you're putting all your ideas down and preserving them silently. Someday I hope one of you writes a book.

In writing explain, to student in the same grade as you are in (5th or 7th) what writing is.

Dear 7th grader,

Writing is a tool that you can express your feelings through silently. Some people love writing and some people don't. No matter what somehow writings always going to be in your life whether you like it or not. You should try to like writing at least a little or become good at it so if you don't like it its not so much a pain to do.

continued on next page

Figure 5.1 continued

In writing explain, to a kindergartener what writing is.

Writing is a way to talk to other people. Like, if I was to write, "D-O-G," what does that tell you? Dog! If I was to write a "C-A-T," what does that tell you? Cat! Once you get really good at writing, you can write bigger words to people, like "happy", and "angry."

In writing explain, to a third grader what writing is.

Writing is a way to talk to other people. Like if I wrote, "E-X-C-I-T-I-N-G," what does that tell you I'm trying to tell you? Exciting! If I wrote "A-N-G-R-Y," what does that tell you I'm trying to tell you? Angry! Once you guys get better at writing, you can write bigger words to people, like "Exuberant" or "Inflamitory."

Figure 5.1 continued

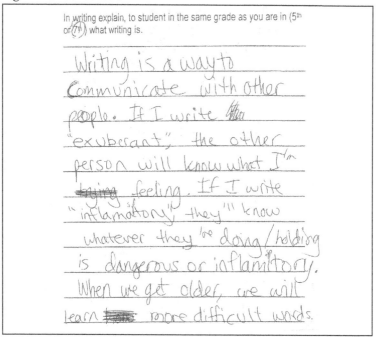

Cross-sectional comparisons of typically developing writers showed the following patterns in the coded themes. First, explanations related to developmental domains were examined. Unexpected was the high frequency of explanations related to tools or medium used in grades 1 and 3, which were not mentioned in grade 5 or less frequently in grade 6. These are included in the sensorimotor domain because both somatosensory and motor feedback from the tool and placement of writing on the medium could influence tool use and medium for writing. In contrast, explanations that *integrated* tool and medium, tool and function, medium and function, or tool, medium, and function were never observed in first grade. A developmental trend was observed in increasing use of multiple levels of language in explaining what writing is—in the first two years of the younger cohort (grades 1 to 2) reference to at least two levels of language and often more than two levels of language from grades 3 to 5, and from grades

3 to 7 in the older cohort reference to multiple languages very frequent across each grade level. Explanations of writing related it to either oral language or reading occurred for the most part only in the seventh grade and rarely before the seventh grade. Likewise, explanations involving cognition occurred most often in seventh grade and rarely before then. In contrast, explanations of writing relating to communication with others or affect toward writing occurred at each grade level, but showed a trend toward greater frequency in the seventh grade. Explanations related to attention and executive functions only occurred in the seventh grade. Overall, the cross-sectional comparisons showed an early focus on tools or media, and an increase across time in explanations that drew on language, social/emotional/motivational, cognitive, and attention/executive functions. See Table 5.1 and Appendix A.

Second, patterns of relationships between explaining what writing is and specific writing skills were examined. Explaining writing on the basis of an analogy to drawing letters occurred mainly in the primary grades and primarily in the first grade. Explaining that writing is related to spelling, punctuation, and capitalization occurred only in the fifth and seventh grades. Translation as idea expression, self-expression of opinions and points of view, and expression of emotions occurred, with rare exceptions, only in the fifth and seventh grades. See Table 5.1 and Appendix A.

Third, other observed patterns related to explaining what writing is appeared to reflect a continuum of metacognition independent of the first two coded themes. At the lower end of this continuum, some developing writers, mainly in first grade but sometimes other primary grades, were unable to define writing. Across the grades explanations were offered that described the functions of writing, but only in the seventh grade did explanations describe the multiple forms of writing. Only in fifth and seventh grade were explanations of writing likely to provide specific examples of writing and integrate multiple component processes or skills. See Table 5.1 and Appendix A.

Finally, patterns related to explaining what writing is related to schooling were observed. Only the older developing writers, not the younger developing writers, explained what writing is with reference to schooling. See Table 5.1 and Appendix A.

Longitudinal comparisons of typically developing writers showed the following patterns in the coded themes. For the set of analyses related to developmental domains, although explanations that integrated tool and medium, tool and function, or medium and function showed a longitudinal trend from third to seventh grade, this longitudinal trend was observed only in cohort 2. The longitudinal trend from first to fifth grade (cohort 1) and from third to seventh grade (cohort 2) was observed across cohorts for integration of tool, medium, and function. Likewise, the longitudinal trends related to language, cognition, and attention/executive function were more evident in cohort 2, from grade 3 to grade 7, than in cohort 1, from grade 1 to grade 5, suggesting that the transition to middle childhood and to adolescence is when changes in these developmental domains in children's explanations of writing are most likely to occur. See Table 5.1 and Appendix A.

For the second set of analyses related to writing skills, only cohort 2 explained writing in terms of handwriting, and more so in third than seventh grade but with low frequency in both grades. Both cohorts showed the developmental trend toward less reference to drawing letters in fifth and seventh grade and more reference, but not frequent reference, to spelling, punctuation, and capitalization in the fifth and seventh grades. Both cohorts showed the longitudinal trend to less focus on handwriting and more focus on spelling, capitalization, punctuation in transcription and idea expression, self-expression of opinions and points of view, and emotions in translations in the fifth and seventh grades than in the primary grades. See Table 5.1 and Appendix A.

For the third set of analyses, the two cohorts did not show the same longitudinal trends for being unable to define writing or the functions of writing. The two cohorts did show the same longitudinal trends for the other indicators of the continuum of metacognitions about writing. See Table 5.1 and Appendix A.

For the fourth set of analyses, cohort 1 never used reference to school in explaining what writing is. In contrast, cohort 2 did. See Table 5.1 and Appendix A.

Study 2

Procedures

Referred children in grades 4 to 9, from the same community near the university as in the longitudinal study, completed comprehensive assessment to evaluate whether they met research criteria based on two decades of interdisciplinary research for dysgraphia, dyslexia, or OWL LD for an SLD in writing (see Berninger et al., 2015). Because these criteria are based on standardized measures with age or grade norms, dysgraphia, dyslexia, and OWL LD could be diagnosed despite the grade range. In fact, sometimes older students were more impaired than younger ones. However, one of the criteria was to document that these were SLDs (specific learning disabilities in that otherwise the developing writer was within the normal range in the cognition, language, sensorimotor, social/emotional, and attention/executive function domains). All of these SLDs impair transcription in some way but not necessarily the same way (see Berninger et al., 2015), and inclusion criteria also took into account histories of persistent written language problems. The parental level of education and the ethnic background of participants were comparable to that of the first study of typical language development.

Children who qualified for (and assented) and whose parents granted informed consent were invited to participate in weekly instructional sessions to complete eighteen computerized lessons. At the completion of many of these sessions, the second author asked the children to explain what writing meant to them through various prompts, similar to how the children in the longitudinal study had been asked. She tested the hypothesis that because of their long-standing difficulties with handwriting and spelling, they might focus exclusively on those skills in explaining what writing is. Some of the specific questions she used included asking them to explain how teachers could help them to become better writers and express their creativity, what styles of writing they liked to use and why, and what kinds of assignments they preferred to write by hand. For each question, students wrote their responses in handwriting on paper.

The third author examined the writing samples produced by students from the same study who also participated in a related brain-imaging study. At the end of the scanning session, the participants were instructed to plan silently before composing and then when they exited the scanner to write the composition they had planned on this topic: "Explain to an astronaut how writing can be used in exploring outer space." Of interest were the coded transcription and translation variables observed for a common writing topic.

Results

As shown in Appendix B, explanations of what writing is, provided by the students with SLDs in transcription, were diverse, reflecting themes in the typically developing writers' explanations. The explanations of those with SLDs did not uniformly reflect a narrow understanding of writing restricted to the transcription skills with which they had difficulty. The hypothesis that transcription problems preclude developing a broader view of the writing process was not supported.

Of educational relevance, the students with SLDs explained that they learn more in the years they have teachers who understand and like them, consistent with a sociocultural perspective on writing development that suggests that student-teacher bonding is as important as the nature of the writing instruction during middle childhood and adolescence, just as parent-child bonding is in the early postnatal period. Moreover, when the second author queried the students with SLDs about the styles of writing they enjoyed, that is, with which they experience positive affect, they reported a wide array of writing they enjoyed despite their own transcription problems (see Appendix C).

The third author's coding of those compositions showed considerable variation in genres for the same topic sentence and in knowledge-telling strategies as well (Wallis, Richards, Boord, Abbott, & Berninger, 2017). The first finding is consistent with recent research by Boscolo, Gelati, and Galvan (2012) and Olinghouse, Santangelo, and Wilson (2012) showing the generativity of genres in typically developing writers. The second finding extends what Hayes (2011) found for young typically developing writers, and adds genre competency to Hayes's family of strategies. Both findings show that translation, while constrained by transcription, is a separable process from transcription and expresses itself in diverse ways. Also illuminating was the number of students who spontaneously used art along with written language to translate their thoughts for communication with others (Wallis et al., 2017). Translation draws on the hand in expressing ideas in both written language and art, which is why many books are illustrated in art or visual displays that combine linguistic and nonlinguistic portrayal of ideas.

Discussion of Studies 1 and 2

Significance for Writing Research

The perspectives of the typically developing writers reflected an awareness that writing develops over time and across space. As one fifth grader explained: "Writing is something you will do the rest of your life." Other developing writers offered the insight that writing helps you to communicate to more people (as one expressed it, "millions"), across time ("lasts long after you write it"), and across space ("far away readers"). However, the initial model based on prior research did not capture all the perspectives developing writers in the current study brought to the task of learning to write. New categories were also identified (see various items in sections I, II, and III in Table 5.1).

However, the developing writers and the adults who interact with them may be not only at different chronological ages but also at very different stages or places in their own writing development; the latter transcends chronological age and may affect how the adult interacts with the child or adolescent developing writer. Indeed, not only teachers but also parents play an important role in writing development as the annual parent questionnaires collected in the longitudinal study demonstrated (Alston-Abel & Berninger, 2017). A wraparound developmental model acknowledges the cross-development influences on writing development, which may be both age-related (generational) and skill-related (individual), and as important as the perspectives of the developing writers themselves.

Writing research too, like other research fields, involves cross-generational collaborations. A research mentor guides the new generation in the research they will pursue in the future, but it is that new generation who will carry the research field forward. For example, the second author is engaged in a larger study seeking developing oral and written language learners' advice for teachers on many topics and communicating the students' perspectives gleaned from their advice to teachers in general. Educational theorists who emphasize the constructive processes of the learner have long acknowledged that the teacher and the learner are coparticipants in the learning process. Yet recently the emphasis has been on what the teacher does—evidence-based instruction—and perhaps we are losing sight of the perspectives learners bring to the instruction that can influence their responses to that instruction. The third author is engaged in interdisciplinary research integrating language with STEM and the arts (L'STEAM) and exploring how technology can support learning and instruction for both. In the process he is discovering amazing generativity in the creativity of written language expression and the genres employed, even in students with diagnosed transcription disabilities (Wallis et al., 2017). At the same time, problems in text organization are observed that cannot be fully explained by transcription disabilities.

It is this cross-generational collaboration among seasoned and new-generation adult writing researchers that sustains the continuity of the field of writing research. Just as writing develops across the lifespan, the field of writing research will also evolve developmentally over time as the collective wisdom continually identifies new research topics and methods. Thus, the field of writing research benefits from the multiple perspectives of writing researchers, both from diverse traditions investigating writing across the lifespan and at different time points in their personal career paths.

Limitations

The explanations of writing of the typically developing writers were collected longitudinally from 2001 to 2005, early in the current era of annual state testing yoked to state standards. Furthermore, the focus was on the developing writers' explanations of what writing is—not necessarily all the processes and skills that may affect their writing development and achievement. That is, the findings only reflect developing writers' ability to explain in language their understandings or metacognitions about what writing is.

The explanations of writing of the students with persisting SLDs-WL were collected in writing, which may have limited what they were able to express. As time permitted, the second author was sometimes, but not always, able to interview the student for oral clarification of their perspectives on the question for each lesson. Nevertheless, it was very instructive how many students shared that they learn the best when teachers show an understanding of students and connect with them socially and emotionally. It is not just what teachers teach but how they create relationships with the students they nurture that contributes to writing development.

Future Research Directions

Future research might also use longitudinal designs of typically developing writers as well as a variety of other methods that have been used to assess student's perspectives on what writing is and that were reviewed in the introduction to this chapter. These methods might be applied both alone and in combination to identify the richness and diversity of perspectives that developing writers might bring to the tasks of learning to write and using writing. Some of these findings may inspire future research on the role of metacognitive understandings of writing in learning to write and test hypotheses generated on the basis of the current findings.

Asking children to explain writing to other students who were younger or in the same grade served as a reminder that writing development may be influenced by others at different time points in their own journeys in writing development. Although we did not find support for a phenomenon like "motherese," which is well established for oral language learning, we did find evidence that during early adolescence at least some developing writers may be developing abilities to express their metacognitions about what writing is, which are affected by the developmental level of the writer and audience for their explanations. See Figure 5.1 and Table 5.1. Future research might explore effects of this increased meta-awareness about writing in some adolescents on their own writing development. Our introduction also discusses past research on such meta-awareness in adolescent writers.

Conclusions

Both typical writing development and writing development in struggling writers with SLDs-WL are best understood from not only the perspectives of researchers' methodologies and paradigms but also the perspectives of developing writers. Also relevant are the perspectives of teachers and parents, which deserve additional research attention.

Acknowledgments

The authors would like to acknowledge a Spencer LifeSpan Grant, the leadership of Charles Bazerman in organizing the collaborations of Life Span Writing Development Group members, and the input on this chapter from Kristen Wilcox, Jill Jeffery, Mary Schleppegrell, and Debbie Rowe. Preparation of this chapter for the Spencer LifeSpan Writing Project was supported, in part, by HD P50HD071764 and HD25858 from the Eunice Kennedy Shriver National Institute of Child Health and Human Development (NICHD) at the National Institutes of Health (NIH). Both the second and third authors participated as doctoral students in this research, on which the first author is principal investigator. The chapter is based on a presentation by V. Berninger, "Understanding What Writing Is and How It Develops from the Perspectives of Developing Writers," at the LifeSpan Symposium organized by Charles Bazerman for the EARLI Writing Conference, Amsterdam, 28 August 2014.

Appendix A

Examples from Protocols for Coded Themes in Table 5.1

Integrating Multiple Writing Components
Examples from seventh graders; also produced by fifth graders.

1. Use letters of the alphabet to form words to get ideas across and write stories, letters, books, and essays.
2. Writing is an art . . . a form of communication that is made up of symbols for words . . . write for all different types of reasons for fun or required for job or school or any other purpose.
3. Writing is an act of forming letters, words, sentences, and paragraphs, to persuade, explain, describe, or show feeling.
4. Communication that is facilitated through a collection of hieroglyphs or letters or numerals drawn on a piece of paper or smaller materials—you can transfer ideas or concepts to millions of others by recording them on a piece of paper.
5. Express by putting your idea into words with vivid descriptions and compelling words and exciting concepts so other people can understand what they mean, also with certain things an emotional response to writing
6. Putting words on paper in sentences that make a story, there is usually a subject, put your imagination on paper, say whatever you want, have fun, usually boring, you do it a lot
7. Use regular or cursive alphabet letters to form words on paper forming sentences with words in order that makes sense, 5 to 9 sentences into paragraphs, express your thoughts or write stories with different plots or ideas, persuasive, narrative, expository, action, an art like painting
8. Examples for sound to letters, morphology transforms words, homophones and word-specific spellings
9. Types of homework teachers give and expect, good word choice, ideas, organization, and creativity
10. Use pen or pencil to make words on paper, make words into sentences, sentences into a story, think about what you want to say that everyone can read, for school, work, fun, write for many reasons, write a book, type it on a computer
11. Use pen or pencil to tell a story or express self on paper using letters of the alphabet
12. Communicating thoughts to other people through symbols on paper using the alphabet to express whatever you want
13. Putting ideas on paper by "drawing" letters to make words, another way besides saying words to tell somebody something by combining letters to make words and sentences

14. More than a bunch of words "It is creating imagination and knowledge all in one word."

Appendix B

Responses Explaining What Writing Is by Students with Persisting Writing Disabilities (Spelling Uncorrected)

From the "In Their Voice" Project (Geselowitz)

Student 1 Writing is when you right down words and tell a story

Student 2 Writing is a form of communication which can be preserved and used/read at a later time.

Student 3 Placeing words on paper to make storys

Student 4 Putting down information

Student 5 It something you do with your hand and the pencil

Student 6 Writing is a way of cominicating with oterhs and it can be records

Student 7 Writing is a form of language

Student 8 I think cause I am reefing to handiting

Student 9 Writing is a form of speaking just on paper. You are writing it not speaking it.

Student 10 doing written work

Student 11 Writing is what you fill and you can write on a piece of paper like I am to tell you what writing is.

Student 12 Writing is makrs or simbles used to communicate

Student 13 Evil, horrible, energy wasting task

Student 14 Putting words on paper.

Student 15 expressing an opionion or docement a time in history

Appendix C

Responses to the Questions "What *kinds* of writing are the most interesting to you? What style do you like to use the most when you

write? Why?" by Students with Persisting Writing Disabilities (Spelling Uncorrected)

From the "In Their Voice" Project (Geselowitz)

"I like essays and stories when I get something to write about. The style of writing that I like depends I like fiction when I'm given something to write about and I like joural entrys about other people."
"Abvencher beause it is fun to right. My favret righting is advencher because its exiting and you can make the caricter do enything like go throw the fucher or space"
"I like free writing. The free writing that I do is for fun I like to write about things that I've done or seen or heard of. I also like to write songs. Rhyming really caches on to me. writing a song you have to be creative and let the words come from the bottom of your heart. They have to truely mean somthing to you or someone else or else you don't understand what your writing."
"I really enjoy fiction, no fiction, poems and etc. When I'm writing I like to write the way poems are written but free verse. I don't really like to rhyme I rather just write my feelings out and not think about what I'm writing or what word rhymes with what. I mostly write about how I feel, sports or just like the weather."
"foot ball writing. Staf I like. like foot ball.
"I guess creative writing but I love to use dialog. I love it! Mostly because if you ask anyone that is close to me they will say, I like to talk. I think it is super fun to skript out what someone will say. Because sometimes life will be unpredictable so it's cool to know what they are going to say before they say it."
"I like narrative writing because I can write about whatever I want to write about and have control on how it ends. But I only like it if I can choose what I want to write about."
"cursive Beacuse it looks cool. its not reaalistic. cusive is not reaalitic, thats why I like it"
"I love to write poems. I don't know why but I do. Actully I do know why. I love poems because you don't have to write in full centenses. I really don't like expressing my self in langhes people understand so I feel free when I write poetry"
"I like writing most about somthing interesting like a book we read in class or a passage. I like writing inforamational writing the most because it is easiest for me."

"I am most instriced in mreanbyology. I like riting facts about it that are true! because it is verry fun!"

"The kind of writing that is most interesting to me is relalistic Fiction or Fiction. a type of writing I can make anything I want happen in the book or story.
The style of writing I like to use is mostly made op writing. But when I have to do an essay for scholl I do something that happened to me but otherwise I mostly make storys up."

"Fiction and naritive writing is more interesting to me.
I like it when I can write little children's books and storys.
Why? I can let my ideas flow."

References

Abbott, R. D., Berninger, V. W., & Fayol, M. (2010). Longitudinal relationships of levels of language in writing and between writing and reading in grades 1 to 7. *Journal of Educational Psychology, 102*(2), 281–98. doi:10.1037/a0019318

Alstad, Z., Sanders, E., Abbott, R., Barnett, A., Hendersen, S., Connelly, V., & Berninger, V. (2015). Modes of alphabet letter production during middle childhood and adolescence: Interrelationships with each other and other writing skills. *Journal of Writing Research, 6*(3), 199–231. PMC4433034. doi:10.17239/jowr-2015.06.03.1

Alston-Abel, N., & Berninger, V. (2017). Relationships between home literacy practices and school achievement: Implications for consultation and school-home collaboration. *Journal of Educational and Psychological Consultation.* NIHMS 874208. Advance online publication. doi:10.1080/10474412.2017.1323222

Applebee, A. N. (1981). *Writing in the secondary school: English and the content areas.* Urbana, IL: National Council of Teachers of English.

Applebee, A. (2000). Alternative models of writing development. In R. Indrisano & J. R. Squire (Eds.), *Perspectives on writing: Research, theory, and practice* (pp. 90–110). Newark, DE: International Reading Association.

Bazerman, C. (2013). *Literate action: Vol. 1. A rhetoric of literate action.* Fort Collins, CO: WAC Clearinghouse. Retrieved from http://wac.colostate.edu/books/literateaction/v1

Bazerman, C., Krut, R., Lunsford, K., McLeod, S., Null, S., Rogers, P., & Stansell, A. (Eds.) (2010). *Traditions of writing research.* New York: Routledge.

Berninger, V. (1994). *Reading and writing acquisition: A developmental neuropsychological perspective.* Madison, WI: Brown & Benchmark.

Berninger, V. W. (2009). Highlights of programmatic, interdisciplinary research on writing. *Learning Disabilities: Research and Practice, 24*(2), 68–79. doi:10.1111/j.1540-5826.2009.00281.x

Berninger, V. W. (2015). *Interdisciplinary frameworks for schools: Best professional practices for serving the needs of all students.* Washington, DC: American Psychological Association. doi:10.1037/14437-000. Companion website at https://apadivision16.org/publications/division-16-books/supplement-to-interdisciplinary-frameworks-for-schools/

Berninger, V. W., & Abbott, R. D. (1992). The unit of analysis and constructive processes of the learner: Key concepts for educational neuropsychology. *Educational Psychologist, 27*(2), 223–42.

Berninger, V., & Abbott, S. (2003). *PAL Research-based reading and writing lessons.* Instructional manual and reproducibles. Retrieved from https://www.pearsonclinical.com/psychology/products/100000221/process-assessment-of-the-learner-pal-research-based-reading-and-writing-lessons.html#tab-details

Berninger, V., Abbott, R., Cook, C. R., & Nagy, W. (2017). Relationships of attention and executive functions to oral language, reading, and writing skills and systems in middle childhood and early adolescence. *Journal of Learning Disabilities, 30*(4), 434-49. NIHMS 721063. doi:10.1177/0022219415617167

Berninger, V. W., & Chanquoy, L. (2012). What writing is and how it changes across early and middle childhood development: A multidisciplinary perspective. In E. L. Grigorenko, E. Mambrino, & D. D. Preiss (Eds.), *Writing: A mosaic of new perspectives* (pp. 65–84). New York: Psychology Press.

Berninger, G.[V. W.], & Garvey, C. (1981). Questions and the allocation, construction, and timing of turns in child discourse. *Journal of Psycholinguistic Research, 10*(4), 375–402. doi:10.1007/BF01067165

Berninger, V. W., & Hayes, J. R. (2012). Longitudinal individual case studies of 20 children on writing treks in grades 1–5. In M. Fayol, D. Alamargot, & V. W. Berninger (Eds.), *Translation of thought to written text while composing: Advancing theory, knowledge, research methods, tools, and applications* (pp. 95–179). New York: Psychology Press.

Berninger, V. W., Nagy, W., & Beers, S. (2011). Child writers' construction and reconstruction of single sentences and construction of multi-sentence texts: Contributions of syntax and transcription to translation. *Reading and Writing: An Interdisciplinary Journal, 24*(2), 151–82. PMC3048336. doi:10.1007/s11145-010-9262-y

Berninger, V. W., Proctor, A., De Bruyn, I., & Smith, R. (1988). Relationship between levels of oral and written language in beginning readers. *Journal of School Psychology, 26*(4), 341–57. doi:10.1016/0022-4405(88)90042-8

Berninger, V., & Richards, T. (2010). Inter-relationships among behavioral markers, genes, brain and treatment in dyslexia and dysgraphia. *Future Neurology, 5*(4), 597–617. doi:10.2217/fnl.10.22

Berninger, V. W., Richards, T. L., & Abbott, R. D. (2015). Differential diagnosis of dysgraphia, dyslexia, and OWL LD: Behavioral and neuroimaging evidence. *Reading and Writing: An Interdisciplinary Journal, 28*(8), 1119–53. PMC4553247. doi:10.1007/s11145-015-9565-0

Berninger, V. W., & Wolf, B. J. (2009). *Helping students with dyslexia and dysgraphia make connections: Differentiated instruction lesson plans in reading and writing.* Baltimore, MD: Paul H. Brookes.

Boscolo, P., Gelati, C., & Galvan, N. (2012). Teaching elementary school students to play with meanings and genre. *Reading & Writing Quarterly, 28*(1), 29–50. doi:10.1080/10573569.2012.632730

Brandt, D. (1998). Sponsors of literacy. *College Composition and Communication, 49*(2), 165–85.

Brandt, D. (2001). *Literacy in American lives.* New York: Cambridge University Press.

Christie, F., & Derewianka, B. (2008). *School discourse: Learning to write across the years of schooling.* New York: Continuum.

Davidson, M., & Berninger, V. (2015). Informative, compare and contrast, and persuasive essay composing of fifth and seventh graders: Not all essay writing is the same. *Journal of Psychoeducational Assessment, 34*(4), 311–21. PMC4939906. doi:10.1177/0734282915604977

Davidson, M., & Berninger, V. (2016). Thinking aloud during idea generating and planning before written translation: Developmental changes from ages 10 to 12 in expressing and defending opinions. *Cogent Psychology, 3*(1), 1276514. PMC5305188. doi:10.1080/2 3311908.2016.1276514

de Oliveira, L. C., & Schleppegrell, M. J. (2015). *Focus on grammar and meaning.* New York: Oxford University Press.

Graham, S., Kiuhara, S., McKeown, D., & Harris, K.R. (2012). A meta-analysis of writing instruction for students in the elementary grades. *Journal of Educational Psychology, 104,* 879–96.

Graham, S., Schwartz, S. S., & MacArthur, C. A. (1993). Knowledge of writing and the composing process, attitude toward writing, and self-efficacy for students with and without learning disabilities. *Journal of Learning Disabilities, 26*(4), 237–49.

Hamilton, E. W., Nolen, S. B., & Abbott, R. D. (2013). Developing measures of motivational orientation to read and write: A longitudinal study. *Learning and Individual Differences, 28,* 151–66. doi:10.1016/j.lindif.2013.04.007

Harris, K. R., Graham, S., Mason, L. H., & Friedlander, B. (2008). *Powerful writing strategies for all students.* Baltimore, MD: Paul H. Brookes.

Hayes, J. R. (2009). From idea to text. In R. Beard, D. Myhill, J. Riley, & M. Nystrand (Eds.), *SAGE handbook of writing development* (pp. 65–79). London, UK: SAGE.

Hayes, J. R. (2011). Kinds of knowledge-telling: Modeling early writing development. *Journal of Writing Research, 3*(2), 366–83. doi:10.17239/jowr-2011.03.02.1

Hayes, J. R., & Flower, L. S. (1986). Writing research and the writer. *American Psychologist, 41*(10), 1106–13.

James, K. H., & Li, J. X. (2016). Symbol learning is facilitated by the visual variability produced by handwriting. *Journal of Experimental Psychology: General, 145*(3), 298–313.

Jeffery, J. V. (2009). Constructs of writing proficiency in US state and national writing assessments: Exploring variability. *Assessing Writing, 14*(1), 3–24. doi:10.1016/j.asw.2008.12.002

Jeffery, J. V., Kieffer, M. J., & Matsuda, P. K. (2013). Examining conceptions of writing in TESOL and English Education journals: Toward a more integrated framework for research addressing multilingual classrooms. *Learning and Individual Differences, 28,* 181–92. doi:10.1016/j.lindif.2012.11.001

Jeffery, J., & Wilcox, K. (2014). "How do I do it if I don't like writing?" Adolescents' stances toward writing across disciplines. *Reading and Writing: An Interdisciplinary Journal 27*(6), 1095–1117. doi:10.1007/s11145-013-9493-9

Kellogg, R. T. (1994). *The psychology of writing.* New York: Oxford University Press.

Lin, S.-J. C., Monroe, B. W., & Troia, G. A. (2007). Development of writing knowledge in grades 2–8: A comparison of typically developing writers and their struggling peers. *Reading & Writing Quarterly, 23*(3), 207–30. doi:10.1080/10573560701277542

Murphy S., & Smith, M. A. (2015). *Uncommonly good ideas: Teaching writing in the Common Core era.* New York: Teachers College Press.

Niedo, J., Abbott, R. D., & Berninger, V. W. (2014). Predicting levels of reading and writing achievement in typically developing, English-speaking 2nd and 5th graders. *Learning and Individual Differences, 32, 54–68.* PMC4058427. doi:10.1016/j.lindif.2014.03.013

Nielsen, K., Andria-Habermann, K., Richards, T., Abbott, R., Mickail, T., & Berninger, V. (2017). Emotional and behavioral correlates of persisting specific learning disabilities in written language during middle childhood and early adolescence. *Journal of Psychoeducational Assessment.* Prepublished March 27. doi:10.1177/0734282917698056

Olinghouse, N. G., Santangelo, T., & Wilson, J. (2012). Examining the validity of single-occasion, single-genre, holistically scored writing assessments. In E. Van Steendam & M. Tillema (Eds.), *Measuring writing: Recent insights into theory, methodology and practices* (pp. 55–82). Leiden, NL: Brill.

Richards, T. L., Berninger, V. W., Stock, P., Altemeier, L., Trivedi, P., & Maravilla, K. (2009). Functional magnetic resonance imaging sequential-finger movement activation differentiating good and poor writers. *Journal of Clinical and Experimental Neuropsychology, 29*(8), 1–17. doi:10.1080/13803390902780201

Rowe, D. W., & Wilson, S. J. (2015). The development of a descriptive measure of early childhood writing: Results from the Write Start! writing assessment. *Journal of Literacy Research, 47*(2), 245–92. doi:10.1177/1086296X15619723

Saddler, B., & Graham, S. (2007). The relationship between writing knowledge and writing performance among more and less skilled writers. *Reading & Writing Quarterly, 23*(3), 231–47. doi:10.1080/10573560701277575

Schleppegrell, M. (2004). *The language of schooling: A functional linguistics perspective.* Mahwah, NJ: Erlbaum.

Silliman, E. R., & Berninger, V. W. (2011). Cross-disciplinary dialogue about the nature of oral and written language problems in the context of developmental, academic, and phenotypic profiles. *Topics in Language Disorders, 31*(1), 6–23. doi:10.1097/TLD.0b013e31820a0b5b

Snow, C. E. (1972). Mothers' speech to children learning language. *Child Development, 43*(2), 549–65. doi:10.2307/1127555

Wallis, P., Richards, T., Boord, P., Abbott, R., & Berninger, V. (2017). Relationships between translation and transcription processes during fMRI connectivity scanning and coded translation and transcription in writing products after scanning in children with and without transcription disabilities. *Creative Education, 8,* 716–48. NIHMS 857277. doi:10.4236/ce.2017.85055

Wilcox, K. C. (2011).Writing across the curriculum for secondary school English language learners: A case study. *Writing and Pedagogy, 3*(1), 79–111. doi:10.1558/wap.v3i1.79

Wilcox, K. C., & Jeffery, J. V. (2014). Adolescents' writing in the content areas: National study results. *Research in the Teaching of English, 49(2),* 168–76.

Wilcox, K. C., & Jeffery, J. V. (2015). Adolescent English language learners' stances toward disciplinary writing. *English for Specific Purposes, 38,* 44–56. doi:10.1016/j.esp.2014.11.006

Wilcox, K. C., Yagelski, R., & Yu, F. (2013). The nature of error in adolescent student writing. *Reading and Writing: An Interdisciplinary Journal 27*(6), 1073–94. doi:10.1007/s11145-013-9492-x

CHAPTER SIX

Adolescent Writing Development and Authorial Agency

KRISTEN CAMPBELL WILCOX
University at Albany, State University of New York

JILL V. JEFFERY
Leiden University

"I speak two languages so sometimes my writing is difficult." (Lila)

"How do I do it if I don't like writing?" (Carlton)

"I like to write stories. I keep it to myself because it's me." (Hillary)

Above are the responses of adolescents who participated in the National Study of Writing Instruction (NSWI), the most comprehensive US study of adolescent writing conducted in recent years. They were asked to talk about how they see themselves as writers and to describe their experiences with writing in their core content classrooms (i.e., English language arts, social studies, mathematics, and science). These kinds of comments were

This chapter is dedicated to Arthur N. Applebee and Judith A. Langer, whose leadership on the National Study of Writing Instruction made this chapter possible. We also acknowledge the support of all members of the Lifespan Writing Development Group who authored this book (Chuck Bazerman, Virginia Berninger, Deborah Brandt, Steve Graham, Paul Matsuda, Sandra Murphy, Deborah Rowe, and Mary Schleppegrell), and who welcomed us after Arthur's passing with encouragement and valuable feedback on our ideas.

not unusual in the data collected across five states and from adolescents in grades 6, 8, 10, and 12 (Applebee & Langer, 2013). Their expressions of pleasure and displeasure with writing, sense of confidence in their ability to write well, and motivations or purposes for writing provide a complex picture of adolescent writers as well as the contextual affordances and constraints that relate to their writing development.

These adolescents represent different experiences with writing in and out of school and different personal backgrounds. Some have enjoyed histories of higher performance in school and some have struggled to meet their teachers' or states' standards for writing. Some are learning to write in English as an additional language and others have grown up writing only in English. Still others have had pleasurable experiences writing for different audiences or for themselves in diaries and journals while others have little experience of or affinity for extended writing in or out of school. However, these adolescents also share a commonality. All of them attended schools with better than average student achievement trends on English language arts (ELA) assessments and they all were exposed to teaching staffs identified for exemplary writing instruction. Thus, these students studying in "better-case scenario" contexts have the potential to provide insight into what factors might contribute to adolescent writing development.

In this chapter we focus on the role of authorial agency in adolescents' writing development as represented in the stances (i.e., positions, perspectives, proclivities) adolescents expressed in their interviews with NSWI researchers. Agency, we define, following Ahearn's (2001) "provisional definition," as "the socioculturally-mediated capacity to act" (p. 112). Linked to concepts such as engagement and motivation, agency, in this view, is conceptualized as socially situated and dynamic and thus is best understood by taking into account the ecologies (i.e., environments, contexts, communities) that offer affordances as well as constraints to the developing writer.

Authorial Agency and the Adolescent Writer

Applebee's foundational vision for writing in secondary schools (1981; 1982; 1984; 2000), provides the guiding framework for this chapter. As he noted in an article published following completion of the NSWI, "Generic writing skills—ones that can be learned in English class and applied everywhere else—just won't do. And neither will a curriculum that focuses on knowledge about writing (the conventions of written English and the structures for paragraphs or whole essays) rather than on the issues and ideas that make a subject interesting in the first place" (Applebee, 2012). We base our discussion on findings from several analyses of NSWI data, specifically students' written work and interviews, and we pick up Applebee's concern for subject "interest" and also the issue of what it takes for a writer to transfer writing "skill" from one context to another. Each of our NSWI analyses has been published elsewhere (see Jeffery & Wilcox, 2014; Jeffery & Wilcox, 2016; Wilcox & Jeffery, 2014; Wilcox & Jeffery, 2015), and in this chapter we approach these separate analyses from a lifespan perspective.

As discussed in other chapters in this volume, the roles writers play and are expected to play across their lifespans hold implications for their development. In this regard, adolescence is a uniquely mutable period of life characterized by individuals' keen attention to social cues and solidifying sense of identity, established through participation in activities in and outside of school. Moje, Young, Readence, & Moore (2000), referring to an earlier publication, *Reconceptualizing Literacies in Adolescent Lives* (Alvermann, Hinchman, Moore, Phelps, & Waff, 1998), articulated two principles about adolescent literacy based on prior research of import to our discussion:

1. Adolescents want to be viewed as already possessing knowledge and skills and plans for the future, and

2. they want to participate in literacy practices suited to the ways they view their day-to-day lives. (p. 402)

Thus adolescents are likely to present a desire to assert agency and to be in the process of developing more refined stances toward many activities, including writing, that contribute to the identity work in which they acutely engage daily. For bi- and multilinguals this identity work may be particularly complex as these adolescents are pressed to navigate different cultural and linguistic norms in and outside of school (Kanno & Harklau, 2012).

As adolescents engage in writing they assert agency, which can be understood as a medium for constructing identity wherein individuals are "agents in the production of their own and others' social selves" (Holland, Lachicotte, Skinner, & Cain, 1998, p. 296). Reciprocally, their developing identities can be understood as mediums through which agency is realized, or "social forms of organization, public and intimate, that mediate this development of human agency" (Holland et al., p. 282). Either way, and as Ahearn argued, any attempt to study agency ought to consider how it is constructed through language use within social contexts, arguing for a "dialogic, co-constructed view of language as a form of social action" (2001, p. 111). This way of conceptualizing agency as socioculturally mediated and realized through language differs from definitions of agency as something one has or does not have. Rather, agency is seen as always manifesting itself, but in different ways in different contexts, and in a dialectical relationship with perceived or real affordances and constraints different contexts offer.

In this view, and the one we hold, agency is central to how we conceptualize adolescent writing development. It is therefore necessary to seek to understand how writing experiences offered in school might invite adolescents to see writing as something one does purposefully and strategically and as an assertion of agency, rather than as an ability or talent one has or does not have. It would also be necessary to take into account the kinds of writing tasks and materials or resources used to promote writing in different contexts.

Qualities of Secondary School Contexts for Writing

Since adolescence is a period of life characterized by acute awareness of social cues, here we draw attention to the role of *contexts of participation* (see discussion in the introduction to this volume) that adolescent writers encounter and that are unique to secondary schools. We do this, however, with a caveat: While throughout this chapter, our focus is on adolescents' experiences with academic school-based writing (as this was the main focus of the NSWI), we are mindful that contexts for writing outside of school may have mutually supportive relationships with academic writing development (see for example, Berninger & Chanquoy, 2012; Brandt, 2001; Rowe & Wilson, 2015). Indeed, we found the adolescents who participated in the NSWI, even unprompted, shared how out-of-school writing affected their understanding of the range of writing and purposes for writing available to them as well as of themselves as writers.

The study of adolescent writing development in secondary school contexts is relatively new. The focus of early writing scholarship, reflected in still-prominent journals such as *College Composition and Communication* (which dates back to 1950), has often focused on the challenges students face in their first encounters with college writing (e.g., "first-year composition"). Initially, little research was conducted within secondary settings, and much early work in adolescent writing drew heavily from the theoretical perspectives of college composition—an imperfect fit given fundamental differences in secondary and postsecondary writing demands as well as differences between adolescents and young adults. For example, while college composition scholars who often work within English literature departments have resisted the term "literacy" to describe their goals for student learning, literacy learning is an assumed focus in K–12 school settings. However, literacy researchers have traditionally focused on reading more often than on writing (Graham & Perin, 2007), and until quite recently literacy researchers have focused more on elementary, rather than secondary, settings (Applebee & Langer, 2013). This indicates a notable gap in the area of adolescent writing research, a gap that has only begun to be addressed in the past few decades.

Qualities of Multilingual Writers

Another gap in scholarship, which we seek to address in our re-search, is the study of bi- or multilingual (L2) adolescent writers in secondary school settings. Research that explicitly examines both native English speakers' (L1) and L2 adolescent learners' academic writing experiences has inhabited a relatively under-theorized and under-researched area (Silva & Matsuda, 2010). Within college composition studies, the field of L2 writing grew from an awareness of the need to understand college classrooms as linguistically and culturally heterogeneous spaces that require differentiated pedagogies and research designs. Reflecting this growing awareness, scholarship regarding L2 writers became more prominent in, most notably, the *Journal of Second Language Writing* (which began publishing articles in 1992).

Though there is much overlap between the concerns for developing writers in the fields of L1 and L2 writing, analyses of scholarship situated in these two fields suggests that they have typically drawn from distinct bodies of research (Jeffery, Kieffer, & Matsuda, 2013; Tardy, 2006). Acknowledging this disconnect between scholarship on L1 and on L2 writers, adolescent-writing scholars have begun to pay more attention to the contextual factors that relate to the development of writing competence among bi- or multilinguals in middle and high schools (Harklau, 2011; Ortmeier-Hooper & Enright, 2011). Given the growing cultural and linguistic heterogeneity of students engaged in academic writing in secondary school classrooms around the globe, scholars have noted that research that avoids the "myth of linguistic homogeneity" (Matsuda, 2006), which characterized early composition scholarship, is needed. This research considers urgent questions regarding how best to differentiate writing instruction for all adolescent learners, whether characterized as L1 or L2, while avoiding stereotypical representations of these writers that inevitably fall short of capturing their uniqueness (Enright, 2011).

Overall, this overview of the emerging field of adolescent writing suggests some unique qualities of adolescence and secondary school settings that present both affordances for and constraints to adolescent writer development. Chief among the affordances is the wider variety of disciplinary genres adolescents are exposed to and asked to craft in their secondary core content classrooms as opposed to in the elementary grades. This variety can build awareness of the ways that genres of writing are culturally and historically rooted in different domains of knowledge and discourse communities (Applebee, 1981; Monte-Sano & Miles, 2014). However, with regard to constraints, if these genres are limited to those tested on high-stakes exams or presented to adolescents as prescribed patterns for them to follow, they are unlikely to see such writing tasks as opportunities for them to engage agentively as writers. Further, constraints in writing opportunities may be more acutely experienced by bi- or multilingual adolescents who are working simultaneously with new academic content and new language structures, and who are more likely to experience what Applebee (2012) described as "a curriculum that focuses on knowledge about writing (the conventions of written English and the structures for paragraphs or whole essays) rather than on the issues and ideas that make a subject interesting in the first place."

Adolescent Writers under Empirical Study

As mentioned at the outset, this chapter presents the overarching patterns identified in a series of NSWI-embedded analyses of student interview and writing-sample data. In these analyses, we examined L1 (Jeffery & Wilcox, 2014) and L2 (Wilcox & Jeffery, 2015) students' perspectives on writing separately. We also compared L1 and L2 interview and writing sample data (Jeffery & Wilcox, 2016; Wilcox & Jeffery, 2014). In this section we describe the NSWI study and how we conducted our embedded analyses.

The Study Background

Informed by a social-constructivist understanding of adolescent writers and their development, the NSWI sought to investigate adolescents' experiences with writing in a variety of contexts (see detailed methods and procedures report: Applebee & Langer, 2011). California, Kentucky, Michigan, New York, and Texas were selected to represent a range of approaches to large-scale writing assessments, including substantial variation with respect to genre demands on high-stakes exams. For each of the five states, two middle and two high schools were selected that served larger-than-average populations of low-income students and had above-average literacy achievement outcomes compared with schools serving similar populations of students. Sites with a demonstrated commitment to implementing schoolwide literacy initiatives and those identified by literacy experts as having enjoyed a history of exemplary ELA assessment performance were targeted for selection so as to highlight exemplary practice.

The students included in the NSWI sample were identified for participation by virtue of having attended one of these twenty "exemplar" schools. Three groups of students participated: (1) L2 writers, who were of intermediate proficiency based on English language tests used within their schools, (2) L1 higher-achieving students based on prior history of school writing performance, and (3) L1 lower-achieving students, again based on prior history of school writing performance. In total, the NSWI included 95 L1 writers and 43 L2 writers. In our series of analyses, we selected a subset of 66 from the larger NSWI sample so as to balance the representation of students across achievement levels and language backgrounds, and also across gender and grade level categories (see Table 6.1). Students from Michigan were not included in this subset as there were no L2 student participants from there, and Texas is most strongly represented in the sample as a larger number of students participated in that state than in the others.

TABLE 6.1. Sample by State, Language Background and Achievement History, Grade, and Gender

	CA	KY	NY	TX	Totals
Language Background and Achievement History					
L2	7	3	5	11	26
L1 low-achieving	1	5	2	11	19
L1 high-achieving	4	3	6	8	21
Grade					
6th grade	3	1	4	9	17
8th grade	4	2	3	10	19
10th grade	3	3	4	7	17
12th grade	2	5	2	4	13
Gender					
Female	9	8	6	14	37
Male	3	3	7	16	29
Totals	12	11	13	30	66

The Analysis

We focused our analysis in the embedded studies on two NSWI data sources: (1) interviews in which adolescents described their experiences with disciplinary writing and (2) these same students' writing samples gathered from their core content classes over one school term (~eighteen weeks). In the interviews students were asked ten questions ranging in focus from their processes of writing to types of writing they do for tests. In alignment with our interest in authorial agency we focused on the following questions: (Q.1) Tell me a little about yourself and how you see yourself as a writer; (Q.2) Tell me about the kinds of writing you do in the different classes you are taking; (Q.5) What were your favorite writing assignments this semester? Why? Which assignments did you like least? Why? (Q.10) How much do you feel that you've been helped to understand the kinds of writing you need to do in each subject and how to do it better? Tell me about it.

Like Du Bois (2007) and Ochs (2004), we were chiefly interested in stances (i.e., verbal expressions of perspectives, positions, and proclivities), as these stances can be taken as important linguistic representations of agency. In our analyses, we became concerned with both affective and epistemic stances—affective being related to attitudes, feelings, and emotional dispositions, and epistemic being related to knowledge and understandings. We focused on these types of stances since prior scholarship has pointed to their reciprocal nature and relationship to student engagement in academic work (Christenson, Reschly, & Wylie, 2012). We were also concerned with students' perceptions of others' (e.g., teachers', peers', family members') assessments of writing quality or value since such assessment has been found to function in a dialectical relationship with personal stances (Martin & Rose, 2007). Accordingly, our analyses focused on adolescents' stances toward themselves, others, and particular kinds of writing tasks and the contexts in which they were assigned.

Since we sought to reveal the relationships among the affordances and constraints for writing in different school contexts and adolescents' stances toward writing, we used a stance analysis procedure similar to that of Du Bois (2007). This procedure entails indexing a subject, a context, an object, a stance or position, and an attribution of a stance. For example, in response to the question "What is your favorite kind of writing?" one sixth-grade student from Texas, "Roberto" (all student names are pseudonyms), answered "In history, when we chose four cities to travel to, what the weather was like, why do people go there, why do I want to go there, what kind of food, and compare currency, it was my favorite because we got to look stuff up on the Internet." We mapped Roberto's response in a matrix (see Table 6.2) that facilitated identifying his stances by (1) context (history class), (2) object (travel essay), (3) stance and directionality of stance (was my favorite: positive affective), and (4) attribution (because got to look stuff up on the Internet).

After we analyzed each interview as in Roberto's example, we then constructed a consolidated matrix that included all participants' responses organized in the same way. Next, we checked for patterns across this matrix and kept memos in which we discussed ongoing interpretations of patterns, noting, for example, whether stances were epistemic or affective in nature and whether they were positive or negative (Miles, Huberman, & Saldaña, 2014). We relied upon both investigator triangulation (i.e., comparison of two investigators' stance matrices and investigators' ongoing

TABLE 6.2. Roberto Stance Matrix Excerpt

Interview Prompt	Stance Subject	Context	Stance Object [Genre]	Stance/ Position	Attribution
Q5. Favorite and least favorite assignments	[I]	in history	when we chose four cities to travel to, what the weather was like, why do people go there, kind of food, and compare currency [travel essay]	was my favorite (+ affect)	
			Because		
	[We]				got to look stuff up on the Internet

shared interpretive memos) and source triangulation (examination of the patterns among different student interview data sources that used the same data-collection and analysis procedures) for our interpretations (Patton, 2001).

Our analyses revealed a great deal of variation in adolescents' stances, yet we also noted some unifying patterns among lower-performing L1, higher-performing L1, and L2 writers that contribute to our understandings of adolescent writers' experiences more globally. Specifically, we identified three overarching themes in the data. The first relates to adolescents' stances toward different types of writing they do in their core content classrooms; the second relates to their perceptions of themselves as writers and their writing abilities; and the third relates to the variable constraints and affordances they encounter in developing their writing.

Patterns in Adolescents' Stances toward Writing

Pattern 1: Although adolescents' stances varied by grade level, language background of the student, and disciplinary context, adolescents in the study expressed many positive feelings toward writing assigned in school.

Even though school-based writing tasks can pose challenges for adolescent writers' experience of pleasure in writing, overall the adolescents in this study, notably attending schools with histories of exemplary writing instruction, expressed many positive feelings about it. For example, approximately two-thirds of them (68%) indicated that they enjoyed some writing experiences in school. Older students in our study in particular, specifically those in tenth and twelfth grades, expressed more positive feelings toward writing overall than their younger peers, who were more likely to express negative feelings toward writing (see Figure 6.1).

When comparing this finding with the kinds of writing these same students reported doing and those that were collected, it is notable that the students in the lower grades engaged in a larger variety of writing tasks than the students in the higher grades, yet many of these tasks were mechanical in nature (e.g., note-taking) and those same mechanical tasks are ones associated with generally negative stances.

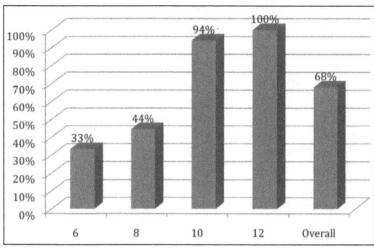

FIGURE **6.1.** *Adolescents in grades 6, 8, 10, and 12 who expressed positive affective stances toward writing.*

When analyzing contrasts by language background, students differed with regard to what kinds of writing they felt positive about. For example, though L1 writers were more likely to voice positive stances toward writing in ELA, where they could be "creative" or express their subjective positions as compared to writing in other disciplines, L2 writers were less likely to view writing occurring within the ELA disciplinary context favorably. Instead, L2 writers held generally positive views toward source-based writing (i.e., writing in which academic texts provided source material) in disciplines other than ELA, particularly when assigned in the forms of research reports in science or document-based essays in social studies. We also noted that L2 adolescent writers tended to refer to negative feedback from their teachers when describing negative feelings toward writing more often than their L1 peers. In addition, some of these L2 writers mentioned literacy and English as a Second Language (ESL) specialists as mitigating negative experiences with writing in their content classrooms. Further discussion of this finding is presented in the portrait of an L2 writer ("Lila") in the next section.

Pattern 2: Adolescents hold different perceptions of their writing abilities and knowledge of writing and these perceptions are related to their prior achievement histories, language backgrounds, and supports for writing in and outside of school.

The patterns we noted with regard to self-perceptions of writing ability and knowledge of writing were varied across grade levels and also between higher-achieving L1, lower-achieving L1, and L2 writers. Overall, slightly more adolescents in this study expressed negative epistemic stances toward writing (51%) than positive ones (47%), with the twelfth-grade students voicing the fewest positive epistemic stances overall compared to their younger peers, indicating relatively less confidence in writing ability (see Figure 6.2).

Not surprisingly, higher-achieving L1 writers expressed the greatest confidence in their writing abilities (i.e., a pattern of greater positive versus negative epistemic stances). This distinction for higher-achieving writers was even more pronounced when they discussed writing in social studies, which lower-achievers generally tended to describe in terms of negative perceptions of their abilities. Overall, fewer lower-achieving L1 writers in our study expressed positive stances regarding their abilities to

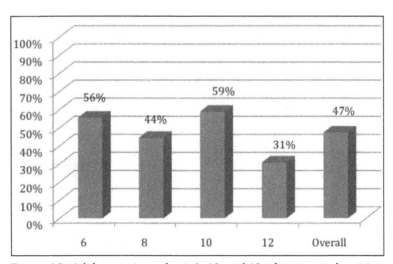

FIGURE **6.2.** *Adolescents in grades 6, 8, 10, and 12 who expressed positive epistemic stances toward writing.*

write well and more expressed negative epistemic stances than higher-achieving L1 writers and even their L2 peers. Social studies writing in particular evoked both negative affective and negative epistemic stances for lower-achievers; a combination that signals a less agentive positioning that will be discussed in more detail in the portrait of a lower-achieving L1 writer ("Carlton").

Pattern 3: Adolescent writers' understandings of the purpose of writing and what makes for good writing are related to the qualities of the opportunities they are offered.

In comparison to other content areas, writing in ELA contexts was seen by most adolescents in this study as providing greater opportunities to develop their writing. Patterns in their responses, however, demonstrated varying degrees of alignment with a conceptualization of writing competence centered on understanding writing as something one does purposefully and strategically to fulfill particular aims in particular contexts.

Our analyses revealed that in general, higher-achieving L1 adolescents' conceptions of writing were more closely aligned with an understanding that good writing differs by disciplinary context, such as in this excerpt from higher-achieving tenth grader "Tessa." Here Tessa notes both intra- and interdisciplinary differences in her comparison of the types of writing she does in different subjects.

> Good writing seems to vary from subject to subject. Good writing can vary within one subject, too. In English, it's the interest of the writer in her subject that makes good writing; English writing allows more time for the individual to be involved. In history, good writing is related to having specific facts. We use a rubric that emphasizes facts. In mathematics, good writing has to do with spelling out the steps and processes used in solving problems and equations. In science, good writing deals with relating things, relating and describing processes.

Tessa's sense that writing in science and math involve explaining one's thinking suggests an agentive view as illustrated in her final comment that this writing is "a way to express myself." Such conceptualizations were rare among lower-achieving and L2 writers, in contrast. For example, statements like this one, from one twelfth-grade L2 writer, "Christiano," illustrate limited understanding of how the aims of writing might differ in different genres and in different disciplinary settings.

> English is a writing class. Writing a poem vs other kinds of writing, for example. Mathematics and physics are formula type writing and number writing. Social studies is formula type writing too. We can revise in English, but not for other subjects because the writing is usually not long enough to revise.

These contrasts are perhaps not surprising considering that higher-achieving L1 students in the study produced more extended writing such as essays and reports than mechanical writing in the forms of short-answer or fill-in-the-blank compared to their peers (see Wilcox & Jeffery, 2014). This pattern will be discussed in more detail in the portrait of a higher-achieving L1 writer ("Hillary") in the next section.

Portraits of Three Adolescents

Here we dive deeper in presenting brief portraits of three adolescent writers to illustrate the patterns discussed above. We highlight an L2 writer, "Lila"; a lower-achieving L1 writer, "Carlton"; and a higher-achieving L1 writer, "Hillary."

Lila: "I speak two languages so sometimes my writing is difficult."

The stances of Lila, an eighth grader from California, provided an illustrative case of the patterns we found in the larger L2 writer data set. Lila attended a middle school with a relatively large proportion of students identified as Hispanic or Latino.[1] Her school was chosen for the study because it had a history of exemplary performance on ELA state exams (taking into account the student population served), and because the district had launched a program of interdisciplinary learning communities focused on using culturally responsive pedagogies in core content classrooms.

The L2 writers who participated in the NSWI, such as Lila, differed from their L1 peers in how they described themselves as writers and what experiences contributed to their stances toward writing. They differed from higher-achieving L1 writers most starkly regarding the greater prevalence of negative epistemic stances overall (indicating a sense of not knowing how to write well) and from their lower-achieving L1 peers in their relatively more agentive positioning toward improving their writing.

Lila characterized herself as a writer who is capable of doing well in school and of writing well with encouragement and opportunities to write about things she has researched or finds personally meaningful, as did her L2 peers in the study. She identified her support teacher's help ("The literacy support class really helps me") as the most important affordance available for her writing development. However, she also expressed facing many challenges, particularly in relation to how to advocate for herself and how to maintain motivation in the face of her teachers' sometimes negative feedback, particularly in her mainstream classrooms.

An important finding was that Lila expressed a sense of responsibility for her school achievement. For example, regarding a relatively weak assessment she had received on an ELA writing assignment, she explained, "I feel it is my fault because I should ask more things and ask for more help." She also said that she was "happy" when she had opportunities to share what she knew in her writing because she identified herself as being "shy" in class, and therefore did not feel teachers always knew what she was capable of doing. Writing provided her with an opportunity to express her knowledge and share something of herself that may not have been clearly expressed orally in class discussion.

In one example (Figure 6.3) of writing that she described as engaging, we see Lila's source-based essay, in which she is tasked to provide facts from texts she has read to explain causes of the Civil War. While Lila generally expressed liking source-based assignments such as these, social studies was particularly challenging for her; as she explained, "Social studies [writing assignments] were my least favorite assignments because it's easy but also hard to explain what I'm saying. It's hard for me to make sentences." For this assignment, Lila composed several paragraphs and was able to perform the task to the level of what was assessed by her social studies teacher as a "C." She expressed her opinion in a thesis statement, provided detail on the topic in the supporting paragraphs, and provided a conclusion restating her thesis. However, the teacher's feedback indicated that Lila needed to provide more explanation based on her thesis statement and that the teacher had partly based the evaluation on identified errors in spelling, mechanics, and tenses.

Nonetheless, overall Lila revealed an agentive, resilient stance toward writing—the development of which was apparently both facilitated and challenged by the learning contexts she experienced

---

CIVIL WAR AND RECONSTRUCTION

What do you think the cause of the Civil War? Compare it with 3 other causes and use facts to support your answer.

The most influence cause of the Civil war will be slavery. A cause of it will be "Uncle Tom's Cabin", a novel by Harriet Becher Stowe. The book had a dramatic effect on the country's attitude toward slavery. In five years the book was sold over a half million copies on the United States, and was translated on 37 languages. It talks about how Eliza, a slave wants to escape with his son of slavery. This shows to the world the emotions of a slave.

A second cause will be the fugitive slave law. Its purpose was to help slave owners find their fugitive slaves. Runaway slaves had almost no legal rights. The law said that any person who helped a runaway slave will be arrested. Many slaves run to Canada, few slaves decides to stand and fight. Some persons that didn't like slavery, helped runaway slaves by giving them food or letting them stay with them for a night.

Missouri Compromise of 1820 will be another cause. Sothern's proposed a bill that will extend the Missouri Compromise line all the way to the pacific. This line would be banned north of slavery and allowed south of it. The Missouri Compromise kept the Union together, but it pleased no one. These three causes talk about slavery disagreement and shows how these cause the most influential cause of Civil War.

Explain how Slavery was a more important cause

watch tenses !

FIGURE 6.3. *Lila's essay.*

in school. Lila's interview reveals an L2 writer who faced challenges she encountered in her writing, and who worked "really hard," in her own words, to overcome them. She repeatedly emphasized the relationships between challenge and pleasure in learning, for example, by identifying her science research project as her favorite "*because* it was hard" (emphasis added). However, we also see a negative-positive stance interaction throughout her interview, one that begins with her characterization of herself as someone whose writing "isn't excellent" but who tries "really hard" to improve. This juxtaposition is perhaps best illustrated in the repetition of "really hard," which works simultaneously as a negative and as a positive stance indicator to describe both the challenges she encounters and her determination to overcome them.

Carlton: "How do I do it if I don't like writing?"

Carlton—a lower-achieving native-English-speaking tenth grader—attended high school in Texas. His school, with a relatively high poverty rate as compared to the national average, included a fairly large number of Latino and African American students. The school was chosen for the study based on relatively good performance on state ELA exams and on its inclusion of a fine arts academy with a particularly strong emphasis on writing in ELA and in social studies.

Carlton represented the stances of other L1 lower-achieving writers in several ways. First, when we examined Carlton's responses to the interview questions, we noted that at times he expressed negative stances toward academic writing tasks, but also expressed that his stances toward writing have been variable and dependent on the audience for and topic of his writing. For example, when asked to reflect on his experiences with writing, he discussed how his brother encouraged him to complete journals for his ELA class and how this encouragement in turn spurred him to engage more fully with these assignments.

I know the one [assignment] I was complaining about to my brother when I was doing it. He said "do your work." I was

> talking to him about my journal and said "I do not like this" and he said "boy, be quiet and do your work." I said "I am."

Carlton is like other L1 lower-achieving NSWI participants, in that his most negative experiences with writing occurred in social studies. In social studies, Carlton reported that his teacher used writing for punishment on occasion. He explained,

> In World History, my class got in trouble and we had to do a 600 word essay, or was it 300? One of those. We had a sub [substitute teacher] and my class was the worst. I already knew we were going to get the essay because of people in my class, so I was expecting nothing different. The teacher came back and she said "I've got some good news and bad news. First, you all won the essay. . . ." We won the essay—that is not a prize. We had to write about some Ghandi thing— the movie that we watched. We had to write about that and it was front and back page.

This example of "punishment writing" is displayed in Figure 6.4.

The counterweight to such negative experiences came from some of his teachers and his family in the form of tasks that allowed Carlton to use writing to express his personal thoughts

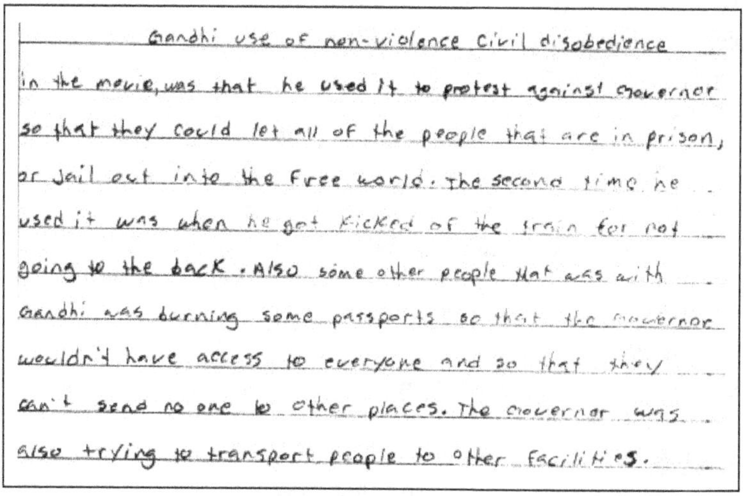

Gandhi use of non-violence Civil disobedience
in the movie, was that he used It to protest against governor
so that they could let all of the people that are in prison,
or jail out into the Free world. The second time he
used it was when he got kicked of the train for not
going to the back. Also some other people that was with
Gandhi was burning some passports so that the governor
wouldn't have access to everyone and so that they
can't send no one to other places. The governor was
also trying to transport people to other facilities.

FIGURE 6.4. *Carlton's punishment writing.*

and experiences. He shared how engaging in a writing assignment with the intended audience of his mother seemed to have purpose.

> I didn't feel important for nobody, so I wrote about how my mom made me feel important to myself and made me feel how school is important for your education, so that later in life, you can have something to look back and tell your kid about this and how education is good for you and to be successful in life.

He further explained that his most positive experience with writing was when he wrote in his journal about his time in an alternative school for at-risk adolescents. He associated that writing with feeling "free." He also associated writing out of school, particularly for his grandfather, as "fun." He explained, "When I'm writing stuff for him, I'm thinking about what I want to write. He made writing look fun the way he was doing it and when I was doing it for him."

Such responses suggest how out-of-school writing experiences, writing tasks of intrinsic interest, and different audiences for his writing helped mitigate more negative experiences such as in the "punishment writing" example.

Hillary: "I like to write stories. I keep it to myself because it's me."

Next we discuss eighth grader Hillary, a higher-achieving native-English speaker from Kentucky. Hillary attended a middle school serving a lower percentage of children growing up in poverty than Lila's and Carlton's schools. Hillary's school was chosen for this study based on its history of students' good writing performance on state exams, high academic standards, and the use of the "Different Ways of Knowing" model that promoted a whole-school use of thematic units that integrate writing across disciplines.

Hillary's responses to interview questions illustrated a larger pattern among the higher-achieving L1 students in her emphasis on the relationship between enjoyment of writing and having opportunities to be "creative." For example, Hillary explained that her most positive experiences with writing were in ELA because in tasks like a persuasive essay she "got to vent," and in a poem (see

Figure 6.5) she could express herself in a way that "comes from my mother like music and acting." Hillary provides an illustration of the importance she and many of her higher-achieving peers place on being afforded writing opportunities to be creative and to go beyond purely mechanical tasks, as illustrated in her poem.

(I used AABB rhyme scheme)

The Pre-K Nightmare

Mommy screams and gasps what is this???
She looks so mad she is starting to hiss
Every brick and all the mortar covered in marker
All the drawing down low is darker and darker

Oh My God is that a drawing of Mickey Mouse?
There must be a graffiti artist in this house
A little boy curse word written in bold
Shut Up Doodyhead it says in gold

A fireplace covered in color and scribbles
The ink running down the hearth in dribbles
Momma is starting to feel really sick
The truth is he wrote on every single brick

SpongeBob Squarepants colored in yellow
Ben thinks he is an artistic little fellow
We sent him to preschool to learn to read and write
And now Mommy sees the fireplace with fright

She grabs the phone and calls up Daddy
She tells him come home Ben is a Baddy
He even wrote a toddler's swearword
He colored it on the wall- how absurd!

He'll need some soap, water and a sponge
His Momma watches him clean, ready to lunge
She thinks he ruined every inch of the den
He's the famous brick artist the great Ben Ben

FIGURE 6.5. *Hillary's poem.*

Hillary explained this perspective on creativity when discussing the constraints of a social studies writing task, which did not afford her such expressive possibilities. She described textbook responses as her least favorite writing assignments because, as she explained, "We have to answer the questions at the end of the chapter. It's not the kind of creative writing I like to do."

An example of a social studies writing task was collected in Hillary's portfolio, which included her teachers' acknowledgment of receipt represented with a check mark, as displayed in Figure 6.6.

Marbury vs. Madison

By ▆▆▆▆▆▆▆

Marbury vs. Madison was a court case filed in 1803. William Marbury verses James Madison.

It starts with John Adams. It was nearing the end of his one and only term as president and he felt the need to appoint men of his choise to different positions in the federal government before he left office and turned the keys to the country over to a Democrate-Republican, which, ofcorse, was a different party than the Federalists. (Adams being a Federalist.)

At the time of his presidency, Adams had John Marshall as his Secratary of State. One of the main jobs of the Secretary of State back then, was to seal commisions. They were the keepers of the seal and validated the commisions that were warrented.

Just before Adams left office, he appointed William Marbury to Justice of the Peace. President Adams signed it and John Marshall sealed it. Everything had been taken care of. The only thing left out of place, was the fact that the commision (or proof that the person had been appointed) had not yet been delivered to Marbury yet.

Well John Adams left office soon after Marbury had been appointed and Thomas Jefferson moved in as president, bringing with him James Madison as his Secratary of State.

Since the commision had not been delivered to William Marbury by the time John Adams left the presidency, he felt that even though Marbury had his paperwork signed and sealed, he didn't have proof in his posession that he was appointed, his appointmenship should have been voided.

This is where Marbury desided to sue James Madison because he refused to send out his signed and sealed commision.

They came up with the three questions that they had to deside on. (in other words)
• Does the plantive have the right to his commision?
• If so, does the government afford him a remedy?
• If the goverment affords him a remedy, who has the power to decide the verdict?

The answer for number one, was yes. The commision had been signed and sealed. It was valid.

The answer to number two was yes again. They gave him the choise to take the job that he had been appointed to by Adams.

The answer for number three was very important. They ruled that the Supream Court should be in charge of the power of desiding the verdict.

Even though William Marbury never took his job as Justice of the Peace, his court case was important to American history.

FIGURE 6.6. *Hillary's social studies homework.*

While most L1 higher-achieving students held generally positive stances toward social studies, these were more epistemic in nature, indicating that they felt confident they could do this writing well, even if they didn't enjoy it. Overall, the L1 higher-achieving adolescents in the NSWI, while expressing the view that that in-school tasks posed constraints for developing their writing and themselves as writers, nonetheless still mainly reported liking such tasks and doing well at them.

In sum, although we noted commonalities among the adolescents who participated in NSWI, we also identified contrasts between them and their variable stances as represented in these three portraits. Their different stances are related to different life histories, affordances, and constraints they experience to write in different genres, for different purposes, and for different audiences. Together, these factors hold implications for their writing development over the lifespan.

Adolescent Authorial Agency in a Lifespan Framework

In this chapter we focused our attention on the concept of authorial agency as it is represented in adolescents' affective and epistemic stances toward writing. We were interested in the affordances and constraints for writing development that adolescents experience in their secondary school classrooms.

What we found from our multiple analyses is that although these adolescents attended relatively "better-case scenario" schools with regard to ELA achievement and teachers' writing instruction, they nonetheless experienced few opportunities to develop an understanding of writing as an agentive act. Although these writers generally expressed resilience when confronted with challenges to their experience of pleasure in writing or to their sense of confidence in their abilities to write, they often did not see writing assigned in school as offering opportunities for expressing their ideas in meaningful ways or for participating in a discourse community.

Our analyses speak to the importance of several considerations for adolescent writers regarding choice, audience, and task constraint. As discussed in the previous section, the adolescents who participated in the NSWI expressed some positive stances toward writing tasks that offered opportunities to choose topics and in some cases genres for the expression of their ideas (Jeffery & Wilcox, 2014; Jeffery & Wilcox, 2016; Wilcox & Jeffery, 2015). In addition, some students, particularly in the lower-achieving sample, were notable with regard to the importance they placed on having audiences for their writing outside of school (e.g., family members and peers) and on having access to opportunities to engage with writing that was more personal or open-topic in nature (e.g., diary or journal writing). These opportunities provide spaces for adolescents who may not meet the relatively narrow norms for what counts as good writing in school to be agents in their writing.

Our analyses also point to the link between adolescents' sense of feeling pleasure in writing and their sense of being able to write well, a link that contributes to an adolescent's motivations to write and growing sense of identity as a capable writer. We identified evidence of this link most notably among higher-achieving L1 writers, as one might expect. Although they, like their L2 and lower-achieving L1 peers, faced challenges in maintaining agentive stances toward writing in the face of high task constraint, they also expressed having experienced positive feedback on the quality of their ideas as well as their expression in writing, fueling their sense of authorial agency. Such a scenario was not as evident among L1 lower-achieving writers and L2 writers. However, L2 writers, unlike their L1 lower-achieving peers, reported reaping the benefits of ESL teachers and other literacy specialists who tended to mitigate negative experiences by providing emotional support, advocacy, and cognitive scaffolds for their learning.

Finally, although the adolescents who participated in the NSWI mentioned some opportunities to write in social studies, and many fewer in science and math, classrooms other than ELA were reported to offer exactly what these adolescents—regardless of achievement history or language background—need and want: opportunities to engage in writing that they see as purposeful and about subjects of interest. So while teachers in classrooms outside of ELA may not see themselves as writing teachers, some genres that are quite appropriate assignments in their classrooms (e.g., research reports) were reported to have been received by the adolescent participants in the NSWI as more accessible than others that require particular cultural, historical, and linguistic understandings (e.g., literary-analysis essays). This is particularly true for L2 and lower-achieving L1 writers. For these adolescents, writing opportunities offered beyond the walls of ELA classrooms not only align well with recent US trends toward standards emphasizing writing in the disciplines (Wilcox, Jeffery, & Gardner-Bixler, 2016), but also provide potential for adolescents to experience pleasure in writing, a sense of purpose in writing, and accomplishment.

Our analyses demonstrate the impressive complexity and variety of students' experiences with writing across disciplines in secondary school settings. Students who reported disliking source-based writing tasks such as literary analysis essays in ELA also reported enjoying other types of source-based writing such as reports in science and social studies. The differences in their reactions had less to do than one might think with the particular disciplinary context within which they were working and more with the way they perceived writing tasks as affording them agency—or not—in those contexts. From this, we take three valuable lessons. First, students' responses provide articulations of agency as the "socioculturally mediated capacity to act," a capacity that varies for individual writers across time and space. Second, authorial agency, as we have argued elsewhere, is essential to social-constructivist understandings of what it means to develop as a writer, and also to students' motivation to write and to their developing sense of themselves as writers. From this we infer that authorial agency is crucial for writing development, perhaps particularly in adolescence. Third, given the importance of authorial agency for adolescent writing development, students need far more frequent, and more varied, opportunities to use writing to express not only their understandings of, but also their feelings about, different topics, and for varied audiences including themselves. Such experiences will ideally extend across disciplines as well as into the home and community. A challenge is, however, how teachers are to exert their own agency as instructors of writing to provide this affordance, in the face of US policy trends that emphasize single-task standardized test performance as the most important measurement of writing development.

While Applebee's seminal book *Writing in the Secondary School* (1981) opened the door for many scholars of adolescent writing to explore what contributes to writing development, there is much yet to do. Applebee's vision for writing pedagogies that enable students to engage in the essential conversations of secondary curricula still circulates and informs how we might respond to such questions as "How do I do it if I don't like writing?," such challenges as "I speak two languages so sometimes my writing is difficult," and such opportunities as "I like to write stories."

Acknowledgments

The authors would like to acknowledge a Spencer LifeSpan Grant, the leadership of Charles Bazerman in organizing the collaborations of LifeSpan working group members, and the input on this chapter from Sandra Murphy.

Note

1. Some states, like New York, combine Hispanic and Latino into one subgroup and since these performance data were used in the process of identifying schools these terms are also used in combination here.

References

Ahearn, L. M. (2001). Language and agency. *Annual Review of Anthropology, 30,* 109–37.

Alvermann, D. E., Hinchman, K. A., Moore, D. W., Phelps, S. F., & Waff, D. R. (Eds.). (1998). *Reconceptualizing the literacies in adolescents' lives.* Mahwah, NJ: Erlbaum.

Applebee, A. N. (1981). *Writing in the secondary school: English and the content areas.* Urbana, IL: National Council of Teachers of English.

Applebee, A. N. (1982). Writing and learning in school settings. In M. Nystrand (Ed.), *What writers know: The language, process, and structure of written discourse* (pp. 365–82). New York: Academic Press.

Applebee, A. N. (1984). Contexts for learning to write: Studies of secondary school instruction. Norwood, NJ: Ablex.

Applebee, A. N. (2000). Alternative models of writing development. In R. Indrisano & J. Squire (Eds.), Perspectives on writing: Research, theory, and practice (pp. 90–110). Newark, DE: International Reading Association.

Applebee, A. (2012, September 27). Great writing comes out of great ideas. The Atlantic. Retrieved from https://www.theatlantic .com/national/archive/2012/09/great-writing-comes-out-of-great-ideas/262653/

Applebee, A. N., & Langer, J. A. (2011). The National Study of Writing Instruction: Methods and procedures. Retrieved from http://www .albany.edu/cela/reports/NSWI_2011_methods_procedures.pdf

Applebee, A. N., & Langer, J. A. (2013). Writing instruction that works: Proven methods for middle and high school classrooms. Berkeley, CA: National Writing Project; New York: Teachers College Press.

Berninger, V. W., & Chanquoy, L. (2012). What writing is and how it changes across early and middle childhood development: A multidisciplinary perspective. In E. L. Grigorenko, E. Mambrino, & D. D. Preiss (Eds.), Writing: A mosaic of new perspectives (pp. 65–84). New York: Psychology Press.

Brandt, D. (2001). Literacy in American lives. New York: Cambridge University Press.

Christenson, S. L., Reschly, A. L., & Wylie, C. (Eds.). (2012). Handbook of research on student engagement. New York: Springer.

Du Bois, J. W. (2007). The stance triangle. In R. Englebretson (Ed.), Stancetaking in discourse: Subjectivity, evaluation, interaction (pp. 139–82). Amsterdam: John Benjamins.

Enright, K. A. (2011). Language and literacy for a new mainstream. American Educational Research Journal, 48(1), 80–118.

Graham, S., & Perin, D. (2007). Writing next: Effective strategies to improve writing of adolescents in middle and high school. Retrieved from https://all4ed.org/wp-content/uploads/2006/10/WritingNext .pdf

Harklau, L. (2011). Commentary: Adolescent L2 writing research as an emerging field. Journal of Second Language Writing, 20(3), 227–30. doi:10.1016/j.jslw.2011.05.003

Holland, D. C., Lachicotte, W., Skinner, D., & Cain, C. (1998). *Identity and agency in cultural worlds.* Cambridge, MA: Harvard University Press.

Jeffery, J. V., Kieffer, M. J., & Matsuda, P. K. (2013). Examining conceptions of writing in TESOL and English Education journals: Toward a more integrated framework for research addressing multilingual classrooms. *Learning and Individual Differences, 28,* 181–92. doi:10.1016/j.lindif.2012.11.001

Jeffery, J. V., & Wilcox, K. (2014). "How do I do it if I don't like writing?": Adolescents' stances toward writing across disciplines. *Reading and Writing: An Interdisciplinary Journal, 27*(6), 1095–1117. doi:10.1007/s11145-013-9493-9

Jeffery, J. V., & Wilcox, K. C. (2016). L1 and L2 adolescents' perspectives on writing within and across academic disciplines: Examining the role of agency in development. *Writing and Pedagogy, 8*(2), 245–74. doi:10.1558/wap.28750

Kanno, Y., & Harklau, L. (Eds.). (2012). *Linguistic minority students go to college: Preparation, access, and persistence.* New York: Routledge.

Martin, J. R., & Rose, D. (2007). *Working with discourse: Meaning beyond the clause* (2nd ed.). London, UK: Continuum.

Matsuda, P. K. (2006). The myth of linguistic homogeneity in U.S. college composition. *College English, 68*(6), 637–51.

Miles, M. B., Huberman, A. M., & Saldaña, J. (2014). *Qualitative data analysis: A methods sourcebook* (3rd ed.). Thousand Oaks, CA: SAGE.

Moje, E. B., Young, J. P., Readence, J. E., & Moore, D. W. (2000). Commentary: Reinventing adolescent literacy for new times: Perennial and millennial issues. *Journal of Adolescent and Adult Literacy, 43*(5), 400–10.

Monte-Sano, C., & Miles, D. (2014). Toward disciplinary reading and writing in history. In P. Smagorinsky (Ed.), *Teaching dilemmas and solutions in content-area literacy, grades 6–12* (pp. 29–56). Thousand Oaks, CA: Corwin.

Ochs, E. (2004). Becoming a speaker of culture. In C. J. Kramsch (Ed.), *Language acquisition and language socialization: Ecological perspectives* (pp. 99–120). London, UK: Continuum.

Ortmeier-Hooper, C., & Enright, K. A. (2011). Mapping new territory: Toward an understanding of adolescent L2 writers and writing in US contexts. *Journal of Second Language Writing, 20*(3), 167–81. doi:10.1016/j.jslw.2011.05.002

Patton, M. Q. (2001). *Qualitative research & evaluation methods* (3rd ed.). Thousand Oaks, CA: SAGE.

Rowe, D. W., & Wilson, S. J. (2015). The development of a descriptive measure of early childhood writing: Results from the Write Start! Writing Assessment. *Journal of Literacy Research, 47*(2), 245–92. doi:10.1177/1086296X15619723

Silva, T. J., & Matsuda, P. K. (Eds.). (2010). *Practicing theory in second language writing.* West Lafayette, IN: Parlor Press.

Tardy, C. M. (2006). Researching first and second language genre learning: A comparative review and a look ahead. *Journal of Second Language Writing, 15*(2), 79–101. doi:0.1016/j.jslw.2006.04.003

Wilcox, K. C., & Jeffery, J. V. (2014). Adolescents' writing in the content areas: National study results. *Research in the Teaching of English, 49*(2), 168–76.

Wilcox, K. C., & Jeffery, J. V. (2015). Adolescent English learners' stances toward disciplinary writing. *English for Specific Purposes, 38,* 44–56. doi:10.1016/j.esp.2014.11.006

Wilcox, K. C., Jeffery, J. V., & Gardner-Bixler, A. (2016). Writing to the Common Core: Teachers' responses to changes in standards and assessments for writing in elementary schools. *Reading and Writing: An Interdisciplinary Journal, 29*(5), 903–28. doi:10.1007/s11145-015-9588-6

CHAPTER SEVEN

"The Faraway Stick Cannot Kill the Nearby Snake"

SANDRA MURPHY
University of California, Davis

MARY ANN SMITH
National Writing Project

Here's a nod to the obvious. No student enters school with the same abilities, background, opportunities, or even, in many cases, with the same native language as the student at the next desk. This phenomenon does not change over time. Students are still different from one another in grade 2, grade 5, grade 9, and so on, in part because they develop at different rates and along different flight paths. Being in school does not level the playing field. Actually, school curriculum contributes to diversity in learning among students.

We use the word *curriculum* here in a broad sense. It includes all of the experiences children have under the guidance of teachers (Caswell and Campbell, 1935). Curriculum is not just subject matter, nor is it limited to a scope and sequence or a plan. It's what happens in the classroom—what some scholars call the "operational" curriculum (Posner, 2004). It includes lessons, events (planned and unplanned), activities, accompanying materials, and assessments. As George Posner explains, the operational curriculum "may differ significantly from the official curriculum because teachers tend to interpret it in the light of their own knowledge, beliefs, and attitudes" (2004, p.13).

As almost every educator knows, curriculum, including writing curriculum, is subject to the pendulum phenomenon—ideas about teaching and learning that swing from one approach to another, leading to wide variations in what goes on in classrooms. For instance, some institutions shape the curriculum in favor of "utilitarian outcomes," for example, writing to get ready for college; others shape the curriculum in favor of "intellectual growth for its own sake," for example, using writing to explore new ideas. Some educators advocate for a "uniform curriculum" in which all students learn the same things at the same time, while others advocate for an "individualized" approach, one that encourages students to develop their own interests and choose their own topics for writing (Gardner, 2000). Clearly, such widely differing points of view contribute to wide fluctuations in what students encounter from class to class or school to school. It is not hard to imagine, for example, how an approach to teaching writing that offers choice and accounts for a student's unique strengths and needs might differ from a program that attempts to run all students through the same mill.

It might be tempting to think that standardizing the curriculum will promote equity. However, prescribing the same over-the-counter treatment for every student dooms many to failure by ignoring the uniqueness of each learner. Rather, we believe *intentional* diversity in curriculum gives students the best chance for success. Indeed, students need curriculum that is sensitive to their individual variations in strengths, abilities, interests, backgrounds, cultures, and so on. It goes without saying that building such a curriculum is a tall order, a next-to-impossible task unless the builder knows the students. Our view is that teachers are best suited to fashion a curriculum that *intentionally* and *purposefully* takes their students into account.

Over the past few years, we have consulted with a number of exemplary teachers to find out what they do in their classrooms and why. Our data include interviews, observations, surveys, written assignments, student writing samples, rubrics, and, in some cases, students' written reflections on their work. We've discovered that these teachers put every lesson through the "my students" test. It's the test that teachers use to adapt, enliven, bump up, or otherwise tailor the curriculum for the students at hand. This kind of fine tuning is not within the grasp of even the most brilliant policymaker. As suggested by the comment of a village elder in our title, "the faraway stick cannot kill the nearby snake." Rather, it is the teacher who knows the nearby students and therefore, who can find the best way for each one to learn.

At the same time, however, "the faraway stick" can play havoc with what teachers need to do for their students, particularly when it comes to writing. Too often teachers run into policies that are unfriendly to teaching writing, that minimize or otherwise distort its place in the curriculum, and that shortchange teacher knowledge and professionalism in the process. In the best of times, writing has a seat at the table in nearly every discipline, for obvious reasons. Scientists write. Historians write. Economists write. Politicians write, sometimes voluminously. In the worst of times, writing mysteriously disappears, nowhere to be seen and often difficult to resurrect.

The amount and kind of attention writing receives in the curriculum varies for other reasons as well—reasons we will examine in the next section:

♦ Reading often monopolizes the available time for literacy instruction at the expense of writing.

♦ Writing of any length and intellectual substance does not always get the time and sustained attention it requires.

♦ How to best teach writing and what to emphasize remains an ongoing debate.

Why Is Writing Curriculum All Over the Map (If It Is on the Map)?

When it comes to writing curriculum, the variety is stunning. Sometimes writing curriculum is ample; at other times it is truncated, or camouflaged, or AWOL entirely.

Reading as the Favored Destination

Clifford (1989) documents the historically "low estate of writing in the schools," noting that "Years of studies of how classroom time is spent" show that "reading instruction dominates the day."

> Investigations of secondary schools by the National Council of Teachers of English (NCTE) have repeatedly shown that more time was spent on literature than on all other aspects of the English curriculum *combined* .... A study of 168 exemplary American high schools during the early 1960s—schools with high state or national reputations—reported that reading (that is, literature) received three and a half times more attention than writing (that is, composition). (1989, p. 28)

But there are certainly other reasons for the fact that writing often plays second fiddle to reading. The most obvious reason is that policymakers influence the scope of teaching in the classroom. During the No Child Left Behind (NCLB) era, policy dictated that external, high-stakes assessments focus on reading and mathematics. The results, according to Applebee and Langer (2013), had "disastrous implications for student learning."

> Over the past decade, for example, writing (as well as other subjects) has been deemphasized in response to the focus on reading and mathematics . . . teachers across subject areas . . . have modified their teaching of writing in response to the exams, leaving out research papers, for example, and personal or creative writing in favor of tasks that would be directly assessed. (pp. 179–80)

Narrowing the curriculum means some things get attention and others get tossed aside. As a consequence of NCLB, a whole generation of students was shortchanged when it came to writing.

Writing as a Drive-By

If reading is a favored destination, where does that leave writing? It's not exactly a pit stop, but it lacks all the characteristics of a desired landing place—somewhere to linger and explore. When Applebee and Langer (2013) observed English classes in twenty schools, they found that in a fifty-minute period "students would have had on average just over 3 minutes of instruction related to explicit writing strategies (the most frequent emphasis observed), or a total of 2 hours and 22 minutes in a 9-week grading period" (p. 22). In another study, Kiuhara, Graham, & Hawken (2009) asked a random sample of high school teachers from across the United States to tell them about writing instruction in their classrooms:

> [T]he teachers said the most common activities that their students engaged in were writing short answer responses to homework, responding to material read, completing worksheets, summarizing material read, writing journal entries, and making lists. Together, these activities involved little extended analysis, interpretation, or writing. In fact, one half of the most common assignments were basically writing without composing (short answers, worksheets, and lists). (p. 22)

Similarly, Applebee and Langer (2013) found that the amount of writing students are doing overall is especially limited when it comes to extended writing assignments. Of the 8,542 assignments that the researchers gathered from their 138 case-study students, in a sampling of all written work in four core content areas during a semester in twenty schools in five states "only 19 percent of assignments represented extended writing of a paragraph or more: all the rest consisted of fill-in-the-blank and short-answer exercises, and copying of information directly from the teachers' presentations—activities that are best described as writing without composing" (p.14).

For writing to receive enough attention in a curriculum, assignments need to blossom beyond mere abbreviations to ones that require intellectual work such as analysis and interpretation. And without a doubt, attention to writing demands adequate time.

> In today's schools, writing is a prisoner of time. Learning how to present one's thoughts on paper requires time. The sheer scope of the skills required for effective writing is daunting. The mechanics of grammar and punctuation, usage, developing a "voice" and a feel for the audience, mastering the distinctions between expository, narrative, and persuasive writing (and the types of evidence required to make each convincing)—the list is lengthy. These skills cannot be picked up from a few minutes here, and a few minutes there, all stolen from more "important" subjects. (National Commission on Writing, 2003, p. 20).

In addition to requiring a hefty amount of time, Kiuhara et al. (2009) suggest, "the teaching of writing is a shared responsibility. It involves not only language arts teachers but students' other content teachers across the high school years" (p. 150). But in their national survey of the kinds and frequency of writing across disciplines, the authors found that "almost one third of language arts and social studies teachers did not assign such an activity [writing multiple paragraphs] monthly . . . and a large proportion of science teachers (77%) did not assign such an assignment monthly" (p. 151).

When the curriculum prunes writing down to a nub, students do not get opportunities to practice the kind of writing they are likely to run into in college and/or in their careers. They miss out on key thinking and composing skills, and in terms of writing in a subject area, they miss out on writing to understand the content material.

Writing Curriculum as a Grab Bag

Yet another reason that writing curriculum is so varied is that over time people have viewed writing in a multitude of ways: as a set of skills, as a product, as a process, as expression, as purposeful communication, as reading and writing woven together, and/or as sociocultural practices. For better or for worse, each of these ways of seeing writing lends itself to somewhat different approaches in teaching.

A skills emphasis in a writing curriculum, for example, might concentrate on the rules-based, step-by-step teaching of grammar and sentence structure. Here, writing becomes a collection of discrete skills or behaviors—conveniently layered so that teachers will systematically teach each skill in a particular order, but not necessarily in a context. Where the debate comes in is around this issue of context. Studies show that decontextualized approaches have little if any effect on improving student writing (Hillocks, 1986; Elley, 1994; Elley, Barham, Lamb, & Wyllie, 1975, Myhill & Watson, 2014). Indeed, Steve Graham and Dorothy Perin (2007) found a small but statistically significant negative effect for grammar instruction that was "mostly decontextualized" (Graham, personal communication, August 4, 2016).

The point here is not to discourage the teaching of grammar. Rather, it's to illustrate how writing curriculum can fluctuate depending on beliefs about what is most important in teaching students to write. Curriculum shifts around other issues as well, such as how much to emphasize process or product or how much time to spend on self-expression as opposed to writing for specific communicative purposes. Even penmanship—whether or not to teach it and to what extent—is a subject for disagreement. While its benefits are debatable in a modern era, some argue that when children learn handwriting to the degree that it becomes automatic, they can then concentrate more fully on their ideas and the content of writing itself.

The sheer number of curricular approaches and their nuances guarantee that no two students encounter the same approach across time. And while some approaches may rise to the top of the charts, based on research and practice, the effectiveness of any approach ultimately depends on a teacher who uses it *intentionally* and *purposefully*—as opposed to rotely—to the advantage of his or her students.

There are certain curricular approaches, nonetheless, that we call "game changers," that is, approaches whose presence or absence in a writing curriculum can substantially alter student achievement. Although research has identified several promising practices, we focus in the next section on three that stand out for us because they represent significant shifts in traditional curricula:

- ♦ Giving students opportunities to collaborate

- ♦ Taking advantage of technology

- ♦ Deliberately tailoring curriculum for the students at hand

Game Changers in the World of Writing Curriculum

Part of the drama when it comes to writing curriculum is that significant practices and resources—what we are calling game changers—may or may not be available to students. While these game changers are not the only ones in the teaching of writing, they highlight the hit-or-miss nature of curriculum, which privileges some students and leaves others in the dust.

Writing as a Participatory Activity

Students who have engaged in collaborative projects or peer-response groups or any other kind of joint writing endeavor in school have experienced the advantages and challenges of teamwork and cooperation. However, some students still work in isolation, confined not only to their desks, but to the limits of their own talent, knowledge, and imagination.

How important is it that students participate in collaborative activities? Because we live in a participatory society, apprenticeship and interaction have an increasingly important role in learning to write:

> Participatory culture shifts the focus of literacy from one of individual expression to community involvement. The new literacies almost all involve social skills developed through collaboration and networking. These skills build on the foundation of traditional literacy, research skills, technical skills, and critical analysis skills taught in the classroom. (Jenkins, Purushotma, Clinton, Weigel, & Robinson, 2006, p. 4)

Another way to answer the question about the value of participation is to look at a real-life example. Middle school teacher Liz Harrington creates a participatory culture in her classroom by inviting her students to write blogs about their reading. The students post their blogs at least once every two weeks and are responsible for commenting on the blogs of each member of their classroom book club. The technology makes possible an out-of-school community of readers and writers, stretching the boundaries of the school day. Blogs are due on a Friday night, long after the last bell. And they are more than just blogs. They serve as the teaching tool for using polite, academic language ("[A]lways consider whether you would be happy to read that same comment on your work") (qtd. in Murphy & Smith, 2015, p. 105).

Consider the intentionality of Harrington's approach to one of the game changers. Her students learn about three essential skills through this collaboration:

1. How to write to a particular audience and purpose

2. How to interact with peers, including what kind of language to use

3. How to communicate online, including practice with a particular online genre

As an added bonus, Harrington's students are building knowledge that will help them with a future genre—literary analysis. These students also have a leg up in their preparation as writers and collaborators and as citizens using social media responsibly. They also have an advantage when they reach their next destination, whether higher education or the workplace, where collaboration is a way of learning and doing business.

Writing and the Technology Factor

New technologies bring unique challenges for students, including, for example, learning to read and write new hybrid kinds of texts that emphasize visual and interactive features (Hocks, 2003) as well as learning how to use new tools and strategies for researching, drafting, revising, and collaborating (Whithaus, 2005; Leu, Kiili, & Forzani, 2015). As a result, new technology can be a significant source of variation in school curriculum that sets students apart. Not all teachers are prepared to teach with technology, and teachers and students alike are not all at the same starting point. Furthermore, technology is not always available, in quality or quantity, to ensure that all students get sufficient exposure: "[T]here is no doubt that the resources for technology available to schools and colleges—including hardware, software, and teacher development—are often inadequate and frequently unequal" (National Commission on Writing, 2003, p. 23).

The problem of access is not necessarily solved by the ubiquitous smartphone or tablet. While most students have phones and may have learned to Google with ease, they are unlikely to use search engines for academic research without supportive instruction and a reason to do so. But when a school computer lab is available and a knowledgeable teacher provides scaffolding, students can learn to conduct meaningful collaborative research. For example, high school teacher Judy Kennedy describes what happened when her students dove into the search process for their civic-action projects.

> The kids really worked together. They talked about different kinds of search words, tried to interpret what they were looking at, and shared everything they found. They delegated—"you look up this and I'll look up that." Kids really liked researching together and finding links. They are naturally curious and don't necessarily do this kind of thing every day. The computer lab was also a place where they could collaborate on setting up their surveys, writing interview questions, coming up with blogs, and taking notes. (qtd. in Murphy & Smith, p. 110)

Note the number of things a student may or may not learn to do with a computer, depending on the skill of the teacher and access to technology: how to conduct online research, how to find and follow appropriate links, how to collaborate in the process, how to use search words, how to read and analyze what pops up on the screen, how to create surveys (and perhaps other methods of firsthand research as well), how to write for a public audience, and, yes, how to keep track of all the information.

Customizing Curriculum

One of the ironies of the NCLB era was its reliance on standardized curriculum to ensure that no child would miss out on what policymakers deemed indispensable. By imposing the same lessons at the same pace with the same instructions, the NCLB "official curriculum" left behind many children, and particularly those who didn't fit into the script. The alternative is for teachers to choose the best path for their students: where to start a lesson, how long to linger on a particular skill or activity, where to scaffold, how to engage students, when and how to evaluate, and so on.

We chose two classrooms at different grade levels with predominantly English language learner populations to illustrate how teachers customize for their students, and in the process, how they solve the "drive-by" and "grab bag" problems that occur so often in writing curriculum.

ENGLISH LEARNERS IN MIDDLE SCHOOL

Most of Zack Lewis-Murphy's students are English learners who need a whole buffet of nourishment, encouragement, and motivation in their 180 days of school, 15 of which are gobbled up by standardized assessments. Thirteen-year veteran Lewis-Murphy dances between a curriculum based on the Common Core State Standards (emphasizing nonfiction reading and argumentative writing) and his own sense of what will give his students a real boost in the long run:

> If all students are reading is nonfiction, what happens to love of reading? How can a kid develop a passion for reading, or get into the pattern—you read this book and then the next book. I tried to tackle the love of reading problem with an eighth-grade class with 20 boys in it, all of them bored and near dropouts. Amazon has lots of high-interest, multicultural teen books. I had the students read these for the first 15 minutes of the period. There was some pushback at first, but they began to read and they were interested in what they were reading. It cost me a lot of money to build up the library. (personal communication, December 30, 2015)

The idea of giving students a choice of high-interest material plays out in the class writing curriculum as well. Recently, Lewis-Murphy assigned Lois Lowry's *The Giver* as a class reading and then asked students to create their own dystopian worlds. He pulled out all kinds of scaffolding for this writing, such as models, graphic organizers, vocabulary work, and a myriad of feedback opportunities, including his own lengthy individualized verbal responses using dictation software. Lewis-Murphy also taught students to respond to each other's writing as they exchanged papers with an "elbow partner." The overall result was full-length stories, composed and revised on computers.

Take a look at some first paragraphs—arranged roughly from the lower end to the higher end—and how they reflect the wide-ranging capacities in a single classroom.

never vote for Trump
by Raiven Brister
The year was 2016 and it was election day and I was at the library voting for the next president. I voted for Bill Carson usually I don't vote but this year I was afraid that if Donald Trump won the election he would deport me back to Mexico. After a few days past for voting the draw came on the tv. Turns out there was only one vote for Bill Carson and I was that one person. Over a million people voted for Trump.

Untitled
by Tia Cooke
In 2019, three years ago the ocean died. All of the vibrant coral reefs and fish were gone. A year after that occurrence the world began to die. There was a huge shortage in food and disease spread. Along with that water became scarce and global warming became bad. I was in the fifth grade when government made everyone start wearing masks outside due to a large amount of greenhouse gasses in the air. People started to die and the government became week. Then as predicted by my father the renegades took over. The renegades is a organization of people who believe they can save the people from the dying world. But in all reality the world needed saving from the people.

U.S. 2130, Alaskan Territory, Academy of the Country Elite
by Brian Zheng
Luke Reinier woke up in a cold sweat. Last thing he remembered was being at this torn up house where he had been living ever since he was a child. His family was poor, but they invested all they could in his education. Luke graduated at the top of his 12th grade class and that had led him here, to ACE. [Academy of the Country Elite] The top school in the world had invited him, a lowly child that grew up in poverty into their ranks. At first he had been amazed at the invitation to ACE, but once the black vans pulled up in his front door he began to regret accepting the letter. They put a bag over his face just like he had seen in the old crime movies. They took him to an airplane, the first he had ever seen. They flew him all the way from his small hometown in the California territory to the far reaches of the frigid Alaskan Mountains.

It's possible from these excerpts to get a sense of each writer's development when it comes to chronology, detail, sense of audience, vocabulary, and conventions. In terms of fluency, the papers ranged from fourteen single-spaced pages to two double-spaced pages. Every paper included dialogue and an attempt to establish time, place, and characters.

What's the secret sauce in this classroom? It seems to be a blend of four essential ingredients:

- ◆ Using research-based practices for teaching writing to EL students, such as teacher and student feedback leading to revision
- ◆ Attending to students' varied abilities and interests
- ◆ Finding a place for every student to plug in
- ◆ Shaping curriculum to help these particular students meet standards

Note, too, that writing is hardly a drive-by in this classroom. If there is a mantra that describes Lewis-Murphy's approach, it is this: Engage . . . Scaffold . . . Linger.

ENGLISH LEARNERS IN HIGH SCHOOL

Tracey Freyre currently teaches long-term English learners in a San Francisco Bay Area high school, many of whom were born in the United States or who came to this country at a very young age, but never reached English proficiency. Some of these students read far below grade level, as low as sixth grade. Understandably, a number of them are unmotivated and resistant to reading and writing. So Freyre has her work cut out for her as she teaches them in English support classes designed to help students catch up with their native-English-speaking peers.

In terms of diversity and degree of development in writing, Freyre's students pose significant challenges:

> Both newcomers and long-term learners tend to have moved a lot. Their schooling has been inconsistent. Some have experienced severe trauma and separation, particularly the new wave of unaccompanied minors who are living with friends or distant relatives. Some just have a language barrier, but others have major literacy issues and, across the board, these students have motivation issues. (All Freyre quotations are from a personal communication, November 24, 2015.)

There are cultural challenges as well. In contrast to school systems in other countries, where the teacher does all the talking, "teachers here want you talking and interacting and collaborating. Students are not used to this kind of environment, nor do they necessarily know what's appropriate when communicating in class." In addition, many students cannot be involved in school life because they are working. In other cases, parents want their children home right after school, which also limits the amount of time they have to speak and practice English, according to Freyre.

With students whose life experiences and levels of development are so different, the trick is how to scaffold to an appropriate level. Freyre explains that she needs "to find the happy medium without over- or under-scaffolding." She has discovered that thematic units that include texts at appropriate levels, opportunities to integrate reading, writing, speaking, and listening, and opportunities to practice skills are the most useful for teaching her students. Less useful, according to Freyre, is the kind of curriculum that goes page by page because—no surprise—students get bored.

The kind of teaching Freyre brings to her classroom could be beneficial in any classroom. For example, when Freyre and her students took up narrative writing, they looked first at features of narrative. Together they noted that good writers often focus on a moment. Through a series of minilessons, Freyre taught her students how to choose a significant moment and how to let it unfold, how to build character, and how to incorporate dialogue. "We did multiple drafts and a combination of individual conferences and response groups." Freyre gave peer responders a set of criteria so they knew what to look for, and she also came up with a rubric tailored to the rhetorical features of narrative. "Here's where you are," she told her students, "and here's where you need to be."

The piece below came from an English Language Development (ELD) class Freyre taught a few years ago. In this class, Freyre worked with students like Fabiola Prieto, who had been in this country for two to three years.

The Disagreement

How can I make two decisions between [people] that I love? Why I have to chose, I ask to myself raising my head up looking at the sky sitting in the school yard.

Hey lets go. "Let do a complot against the teacher" said Luis Enrique one of my classmates.

Yes! Answered Alejandro

"But I don't think Fabiola wants to go, she is the spoiled of the teacher," replied Vanessa.

The student wanted to make a revolution against the teacher like Mexico did in 1910. It was a big deal. But the worst thing was that I was between them.

The teacher was an English teacher and his nick name was "el teacher" he was like a second father to me, he gave me advice, he knew when I was sad and when I had problems in my house. I loved him.

"Fabiola you have to come with us. We are a united group. We know that the teacher is very nice with you but you have to understand us. If we don't know one word in English he wants us to repeat the word 100 times. It is not fear." Insisted Luis Enrique with a frightened look.

"I will think about it." That was all that I said. "The teacher is my best teacher, I know that sometimes he yell at me too but he has reason all the time he just wants us to be good students" I was thinking to myself.

"What should I do? Should I go with my classmates? Or stay in the classroom being like the dark dunk." I questioned.

The bell rang. We went to the classroom my classmates made a circle they were whispering.

"Fabiola we have a plan when the teacher say something bad to us like that I have sh*t in my head, we all going to outside and tell father Jose."

We heard steps. The teacher was coming dressing like a lawyer with a tie and a briefcase. He was sitting on the big chair. He screamed "you guys are my worst group except for a few of you. You guys have Teflon heads" He said that very angry.

The students were standing up one bye one. I was the last one. I looked at the teacher and he looked at me, I can remember his sad look while I was standing up slowly. It was one of the wrongs decisions that I have made.

We went with the principal the father Carlos just ignored us. "All of you guys have to say sorry to the teacher." He demanded that pointing to us.

I ran back to the classroom. There was el teacher almost crying.

"Teacher, teacher sorry I am sorry." "I know I know I know." That was all that he said, hugging me.

When I look back on that day I think of how fortunate I was in having el teacher next to me giving me advice. That day I learn that he wanted me to be good, even if he yell me. I miss him a lot. I hopes one day see him again and say thanks to him.

In Freyre's notes to Fabiola, she praises the way the writing demonstrates "the conflict you faced between following your classmates or defending your teacher. Your narrative makes the reader feel like he or she is there with you!" We would add that this relatively recent arrival to the United States has learned how to unfold a moment. While her paper reveals typical second language errors, it also shows that Fabiola can incorporate key narrative strategies in her writing: dialogue, detail, conflict, a brief character sketch of "el teacher," a bit of reflection, a sense of drama, and a structure that works.

Working with developing writers is a juggling act—teaching sophisticated rhetorical features while supporting language development—and certainly calls for more than a grab-bag writing curriculum. Freyre makes teaching decisions based on what she has learned over time about exactly what benefits her students, for example, integrating the language arts. In this classroom example, she maintains a balance so that reading does not eclipse writing, but rather serves as a model for writing.

More about Remodeling Curriculum

If customizing or otherwise remodeling curriculum is a game changer, what else can we learn about it? How do teachers like Harrington, Kennedy, Lewis-Murphy, and Freyre approach writing curriculum and make it work in their classrooms? One answer is that they think first about the students themselves.

After more than thirty years in the English language arts classroom, Harrington puts her students up front. Rather than adopting ideas wholesale, she runs "great ideas" through several filters, all having to do with who is in the classroom at the moment:

When I adapt an idea, I first consider my students, and ask myself what their needs are, and how this idea will address those needs. I think about the diversity of cultural and ethnic backgrounds in my classroom, and wonder about what kind of prior knowledge or frontloading of vocabulary and information my students might need. I consider whether the suggested text is appropriate for my students, or whether I might need to find a different text that is more in their comfort level, or in mine. In many cases, I will merge several ideas gained from several sources to construct a lesson that meets my particular needs at that time. (personal communication, December 29, 2015)

One of the striking features of the way Harrington approaches the teaching of writing is the absence of dogma or "shoulds." Instead, she tailors her large repertoire of strategies to the immediate situation. Harrington knows a lot about writing, but she also has a firm grip on the elements that will support her students' learning, for example, introducing vocabulary and essential information.

For Judy Kennedy, who teaches US history, government, and economics, both mainstream and sheltered, ideas for teaching content and academic literacy come from the Stanford History Education Group (SHEG), the Civic Action Project of the Constitutional Rights Foundation, the Bay Area Writing Project, and Facing History. But like other skilled teachers we have interviewed, she does not simply drop ideas into her classroom without customizing them for her students:

I rarely adopt writing ideas wholesale without modification. Most times I have to try the writing assignment myself and see how I would need to scaffold it for my students. I try to think of prewriting activities that will help my students on the actual writing assignment itself. Also, I need to think about what the purpose of the assignment is and how I am going to evaluate it. (personal communication, January 3, 2016)

To understand firsthand what kinds of interventions might be most helpful to her students, Kennedy, now in her fourteenth year of teaching, comes to key decisions about scaffolding and assessment—not in the abstract—but in the process of trying out and possibly modifying her own assignments.

Skilled teachers also stay on top of changes, whether that means using more current technology or assuring that the content is current. Corine Maday teaches grades 8–12 classes such as Girls Physical Education, Health Science, Nutrition, Drug Alcohol and Tobacco Abuse, HIV/AIDS, and Sexual Health, and she has done so for twenty-six years. Note how she tailors information to make it interesting for her students:

> Many times I have to use very up-to-date information because health information is always changing so that means changing information that may be in the curriculum. I also change the way in which it may be presented to better fit my audience. I often have to supplement the curriculum with "real-life" stories or events to help my students make a connection. (personal communication, January 4, 2016)

Maday represents those thoughtful teachers of content who work to make information both timely and interesting, in particular, by reaching beyond the school context for authentic examples that will be meaningful to students.

We finish this brief but firsthand look at how experienced teachers make their way to a writing curriculum shaped for their students with the adamant words of Gail Offen-Brown, recently retired from the UC Berkeley composition program after thirty-eight years. She is unequivocal about redesigning curriculum with her students squarely in sight:

> I NEVER adopt ideas wholesale, not even from colleagues in my own program. I think hard about my own students, my goals for the particular assignment within the context of the unit, the class, the semester. I ask myself whether the students have the requisite cultural capital and background knowledge to understand the materials and tasks, and if not how to address that. I consider what kinds of scaffolding are needed. I consider reflective/metacognitive elements. I ask myself how this assignment might stretch my students' minds and hearts. (personal communication, January 6, 2015)

What these teachers tell us is that education is about more than delivering instruction. It's about reaching diverse learners and taking them as far as they can go. To do this, teachers must have the capacity and freedom to "meet them on their own terms, at their own starting points, and with a wide range of strategies to support their success" (Darling-Hammond & Snyder, 1992, p. 11).

Building the Capacity of Teachers to Teach Writing *and* Writers

In this chapter we have featured the thinking of experienced teachers and their message is clear. Assignments, lessons, and materials, no matter what their source, are insufficient. Teachers play a critical role as the key architects in designing or remodeling curriculum for their students.

While policymakers have sometimes worked overtime to eliminate teachers from the equation, others like Lee Shulman insist that nothing can replace teachers:

> The teacher remains the key. The literature on effective schools is meaningless, debates over educational policy are moot, if the primary agents of instruction are incapable of performing their functions well. No micro-computer will replace them, no television system will clone and distribute them, no scripted lessons will direct and control them, no voucher system will bypass them. (Shulman, 1983, p. 504)

Darling-Hammond agrees that education needs to make a radical departure from past practices that put "test prescriptions, textbook adoptions, and curriculum directives" ahead of investments in increasing the ability of teachers to make key decisions on behalf of their students. The mission of education, according to Darling-Hammond, should be "that teachers understand learners and their learning as deeply as they comprehend their subjects ...."(1996, p.4).

The recurring debate about where teachers fit into the equation—are they or aren't they the basic, if not central, learning resource available to students?—becomes even more pressing when the students are disadvantaged and underachieving. In her article, "Good Teaching Matters: How Well-Qualified Teachers Can Close the Gap," Kati Haycock, president of the Education

Trust, reviews research from Tennessee, Texas, Massachusetts, and Alabama that compares the development of disadvantaged students in situations where teachers are highly skilled and less skilled. In every case, students in the presence of highly skilled teachers are the winners. For Haycock, the research is clear: the factor with the most significant impact on student achievement is the teacher:

> After all, poor and minority children depend on their teachers like no others. In the hands of our best teachers, the effects of poverty and institutional racism melt away, allowing these students to soar to the same heights as young Americans from more advantaged homes. (1998, p. 13)

In the next sections, we argue that our most important investment—if we are to *intentionally* and *purposefully* take students into account—is in teachers and in their capacities to teach America's ever-changing student population.

Investing in Teacher Knowledge

As a start, investing in teacher knowledge means preparing teachers for the complex task of teaching writing and writers. The National Commission on Writing recommends requiring "all prospective teachers to take courses in how to teach writing" (2006, p. 43). But this initial investment is not enough. Teachers should have ongoing opportunities to develop their knowledge and skills.

Darling-Hammond and Snyder (1992) describe the kinds of investments that support teachers and their continued growth and development, including "opportunities for teachers to jointly plan and evaluate their work; to reflect together about the needs and progress of individual students and groups of students; and to share teaching ideas, strategies, and dilemmas for collective problem solving" (p. 23). Commonsense investments like these, however, mean a cosmic change from past top-down policies and financial priorities. They call for devoting considerable time and resources to increasing teacher expertise as opposed to deskilling teachers with scripted materials. They call for making space for teachers to interact instead of keeping them in the silos of their classrooms.

The kind of investment recommended by Darling-Hammond and Snyder offers an excellent return. When teachers participate in long-term professional development networks, for example the National Writing Project, not only do they learn specific techniques, they also grapple with and refine "big ideas" in writing instruction, ideas such as focusing on purposes for writing, scaffolding students' writing processes, and linking their teaching to their own experiences as writers (Whitney & Friedrich, 2013). They challenge, inquire into, and revise such ideas in ongoing interactions with other teachers. And they use these "big ideas" to develop and revise curriculum.

The best teachers we know are always building their banks of research-based strategies for teaching writing because any single approach can hardly do the job in today's classrooms. Moreover, successful teachers understand that the bank is never full. New strategies are always in the making. Furthermore, because teachers are on the front line, they know what challenges and issues need attention.

What kinds of things do teachers themselves find valuable in professional development? One answer comes from a seven-year Inverness Research survey study of 22,000 participating teachers in National Writing Project summer institutes. Teachers reported that they benefit from professional development that "increases their ability to teach students of diverse backgrounds" and from information on how to "help students meet standards." They also cited as helpful information about "up to date research and practice," "ways to assess student work and plan teaching," and "concrete teaching strategies" (Stokes & St. John, 2008, p. v).

The survey also indicates that teachers are interested in learning about practices that have immediate relevance and use in the classroom. It makes sense, then, to let teachers identify their most pressing issues. In that regard, the National Commission on Writing (2006) recommends "districts *transform professional development* by turning the responsibility and funding for it over to teachers." The Commission also recommends "embedding professional development in the job." It finds alternatives like one-shot sessions, also known as "drive-by" training, ineffective because they provide "little tangible or long-term benefits to teachers." Instead, the Commission recommends "making professional development part of the daily working lives of teachers—by providing time for it during the school schedule on a regular and recurring basis" (p. 26).

Investing in Opportunities for Teachers to Share Their Knowledge and Expertise

For an outsider looking into the daily life of schools, it's hard to imagine that teachers wouldn't find *some* time to talk together about what's happening in their classrooms or to share some of the work of their students, or better yet, to consult each other when they run into some kind of road block. But in fact, teachers have little time or inclination to sit down together—not when there are lessons to plan, papers to grade, and, in this era of social media, curriculum, assignments, and messages to post for students and their parents. The situation is deceiving:

> The "structural isolation within which the teacher has to operate," each working within his or her own classroom, has created a vision of the self-made teacher, a vision in which "teaching comes to be seen as an individual accomplishment," rather than a collaborative venture, and "a natural expression of a teacher's personality" rather than an enactment of disciplinary knowledge and professional expertise. (Labaree, 2004, pp. 51–52)

So finding a place, a time, and a relevant agenda for teachers to share their knowledge and expertise requires special attention and structured support. One not-so-new invention that brings teachers together are teacher networks. Ann Lieberman and Milbrey McLaughlin (1992) note:

> [N]etworks, committed as they are to addressing the tough and enduring problems of teaching, deliberately create a discourse community that encourages exchange among the members. Being a part of the discourse community assures teachers that their knowledge of their students and of schooling is respected. Once they know this, they become committed to change, willing to take risks, and dedicated to self-improvement. (p. 674)

Certainly, James Gray was thinking about the value of teachers sharing their knowledge when he founded the Bay Area Writing Project. Gray was keenly aware that there were teachers in the community who knew a lot about the teaching of writing, although they had few opportunities to share their expertise:

> I knew that the knowledge successful teachers had gained through their experience and practice in the classroom was not tapped, sought after, shared, or for the most part, even known about. I knew also that if there was ever going to be reform in American education, it was going to take place in the nation's classrooms. And because teachers—and no one else—were in those classrooms, I knew that for reform to succeed, teachers had to be at the center. (2000, p. 50)

Gray's plan was to invite outstanding teachers from the schools and the university and put them to work together in a summer institute, after which they would teach their colleagues how to teach writing during the school year. The mantra was "teachers teaching teachers." In the years that followed, the writing project became a national model for effective professional development, one that provides significant opportunities for teacher learning and collaboration.

Commenting on the value of teacher networks, Darling-Hammond observes:

> [P]rofessional communities of teachers can have a large and positive impact, doing much more than simply sharing teacher tips. Teachers who are able to collaborate with other teachers are really engaged in work where they are rolling up their sleeves to design and evaluate curriculum and instruction together in a way that allows them to share their expertise deeply and in a sustained and ongoing fashion. (Darling-Hammond, qtd. in Collier, 2011, p. 12)

Another example of "rolling up their sleeves" occurs when teachers pull out their students' writing and invite their colleagues to take a look. Analyzing student work together opens up all kinds of conversations, from the strengths and limitations of the writing to possibilities for next steps. These discussions zero in on what happens when students are learning to write with all the messiness, frustrations, and complexities that involves.

The advantages of inviting teachers to the table and of giving them multiple forums for sharing what they know are numerous:

◆ Teachers generate and gain more knowledge each time they interact with their colleagues.

◆ Teachers gain deeper insights into the range of student abilities and how to address that range when they assess student work together.

◆ Teachers who work together do things that are impossible to do alone, like developing a common language for teaching writing.

◆ Veteran teachers up the game of novice teachers.

◆ Teachers bring needed support directly to the classroom when they mentor one another in positions like literacy coaching.

◆ Teachers become more motivated and energetic when they can turn to one another to solve problems.

◆ Teachers are more likely to examine new resources or take risks with tools like technology in collaboration with their peers.

Given half a chance, teachers naturally gravitate toward sharing with each other. During his tenure as English department chair in a Pittsburgh, Pennsylvania, high school, Jerry Halpern actively looked for ways to get teachers together, including weekly meetings for talking shop. As an outgrowth of these meetings, Halpern and two colleagues began observing one another and then decided to teach one another's classes:

> Each worked up a set of minilessons or minicourses and began trading classrooms. Afterward they shared what happened—the good and the not-so-good. "The professional dialogue kept us focused. We were talking about curriculum and student writing and how to use our individual strengths to help these kids," remembers Halpern. (Murphy & Smith, 2015, p. 128)

In the end, teacher sharing is a kind of professionalism that has particular characteristics, according to Halpern: "a fundamental focus on teaching and learning; a high degree of collegiality and collaboration; a willingness to put yourself and your work forward for examination" (Murphy & Smith, 2015, p. 127).

As impressive as the Halpern example is, it's unrealistic to expect individual teachers to initiate all the conversations that need to happen. Here again, networks give teachers the kind of boost they need to adopt new teaching approaches for the benefit of their students:

> When they construct ideas about practice with their colleagues, teachers act as both experts and apprentices, teachers and learners. Members of networks report an intellectual and emotional stimulation that gives them the courage to engage students differently in the classroom—an opportunity especially valued by teachers working in urban schools. (Lieberman & McLaughlin, 1992, p. 674)

Investing in Teachers as Writers, Scholars, and Leaders

In 1984, Marian Mohr, a teacher in Northern Virginia, published a book called *Revision: The Rhythm of Meaning*. It quickly became a classic among writing teachers, not just because of its 248 pages of ideas about teaching students to revise, but because it was a window into a real classroom. Mohr's publisher, Bob Boynton, a former English teacher at Germantown Friends School in Philadelphia, devoted himself to publishing what teachers had to say on all kinds of subjects, including the still popular teachings of Boothbay Harbor's Nancie Atwell (1987) in her book *In the Middle: Writing, Reading, and Learning with Adolescents*. Boynton also put his teacher-writers on planes to fly wherever there were conferences or institutes, and no surprise, there was a huge audience of teachers waiting at the other end to hear what another colleague—someone who walked the walk—could tell them about teaching and learning.

Not everyone who writes in the field of composition writes about classroom practice. In fact, it's likely that teachers are the primary authors of what goes on in classrooms, while college faculty contribute a greater percentage of research reports, and fewer descriptions of practice. In her analysis of contributions to three NCTE publications—*Language Arts, Voices from the*

Middle, and *English Journal*—Anne Whitney (2009) notes that K–12 teachers write mostly about teaching practices. Thus, if we want to read about on-the-ground practices and issues, we look to teachers to carry the bulk of the conversation.

And who knows the audience of teachers better than teachers? According to Whitney et al. (2012), from their interviews with thirteen teacher-authors, the teacher-authors "wanted to produce something that classroom teachers could use. They wanted to share their own experiences of what worked and sometimes of what did not." As one of the teacher-authors put it, "How can I make this make sense, and appealing also, to another English teacher?" (p. 404).

Recent examples of teacher scholarship can be found in the work of teachers Jim Burke, Kelly Gallagher, and Carol Jago, who have collectively authored thirty books, along with contributing to textbooks and other collections. They make podcasts and DVDs for their colleagues, conduct workshops, and frequently show up as conference keynote speakers. Jago has edited the professional journal *California English* for the past twenty years. This scholarship translates easily into leadership. When any of these three is in front of a group of teachers, the audience reacts with laughter, applause, nodding heads, pertinent questions, and copious note taking.

It makes sense that teachers gravitate to reading about and listening to their colleagues' experiences. But beyond what's published, investing in opportunities for teachers to write about their practice has big rewards for students. As Whitney and Friedrich (2013) explain, teachers use "their ongoing experiences as writers to gain insight into the supports their students would need as they worked" (p. 11):

> Seeing oneself as a writer and linking that to students' experiences as writers offers at least two main benefits cited by NWP teachers: first, it provides empathy for student experience and firsthand knowledge of the challenges student writers might face when writing; second, it positions the teacher relative to students as a writer among writers. (p. 24)

There is a theme here: investing in teacher scholarship, leadership, and writing pays off. What's more, the payoff increases when the investment is in *putting teachers to work* teaching their colleagues. Effective professional development, like classroom teaching, is more than a delivery system. When teachers are in charge of workshops, seminars, study groups, institutes, conferences and the like, the content more closely relates to the realities of the classroom. For example, Stokes (2010) explains how writing project teachers prepare to lead professional development sessions:

> Individual teacher-consultants focus on teaching problems that they find most vexing in their own practice and important to their students. In so doing, they amass resources and develop classroom practices that will be germane to their colleagues who face similar challenges. (p. 149)

Perhaps the most compelling reason to invest in opportunities for teacher leadership is the potential for expert, veteran teachers to stay in the profession—a phenomenon that greatly improves student learning. In its study of 5,534 individuals who participated in summer institutes from 1974 to 2006 and who completed a professional history survey, NWP researchers found that 99 percent of institute participants stayed in classrooms and in the profession for over seventeen years. Of these teachers, 72 percent remained in the classroom while 27 percent played other roles in education, for example in administrative positions. Fewer than one percent worked outside of education (Friedrich et al., 2008, pp. 10–11).

Investing in Teacher Research

One mutual activity that attracts many teachers, to the benefit of their students, is classroom research. As long ago as 1978, Northern Virginia Writing Project teacher Marian Mohr began her foray into conducting research by retitling her teaching journal "Research Log" (Gray, 2000, p. 91). Later coauthor Marion MacLean and Mohr (1999) shared their discoveries about what happens when teachers become researchers:

> Teacher-researchers raise questions about what they think and observe about their teaching and their students' learning. They collect student work in order to evaluate performance, but they

also see student work as data to analyze in order to examine
the teaching and learning that produced it. (p. x)

One of the notable advantages of this kind of research is that
teachers conduct it in the context of the classroom (Mohr &
MacLean, 1987). In terms of classroom practice, teacher research
provides "interpretive frames that teachers use to understand
and to improve their own classroom practices" (Cochran-Smith
& Lytle, 1993, p. 7).

Another advantage when it comes to curriculum design is
that when teachers closely analyze various aspects of their teaching, including the results, they are more likely to make ongoing
adjustments. In other words, the curriculum, rather than being
static, becomes dynamic and responsive to real classroom events.

Many teacher-researchers collaborate with their students to
answer mutually interesting questions—a strategy that transforms
roles in the classroom because the research process and findings
belong to both. And because the research involves teaching and
learning, teachers also have something useful to pass along to
their colleagues:

> As their research becomes integrated into their teaching, their
> definition of teacher-researcher becomes *teacher*—a teacher
> who observes, questions, assists, analyzes, writes, and repeats
> these actions in a recursive process that includes sharing their
> results with their students and with other teachers. (Mohr &
> MacLean, 1987, p. 4)

No doubt teacher research, among other professional activities,
has contributed to improving what happens in classrooms and
schools. And that's the goal of any investment in education—to
get it right for every student in every classroom and school.
Placing bets on teachers is not a gamble, especially in the area of
classroom curriculum and its relevance to the students at hand:

> Once the important concepts and generalizations are identified
> at a national level for a particular field of study, the way in
> which they are transformed into an operational curriculum for
> students is a task for the teacher or the faculty of the school.
> In this way both national and local needs can be met. (Eisner,
> 1985, p. 139)

To make relevant improvements in teaching and learning, tailored to the current needs of diverse students, it takes those on the ground who have the essential knowledge and experience.

Investing in Teachers to Help Solve Educational Problems: The Power of Positive Deviance

How do people in professions other than education solve some of their most difficult problems? One key strategy is to look to those on the inside for solutions. Atul Gawande describes a long-standing problem with hospital infections in the United States due to lack of proper handwashing. At a veterans' hospital in Pittsburgh, Pennsylvania, those in charge had made every possible move to encourage handwashing, including cajoling, reprimanding, and pointing to gel dispensers. However, the infections continued. In some cases, medical staff actually rebelled against outsiders' telling them what to do.

Even with the most innovative solutions, the hospital failed to create lasting change. Still, there was a desperate need to turn things around. One of the hospital surgeons came across the idea of *positive deviance*—a notion about working from the inside, building on the capacities people already have as an alternative to bringing in outside "experts" to tell them what and how they need to change. In March 2005, food-service workers, janitors, nurses, doctors, and even patients participated in a series of small-group discussions. To introduce the first session, the leaders, headed by the surgeon, said, "We're here because of the hospital infection problem and we want to know what *you* know about how to solve it." What happened next was nothing short of a landslide:

> Ideas came pouring out. People told of places where hand-gel dispensers were missing, ways to keep gowns and gloves from running out of supply, nurses who always seem able to wash their hands, and even taught patients to wash their hands too. Many people said it was the first time anyone had ever asked them what to do. The norms began to shift. When forty new hand-gel dispensers arrived, staff members took charge of putting them in the right places. Nurses who would never speak up when a doctor failed to wash his or her hands began to do so after learning of other nurses who did. (Gawande, 2007, p. 26)

The *inside* team managed all the follow-up by posting monthly results and promoting their ideas on the hospital website and in newsletters. Gawande explains the result: "One year into the experiment—and after years without widespread progress—the entire hospital saw its MRSA [infection by antibiotic-resistant bacteria] wound infection rates drop to zero" (pp. 26–27).

Jerry Sternin and his wife Monique developed the idea of positive deviance—finding solutions from insiders. In his YouTube video, Sternin (2015) offers this metaphor for positive deviance: "The faraway stick cannot kill the nearby snake." In the world of education, the faraway curriculum cannot serve all the nearby students with their various cultures, languages, and abilities.

Positive deviance is a loaded term, without a doubt, and its application to date has often privileged uncommon solutions, although with some excellent outcomes. However, it's the mental shift that interests us. In a profession like education, with a history of pendulum swings and winner-take-all arguments about how to teach one thing or another, for example the reading wars of the recent past, there is a crying need for openness to what insiders have to say. Further, given the complexities of teaching a wide range of learners, it seems that insider knowledge should be a precious, sought-after commodity.

Taking teachers into account is not a new concept, but the concept sorely needs staying power and policies that support rather than weaken it. Certainly, control from the top has had less than stellar results, and as our population becomes more heterogeneous, top-down approaches are bound to be less and less successful.

Teachers are much more than a conduit for a prepackaged curriculum. Without thoughtful adaptation, this kind of curriculum is dead on arrival, at least if we expect it to support the learning of each student in the local classroom. Since teachers are the ones to work directly with students, they are the ones to customize "official" curricula for their students or to create their own curricula as the case may be.

But the development and use of teacher knowledge, leadership, and expertise has to happen on a larger scale than is possible in preservice education or in worthy, but relatively small, professional development programs. It must be built into the way schools, districts, and universities operate. It must be systemic, not here and there on the sidelines. And for good reason. What local teachers know is critical to giving all students a fighting chance at a real education.

References

Applebee, A. N., & Langer, J. A. (2013). *Writing instruction that works: Proven methods for middle and high school classrooms.* Berkeley, CA: National Writing Project; New York: Teachers College Press.

Atwell, N. (1987). *In the middle: Writing, reading, and learning with adolescents.* Portsmouth, NH: Boynton/Cook.

Caswell, H. L., & Campbell, D. S. (1935). *Curriculum development.* New York: American Book.

Clifford, G. J. (1989). A Sisyphean task: Historical perspectives on writing and reading instruction. In A. H. Dyson (Ed.), *Collaboration through writing and reading: Exploring possibilities* (pp. 25–83). Urbana, IL: National Council of Teachers of English.

Cochran-Smith, M., & Lytle, S. L. (1993). *Inside/outside: Teacher research and knowledge.* New York: Teachers College Press.

Collier, L. (2011, November). The need for teacher communities: An interview with Linda Darling-Hammond. *Council Chronicle, 21*(2), 12–14.

Darling-Hammond, L. (1996). The quiet revolution: rethinking teacher development. *Educational Leadership 53*(6), pp. 4–10.

Darling-Hammond, L., & Snyder, J. (1992). Framing accountability: Creating learner-centered schools. In A. Lieberman (Ed.), *The changing contexts of teaching* (pp. 11–36). Chicago: National Society for the Study of Education.

Eisner, E. W. (1985). *The educational imagination: On the design and evaluation of school programs* (2nd ed.). New York: Macmillan.

Elley, W. B. (1994). Grammar teaching and language skill. In Asher, R. E. (Ed.), *The Encyclopedia of Language and Linguistics* (Vol. 3, pp. 1468–71). Oxford, UK: Pergamon.

Elley, W. B., Barham, I. H., Lamb, H., & Wyllie, M. (1975). The role of grammar in a secondary school curriculum. *New Zealand Journal* of *Educational Studies, 10*(1), 26–41. Reprinted (1976) in *Research in the Teaching of English, 10*(1), 5–21.

Friedrich, L., Swain, S., LeMahieu, P., Fessehaie, S., Mieles, T. (2008). *Making a difference: The National Writing Project's inculcation of leadership over 30 years.* Paper presented at the 2007 meeting of the American Educational Research Association, Chicago, IL, and rev. May 2, 2008. Retrieved from https://www.nwp.org/cs/public/print/resource/2754

Gardner, H. (2000). *The disciplined mind: Beyond facts and standardized tests, the K–12 education that every child deserves.* New York: Penguin Books.

Gawande, A. (2007). *Better: A surgeon's notes on performance.* New York: Picador.

Graham, S., & Perin, D. (2007). *Writing next: Effective strategies to improve writing of adolescents in middle and high schools.* Retrieved from www.all4ed.org/wp-content/uploads/2006/10/WritingNext.pdf

Gray, J. (2000). *Teachers at the center: A memoir of the early years of the National Writing Project.* Berkeley, CA: National Writing Project.

Haycock, K. (1998). Good teaching matters: How well-qualified teachers can close the gap. *Thinking K–16, 3*(2). Retrieved from http://eric.ed.gov/?id=ED457260

Hillocks, G., Jr. (1986). *Research on written composition: New directions for teaching.* Urbana, IL: ERIC Clearinghouse on Reading and Communication Skills and National Conference on Research in English.

Hocks, M. E. (2003). Understanding visual rhetoric in digital writing environments. *College Composition and Communication, 54*(4), 629–56.

Jenkins, H., Purushotma, R., Clinton, K., Weigel, M., & Robison, A. J. (2009). *Confronting the challenges of participatory culture: Media education for the 21st Century.* Retrieved from http://www.newmedialiteracies.org/wp-content/uploads/pdfs/NMLWhitePaper.pdf

Kiuhara, S. A., Graham, S., & Hawken, L. S. (2009). Teaching writing to high school students: A national survey. *Journal of Educational Psychology, 101*(1), 136–60. doi:10.1037/a0013097

Labaree, D. F. (2004). *The trouble with ed schools.* New Haven, CT: Yale University Press.

Leu, D. J., Kiili, C., & Forzani, E. (2015). Individual differences in the new literacies of online research and comprehension. In Afflerbach, P. (Ed.), *Handbook of individual differences in reading: Reader, text, and context* (pp. 259–72). New York: Routledge.

Lieberman, A., & McLaughlin, M. W. (1992). Networks for educational change: Powerful and problematic. *Phi Delta Kappan, 73*(9), 673–77.

MacLean, M. S., & Mohr, M. M. (1999). *Teacher researchers at work.* Berkeley, CA: National Writing Project.

Mohr, M. M. (1984). *Revision: The rhythm of meaning.* Upper Montclair, NJ: Boynton/Cook.

Mohr, M. M., & MacLean, M. S. (1987). *Working together: A guide for teacher researchers.* Urbana, IL: National Council of Teachers of English.

Murphy, S., & Smith, M. A. (2015). *Uncommonly good ideas: Teaching writing in the Common Core era.* New York: Teachers College Press; Berkeley, CA: National Writing Project.

Myhill, D., & Watson, A. (2014). The role of grammar in the writing curriculum: A review of the literature. *Child Language Teaching and Therapy, 30*(1), 41–62. doi:10.1177/0265659013514070

National Commission on Writing for America's Families, Schools, and Colleges. (2006). *Writing and school reform: Including the neglected "r": The need for a writing revolution.* Retrieved from http://www.collegeboard.com/prod_downloads/writingcom/writing-school-reform-natl-comm-writing.pdf

National Commission on Writing in America's Schools and Colleges. (2003). *The neglected "r": The need for a writing revolution.* Retrieved from www.collegeboard.com/prod_downloads/writingcom/neglectedr.pdf

National Writing Project with DeVoss, D. N., Eidman-Aadahl, E., & Hicks, T. (2010). *Because digital writing matters: Improving student writing in online and multimedia environments.* San Francisco: Jossey-Bass.

Posner, G. J. (2004). *Analyzing the curriculum* (3rd ed.). Boston: McGraw-Hill.

Shulman, L. S. (1983). Autonomy and obligation: The remote control of teaching. In L. S. Shulman & G. Sykes (Eds.), *Handbook of teaching and policy,* pp. 484–504. New York: Longman.

Sternin, J. (2015, April 30). *Positive deviance approach* [Video]. Available from https://www.youtube.com/watch?v=9Pj4egHN0-E

Stokes, L. (2010). The National Writing Project: Anatomy of an improvement infrastructure. In C. E. Cobur & M. K. Stein (Eds.), *Research and practice in education: Building alliances, bridging the divide* (pp. 147–62). New York: Rowman & Littlefield.

Stokes, L., & St. John, M. (2008). *Teachers' assessments of professional development quality, value, and benefits: Results from seven annual surveys of participants in National Writing Project summer institutes: Executive summary.* Retrieved from http://inverness-research .org/reports/2008-03-nwp-survey-resultsfor7yrs/2008-03-Rpt-NWP-DOE_SurveyResultsReport-ExecSum.pdf

Whithaus, C. (2005). *Teaching and evaluating writing in the age of computers and high-stakes testing.* Mahwah, NJ: Erlbaum.

Whitney, A. (2009). NCTE journals and the teacher-author: Who and what gets published. *English Education, 41*(2), 101–13.

Whitney, A. E., Anderson, K., Dawson, C., Kang, S., Olan, E. L., Olcese, N., & Ridgeman, M. (2012). Audience and authority in the professional writing of teacher-authors. *Research in the Teaching of English, 46*(4), 390–419.

Whitney, A. E., & Friedrich, L. (2013). Orientations for the teaching of writing: A legacy of the National Writing Project. *Teachers College Record, 115*(7), 1–37.

CHAPTER EIGHT

Writing Development and Life-Course Development: The Case of Working Adults

DEBORAH BRANDT

University of Wisconsin–Madison

Fifty-two-year-old Alejandro Ortega serves as public housing director for a midsized city not far from where he grew up in Iowa. Over the course of his twenty-five-year career in public service, he has written successful grant proposals for awards totaling more than $25 million, awards that have secured a variety of goods and services including construction supplies, literacy tutoring, wheelchairs, maternal education, and mental health assistance. He also mentors other grant writers on the housing staff, teaching them a writing strategy that he calls "making the case." When asked how he learned to "make the case," Mr. Ortega first referred not to his schooling (which included earning a master's degree in urban planning) but to this childhood memory:

> In growing up I noted that my father was active in the Mexican American community. There were things that were not going well in the community, and people would come to my father with problems. How do I file the papers to become a citizen? How do I get the assistance that I need? My son is in trouble with the police. So I saw what he did for people. He was a spokesperson for the community. So I guess I got that orientation. It's all a matter of making the case, and I like it.

This account brings attention to powerful aspects of writing development that are easy to miss when developmental models are too simple, too narrow, too linear, or too disconnected from context. Mr. Ortega's model locates the beginnings of his adult grant writing expertise in orientations passed to him in childhood as he observed his father respond to neighbors in need and take action on their behalf. Long before encountering the genre of the grant proposal, Mr. Ortega experienced the forms of life that would give that vehicle meaning, value, and attraction as he also gained early access to connections between rhetorical efforts—making the case—and their outcomes for people. Above all, Mr. Ortega was given means to understand early on that his own writing development could be tied to the human development of those around him and that they could develop together.

This chapter explores the writing development of working adults through the lens of human development, drawing specifically on insights from multidisciplinary studies of life-course human development (Elder, Johnson, & Crosnoe, 2004; Sørensen, Weinert, & Sherrod, 1986). This scholarship, located in such fields as genetics, sociology, history, and psychology, offers rich conceptual guidance for lifespan writing research. Across fields, life-course development research focuses on change and aging as continual, multidimensional and mutually influencing processes that are in analyzable relationships to processes and changes in wider environments. This work emphasizes how development comes to people through the roles they play or are expected to play at different times of life; the historical events to which they are exposed; and the reconfigured meanings and potentials that accumulate around these experiences (Elder, 1999; Elder & Conger, 2000; Mortimer & Shanahan, 2004). This orientation resists a view of human development as a timeless, universal, unidirectional, stable, or normative property of individuals. Rather development is defined in terms of changes that occur in relationships between people and their life worlds over time, changes that gather lasting consequence for the workings of those relationships going forward (Sroufe, Egeland, Carlson, & Collins, 2005; Bronfenbrenner, 2004). Human development, from this perspective, is a deeply interdependent endeavor, what psychologist Urie Bronfenbrenner (1979) calls an ecological endeavor, in which one's developmental efforts and outcomes are constituted with and through the lives and events to which one is connected (also see Elder & Rockwell, 1979). Development is reciprocally realized and maintained, outwardly as well as inwardly motivated, temporally situated, and, in essence, an ongoing process of adaptation that shares its forms, meanings, and potentialities with its contexts. Life-course researchers are committed to applying this perspective even when their studies or interventions focus on particular age groups or present-tense situations (Sørensen et al., 1986).

Life-course developmental research, both sociological and psychological, pays attention to people's patterns of exposure to enduring and changing environments and to the significance of place in developmental processes. It also offers a complex, multidimensional concept of time and timing as central to the contours of development. For the analyst, this means that development can be approached not merely in terms of biological or chronological age but in terms of roles and expectations that society associates with different stages of life (Elder, 1994; Elder & Giele, 2009). How a person's life course conforms with or deviates from the conventional expectations of social age carries implications for development (Settersten, 2004; also see Mayer, 2009). So too does the timing of one's birth and how one is moving through (and contributing to) large- and small-scale historical events and change. Anyone's life trajectories, including his or her choices and actions, will be in relationship to these multiple dimensions of time, timing, transition, and reciprocal change (Elder, 1998). So too will the emergence of individual dispositions—what Bronfenbrenner (2004, p. 97) calls "structuring proclivities" or "instigative characteristics"—which help to animate, mediate, and modulate developmental processes of self and others. Dispositions must be treated not as innate features of personality but as performances of adjustment across time, change, and contexts. Also contributing to developmental ecologies and outcomes are members of one's "social convoy" (families, community members, school and work associates) and the ways those people develop from their historical and social positions and environmental experiences (Antonucci, Fiori, Birditt, & Jackey, 2010; Moen & Hernandez, 2009). In this framework, human development becomes both a project and a reflexive product of social demands and experience (Heinz & Krüger, 2001). It is reflected in the range of socially contributive activities that an individual can instigate, coordinate, and maintain with increasing success.

Using the term *life-course* vs. *lifespan* development is a deliberate choice in this chapter as the aim is to bring attention to social structure as an active agent in the formation of individual literacy. In anyone's development one can discern what Mayer (2003) has called a patterned expression of social structure. This structure does not determine development but seriously conditions it as individuals participate in a social order across time. Life-course perspectives emphasize how earlier events influence later events and how getting selected for different roles and strata affects development. One can read from a developmental history the way a person has accommodated social norms. "Life course" denotes a difference from a "lifespan" perspective, preferred in the fields of biology and psychology, where the focus is more on the ontogenesis of development and the physical and cognitive structures and functions that change over time. But these two perspectives can be complementary and have been productively fused, for instance, in the work of the brilliant psychologist Urie Bronfenbrenner, whose concepts are explored later in this chapter.

When applied analogically, the life-course orientation has much to offer the field of writing studies. It helps to get beyond treating writing ability as a skill set that accumulates as a property of the individual—a view that dominates curriculum, assessment, policy, and public perception. But this orientation also has something important to say to those who take a more contextual approach to writing, as it eschews a view of context as a container or social address that emits influence on people in some kind of predictable (but not deeply examined or explained) way (Bronfenbrenner, 2004). Rather analysts must scour contexts for evidence of developmental processes occurring (or not) as part of historically specific systems of people, places, and times. From this perspective, contexts are understood as constituents (indeed even beneficiaries) of individuals' development. This dynamic perspective brings attention to how people develop—or not—together (i.e., parent and child; teacher and student; colleague and colleague; writer and reader) and how real development registers as change not only in one's self but also in one's environment. Development is action, not a state of being. Such an active and outward-looking view of development is an obviously appealing lens for our purposes here, as writing, in its barest elements, projects language outward toward responsive others and, as a set of speech acts, bends toward altering worlds or possible worlds even as it changes a writer in the process.

Life-course scholarship, then, provides analytical frameworks that are relevant and resonant for literacy researchers even as it compels us to adopt more longitudinal, multifaceted, and integrated approaches to writing development. This orientation asks us to look broadly for life events and experiences that trigger and suppress writing development and to consider what stays stable and what changes in writing development (including when, where, why, and under what conditions). This orientation also requires us to approach writing development more collectively and interrelationally than we typically do, considering how people's development is linked to the developmental conditions and gains of those around them. It invites us to pay attention to phenomena that involve times, timing, place, duration, spacing, order, role, transition, variance, process, context, system, action, and change.

This chapter tries, then, to bring some of these conceptual tools of life-course studies to bear on processes of adult writing development. It is based on a qualitative reanalysis of in-depth interviews I conducted between 2005 and 2012 with sixty adults ages 25 to 80 who were employed in a range of public- and private-sector jobs or in volunteer civic positions that required them to write for a minimum of 15 percent of the workday and, in most cases, much more than that. They held jobs in a wide range of enterprises—health care, insurance, finance, accounting, business, farming, ministry, public relations, technology, education, law, military, science, politics, social service, public policy, art, publishing, and communications, among others. They served at various ranks, from entry level to supervisory, and in large and small concerns. Their length of employment ranged from a few months to more than thirty years. The original research project for which the interviews were collected sought to track relationships between reading and writing in the everyday lives of writing-intensive individuals and the effects of writing intensity on the ways these individuals understood and valued their literacy. The study was published as *The Rise of Writing: Redefining*

Mass Literacy (2015). The focus of that study was not explicitly on writing development; however, conversations did focus quite a bit on how, over time, people learned to do the writing they were currently pursuing. In addition, several interview questions invited wide-ranging reflections about the meaning and value of writing across the lifetime. (For the value of retrospective life accounts for life-course research, see Elder, 1998; also Cohler & Hostetler, 2004.)

As I engaged with the other scholars represented in this volume in exploring writing development from a lifespan perspective, I wondered what this existing interview data might yield for our collective purposes. I decided to reanalyze the interviews for patterns and processes of writing development, even as I recognized the limitations of the study's original design for such purposes. Obviously had writing development been the explicit focus of the inquiry, the design of the study would have been more inclusive; different questions would have been asked; and participation would have been organized around cohorts and convoys to allow more systematic comparisons and contrasts of people's experiences across time. Instead, by intention, the original study excluded people who did little or no writing on a daily basis and focused instead on adults who did a lot of writing for work. Consequently, the participants had higher levels of education and higher-paying jobs than the population overall. So what is presented here comes with some challenges in design, interview format, and participant representation. But with those limitations stated, and even acknowledging the security that higher education and employment can provide, adult writing still emerged in the new analysis as sensitive to change, vulnerabilities, and shifting dependencies—all of which mattered, for better or worse, to how people experienced writing development and its outcomes. Indeed I hope it will prove an asset to theory development that individuals in this study had such sustained exposure to powerful processes of writing development across multiple and diverse places and times. At the very least, the fact that the interviews, even unintentionally, contained references to development suggests how deeply developmental processes are embedded in routine writing experiences and self-reflection about them.

Workplaces as Sites of Writing and Human Development

In contemporary workplaces, writing is both a means and an end of production. Particularly as the country's economic base has shifted over the last seventy years away from the manufacturing of things and toward the providing of services, writing has become a dominant form of labor for millions of Americans. In many public and private concerns, written texts are the only products made. It is not unusual for people in many occupations to spend three, five, eight, or more hours a day with their hands on keyboards and their minds on audiences. As a result, the development of writing—as a human resource and a transactional product—has come to be built into the structures and processes of many businesses and institutions, embedded in routine activities of planning, production, and oversight. It is through these larger productive efforts that individual writing development emerges—not as an explicit goal of the workplace but as a by-product or residue of work, as people labor to write in rhetorically consequential conditions with powerful technologies at hand and with regular invitations to reflect, revise, and talk about writing. In these conditions, people find their writing literacy shaped and often amplified by the economic, political, and cultural power of the groups for whom and with whom they work. But, in these conditions, access to instruction, opportunity, and reward for writing are stratified as a matter of economic principle—dependent on one's position in the production process—and also highly susceptible to disruption, change, and, of course, cessation, as workplaces adapt (or not) to shifting economic, technological, and political conditions. Workplaces, then, provide especially clear windows into the powerful yet often fragile ecological processes that feed and condition writing development.

The Role of Roles in Workplace Writing

One of the main tenets of life-course scholarship is that human development is catalyzed and modulated by the social roles one plays or is expected to play across the lifespan (Bronfenbrenner, 1979; Elder & Giele, 2009; Kohli, 1986; Sørensen, 1986). Roles situate people in particular activities and sets of obligations or cultural regimes that demand, invite, or suppress particular kinds of growth and experience. While often congruent with certain stages of life (i.e., youth, middle age, old age) the multiple and simultaneous roles most people play in families, communities, and workplaces condition developmental trajectories and possibilities even as they interact with one another. Roles in some sense are opportunity structures for development and, as such, are one of the biggest sources of developmental variation and stratification.

As a lens for approaching writing development, role lends much conceptual assistance. The role(s) one occupies at work position writers within particular hierarchies or networks of production; dictate the amount and timing and genres of their writing; set the audiences they address; and determine the convoys of other writers with whom they move, among other variables. Roles also have implications for gaining access or not to tools, assistance, learning, and feedback that can matter to writing development. Roles are not static. In the workplace, promotions, staff reductions, reorganization, the arrival of new technologies and other innovations—not to mention the loss or change of jobs— can alter work roles and the role of writing in work. Roles are often the prisms through which general events in the immediate or global environment are refracted into an individual's writing context. In sum, roles are one of the major sources of dynamism and contingency in adult workplace writing development.

Consider the following observation of Anne Schmidt, who, when I interviewed her in 2005, was 36 years old and running her own one-person freelance writing business. Over the previous fourteen years she had held five different positions in both mid-sized and large organizations in the East and Midwest, working as a technical writer or editor in the areas of media, software, finance, and academia. Here Schmidt recalls her first full- time job out of college. For one year in the early 1990s, she was on the staff of a national optometry trade journal in New York City. "My job," she explained, "was to write little blurby pieces, captions, feature articles, that kind of work" and went on to disclose the role of roles in workplace writing.

I was the low person when I started out. Above me there were other people who wrote their own stories who had more seniority than I did. They didn't particularly oversee what I did. But supervising the staff was an executive editor, a managing editor, and also an editor-in-chief. The executive editor did the first-level edit and proofreading. The managing editor took care of the production part of it. And the editor-in-chief signed off on all the galleys. She and I had a very close relationship. She sat two desks away from me and I could talk to her. If I had a concern about a piece of information I was trying to communicate I would bring it to her attention. So we would collaborate on that sort of thing all the time. But often I was in a position of being asked to do a final proofing of everybody's work at the galley stage. This editor would come to me and say that she would like another set of eyes on this and she trusted me to do that. So I often ended up proofreading my own work and everybody else's too.

This description makes obvious how roles are partly structural. Schmidt entered a production hierarchy where tasks were segmented by job title and where writing assignments were meted out in part by seniority. But roles also can be emergent, stemming from conditions and relationships particular to a setting. These conditions can be material; for instance, the positioning of desks seems integral to the tutor-tutee roles that developed between Schmidt and her editor. But they also can be political, as when Schmidt says she was "in a position of being asked" to help the editor with proofreading. So while occupying a structural role as "the low person," Schmidt's collaborative relationship with the chief editor brought a reciprocal obligation. As a result, she crossed the usual organizational lines and gained some oversight over other people's work, as well as her own.

This recollection also shows how even structural roles at work share something of the characteristics of the people who occupy them. Being the "low person" often means being one of the younger people in a setting, part of a complex power dynamic that is associated with any workplace role. This dynamic can invite pedagogical overtures from more seasoned employees but it also sometimes means getting assignments that other people do not want to do. One interviewee described how, in his early years working in the petroleum department of Citibank, he was made to ghostwrite a condolence letter that was to be addressed from the bank president to the widow of a major client. "The head of the department didn't want to do it so it went all around and way down to the lowest guy in the room," he recalled. At the same time, people of younger age can be perceived to have some advantages over older or more entrenched staff, especially when it comes to knowledge of emerging technology. Here is Schmidt again discussing how she gained her first exposure to desktop publishing while interning, along with her college roommate, at a public television production company:

> One day they said we need somebody to lay out a thirty-page training manual for a session we are having next week, and this is the kind of thing that often fell on interns to do. So my roommate and I took an afternoon off and she showed me everything she knew about how to do desktop publishing. This was back in 1989 when nobody was really doing it. And there is a theme here. Most of what I know how to do has come to me that way.

For people in "higher" positions, the stakes that surround so much workplace writing and the potential for liability if something goes wrong often shape the oversight and mentoring roles they take toward less experienced or subordinate staff. "We have more on the line," explained a senior partner in a midsized accounting firm as to why he and the other partners undertook all the document review, "in case something would get us in trouble or something." Here other supervisors describe the delicate teaching dimensions that accompany their oversight of subordinates' writing, a responsibility that requires metalanguage for writing as well as sensitivity to writing egos:

> If somebody hands me something, I will edit it and go back to their desk or say, here, I made a couple of changes. In some cases I'll say let's do it this way. It's not like I'm gathering people around me and saying here is how we're going to write, although I don't think that's a bad idea. (government unit head)

> I don't use a red pen. I don't highlight. But I suggest. And it might be something like, if I were writing this, I don't think I'd send this out in this form. Look at this. There was a time in my

life when I would have underlined it. I don't do that anymore. (branch manager of a brokerage)

I use a couple of different feedback methods depending on the person. I either sit down with them and review the document, point out some things to them, or I will print the document and put some notes on it and send an email with some feedback. (social service director)

But such give-and-take review was not available in all work environments. Especially where people worked in small or under-funded enterprises, and perhaps where stakes were lower, review of writing was less common. A librarian at a historical society, for instance, discussed how even in the first weeks of his job he was on his own to respond to researchers who inquired about the collections: "In some libraries it was common for supervisors to read letters before they went out but we never had enough people for that." Another interviewee recalled being hired early in his career to write user documentation for a financially failing weather-graphics company: "I made vain attempts to get people to review my work," he said. "Rarely would they read it. But that was okay because customers weren't going to read it either. So if it was wrong it didn't matter."

So roles are partly structural and official. But they also partly partake of the contingent material conditions of the workplaces and their comparative relationships to a wider economy (see Mayer, 2009). Roles also partake of the sociological relationships among individuals who occupy them, including the stereotypical expectations that might be placed on individuals by virtue of their age, race, gender, or standing in a wider society. For writers from groups that are often negatively stereotyped or stigmatized, these expectations can register as differential treatment leading to a sense of heightened pressure. A Latina police detective, aware that some of the people who read her work "might not think I can produce," paid careful attention to her reports. "I try to do them as best I can because sometimes that is all people will see and I'll be judged by that." Her writing efforts could blunt what she saw as gender and race bias. As a result of the care she took, she said, "I probably write better than a lot of other people around here." An African American business professional discussed a cycle of pressure under which he wrote: "I think I have been very effective but the more effective you are, the more people expect of you. The more effective you are, the more you attain goals and achieve them, the more people will raise the bar. And it's not like people say, that's great. They just raise it again."

Roles, then, and their interactions lend a crucial lens through which to observe writing experience and development. In the broad life course, those I interviewed played a breadwinner role for themselves and dependents; writing at work was a requirement of that general role. But the writing roles they played at work were particular, stratified, fraught, formative, and elastic. Roles position people within sets of formal responsibilities, organizational arrangements, material and political conditions, reciprocating collegial relationships, and cultural biases and changes, among other variables, all of which can shape writing experience and invite and constrain growth. Workplace writing roles and their fluid configurations in different locations introduce inevitable variation into the course of writing development, even as individuals may hold similar job titles or compose in similar genres across contexts or have similar career trajectories. Indeed when we look closely enough we can see that what people write and how they write it will embody an interpretation of role—what it calls for and what it makes possible or not at the time of composition—contributing to individual variation in writing. As the discussion moves to additional processes that feed and condition adult writing development at work, the role of role will continue to be visible in the dynamic.

Historical Times and Timing

One of the most valuable contributions of life-course development research is the way it attends to history, time, and life stage as material influences on human development. In his pioneering studies of children raised during the Great Depression and men inducted into the military during World War II, the developmental sociologist Glen Elder showed how major historical events—and the social disruption and change they can engender—matter (and can matter differently) to individual life outcomes. Life trajectories and possibilities are nested in interactions between historical time and developmental time (i.e., one's place in the aging process and in the social process). Through his use of longitudinal survey data, Elder documented how the younger a child was when the Depression hit and the older an inductee was when drafted into the military, the more disruptive these events were likely to be on his or her subsequent social, educational, and economic development, in some cases lingering negatively for years to come.

Elder's interest is in how disruptive historical events take people out of their expected life trajectories and put them on a changed path. Many younger children of the Depression were forced to enter the labor market early, forgoing opportunities for additional schooling that older siblings had attained. During the Second World War, older draftees were forced to leave the labor market, interrupting careers and in many cases disrupting the economic well-being of their children and spouses, challenges that affected younger inductees much less.

As Elder's research demonstrates, when events change the life script, considerable adaptation is required. Certainly these themes could be found among the people I interviewed when it came to technological changes that began to disrupt writing practices in the late 1970s and 1980s and continued into the 1990s and beyond. Those of a certain age who had made considerable investment in the practices and technologies of traditional print culture found their literacy skills becoming inadequate if not maladaptive. Many adapted (often with the support of employers who embraced the changes); others did not. Several of those I interviewed lost jobs or were reassigned or fitfully embarked on new learning and relearning during the especially tumultuous years of early personal computing and the emergence of the Internet (for more on this experience, see Selfe & Hawisher, 2004). Some felt they never adequately adapted, including a lawyer, born in 1962, who discussed her research processes, saying: "I can get a lot of statutes and federal materials online now. It saves our firm a lot of money. But I still have a hard time finding them. It is much easier conceptually to do it in the books. I've always been better researching in the books." For several of the older professional men I interviewed, their inability to type was turned from a privilege of status into a dysfunctional drawback as writing technologies changed, gender expectations changed, and work environments became more fast-paced and competitive. In his mid-fifties, the branch manager of a financial advising firm enrolled in a night class in keyboarding at his local community college. He explained:

> Guys like me have been lucky by surrounding ourselves with smart women who did stuff for us. But my associate is so good she can't waste her time doing what I should be doing. She should be using her full skills, not doing menial things that I can't do. It's just not efficient. But typing is laborious. I'm still not very good at it.

While Elder directs our attention to age differentiation within cultural upheaval to show the influence of history and time in human development, these processes are in fact broad and diffused. All of the accounts I collected about people's writing lives are drenched in historical particularity, demonstrating how trajectories of individual writing development relate to larger cultural and economic developments with which they meld. In other words, writers and their times develop together and with mutual impact. If, as Elder (1994, p. 5) has observed, historical sensitivity helps us see "the impact of changing societies on developing lives," it also helps us see the impact of developing lives on changing societies. So just as we must look at how people of different ages intersect with historical trends, the age of historical trends at the time of the intersection will also matter to developmental trajectories. This is especially true given the technological changes that have helped condition the transformation of writing into a form of mass labor and have catalyzed new capacities of writing for identity formation and political activity. Within these general transformations, the timing of economic and cultural developments and individual writing careers converge.

Consider the remarkable case of Margaret Warrick, who fell into a writing-intense career in the 1970s, as US corporations began pouring new investments into upgrading the training of staff, a transformative process that became critical to competition among technical and other knowledge-reliant industries in this era. Warrick, who had been born in 1951, graduated from college in 1972 with a degree in elementary education. After taking what she thought would be a temporary summer position within a national telephone company, she was suddenly plucked from her desk and reassigned to the training department, which was undergoing reorganization. She recalled:

> Training was lacking. It was all lecture-based and done by people who used to do the jobs themselves. They knew it was inadequate. So they began grabbing up any employee who had any knowledge at all about education and sending us to classes in adult education. The salaries they were paying for trainers in the corporate world were almost double what teachers were being paid so it was good for me to stay there.

Warrick indeed stayed in this field for most of the rest of her career, although she moved over time from the telephone company to a mutual-fund company and eventually to the headquarters of a national trade organization for credit unions. There she took charge of producing educational materials for thousands of members, boards of directors, and staff. This publishing enterprise, which sold its materials to local credit unions all over the country, remained healthy and busy through the early 1990s. During her more than twenty years in the training field, Warrick was sometimes instructor; sometimes author of instructional material; sometimes researcher of learning effectiveness; a pioneer in organizing and assessing distance education in her field ("it was very antiquated when you look back on it") and eventually executive editor of a commercially successful line of credit-union publications, producing dozens of books on as many topics with sales exceeding 100,000 copies. "It was an ever-evolving process," she reflected, "because things never did stay the same for any great period of time."

By the time of our interview in the mid-2000s, book sales had sunk, the organization's educational activities had moved on-line, and Warrick had been recruited to a different position: maintaining the integrity of her organization's management software and database. Interestingly, her new position was created out of the odd millennial crisis known as Y2K, a reference to a glitch in the coding of computers' calendar systems that people feared would wreak havoc worldwide when the century ended. She explained:

So in 1999 when Y2K was coming around the corner they realized that the software we were running was not Y2K-compliant
and, besides, the CFO had a new concept for how to run the
association. So they pulled me out of education and put me in
charge of the transition from the legacy software to the new
software. So these days I do a lot more writing of procedures—
here is exactly what you need to do to run a report, how to get
that information you need and understand it. I write for senior
vice presidents and I write for clerks. My writing has changed
so much. No more examples and lengthy descriptions. It needs
to be quick to read and cleared of clutter. Now that I think
about it, it is such a swing.

As we can see, the forms of Warrick's writing are stimulated,
sustained, and repurposed as a function of the economic histories
of the institutions in which she works. As corporations strive
to grow, compete, and transform, they recruit and develop the
mental and scribal skills of employees in particular ways. Warrick was not the only individual I interviewed who found herself
writing as part of an emergent enterprise that required her to
invent writing procedures and even text types from scratch. A
man I interviewed, born in 1934, who ran an advertising agency,
remembered teaching himself how to write and produce live
television commercials as TV and TV advertising emerged in the
1950s. Another man I interviewed, born in 1946, worked for the
credit-card department of a major bank that was international-
izing in the 1970s. He traveled to Europe and South America to
enlist bank customers. With limited language skills, handwritten
notes, ad hoc banking forms, and a telex machine, he tried to
build a workable infrastructure for credit exchange. Interestingly,
he referred to this task as "heavy writing" (by which he meant
the weight more than the amount).

On the other end of the spectrum, younger people I interviewed, who were born well into the so-called information age,
spoke of the sometimes paralyzing glut of other people's texts that
surround their writing efforts, texts that serve as potential sources
for their writing and also as competitors for attention (Lanham,
2006; Spinuzzi, 2008). Rather than invention of new text types,
the situation seems to call at times for the deconstruction of old
ones. Here a communications specialist for a state government

agency, born in 1981, talks about the potential exhaustion of his bread-and-butter text: the press release.

> Some people say the press release is dead. It could be. I'm not sure. Everybody writes them. Everybody sends them. There is no club you have to join to send out a press release. I am sure with email and fax the news organizations get more of them than they know what to do with. So maybe from that standpoint the formalized here's-the-story press release might be going away and maybe there will be more of an emphasis on building relationships and feeding [reporters] raw materials. Hey, we're doing this and that. Here's some really neat stuff. Maybe it's not formalized as a press release.

Historical processes and events (and especially the ongoing history of literacy itself) shape the horizons of writing develop-ment both as a shared cultural resource and as an individual set of experiences. As we have seen, these horizons can take their character from forces made up of advancing and receding eco-nomic currents, advancing and receding writing technologies, and advancing and receding genres, among other factors. Anyone's writing development will bear these (and other) striations of history.

Economic forces are vital to these processes but are not the only factors that matter. Cultural and political developments are also consequential to the literacy life course. Particularly given their collective character, cultural and political movements in dif-ferent historical times help to organize social convoys of people who develop their literacy together within a particular historical horizon of consciousness.

As but one example, LGBTQIA visibility and activism in the late twentieth and early twenty-first centuries have been broadly influential in this regard (Pritchard, 2016). One woman I inter-viewed, Stella Kind, explained to me how her writing development rested inside a local instantiation of the queer rights movement, an organization that was using writing and performance to sup-port individuals in the process of coming out. When I interviewed Kind in 2012, she was 25 years old and working as a bank teller, but our conversations turned quickly to the writing she was do-ing outside of work. From childhood Kind had written fiction, poetry, and screenplays, and had pursued a creative writing degree in college. But her creative development had recently taken a significant leap after she joined an LGBTQIA narrative activist-writers' group that had organized several years previously in her local community. Group meetings, where she said she found unconditional acceptance for the first time in her life, were giving her the courage to write explicitly as a lesbian. The group, which Kind called "family," consisted of writers, musicians, artists, teachers, and others who shared their works in progress and were coauthoring a collaborative, mixed-genre book for use by other LGBTQIA narrative groups. Kind explained that whereas, as a younger person, she had often restricted her writing to what she called "fantasy" and "escapist" genres, she was now venturing into riskier, more meaningful nonfiction prose that she intended to publish. Here we can see both the critical role of social convoys and the way that writing development, like human development overall, involves a changed relationship between a person and a wider society, with implications for both going forward. She said:

> Part of my growing as a person has been to share really vulnerable parts of myself with other people and realize that they will love me on the other side of it. And I think that the difference between my writing now versus even two years ago is that I think I have seen how rewarding it is to share myself with other people and have them understand more about me, understand more about themselves, understand more about the world. So one thing that I feel that my writing is doing is helping people, whether that is by seeing that someone who identifies as queer is worthy of love and kindness and compassion and isn't just a piece of gum on the bottom of somebody's shoe, or by learning more about how gender is complex and not binary. But if I didn't have the group supporting me, I wouldn't be able to write what I am writing now.

Perhaps more acutely than any other tool of life-course analysis, historical perspectives illuminate how writing development is a contextual and relational phenomenon, suspended in material and interactional processes and efforts that are dynamic, contingent, collectively produced, and mutually sustained. Our capacity to write cannot be found in us: it lies between—in our relationships to the contexts through which we live. The historical events that are part of these contexts serve as powerful magnets, organizing and disrupting the timing and paths of writing development. Through historical awareness, literacy researchers can learn much about how economic, cultural, and political networks in particular times (and places) will carry, feed, divert, expand, contract, reroute, make possible, make impossible, in short, delineate anyone's literacy life course.

Dispositions for Writing Development

This final section returns to the brilliant research of developmental psychologist Urie Bronfenbrenner, whose ecological perspective on human growth brings attention to how individuals contribute to their own psychological development. At various ages and stages, beginning from birth, individuals work deliberately, selectively, and progressively with their environments, human and nonhuman, to gain what they need for social learning and psychological growth, using what Bronfenbrenner (2004, p. 97) calls "developmentally instigative characteristics" of their personhood to fulfill these efforts. Of course, because environments will vary in their capacity and manner of response to these characteristics, such attempts will have unpredictable and varied developmental outcomes for individuals and environments. Still, Bronfenbrenner calls on life-course researchers to pay rigorous, systematic and comparative attention to what individuals are doing in their contexts that have developmental implications, including how they use cumulative experience to formulate and apply beliefs about how to progress. He calls these orientations structuring proclivities or, more generally, dispositions. While dispositions overlap with more traditional psychological concepts like motivation, efficacy, or personality, they are always constituted in interactions. Dispositions often gather continuity and stability over time; yet they are an ever-renewing coproduction of persons and their lifeworlds—constituted out of inner and outer resources, permeable, dynamic, and performative. Human development, then, is associated with an ability to solicit support for one's growth from the environment and to coordinate one's own development with the development of others.

While Bronfenbrenner focused on young children and their interactions in contexts of caregiving, his concepts lend fascinating direction for theories of writing development across the lifespan. What are psychological characteristics that enhance writing development at different stages of life? In what kinds of contexts do they emerge? Concomitantly, what characteristics of writing development enhance personal development over time and in what kinds of contexts do they emerge? Systematic answers to these questions must await further ecologically oriented writing research. (For important leads, see Herrington & Curtis, 2000.)

Here I am able to offer only rudimentary and exploratory observations about writing dispositions as they arose, by happenstance, as ancillary or implied topics in the interviews. This section in fact depends on a serendipitous aspect of the original interview project by which some of the participants chose to range widely over their pasts—including childhood experiences—in order to address basic interview questions about how they learned to do their workplace writing. In other (also serendipitous) cases, interviewees chose to expand narratively in their answers to basic demographic questions having to do with the work histories of earlier generations or their own educational histories. Where these elaborations occurred, interviews provided glimpses into formative and enduring aspects of writing development. In this analysis, as incomplete as it must be, I tried to capture references to dispositions that people said they brought from other contexts into their workplace writing as well as dispositions that they said developed from force of writing at work that then carried over into other aspects of life.

As with the experience of the grant writer with whom this chapter began, several of the people I interviewed linked their interests or skills in writing to formative childhood experiences at home or school. Two men, one a public information officer for a high-profile municipal police department and the other a policy analyst for the human resources department in a large institution, both linked their orientations to writing to the adaptations they made as children when they were forced by family circumstances to move around a lot. Here the police officer reflects on his experience as a child of divorce, who lived intermittently with his mother in the South and his father in the North, and its impact on his adult ability to communicate with a wide range of people in his public writing:

> I really think I'm the person I am because I had to adapt to different school environments, different people, and just a whole different set of circumstances. I was a kid having to make some adult-type adaptations. As time went on, moving didn't scare me and it didn't detract from my ability to do what I needed to do. It was definitely one of those developmental plusses. So it helps me now when I must write to a wide audience with different educational levels and backgrounds, that 80-year-old grandpa or that 16-year-old high school student who is assigned by his teacher to read the paper. My audience is not just local. It expands out across the United States and even internationally. So I have to be conscious of that too.

Below a human resources planner talks about a relationship between his childhood background and the writing niche he developed in his department, specializing in what he referred to as "change management." Having lived in five different states by the time he was 13 because of his father's employment changes, he now writes texts that guide employees through new policies and procedures or departmental reorganizations:

> If I send out an email, right in the first paragraph I will say that I recognize this is going to be difficult for you or I understand that this is going to be a challenge and that we are trying to do everything we can to minimize that. I try to talk at a certain level. I try not to condescend. But I think it starts with acknowledging the difficulty. I learned to do that by moving around so much, constantly finding myself in new situations where you have to take the lay of the land and be sensitive to people's emotional and psychological position, where they are coming from. I don't think it was ever a conscious thing but I just got very used to it and it almost became second nature.

This idea of a second nature for writing arose in other interviews as well, sometimes attributed to language environments in early childhood households as well as to a growing sense of a match between background experiences and certain kinds of writing. In the following fascinating assessment of her ability to carry out her workplace writing, a 36-year-old governmental policy analyst discusses the deep, interflowing origins of her writing disposition:

> I can't say that I ever consciously learned to do this kind of writing. It probably had something to do with growing up with parents who had a wide range of interests and strong backgrounds in writing. I was always being asked: Why did that happen? You did something. It didn't come out the way you wanted it to. Why not? So I became the kind of person who thought ahead of the consequences of my actions. My mom says I am a jack of all trades and master of none but by having that broad, diverse background you're able to start to see where things have some similarities or where they touch on each other and what's the tangential relationship of things and then you can kind of start to form the broad, overarching view of how the interrelatedness works and then you have to try to somehow concisely put that on paper. I think that's why in general I tend to think about things for a long period of time but write for a short period of time because I'm spending my time forming those relationships.

All of these accounts together provide insight into how early life experiences can be creatively transformed into productive orientations to writing (see Gonzáles, Moll, & Amanti, 2005). These experiences range far wider than what we normally think of as literacy experiences, even though they hold the seeds for writing. As a result of childhood experiences, these writers gathered to themselves enduring feelings, realizations, habits of mind, and sets of commitments that—when given the opportunity—could be melded into dispositions for particular kinds of writing and writing careers and turned into particular writing strategies. Certainly their accounts force an expansion of what is considered transfer in writing, as not merely an ability to carry over writing experiences from one context to another or to translate background knowledge from one task to the next but rather a more abstract ability to turn raw experiences into "structuring proclivities" for literacy learning and, indeed, textuality itself. As a field we need to continue to expand the search (and what we consider searchable) for the psychological processes that make up life-to-writing transformations, transfers, and amalgamations. And we need to recognize that what may well be at the center of writing development are opportunities to seek and find one's second nature in the world of writing.

Before leaving the topic of writing dispositions, however, attention turns to an inverse process by which writing orientations developed through workplace practice are incorporated into a person's more general dispositions toward life. While in the standard interview protocol I asked people how their workplace writing might influence writing, reading, or speaking in other arenas of life, some people chose to answer more generally, addressing how their work and work writing affected them as people. In these usually short and offhand remarks are glimpses into how routine daily engagement with powerful institutional or professional dispositions embodied in work roles, genres, and production processes get under the skin, so to speak. Talking about the imprint that fact-based writing had on the way he engaged with friends and even family, an FBI agent remarked: "It's just habit-forming. If you do something for ten hours a day it is going to carry over into the rest of your life." The software manager encountered earlier in this article said the technical process-base of her current writing "makes me left-brained in the way I manage the household, negotiate an airport or a foreign country, how I put together IKEA furniture, how I learn or how I encounter any situation that is new to me. That process is just so engrained." A policy analyst who had been studying environmental issues for the past five years as part of her job responsibilities observed: "The more you learn about a subject, the more you start seeing things. Once you learn about nonpoint pollution and the fact that cows should not be standing in a stream the less you start seeing nice pastoral scenes and the more you are like, get those cows out of the stream. In some ways you know more than you want to." Relatedly and unsurprisingly, several people told me that their political viewpoints had changed as a result of the writing they did at work. Here a longtime executive budget officer explains:

> The work I do on state budgets has made me more moderate in some ways politically. You start to realize how difficult the process is, how complicated, the sheer number of deserving people and social institutions and costs. As a child of the sixties you begin to realize that some of the solutions people thought

up then were simple-minded. The people I related to then would scare the hell out of me now.

But the most mentioned impact of workplace writing was on general language dispositions, particularly as they pertained to interactions with family. The care that must be taken with language at work, the thought that must go into it, seems to carry over into habits of personal interaction. Here are two typical examples: "I would say I'm more conscious of what I am saying and how I am saying it," explained a finance clerk. "I take more time to think about my words instead of just blurting out whatever is on my mind. It may partly be age and maturity but I think my work has helped my communication skills with my husband." The public information officer for a police department said: "I am more thoughtful now. I used to shoot from the hip with comments or the way I'd react to things. Now due to the writing, and talking with the media, there is more thought put into what I'm saying, whether it's in this job or at home."

This has been a brief foray into relationships between human development and writing development as they pertain to the emergence of adult writing dispositions. Though the evidence presented here is scanty, it does point us, as ecological theory would suggest, to look for interanimating processes by which psychological growth feeds and directs writing growth and vice versa. We have much more searching to do within the experiential and action contexts of the life course to identify these processes, their exact workings, their patterns, and their consequences. But as we find them we will begin to fill in the neglected story of the psychology of mass writing and the contributions it is making right now to social, intellectual, and cultural growth among individuals, families, and societies. We will begin to appreciate the intergenerational, long-term, and deeply contextual origins of writing dispositions. We also may reach clearer understandings of how people at different ages are appropriating life events for literacy growth, and consider how workplaces serve (and fail to serve) the larger projects of individual human growth.

Conclusion

This chapter has examined three fundamental concepts from life-course research—roles, historical timing, and dispositions—that offer generative directions for further research in writing development. Life-course perspectives—social and psychological—expand the lens through which we look *for* and *at* development and encourage a much more relational way of thinking about it. The adult working writer is an accessible figure for exploring the slow-growing, dynamic, fragile dimensions of development because of the contexts in which they work and write across the lifespan. When writing functions as an engine of economic development, as it does in many situations today, writers are necessarily caught up in the propulsion of those forces. Development emerges from particular—and stratified—locations in organizations and from expectations associated with particular jobs and occupations, factors that set the composing conditions that accompany daily writing tasks, including their rhythms, their genres, and the degree of authority and control they offer. At the same time, economic processes rarely stand still, so writing development among working adults will occur in contexts of change and disruption and will require adaptation—conditions that have been especially palpable in the past several decades. The longer the life, the more of this experiential history accumulates, as work, life, and writing shape dispositions and orientations going forward.

While the experience of the adult working writer may not have obvious parallels to that of the student writing in school, it is still worth considering the relevance of these perspectives to the teaching and learning mission. The more narrowly we treat curriculum or classroom context as the focus of inquiry, explanation, or assessment, the more likely we will be missing the dynamic life processes that flow in and around teachers, students, and administrators at school. Developmental gains will be more robust and life-lasting when these processes are recognized, harnessed, and incorporated into what counts as teaching and learning. Among the questions that life-course perspectives have raised in my own mind as a teacher of writing are these: How is my students' development related to the institution where we teach and learn? How is my students' development related to my own development as a writer and teacher? Where do my areas of underdevelopment influence shared experiences and outcomes? How and when do students enter into one another's writing development and with what effects? How do teacher and student locations in the life course and in historical times matter to what is happening in the classroom? How do social-age expectations function as resources or hindrances in our work together? What roles are available to students when they write? What kinds of dispositions are invited to take shape? How do their interpretations of those available roles and dispositions matter to writing performance? How does writing development register as change in the world of the classroom and beyond?

References

Antonucci, T. C., Fiori, K. L., Birditt, K., & Jackey, L. M. H. (2010). Convoys of social relations: Integrating life-span and life-course perspectives. In M. E. Lamb & A. M. Freund (Eds.), *Handbook of life-span development: Vol. 2. Social and emotional development* (pp. 434–73). New York: Wiley.

Brandt, D. (2015). *The rise of writing: Redefining mass literacy.* Cambridge, UK: Cambridge University Press.

Bronfenbrenner, U. (1979). *The ecology of human development: Experiments by nature and design.* Cambridge, MA: Harvard University Press.

Bronfenbrenner, U. (2004). *Making human beings human: Bioecological perspectives on human development.* Thousand Oaks, CA: SAGE.

Cohler, B. J., & Hostetler, A. (2004). Linking life course and life story: Social change and the narrative study of lives over time. In J. T. Mortimer & M. J. Shanahan (Eds.), *Handbook of the life course* (pp. 555–78). New York: Springer.

Elder, G. H., Jr. (1994). Time, human agency, and social change: Perspectives on the life course. *Social Psychology Quarterly, 57*(1): 4–15.

Elder, G. H., Jr. (1998). The life course as developmental theory. *Child Development, 69*(1): 1–12.

Elder, G. H., Jr. (1999). *Children of the Great Depression: Social change in life experience.* 25th anniversary ed. Boulder, CO: Westview Press.

Elder, G. H., Jr., & Conger, R. D. (2000). *Children of the land: Adversity and success in rural America.* Chicago: University of Chicago Press.

Elder, G. H., Jr., & Giele, J. Z. (2009). Life course studies: An evolving field. In G. H. Elder, Jr., & J. Z. Giele (Eds.), *The craft of life course research* (pp. 1–24). New York: Guilford Press.

Elder, G. H., Johnson, M. K., & Crosnoe, R. (2004). The emergence and development of life course theory. In J. T. Mortimer & M. J. Shanahan (Eds.), *Handbook of the life course* (pp. 3–22). New York: Springer.

Elder, G. H., Jr., & Rockwell, R. C. (1979). The life-course and human development: An ecological perspective. *International Journal of Behavioral Development, 2*(1), 1–21.

Gonzáles, N., Moll, L. C., & Amanti, C. (Eds.). (2005). *Funds of knowledge: Theorizing practice in households, communities, and classrooms.* Mahwah, NJ: Erlbaum.

Heinz, W. R., & Krüger, H. (2001). Life course: Innovations and challenges for social research. *Current Sociology, 49*(2), 29–45.

Herrington, A. J., & Curtis, M. (2000). *Persons in process: Four stories of writing and personal development in college.* Urbana, IL: National Council of Teachers of English.

Kohli, M. (1986). Social organization and subjective construction of the life course. In A. B. Sørensen, F. E. Weinert, & L. R. Sherrod (Eds.), *Human development and the life course: Multidisciplinary perspectives* (pp. 271–92). Hillsdale, NJ: Erlbaum.

Lanham, R. A. (2006). *The economics of attention: Style and substance in the age of information.* Chicago: University of Chicago Press.

Mayer, K. U. (2003). The sociology of the life course and lifespan psychology: Diverging or converging pathways? In U. M. Staudinger & U. Lindenberger (Eds.), *Understanding human development: Dialogues with lifespan psychology* (pp. 463–82). New York: Springer.

Mayer, K. U. (2009). New directions in life course research. *Annual Review of Sociology, 35*, 413–33.

Moen, P., & Hernandez, E. (2009). Social convoys: Studying linked lives in time, context, and motion. In G. H. Elder, Jr., & J. Z. Giele

(Eds.), *The craft of life course research* (pp. 258–79). New York: Guilford Press.

Mortimer, J. T., & Shanahan, M. J. (2004). *Handbook of the life course.* New York: Springer.

Pritchard, E. D. (2016). *Fashioning lives: Black queers and the politics of literacy.* Carbondale: Southern Illinois University Press.

Selfe, C. L., & Hawisher, G. E. (2004). *Literate lives in the information age: Narratives of literacy from the United States.* Mahwah, NJ: Erlbaum.

Settersten, R. A., Jr. (2004). Age structuring and the rhythm of the life course. In J. T. Mortimer & M. J. Shanahan (Eds.), *Handbook of the life course* (pp. 81–102). New York: Springer.

Sørensen, A. B. (1986). Social structure and mechanisms of life-course processes. In A. B. Sørensen, F. E. Weinert, & L. R. Sherrod (Eds.), *Human development and the life course: Multidisciplinary perspectives* (pp. 177–97). Hillsdale, NJ: Erlbaum.

Sørensen, A. B., Weinert, F. E., & Sherrod, L. R. (1986). *Human development and the life course: Multidisciplinary perspectives.* Hillsdale, NJ: Erlbaum.

Spinuzzi, C. (2008). *Network: Theorizing knowledge work in telecommunications.* New York: Cambridge University Press.

Sroufe, L. A., Egeland, B., Carlson, E. A., & Collins, W.A. (2005). *The development of the person: The Minnesota study of risk and adaptation from birth to adulthood.* New York: Guilford Press.

CHAPTER NINE

A Writer(s)-within-Community Model of Writing

STEVE GRAHAM

Arizona State University

This chapter presents a new model of writing that merges sociocultural and cognitive perspectives. It provides a single ideation of how writing is enacted.[1] While other models are possible, including ones that blend cognitive, sociocultural, and other perspectives, new conceptualizations such as this one are useful, as they spark dialogue and new ways of thinking within a discipline (Mitchell, 2003). The chapter further proposes mechanisms that promote development of the two basic units in the model: writing community and writer(s).

The development of this model grew out of a personal dissatisfaction with current models describing writing from either a cognitive or a sociocultural perspective. Available cognitive models mostly ignore cultural, social, political, and historical influences on writing, and devote little attention to specifying the mechanisms that advance writing development (Graham, 2006). Likewise, sociocultural perspectives on writing often "do not speak particularly well to the process of becoming literate" (Perry, 2012, p. 65), and they generally ignore the cognitive and motivational resources writers bring to the task of writing. These criticisms are not meant to distract from the contributions of prior models of writing, but to suggest that a model that embraces both of these perspectives is likely to result in a fuller and richer understanding of writing.

The basic tenet underlying the model presented here is that the community in which writing takes place and the cognitive capabilities and resources of those who create writing simultaneously shape and constrain the creation of written text.[2] In essence, writing involves an interaction between the social context in which it occurs and the mental and physical actions writers are able to enlist and engage. In turn, I propose that writing cannot be fully understood without considering how the communities in which it takes place and those involved in creating it evolve, including how community and individuals reciprocally influence each other.

In presenting the model, I first examine the concept of *writing community* and describe its components and operation, illustrating how they shape and bind what is written. Next, I describe the cognitive architecture *writers and their collaborators* bring to the act of composing, specifying the components of this architecture and how they interact to shape and constrain text production. While I describe the cognitive architecture of writers and collaborators separate from the description of writing community, this should not be taken to imply that they are somehow disconnected. What members of the writing community bring to the act of writing is an integral part and resource of the writing community.

After describing the concept of writing community and the cognitive architecture of its writing members, I provide an example of how features of the writing community and writers' cognitive capabilities and intentions work in tandem. Finally, I propose mechanisms that promote change in writing communities and the capabilities of writers within the community.

The Writing Community

The model presented here assumes that writing is inherently a social activity, situated within a specific context (i.e., writing community). This is consistent with the view that writing is a socialized activity (Barton, 1991; Hull & Schultz, 2001) that almost always involves multiple people (i.e., author and collaborators, author and readers, the author as own reader). A writing community then is a group of people who share a basic set of goals and assumptions and use writing to achieve their purposes.[3] Moreover, it is a community in which writing takes place. Other activities can occur and can even be more central, but one or more members of the community must engage in writing as part of community pursuits. An example of this is a seventh-grade science class that decides to clean up a local stream polluted by littering, and as part of this endeavor engages in writing designed to highlight the problem and solve it by writing letters to local newspapers and designing flyers encouraging local residents not to pollute the stream.

The basic components of a writing community are described below and their interaction is visually depicted in Figure 9.1. This conceptualization draws heavily on activity theory (Greeno & Engeström, 2014; Lave & Wenger, 1991) and the concept of genre as typified ways of engaging in activities for social purposes (Bazerman, 1994).

Basic Components of a Writing Community

PURPOSE

Purpose involves how writing is used within a community (e.g., Shanahan, Shanahan, & Misischia, 2011), and includes the goals writing is intended to achieve (e.g., facilitate learning or display knowledge in a college anthropology class), the value of different writing activities to the community (e.g., brevity and accuracy in writing is valued in many businesses), norms for what constitutes specific types of writing (e.g., prized attributes and evaluative criteria), stance/identity the community wants to project (e.g., *Mad Magazine* projects an irreverent persona), and the audience that is the object of the community's intentions.

In some instances, the purpose of writing in a community is singular, as when an adolescent is charged with tweeting parents periodically to give updates on activities or location. In other instances, the purposes are broader and more varied, as is the case with a newspaper in which writing is used to report daily events, shape opinions, and entertain. Purposes can further range in intent from communities like the Iowa Writers' Workshop, where the primary purpose is to become a better writer, to a blogging community focusing on fostering and maintaining social connections and friendships, to a fan fiction site where members share a common passion.

MEMBERS (INCLUDING WRITERS AND COLLABORATORS)

Members of a writing community include those who compose text (writers and collaborators)[4] as well as those who serve as an audience for it (Cameron, Hunt, & Linton, 1996). In some writing communities, one or more individuals may serve as mentors who help others acquire the cognitive skills, knowledge, dispositions, strategies, and modes of action needed to successfully achieve the communities' writing goals (Freedman, Hull, Higgs, & Booten, 2016). In a school setting this can be a teacher. At work it might involve one or more colleagues. At home it is usually another family member.

Membership in a writing community can vary considerably, ranging from small, as when a married couple write love notes to each other, to much larger, as when friends communicate via social media. It can further range from exclusive, as when restricted to a college writing class, to more inclusive, such as an Internet forum site open to all.

Members can differ in their familiarity with the purposes and practices of the community. Some members may be new to the group, or sporadic participants, while others may be quite knowledgeable and regularly involved. Additionally, members of a community can differ in their identities as writers, presumed value to the community, and level of commitment and affiliation (Freedman et al., 2016).

Roles and responsibilities of members also differ (Kalman, 1996). For instance, a supervisor may assign different people to write specific sections of a report or allow them to decide how to distribute the workload. As this example illustrates, how power is distributed can affect how a writing community operates (see also Moje & Lewis, 2007). A writing community can have a hierarchical structure, as is common in schools, where an adult assumes the role of teacher. Or the power structure can be more horizontal, as when writers voluntarily come together to act as sounding boards for one another's writing.

Tools

The tools a community employs to accomplish writing tasks vary between and within communities (Yancey, 2009). They can range from paper and pencil to a digital writing tool such as a word processor. It is now possible to write via hand, dictation, typewriter, word processor, or speech synthesizer, to name some of the more prominent options (Gabrial, 2008). Some of the newer writing tools make it possible to produce compositions with text, narration, pictures, and videos. Others such as the Internet provide ready tools for acquiring information for writing, soliciting help from other writers, and sharing the final product broadly.

A writing community can also elect to use one or more writing tools that provide specific assistance to writers (Morphy & Graham, 2012), such as spellchecking or automated essay scoring. A digital writing workbench developed by a team at the Center for Applied Special Technology (http://www.cast.org/) that included Tracey Hall and me provides an example of a tool with multiple forms of assistance. This Web-based tool includes production options that allow students to create single or multimodal versions of their writing plans or paper through typed text, drawn images, or recorded narration. The tool further divides the writing process into distinct stages (e.g., planning, drafting, revising, and editing), providing options to assist writers at each stage of writing. These options include mechanisms that help students generate and organize possible writing ideas, videos and descriptions illustrating how to carry out specific writing processes, and methods for acquiring feedback from peers about plans or the composition itself. These forms of assistance distribute the cognitive load of writing, as help is available from the machine, teachers, and peers.

Actions

Actions are the typical practices that a writing community employs to achieve writing objectives (Russell, 1997). These include the activities members of the community commonly engage in to define the writing task; structure the writing environment;

distribute responsibility; carry out the process of composing; and manage the social, motivational, emotional, and physical aspects of writing (including disagreements when necessary). To illustrate, a newspaper develops multiple typified patterns of practice so that it can reliably and efficiently produce a daily or weekly broadsheet. These include practices that reporters use to gather information for articles, the form articles take in different sections of the paper (e.g., international news, business, sports, entertainment, local news, and editorial), decisions by editors of each section on which articles to include and how they are edited, how and where selected articles are positioned and formatted, and how the paper is distributed to the public. Production and dissemination of the paper are further shaped by the values, norms, identities, forms of reasoning, and types of text valued by the newspaper industry at large and said newspaper in particular.

Typified patterns of action that writing communities adopt are best viewed as temporary, subject to change as new circumstances and needs arise (see for example Many, Fyfe, Lewis, & Mitchell, 1996). This means that the boundaries and actions of a particular writing community are not sealed shut, but permeable and flexible.

WRITTEN PRODUCT

As members of a writing community engage in the process of composing they produce written products. This includes completed text and not fully completed text as well as pictures, narration, or videos if these are part of the composition (Moje, 2009).

Written products include not only what is written, but other tangible artifacts writers use while composing such as notes, drawings, past drafts of text, or recordings of an author's ideas for a piece of writing. They also include text, pictures, film, and recorded interviews produced by others, such as a model text to be emulated or a recorded interview that provides content for the envisioned text. These products reside within the writing community, whether they are housed in a physical or a digital environment.

Physical and Social Environments

Writing communities operate in a range of physical and social environments (Jones, 1998; Hsiang & Graham, 2016). This includes almost any physical place where people congregate (e.g., homes, classrooms, offices) as well as digital locales (e.g., email, social media, websites devoted to writing). These locales influence a writing community in multiple ways (Stedman, 2011), as they affect how many members of a community can be present at any given time, the types of tools available to writers, how writing is carried out, and even the goals set by a community (e.g., the reach of a community can be increased by including digital environments).

The social environment involves the relationships among members of the community (i.e., writers, collaborators, audience, and mentors), and includes a variety of factors that may enhance or impede writing, such as the health of the social relationships among community members (Allodi, 2007), members' sense of belonging and affiliation (Brandt, 2001), stereotypical beliefs about community members (Kwok, Ganding, Hull, & Moje, 2016), and how power and autonomy are perceived and enacted (Bazerman, 2016). The social environment can be supportive, neutral, or hostile; pleasant or unpleasant; competitive or cooperative; controlling or self-governing; or any combination of these. It is generally assumed that work in a community is facilitated when the environment is pleasant, supportive, cooperative, and encouraging of choice and agency (Graham, Harris, & Santangelo, 2015). While most of us prefer such conditions, there are many situations, especially at work, where one or more of these attributes is absent, but the goals of the community are still accomplished (Locke, Shaw, Saari, & Latham, 1981).

Collective History

The work carried out by a writing community does not occur by happenstance, but is shaped by a collective history (Schultz & Fecho, 2000). As a community (e.g., a writer and an editor; a college composition class, a police officer writing a crime report) operates over time, its business becomes codified (Bazerman, 2016; Brandt, 2001; Greeno & Engeström, 2014). The types of writing it conducts and its intended audiences become more defined, as do the values, norms, and stances evident in the writing it produces. Selected writing tools become preferred, and the community devises common practices for carrying out the act of composing. The social dimensions of the community also become defined, for better or worse, with members of the community developing specific identities, roles, and responsibilities. By creating a community of members who know how to participate in the same shared practices, this collective history shapes the purposes, actions, tools, environment, and even the membership of the community, and ultimately the writing products produced. The permanence of these regular and recurring practices, however, as well as the narrative underlying the history and purpose of the community, are open to change, from both within and outside (Dyson, 1999; McCarthy, 1994).

Operation of the Components of a Writing Community

Figure 9.1 presents the basic components of the writing community and how they are related to one another. At the center of the figure is a diagram of the way one or more writing goals are accomplished through the use of writing tools and actions to create the desired written product. This is accomplished by members of the community and includes one or more writers and possible collaborators (represented by the first ring moving outward from the center of the figure).

The involvement of multiple members of the writing community, as either writers or collaborators, requires accommodation and coordination if the writing goals are to be accomplished (represented by directional arrows between writers and collaborators in Figure 9.1). For example, if a writer seeks feedback on a first draft of a composition from another community member (i.e., a collaborator), then the writer must be willing to accommodate and consider possible alternatives to the current written product. The feedback from the collaborator must also be provided in a useful form and in a timely way.

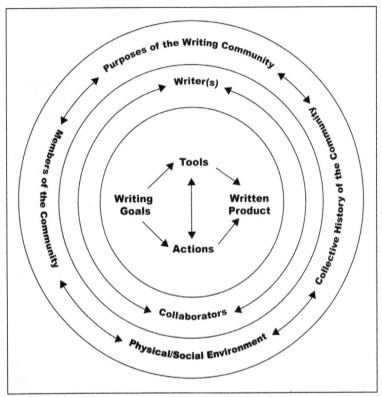

FIGURE 9.1. *Basic components of a writing community.*

How the writer and possible collaborators achieve the desired writing goals through the use of specific writing tools and actions depends on multiple interacting features of the writing community including its purposes, members, physical/social environment, and collective history. This is represented in the outer circle of Figure 9.1 (the arrows illustrate the reciprocal interactions among these features).

First, the desired goals the writer and possible collaborators are trying to achieve through the use of specific tools and actions commonly reflect one or more of the community's central purposes. Writing goals and the resulting written product are further influenced by the kinds of writing the community values as well as its norms, stance/identity, and audience of interest.

Second, who is involved in creating the desired written product depends on members' roles and responsibilities as well as their availability and willingness. Commitment to the community, perceived capabilities, identities as writers or collaborators, and interest in the writing project at hand can further influence who participates. These influencing factors, however, can be ameliorated by how power is distributed among community members, as when a teacher assigns one child to write a text and another to provide feedback on it.

The physical environments in which the community operates affects how many members are likely to engage in a writing activity (e.g., if chairs and desks are not arranged for collaborative work), the types of tools applied (e.g., only paper and pencil are available), as well as the goals and resulting written product (e.g., digital resources allow a diverse audience and multiple forms of text). Likewise, the social context influences writers and collaborators in multiple ways. For instance, members' desire to work together and level of engagement and commitment are influenced by the social climate of the community and the social interactions among its members.

Lastly, the collective history of the writing community not only determines its membership, but gives direction to the types of writing goals members typically undertake, the preferred tools and typified actions used to achieve these objectives, and the form the subsequent written product takes. This collective history further shapes the physical and social dimensions under which members of the community carry out the process of writing.

As this examination of the writing community illustrates, multiple features of this organization and their interactions shape and bind the resulting written product. For example, how writing is conceptualized within a community (i.e., purposes) greatly influences the nature and form of writing. Consider argumentative writing in a biology and in a social studies class. In both classes, students generally apply the same structural components for building an argument (claim, grounds, warrant, support, rebuttal, and qualifications; see Smagorinsky & Mayer, 2014). These components, however, do not necessarily appear in the same form or even to the same degree across these two areas of study (e.g., what counts as legitimate support can differ from one discipline to the next).

I have defined a writing community as a group of people who share a basic set of goals and assumptions and use writing to achieve their purposes, suggesting homogeneity, cooperation, and symmetry. While this may be the case, writing communities as conceptualized here are likely to involve considerable variability in their operation. Within a particular writing community, such as a third-grade classroom, contradictions, disparate elements, conflict, multiple voices, and heterogeneity will exist (Bazerman & Prior, 2005; Swales, 1990). Although most of the members of this classroom may share a common understanding of their and each other's roles and obligations, how to operate within the physical and social confines of the classroom, and how to use specific tools and sanctioned forms of actions to achieve writing objectives, these understandings will not be uniform or consistent across or within individuals. Students will differ in terms of their familiarity with each of these factors as well as their acceptance of them. Relationships between students as well as between teacher and students will fluctuate across situations and time. Further, some students may passively or actively work against the goals of the community by limiting participation or by being disruptive, with some children applying both of these options.

Writing community as envisioned here also involves multiple structural components (e.g., purposes, members, tools, actions, collective history). This should not be interpreted to suggest greater permanence than intended. Writing communities are not static entities, but should be viewed as continually emerging. They can also cease to operate. For instance, a writing community may be short-lived, such as the example provided earlier of an adolescent charged with tweeting parents periodically to give updates on activities or location. With the youngster's increased maturity, the purpose for this community may no longer exist.

While reducing the description of writing community to specific structural components provides a useful means for presenting this construct, it has the potential disadvantage of obscuring its complexity and multiplicity. Each of these components consists of multiple elements that allow for a broad array of interactions and combinations, which are subject to change across time and situations. This allows for considerable variety across and within writing communities.

Finally, any attempt on my part to foreground the concept of writing community does not mean that other socially derived communities are not important. A single writing community coexists with many other communities, including other writing ones. Consequently, writing communities operate across integrated networks (Bazerman & Prior, 2005), and cannot be fully understood in isolation (I will return to this later in the chapter).

Writers and Collaborators

Writing is accomplished by members of the writing community and includes those who compose text (individually or collectively) or collaborate in its construction (e.g., provide direction, give feedback). They are represented in Figure 9.1 as writers and collaborators. This section foregrounds these members of the community to examine how their cognitive capabilities, resources, and intentions also shape writing.

If the writing community is the social context in which writing takes place, then *individual* writers and their collaborators are the keys that turn the engine and initiate the process behind meaning making in writing. The fact that writing takes place in a social context does not mean that it is driven solely by a community's regular and recurring practices, including how writing is conceptualized. Just as writing communities are a driving force behind what is written, so is the agency of individuals (Zimmerman & Risemberg, 1997). I provide two examples below to illustrate this.

One of my favorite examples of agency in writing involves the author and drama critic Robert Benchley (Hendrickson, 1994). As a student at Harvard, he took a final examination where he was asked to discuss how the United States and Great Britain viewed problems that existed in the arbitration of issues surrounding international fisheries. He chose to discuss the problem from the point of view of the fish!

A second example involves Samuel Steward, who ran a tattoo parlor in Chicago while teaching English at Loyola University

(Mulderig, 2015). He wrote a column in the *Illinois Dental Journal* from 1944 to 1949 that had virtually nothing to do with dentistry, addressing topics that ranged from body-building to getting drunk. His writing "gig" started simply enough, with his dentist asking him to write a column for the journal entitled "The Victim's Point of View." While he started off by creating essays that fit the purpose of the column, he soon abandoned this approach to write about things that interested him. He basically hijacked the historical purpose and collective history of the journal to create a venue where he could write about his prejudices, likes and dislikes, and foibles. This does not mean that context did not matter. For example, his articles were shaped by the allowable page length for a paper published in the journal.

The Cognitive Capabilities of Writers and Their Collaborators Shape What Is Written

The two examples above demonstrate a fundamental tenet of the model of writing presented in this chapter. While context shapes and constrains the creation of text and the ultimate form of the written product, it is not the only force at play. Writers and their collaborators make a multitude of decisions that drive and shape what is written. In effect, they exert some degree of agency over the writing process that extends beyond the influence of the writing community. For instance, even when writing is assigned, as often happens in writing communities such as classrooms or at work, the designated writer or writers must decide to undertake the task, determine how much effort to commit, formulate their intentions, determine their ownership over the writing task, decide what cognitive resources to apply, pick what tools to use, and consider how to distribute the various tasks involved in writing (Zimmerman & Risemberg, 1997). These decisions are fueled at the individual level by one's perceived value, utility, and interest in the writing task under consideration; emotional reaction to the writing tasks, motivations for engaging in it; knowledge about the topic, expectations for success, and beliefs about causes of success; dispositions for approaching new tasks, and identities as a writer. It is also influenced by one's beliefs about the value of the writing community as well as one's assumed role, identity, and success in said community.

Writers' and their collaborators' sense of agency, intentions, ownership, values, expectations, and identities, in turn, fuel effort and provide the impetus for drawing on available cognitive resources, regulating the writing process, and executing production procedures. Cognitive resources include acquired knowledge about speaking, listening, and reading as well as specialized knowledge about writing, the topic under consideration, the presumed audience, the writing tools to be used, and knowledge about the purposes and practices of the writing community in question. The use of these resources is initiated and coordinated through control mechanisms that one brings to bear to regulate attention; the writing environment; tools for writing; and the processes involved in planning, producing, and polishing text. These control mechanisms also regulate the motivational beliefs, emotions, personality traits, and physiological factors that influence writers and their collaborators as well as the social situation in which writing takes place. This allows those composing text to engage in production processes including conceptualizing the writing assignment, generating and gathering ideas, translating ideas into acceptable text, transcribing this text onto paper or in digital form, and engaging in reconceptualization with any or all of these production processes.

The beliefs, knowledge, control mechanisms, and production procedures that writers and collaborators bring to a writing task are not always benign. Just like context, they shape the composing process and what is written (Graham, 2006). As we shall see later, development of these cognitive resources is shaped by one's experiences writing in socially derived communities.

Limitations in Cognitive Architecture Shape and Constrain Writing

The writing model presented here is based on the assumption that writing is a cognitively demanding task, and that limitations in humans' cognitive architecture constrain the process of writing. Research with adults demonstrates that writing does "not simply unfold automatically and effortlessly in the manner of a well learned motor skill . . . writing anything but the most routine and brief pieces is the mental equivalent of digging ditches" (Kellogg, 1994, p. 17). Writing is challenging because it is a very complex skill involving the execution and coordination of attention; motor, visual, and executive functioning; memory; and language skills (Hayes, 1996). It is also challenging because the cognitive apparatus we possess has specific limitations (Mayer, 2012; Paas & Sweller, 2014). To illustrate, the cognitive processes we use to process information as we write are limited by how much information can be handled at any given time (about seven elements at a time) and for how long (about twenty seconds without rehearsal). Likewise, while the amount of information we retain over time is quite large, accessing this information is not always an exact process (Torrance, Thomas, & Robinson, 1996).

The capacity problem is especially problematic for writing. There are many competing actions that writers (as well as collaborators) can and often must attend to during writing. Let us consider a writer's creation of a single sentence by hand. The writer must decide what to say. This is shaped by the writer's intentions in writing the sentence in the first place, and requires bringing one or more ideas forward and determining whether they are suitable given the author's intentions, the audience, and the context. The writer must give the idea more precise form by crafting the idea into a grammatically correct sentence, selecting just the right words to convey his or her intentions, make sense to the reader, and be appropriate to the situation at hand and the writing community in which it is created. This sentence must then be transcribed into text where words are spelled correctly and punctuation and capitalization occur according to convention. While doing this, the writer must manage both pencil and paper so that the created text is legible. Failure to adequately attend to these transcription processes increases the risk of the reader's misunderstanding the intended message. This process does not necessarily proceed so neatly, though, as the writer may be refining, reconsidering, and revising the idea and intentions throughout the process as well as constructing, transcribing, and reworking the sentence in parts rather than as a whole. Of course, I have not catalogued everything that happens here, as the writer has to focus and maintain attention, inhibit shifting attention to distracting stimuli, and shift attention to appropriate processes while creating the sentence. This whole process becomes even more complex if we consider the construction of a larger piece of text, as issues such as coherence, organization, text features, and so forth become relevant.

If the cognitive actions the writer (or a collaborator) takes require conscious attention that exceeds the capacity of the processing system, then the result is cognitive overload and interference (McCutchen, 1988; Paas & Sweller, 2014). Having to consciously think about how to spell a word while writing, for instance, can impact a writer in three ways (Graham & Santangelo, 2014). It may tax the writer's processing capacity, leading him or her to forget ideas not yet committed to paper. Uncertainty about how to spell a word may lead to the selection of a different word the author knows how to spell, potentially undermining the preciseness of the intended message. Lastly, having to apply cognitive effort to either of these two situations means the applied resources are not available for engaging in other effortful writing processes.

Cognitive overload has multiple consequences for writing development. Many of the cognitive actions involved in writing require conscious attention, effort, and resources for young beginning writers (McCutchen, 1988). To prevent cognitive overload, they devote their processing capacities mainly to generating ideas for writing via a knowledge-telling approach (e.g., writing by remembering) and transcribing ideas using their developing but effortful handwriting and spelling skills. In the process, other resource-intensive cognitive actions such as planning, monitoring, and evaluating are minimized.

In their different writing communities, writers and collaborators learn multiple tactics and strategies to deal with the processing limitations of the human cognitive architecture. For example, a writer may alter the nature of the task by dividing writing into smaller tasks, such as developing a basic plan for the composition and then using the plan to guide the process of producing text. Responsibility for writing may also be distributed by putting one person in charge of gathering and organizing relevant information, putting different persons in charge of writing specific sections of the report, and charging yet another person with rewriting and polishing the composition so that it speaks with a single voice.

So, just as writing communities shape and bind writing, so does the cognitive architecture of writers and collaborators. This has important implications for writing communities, as the demands on the processing system can be reduced when cognitive actions are firmly established through the typified actions or routines of the community (Paas & Sweller, 2014). For instance, I have to spend very little cognitive effort thinking about the structure of a letter of recommendation for a student, as I have created a schema that is well entrenched in my memory. Likewise, when developing writers master the intricacies of typing, handwriting, speech synthesis, or some other writing tool, the instrument becomes so automatic that it operates in a modular fashion exacting little if any toll on a writer's processing system (Graham & Harris, 2000). As a result, writing communities can and often do provide instructional assistance to their members on specific aspects of writing so that they can operate more successfully within the community (Bazerman, 2016).

Components of the Cognitive Architecture of Writers and Collaborators

Figure 9.2 presents a schematic diagram of the relationship among the different cognitive components involved in writing. This schematic structure is presented for a single writer, even though multiple members of a community may be involved as writers and collaborators in carrying out a writing project. It is assumed that the basic components are universal, even if there are individual differences in the capacities and functioning of each component. These components develop with experience and age, and beginning writers are less adept at using their cognitive capabilities and have fewer resources to draw upon than their more skilled counterparts (Graham, 2006). Thus, how beginning and more mature writers compose differs[5] (see Scardamalia & Bereiter, 1986, for example). Likewise, the writing capability of a more mature writer is not a single thing, as writers may have more or less experience with different kinds of writing in different writing communities, resulting in different resources for each (Bazerman et al., 2017).

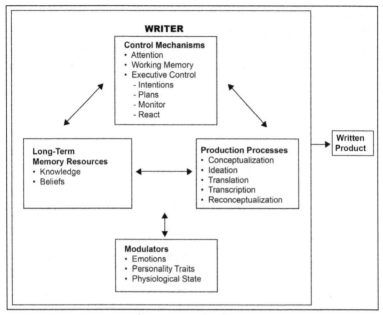

FIGURE 9.2. *Cognitive mechanisms involved in writing.*

LONG-TERM MEMORY RESOURCES

Our writing lives owe much to the richness of our long-term memory. It holds our beliefs and knowledge about the value of writing and expectations for success; interest and knowledge about possible writing topics; identities as writers and views and knowledge about various writing communities; knowledge and beliefs about our emotional reactions and personality traits; specialized knowledge about writing and audiences; and knowledge about how to speak, listen, and read. While not all of these beliefs and knowledge are called upon each time we write, each can potentially impact how and what we write.

In this model (see Figure 9.2), I refer to such beliefs and knowledge as long-term memory resources (see also Hayes, 2012). These are not the only resources a writer can draw upon, as other resources that reside outside the writer in one or more writing communities are likely available too. This includes other collaborators as well as various tools that support the process of composing, as noted earlier.

Knowledge. One form of knowledge that forms a platform for writing is oral language skills, as writers draw on their speaking skills as they write (Shanahan, 2006). The role of oral language skills in writing is evident in many situations, such as dictation or the use of speech synthesis whereby text is created through speaking. Likewise, as we engage in the process of turning ideas into sentences, we often vocalize the text to be produced, allowing us to try out, evaluate, and modify the form the sentence takes (e.g., Chenoworth & Hayes, 2001). In essence, oral language serves as a platform for creating written text.

Oral language includes many different sources of knowledge that writers draw upon. These include phonological, semantic, syntactic, and pragmatic knowledge (Brown & Attardo, 2009). Such knowledge helps writers spell words (phonological knowledge), choose the right words to capture their meaning (semantic knowledge), create a sentence that is grammatically correct and conveys the writer's intentions (syntactic knowledge), and use the appropriate idiom or expression at the right time (pragmatic knowledge).

Many writers are able to draw on resources from more than one language (Cumming, 2016). This is true even for those learning to speak and write in a second language. First language skills (L1) serve as an asset to second language writing (L2), as writing skills in the first language can transfer to and support writing in a second language (Fitzgerald, 2006).

Another language resource that resides in long-term memory is listening skills. Writers use their skills at listening when they interact with other collaborators, listen to source material such as an oral interview, or listen to the text as it is read aloud or to them.

A third language long-term memory resource is reading. Reading plays multiple roles in writing. This includes reading to evaluate text already written, reading to understand and analyze the writing task (when directions are written), and reading to understand and critically analyze source text, locate possible writing ideas and content from it, and connect and organize said content with other source material and prior knowledge (Hayes, 1996). Reading and writing also draw on similar knowledge, skills, and strategies (Shanahan, 2006). For example, a reader who has acquired extensive knowledge about how to decode words encountered in text can apply these same skills to figure out how to spell a word (Graham, 2000). Likewise, readers acquire knowledge about the basic elements or features of a particular type of text as a result of reading such text (Bereiter & Scardamalia, 1984).

Long-term memory also contains all of the specialized writing knowledge that individuals acquire as a result of their collective experiences in writing communities. This includes knowledge about text transcription skills (e.g., spelling, handwriting, typing, keyboarding, and thumbing when text messaging); written sentence construction (e.g., punctuation, capitalization, the more frequent use of subordinate clauses when writing specific types of text); text purposes and features (e.g., how writing is used to accomplish different purposes, the features of different types of text, quality indicators of strong writing, specialized vocabulary for specific types of text, and rhetorical devices for creating a specific mood); processes for producing and revising text (e.g., schemas for text construction and strategies for setting goals, gathering and organizing possible writing content, and drafting text, as well as monitoring, evaluating, and revising plans and text); tools for writing (e.g., facility in and experience using word processing as a tool for composing); attributes of specific audiences (e.g., assumptions about how much a specific audience will know about the targeted topic); and schemas for controlling thoughts, behaviors, inclinations, or the writing environment. Long-term memory further includes knowledge about one's emotional reactions to writing under different conditions and how one's personality traits typically influence writing and working with other writers.

Writing is ultimately dependent upon having something to write about. All or some of the content for writing may come directly from long-term memory resources. Studies have shown that one's knowledge about a topic predicts the quality of the text produced, but this can depend upon what one is writing about (Olinghouse, Graham, & Gillespie, 2015).

A final, but equally important, source of knowledge for writing is knowledge about different writing communities. For a specific writing community, this includes one's knowledge about its purposes (e.g., goals, norms, group identity, intended audience, and value of writing to the community), members (e.g., roles, status, and number of members), actions (e.g., how writing is typically undertaken, how writing tools are commonly used, and how the act of writing is distributed among community members), physical and social environment (e.g., knowledge about where writing takes place, social and power relationships and how to negotiate them, and assumed identities and affiliations of various members in the community), and collective history.

Beliefs. In addition to the potentially rich knowledge base individuals bring to the act of writing, long-term memory resources also include a host of beliefs (see Figure 9.2). These beliefs can foster or hinder writing, as they influence whether one engages in writing, how much effort is committed, and what resources and tools are applied. They can also determine how one interacts with other members of the writing community. Drawing on contemporary models of expectancy-value theories in motivation (Eccles, 2005; Wigfield, Tonks, & Klauda, 2009) and other recent research in motivation (Duckworth & Yeager, 2015; Graham & Weiner, 2012), I identify six broad sets of beliefs that influence individual writers.

One set of beliefs that individuals bring to the act of writing involves their judgments about the value and utility of writing (Graham & Weiner, 2012). These are task-specific beliefs that encompass one's attitudes toward writing and its usefulness. These includes one's beliefs about the: (1) importance of doing the writing task well (attainment value), (2) enjoyment derived from doing the writing task (intrinsic value), (3) how the writing task relates to future goals (utility value), and (4) what has to be given up to engage in the writing task (cost). These expectancy-values are likely influenced by one's interest in the topic that is the focus of the writing task.

Another set of beliefs that writers develop though experience involves their views of their competence as writers. This encompasses the basic question of whether a writer can expect to carry out the writing task successfully. Central to this question is the self-concept of efficacy, which involves beliefs about one's writing capabilities. Writers with a higher sense of efficacy ("can do" beliefs) tend to choose more challenging writing tasks and exert more effort when writing (Pajares, Johnson, & Usher,

2007). In contrast, writers who develop a sense of helplessness when it comes to writing ("cannot do" beliefs) attribute their performance difficulties to personal inadequacies, express anxiety and boredom, and show marked deterioration in performance during tasks (Dweck, 1999). These two different beliefs are likely shaped not only by writers' experiences in various contexts, but by writers' epistemological beliefs, which include their implicit theories about whether ability is fixed or modifiable through effort (Dweck & Leggett, 1988).

A third set of beliefs involves judgments about why one engages in writing. One dimension of these beliefs (Deci & Ryan, 2000) is that a person engages in a writing task because it provides enjoyment or inherent satisfaction (intrinsic motivation) as opposed to engaging in it because of promises of reward or fear of punishment (extrinsic motivation). A second dimension involves a person's goal orientation (Elliott, 1999). Persons with a mastery goal-orientation engage in a task because they seek to gain competence, whereas those with a performance goal-orientation seek to display their competence or experience the feelings of pride that come with success (performance approach goals) or seek to avoid doing worse than others, displaying low ability, or experiencing the feelings of shame that accompany failure (performance avoidance goals). Both mastery and performance approach goals have been associated with better performance, whereas performance avoidance goals have not. As with beliefs about competence (see the paragraph above), implicit theories about intelligence are related to performance goals (e.g., those who view intelligence as malleable are more likely to adopt mastery goals; Elliott & Dweck, 1988).

Writing beliefs also involve judgments about why one is successful (or not) when writing. Perceived causes of success can be attributed to at least three factors (Weiner, 1985): locus (success is viewed as being due to factors within or outside the individual), controllability (causes of success are viewed as amenable or not amenable to personal control), and stability (causes are viewed as fixed, such as ability, or not fixed, such as effort). These beliefs can influence writers' persistence and performance. To illustrate, if a student receives a low grade on a writing assignment and attributes that grade to low aptitude, he or she may experience reduced expectancy for success on future assignments and may be less inclined to devote as much effort to them, resulting in lower grades on future assignments. In contrast, successful performance attributed to effort is likely to promote expectancy for future success, resulting in greater effort and better writing on upcoming assignments.

Writers also develop beliefs about their identities as writers, including beliefs about the voice and stances they project when writing (Bazerman, 2016). These beliefs are not uniform, as writers can assume multiple identities depending on their experiences in different communities (Hull & Schultz, 2001). For instance, Knobel (1999) described a 13-year-old who had one identity as a writer at school ("I'm not a pencil man," p. 104) and another out of school, where he designed advertisements for his lawnmowing service. The identities that writers form are not just about writing, but interact with other identities they establish over time, such as their ethnic, racial, cultural, and peer-group identities (Graham & Weiner, 2012).

Writers further develop beliefs about specific writing communities. These include beliefs about the value of the writing community, the tasks it undertakes, and why it undertakes them. They also include beliefs about a writing community's success in achieving its writing goals, and the reasons the community is successful. This set of beliefs also includes judgments about identity (as discussed above) as well as about social belonging, social climate, and interactions within the community.

CONTROL MECHANISMS

The control mechanisms in the writing model (see Figure 9.2) enable a writer to direct, maintain, and switch attention as needed when writing; establish agency by making decisions about what is composed and how; determine the degree of ownership over the writing task; regulate multiple aspects of writing (i.e., thoughts, beliefs, emotions, behaviors, writing tools, interactions with collaborators, and the arrangement of the writing environment); and monitor, react, and make adjustments for all of these actions. The three specified mechanisms in Figure 9.2 (attention, working memory, and executive control) are drawn mainly from the literature on executive functioning (Diamond, 2006; Jacob & Parkinson, 2015), but were also shaped by theories from self-regulation (Bandura, 1986; Zimmerman & Risemberg, 1997). Each is described in turn below. The three control mechanisms are included in one form or another in the Hayes (1996, 2012) model, but I arranged them differently and I did not conceptualize them in exactly the same way he did.

Attention. The processes involved in the control mechanism of attention (see Figure 9.2) allow writers to choose what is attended to and what is ignored (Jacob & Parkinson, 2015). This includes five basic actions: focusing attention on a selective or relevant aspect of the writing enterprise (e.g., brainstorming and writing possible ideas on paper), maintaining attention on that aspect as needed (continuing to brainstorm until a reasonable number of ideas is produced), ignoring distracting aspects or features (e.g., suppressing the urge to correct the spelling of an idea as it is written down), inhibiting automatic responses (e.g., forgoing evaluating an idea as it is generated), and switching attention (e.g., switching attention between mental generation of an idea and committing it to paper). The processes of focusing, maintaining, inhibiting, and switching attention, as well as ignoring distractions, occur at all stages of the writing process, and involve what a writer does in solitude, in conjunction with the tools selected for writing and the actions undertaken with collaborators.

Working Memory. While attentional processes allow a writer to choose where attention is or is not focused, working memory (see Figure 9.2) provides a limited and temporary storage system where information is held and acted upon (I draw heavily on Baddeley's 2000 conception of working memory). Working memory is where the internal work of writing occurs. It provides a space where all nonautomated composing activities take place, as knowledge and beliefs from long-term memory and external information delivered via the senses are brought into working memory, processed, and acted upon in order to regulate attention, writing processes, writing tools, motivations, emotions, personality traits, and the environmental and social situation in which writing takes place. While actions in working memory are internal, they are the source for the production processes (see Figure 9.2) writers engage in when writing.

I represent the executive control processes (to be covered next) as separate rather than as part of working memory as was done by Baddeley (2000), because this provides a way to bring executive functioning and self-regulation together under the same umbrella. Similar to Baddeley's revised 2000 model, the model of working memory here includes three storage systems: a phonological loop for temporarily holding verbal material; a visuospatial sketchpad for briefly storing visual, spatial, and kinesthetic information; and the episodic buffer, where information from the other two temporary stores and long-term memory are bundled together to form integrated units of visual, spatial, and verbal information.

Executive Control. Executive control (see Figure 9.2) involves the processes of setting goals (formulating intentions), initiating actions to achieve them (planning), evaluating goal process and impact (monitoring), and modifying each of these as needed (reacting). These processes are the mechanisms by which writers and collaborators establish agency over the writing process. They are not separate from the confines of the writing community, but operate in conjunction with them. Even when writers have no control over the writing task assigned (as often happens in school or the world of work), writers and collaborators use these executive-control processes to shape what is produced, personalizing what is produced and how it is produced.

The four actions of formulating intentions, planning, monitoring, and reacting can be applied to all aspects of the writing process (e.g., defining the writing assignment, developing a writing plan, gathering possible writing content, organizing that content, constructing sentences, transcribing sentences into text, integrating visual and verbal features into text, reading and rereading plans and text for evaluative purposes, reformulating plans or text based on these evaluations, and editing and creating a polished final product). They can also be applied to managing one's emotions and dispositions, interacting with collaborators, using selected writing tools, and arranging the writing environment.

The first phase of executive control involves formulating intentions. Intentions are goals. They direct how attention is allocated and what the writer and collaborators do. Writing often involves multiple, hierarchically structured goals (Conway, 2005). For instance, a child may be given the task to write a summary of a passage read by the class. The quest to achieve this goal can lead to the formulation of a host of smaller intentions, such as identifying the gist of the passage, noting important details in it, structuring the summary so that the gist is presented first followed by important details, converting ideas into sentences that are paraphrased and not taken verbatim from the read material, making the produced text legible, and eliminating grammatical and spelling errors. The writer may also decide to ask another student to provide feedback on the summary before submitting it or to write it at home after supper when it is quieter. While the student is engaged in writing the summary, new intentions or goals may surface (e.g., the student decides to add personal asides in the summary), whereas other intentions may advance, retreat, or disappear (e.g., legibility is no longer important as the student decides to write the summary on a word processor). The process of formulating intentions is potentially active and ever evolving as the composing process proceeds (Hacker, Keener, & Kircher, 2009).

Once an intention is formulated then a plan is put into place for achieving it. I propose two possible mechanisms for generating this solution. One, the writer may draw on a schema held in long-term memory that provides a reasonable solution for achieving the intended goal (Hayes, 2012). For example, if a writer's goal is to clean up spelling errors in text, he or she may write a second version or even a third version of misspelled words to see if they look right because he or she remembers that this approach or schema worked in the past.

If a ready schema is not available for achieving a formulated intention, then the writer can generate solutions by engaging in problem solving (Paas & Sweller, 2014). For example, when developing this model, I was unsure how to handle my goal of drawing broadly on many different literatures, so I generated a solution that involved consulting handbooks that focused on many aspects of learning and development. A writer can also modify an existing schema taken from long-term memory so that it is relevant for the intentions at hand.

Just because a plan is selected/created does not mean that it will be successful or even that the intention it was designed to achieve was a good choice. Thus, another important phase in the executive-control mechanism is to monitor the effectiveness of the intention and its plan. Because a writer typically formulates multiple intentions when writing, evaluation for some goals will occur at the point the plan is executed, for others it will occur again sometime after the fact, and for still others it will pop up consistently throughout the act of writing. To illustrate, a writer who is writing an article for a magazine for 20- to 30-year-olds may decide that one of the overriding goals for the piece is to sound young and smart by using certain words and employing ideas that resonate with these readers. The author may frequently evaluate the text as it is being produced to see whether this goal and plans for achieving it are working. While creating the text, the author may set a goal to immediately capture the audience's attention by using a hook that appeals to their sense of irony. As soon as the hook is created, it may be evaluated, but the writer may also return to it the next day to evaluate it anew. The evaluation criteria a writer applies will not be the same for different goals and will vary by writing community.

The fourth phase involves the writer's reaction to the evaluation conducted as part of monitoring. A writer may view the desired intention and its plan as useful and effective, and move on to formulating another intention or returning to a previous intention put it into play. Or the writer may be unsatisfied with the outcome, and will be faced with a decision: make a change, move on, or move to another goal?

As noted earlier, executive-control mechanisms not only direct and regulate a writer's thoughts and behaviors, but help the writer direct and manage work within the writing community. This includes applying strategies for regulating the writing assignment (e.g., changing the assignment so it is more interesting), writing community (e.g., modifying a typified way that the writing community carries out writing activities), writing environment (e.g., restructuring the writing environment so that it is conducive to success), social situation (e.g., choosing whom to work with or how the writing task is to be distributed), writing tools (e.g., choosing what tools to use or what features of a tool to activate or switch off), writing process (e.g., setting rhetorical goals, creating an advanced plan, self-vocalizing while crafting sentences, setting writing aside for a day before making revisions), attention (e.g., monitoring and recording the amount of time spent writing), motivation (e.g., engaging in self-reinforcement or goal-oriented talk), emotions (e.g., purposefully controlling excitement, counting to 10, reminding oneself that getting frustrated is not helpful), personality traits (e.g., creating a strategy to manage time more effectively), and physical readiness (e.g., making sure not to come to the writing task sleepy or hungry).

Summary. Control mechanisms provide writers with a temporary storage space where intentions and plans can be formulated (through reasoning, problem solving, and decision making), resulting in thoughts, actions, emotions, and behaviors that can be regulated, monitored, evaluated, and adjusted as needed. This temporary storage space draws on long-term memory resources (knowledge and beliefs) as well as input from outside the writer. In turn, acting on ideas for writing in working memory as well as establishing goals and plans for writing, monitoring their success, and deciding to make changes when needed can provide new insights, knowledge, and beliefs that are added to long-term memory resources.

PRODUCTION PROCESSES

Production processes (see Figure 9.2) are the mental and physical operations writers apply to produce text (similar operations are included in the Chenoweth & Hayes 2001 model). These production processes are guided by decisions made in the writing community (e.g., to produce a specific type of text) and/or by decisions made by the writer through the control mechanisms involved in setting writing goals (intentions), initiating actions to achieve them (plans), evaluating goal process and impact (monitoring), and modifying goals and plans as needed (reacting). Production processes draw on long-term memory resources, such as topic knowledge, language, and specialized writing knowledge, as the writer constructs a mental representation of the writing task (conceptualization), draws ideas for the composition from memory and/or external sources (ideation), takes the most pertinent of these ideas and transforms them into acceptable sentences (translation), commits the sentences to paper or digital print (transcription), and engages in the act of revision (reconceptualization). Engagement and persistence in employing these production processes are likely influenced by some combination of beliefs writers hold about the value/utility of writing, their capabilities as writers, motivations for engaging in writing, reasons for success, and identities as writers. In turn, engagement in these production processes can lead writers to acquire new knowledge and affect how they view writing and themselves, adding to their long-term memory resources (Graham, Harris, & Mason, 2005).

Conceptualization. One production process involves forming a mental conceptualization of the writing task or assignment (see also Hayes, 2012). The starting point for this may be goals established by the writing community (e.g., an employer assigns a writing task with specific goals), goals established by the writer, or some combination of the two. This resulting mental conceptualization, which includes remembered goals and text produced so far, serves to guide other production processes, as it provides a mental road map of what has been done and what was intended. It is open to modification, as the writer engages in evaluations of the intentions, plans, and text produced.

Ideation. A second production process is ideation. This involves accessing possible ideas or content for writing from internal memory sources or external sources within or outside of the writing community (see Torrance, Thomas, & Robinson, 1996, for a discussion on idea generation during writing). Ideas can take more than one form, as they can involve language, an image, or an abstract thought. In some instances, an idea may undergo intense scrutiny by a writer to determine whether it is suitable given his or her conceptualization of the writing task. In other instances, as may happen when writing an entry in a diary, it may receive only a passing appraisal.

Translation. Ideas viewed as pertinent for the text being assembled must be turned into acceptable sentences (translation).

This involves deciding which words and syntactic structures best convey an author's intended meaning (see Kaufer, Hayes, & Flower, 1986, for a study of sentence production). Writers draw on their own knowledge of grammar, sentence structure, usage, and vocabulary to do this, but may also rely on external aids from the writing community such as a thesaurus or grammar checker.

Transcription. Sentences must also be converted to text, either on paper or digitally (transcription). Transcriptions skills include handwriting, typing, and spelling, but are expanding to include other production methods such as speech synthesis, using thumbs to create a message on a smartphone, or inserting pictures, videos, or narration into a digital text. Developing facility with most transcription procedures is important, as slow transcription skills can interfere with other production processes like conceptualization, ideation, and translation (see Graham, 2006).

Reconceptualization. The production process of reconceptualization applies to all aspects of writing, as writers can rethink and revise whatever is produced, including their writing goals, plans, notes, and text as well as procedures for producing and presenting a paper. This reconceptualization not only involves adding to, rearranging, or taking away from what is produced already; it can involve transformation, too, as when writers reformulate their intentions (Scardamalia & Bereiter, 1986).

Of course, production processes cannot be considered as separate from the material experiences and tools writers use to produce text within their writing communities. For instance, when reconceptualization takes place and how frequently it occurs is related to the tools writers use to produce text (MacArthur & Graham, 1987).

MODULATORS

The fourth component of cognitive architecture (see Figure 9.2) involves the physical and psychological factors that modulate the workings of the other components: long-term memory resources, control mechanisms, and production processes. The modulators are emotions, personality traits, and physiological states.

— 301 —

Emotions. Emotions are "affectively charged cognitions, feelings, mood, affect, and well-being" (Boekaerts, 2011, p. 412). They include joy, surprise, sadness, anger, disgust, and fear as well as secondary emotions such as hopefulness, hopelessness, jealousy, disappointment, guilt, shame, embarrassment, excitement, pride, relief, envy, anxiety, annoyance, and gratefulness (Fridja, 1988). Emotions make writers want to do things or not do them (Pekrun, Frenzel, Goetz, & Perry, 2007). For instance, the anger that results from reading a newspaper article that espouses an objectionable viewpoint may lead a person to write a letter of rebuttal. Further, if one believes he or she is a good writer, a writing task may activate positive emotions such as joy and pride and result in greater effort and persistence. In contrast, if a writer has serious doubts about his or her competence, this may activate emotions of shame and anxiety, resulting in difficulties starting writing tasks, focusing on them, and managing them (Daly, 1985). Positive or negative emotions can enhance or reduce effort allocation and management (Boekaerts, 2007) and can combine with cognitive information in long-term memory, such as beliefs about capabilities, causes of success (or failure), and the value and utility of writing, to further moderate the relationship between emotions and writing performance.

Emotions can affect more than attention, as they can influence recall, problem solving, and decision making (Fridja, 1988). As noted earlier, these cognitive processes are central to executive-control processes of formulating intentions, initiating plans, monitoring goal process and goal impact, and reacting as needed. It should not be assumed, however, that negative emotions toward writing such as writing anxiety mean that those experiencing these emotions are weaker writers than those not experiencing them. Rather, they tend to worry more about writing, judge their text more harshly, and engage in more negative self-talk (Madigan, Linton, & Johnson, 2006). While emotions can modulate what a writer does cognitively, it is possible that the emotions of individuals in a community of writers influence the mood and work of the community, too, just as emotions themselves are responsive to social situations and relationships within that community.

Personality Traits. Another modulator that can potentially influence what a writer does is personality traits. Personality is defined as "relatively stable individual differences in behavioral dispositions that generalize across a range of environments" (Zeidner & Matthews, 2012, p. 111). According to contemporary approaches to the study of personality, this construct involves multiple and relatively enduring traits that are not viewed as fixed, but probabilistically affect a person in his or her interaction within a situational context. These traits center on openness to experience, conscientiousness, extraversion, agreeableness, and neuroticism (see Costa & McCrae, 1992).

The work of Galbraith (1999) provides an example of how personality traits influence the writer. He found that students who control their expressive behavior to present themselves in a pleasing way versus those who are less likely to filter their expressions differ in how they plan, with the former producing more new ideas when planning and the latter doing this as they wrote.

Just as emotions can influence the writing community, so may personality traits (see Zeidner & Matthews, 2012). For instance, interactions within a community are influenced by the agreeableness, openness, conscientiousness, sociability, and self-consciousness of its members.

Physiological States. A writer comes to the task of writing in varying physiological states (see Figure 9.2). From one situation to the next, a writer may be more or less hungry, stressed, tired, or healthy. This matters, as these factors influence performance. For example, too little sleep can lead to problems with concentration and memory (Curcio, Ferrara, & De Gennaro, 2006). Performance is also negatively impacted when daily nutritional needs are not met (Kleinman et al., 2002). Stress influences cognitive processes like decision making, but also affects people working together toward a common goal (Driskell & Salas, 1996). As a result, physiological status can impact a writer affectively and cognitively, and may under the right circumstances influence the work of a writing community as well, just as the demands imposed by a writing community can influence one's physiological state.

An Example of How Community and Writers Work in Tandem

A basic assumption of the writing model is that writing involves an interaction between the social context in which it occurs and the mental and physical actions writers are able to enlist and engage. While the two previous sections (i.e., writing community and writers/collaborators) provide some illustrations of this interaction, I demonstrate this here with a more detailed example involving the conceptualization of a writing task.

Writing tasks can be assigned by one or more members in a community, determined individually, or created collectively. For example, a high school teacher may ask students to complete a written report on the impact of hip-hop on poetry, a student in the same classroom may decide to pursue this topic independently, or the teacher and students may negotiate the topic of the report to include other types of music and poetry.

Whether writing is assigned, self-determined, or collectively determined, a starting point in the writing process is to create goals for the task and an initial conceptualization of it. This is directly influenced by the specific features of the writing community as well as what the writer(s) bring to the situation. In turn, how writers conceptualize the writing task influences what they do cognitively (Many et al., 1996) and can further influence the writing community (e.g., a teacher may provide more time for completing the hip-hop report if students working on it have different ways of conceptualizing it).

In constructing a mental conceptualization for a report on hip-hop and poetry, students in a class are likely to have overlapping but not exactly identical ideas for the goals of this task because of their collective history (much of this information will be held in community members' long-term memory, but can also be represented in the community as well through posted rules, example text, and so forth). Students in our fictional class, for example, know their teacher prefers that students work together as they plan and revise their compositions and that the end product is a multimodal writing composition. They also know that the audience for writing projects developed in this classroom is the teacher, and that the purpose of such writing is mainly evaluative. They further understand that other members of the class have specific beliefs about one another's skills as writers and their knowledge about hip-hop and poetry. They know what tools for writing are available in the classroom (mostly paper and pencil and several computers), and they will likely need to do some or most of their work at home or in the library (physical environment) where other needed tools are available. They realize that they need to choose whom to work with and where (social environment), and that there are specific actions that the teacher expects them to engage in as they work on this project, including deciding whom to work with as they plan and revise their paper, how to distribute the collective load during each of these activities, and the creation of an initial writing plan and timeline for the teacher to review. As this example illustrates, the various features of the writing community shape and bind the conceptualization and goals for the writing task in multiple ways.

The knowledge, beliefs, emotions, personality traits, and physiological states of each writer further shape and bind how the writing task is initially conceptualized. For instance, the writing task is likely to be conceptualized differently by those with more or less knowledge about hip-hop and poetry or students who value this type of report writing versus those who do not. Similarly, students' emotional reactions to the writing assignment (e.g., excitement, anxiety), their basic personality traits (e.g., conscientiousness, willingness to entertain new ideas), and their physical states (e.g., healthy versus sick) will determine how the writing task is defined, how the goals for writing are refined, and how much effort is expended in achieving them.

A writer's initial conceptualization for the hip-hop and poetry task may range from minimal (e.g., I want to work with Alfredo and include hip-hop lyrics from Jay-Z) to more extensive (e.g., a detailed outline with rhetorical and content goals, possible writing partners, specific writing tools, and a timeline). With the exception of very limited writing tasks (e.g., writing a note to tell your spouse where you are), this initial conceptualization is likely to evolve as the writer or writers: (1) monitor and react to the success of initial intentions/plans, (2) discover new intentions/plans as a result of the text and byproducts of writing that are created through the composing process, and/or (3) interact with members of the community to shape the intentions and the developed text. For example, an initial conceptualization may become richer, as the writer thinks of new ideas as text is created or after others provide feedback about the text produced so far. Similarly, these processes may lead to replacing part or all of an initial conceptualization and goals. The point here is that conceptualization and goals for writing are usually not stagnant, but are dynamic and changing. It is important to note that the fluidity of this mental representation can be affected by changes in the community (e.g., the original teacher becomes ill and a substitute teacher takes over the class and decides to place additional boundaries around the writing task) as well as events that affect individual writers (e.g., a student's parents purchase a home computer that makes it easier to add video and narrative clips). Conceptualizations can further involve shared community intentions that develop as students work with peers and teachers to develop their projects.

Before turning to mechanisms that promote development, it is important to reiterate that writing occurs within both the writing community and the heads of writers. As students engage in the hip-hop/poetry assignment above, considerable work will take place in both. Teachers will likely confer with students about their paper, asking questions and providing suggestions. Students may talk among themselves, sharing and gathering ideas and feedback from one another. They may further collaborate with classmates on all or parts of the writing process. External resources such as the Internet, records, autobiographies, or interviews may be accessed. Students may share drafts of their paper with others for feedback, or they may use their peers as a sounding board for their ideas, frustrations, and accomplishments.

At the same time, students will bring their cognitive architecture to bear to help them focus and maintain attention, decide how much effort to invest (including their level of ownership of the writing task), access relevant beliefs and knowledge, plan and evaluate, as well as monitor and react so they can operate successfully within this writing community and carry out the processes involved in composing their paper. The interplay between cognition and community is complex, as it involves reciprocal relationships that do not remain constant. To illustrate, as students work alone and together with peers and teacher, the multiple voices, contradictions, disparate elements, conflicts, and heterogeneity described earlier will surface. As students and teachers monitor what happens within the community and with their own writing projects, reactions by each may result in shifts in how the community or individual students operate. For example, the teacher may modify the writing assignment because of time constraints, or individual writers may become more or less engaged in completing the assigned writing project.

Mechanisms That Promote Development

A model of writing is not complete without addressing how development occurs. The model presented here proposes that writing development is shaped by participation in different writing communities, engagement in the practice of writing, and changes in the cognitive and affective properties of the writer. Writing development is not just about the individual, though, as writing communities are shaped by the collective actions of their members, writing communities influence one another, and writing communities are influenced by larger forces involving history, culture, politics, institutions, and society.

Before turning more specifically to the mechanisms that shape development of writing communities and individual writers, it is important to note that writing development is not a single thing. Writers develop expertise with a variety of different types of writing. The purposes and situations in which these forms of writing are applied vary, as do the audiences to which they are directed. In fact, it is difficult to obtain a general measure of writing achievement (Coffman, 1966; Graham, Hebert, Sandbank, & Harris, 2016), and there are relatively low correlations between writing within and across genres (Graham, Harris, & Hebert, 2011).

Mechanisms That Shape the Writing Community

Writing communities are built by and in turn shaped collectively by individuals. The purposes and ultimately the actions of writing and other socially derived communities are initially constructed by people, drawing on their experiences in other communities (Moll, 1990). For example, a writing program may be implemented by parents at home that is similar to the writing practices applied at school (Morrow & Young, 1997) or writing practices from home can be brought directly into the school (Dyson, 1999).

It is important to note that writing communities can influence other socially derived groups. A famous illustration of this point involves *The Origin of Species,* written by Charles Darwin for a scientific writing community. The ideas in this book have been applied not just to views about biological development, but to other areas too, such as economic evolution (Hodgson & Knudsen, 2010) and the evolution of learning (Geary, 2008). In addition, writing in one community may provide capital in other socially derived communities. For instance, learning to write makes one a better reader, and writing about material presented in other learning situations enhances comprehension of material read (Graham & Hebert, 2011). This provides individuals with skills that can be applied beyond the writing communities where they were first developed, as reading is a fundamental skill in a variety of socially derived communities today.

Writing communities can further develop as a function of changes in the community itself (Greeno & Engeström, 2014). This can include changes in the tools used by a writing community. For instance, Charley Kempthorne was a writing community of one for more than fifty years, writing a diary entry each day for himself, where he reflected about his past experiences and his burgeoning belief in God (Ansberry, 2016). This writing community evolved considerably after he started posting his diary entries on Facebook. Similarly, Wikipedia evolved from a companion site to a free online encyclopedia (i.e., Nupedia) that used highly qualified volunteers and a peer-review process to a more catholic community in which the users of Wikipedia created and curated entries.

Writing communities are also shaped by larger forces. Consider the interaction between history and writing tools. Five thousand years ago, the purposes of Sumerian writing communities revolved around the activity of recording goods (Cook, 2003). As writing tools evolved from marks on clay to marks on paper to marks on computer screens, the number and types of writing communities exploded, especially with the advent of the printing press (Hendrix, 2016). Today, almost nine out of ten people worldwide write (Swerdlow, 1999).

Another example involves the impact of culture on writing communities. A classic study by Scribner and Cole (1981) provides an excellent demonstration of this point. They studied the Vai, who operate between multiple cultures, learning to write in English in school, using Arabic to study the Quran, and learning an indigenous script at home.

Finally, political and institutional factors influence the nature of writing communities and ultimately the development of writing. Formal schooling in the United States provides an excellent example. Writing instruction in schools (K–12 and college) has been shaped by a variety of professional institutions such as the Committee of Ten, the National Council of Teachers of English, the Modern Language Association, the Conference on College Composition and Communication, and the Dartmouth Seminar (Sperling & DiPardo, 2008). Perhaps even more influential in recent years are edicts and mandates from local, state, and federal governments. These have resulted in reforms emphasizing accountability (e.g., standardized tests) and the privileging of specific approaches to instruction (e.g., California's proposing a literature-based/whole language approach to instruction in 1989). These mandates have specific consequences for the writing communities targeted. For instance, periodic standardized writing assessment can make writing more central to the mission of schooling and change teachers' writing practices in positive ways (see Graham, Hebert, & Harris, 2011), but it can also narrow the writing curriculum in unintended and negative ways (Hillocks, 2002).

Mechanisms That Shape Writing Development at the Individual Level

I propose five mechanisms that shape writing at the individual level (they are not completely separate from one another). They occur within the context of specific writing communities, but cut across them too.

LEARNING BY DOING

One mechanism that promotes writing development is learning by doing or learning through experience. I highlight three approaches to learning by doing here. One, through participation in a writing community, an individual writer learns a community's goals, identity, norms, specialized knowledge, evaluative criteria, forms of reasoning, action routines, tool use, and the identities, affiliations, roles, attitudes, beliefs, relationships, and expectations of other members in the writing community (Bazerman, 2016; Greeno & Engeström, 2014). Participation further allows the individual writer to gain a sense of the physical and social conditions under which the writing community operates, including how power is distributed. Participation in a writing community can lead an individual writer to develop a sense of belonging and identity (Hull & Schultz, 2001), but it can also lead to negative outcomes as well, such as rejection of the goals of a community and passive or even aggressive resistance to it (e.g., those who find writing challenging at school may act out in inappropriate ways when it is writing time).

A second way of learning by doing is to learn as a consequence of action (Graham & Harris, 1994). As students write, they put into play various mental operations and behaviors to achieve their goals. These vary from routine actions to ones that are applied for the first time; personally created actions to ones prompted by a mentor or collaborator; and actions that involve personal judgments to ones that involve external judgments of success. These actions have consequences: they are successful or not successful. If a writer views a particular action as successful, then it is more likely to be used in the future. If it is not successful, then it is less likely to be applied later. Evaluations of these actions can also influence a writer's beliefs (Zimmerman & Campillo, 2003). A writer who routinely views writing actions in a specific writing community as unsuccessful is likely to become less confident about his or her writing capabilities in that situation.

A third means for learning by doing involves learning by expansion. As writers engage in the act of reading, for example, they may acquire important insights into writing, as they think about why an author used a particular word, phrase, sentence, or rhetorical device to deliver the intended meaning (Tierney & Shanahan, 1991). This learning can be deliberate, as when a writer is asked to read and emulate a model text (Knudson, 1989), or unintentional, as when writers extract rhetorical knowledge (Bereiter & Scardamalia, 1984) or knowledge about spelling (Graham, 2000) as a consequence of reading. Another example involves the acquisition of content or vocabulary knowledge as a result of listening to a lecture or reading a book. Both types of knowledge may be applied by a writer when creating future texts. The acquisition of these different types of knowledge can influence one's beliefs, as an individual may be more interested in writing about a topic after acquiring new information about it or may feel more confident as a writer as a result of writing skills acquired vicariously through reading.

LEARNING BY OBSERVING

Writers also develop as a result of learning by observing. This involves observing other writers and readers (Couzijn, 1999). Examples of this kind of learning activity include observing another writer carry out the processes involved in writing or watching a reader try to carry out directions written by oneself or someone else. The success of learning by observations depends on the writer's focusing attention on relevant features of the event observed, retaining in long-term memory the pertinent information, and translating the retained information into successful action when writing (Schunk, 2012).

LEARNING FROM OTHERS

Writers further develop as a function of learning from others. This typically involves learning from other people within specific writing communities (Graham, Harris, & Santangelo, 2015), but it can involve learning from a machine, as when feedback is given via automated essay scoring (Graham, Hebert, & Harris, 2015). One way in which learning with others occurs is through a writer's collaboration with another student to create a composition. Collaborations such as these can result in one or both writers learning something new from the other about how to write. They can also result in changes in beliefs. For instance, one of the writers might decide, as a result of the experience, that she is a very good editor.

Another way that learning from others occurs is through one or more individuals in a writing community serving as mentors to teach skills a writer needs to be successful. Teaching or mentoring can involve an array of activities, including discussion about text and writing, modeling specific writing skills or behaviors, providing guided practice, sequencing learning activities, coaching, creating a supportive writing environment, designing writing tasks that engender specific writing processes, providing feedback, facilitating self-reflection, and displaying a positive attitude toward writing, to provide a few examples. For school-age developing writers, most of these activities result in improvements in the quality of what they write (Graham, McKeown, Kiuhara, & Harris, 2012; Graham, Harris, & Chambers, 2016).

LEARNING THROUGH DELIBERATE AGENCY

Writers can develop as a result of learning through deliberate agency. This involves a deliberate decision on the part of the writer to: (1) become more skilled (Kellogg & Whiteford, 2009), (2) apply what was learned in a previous situation or community to new ones (Bazerman, 2016), or (3) build new ideas about writing within the context of old ones (diSessa, 2014). The first deliberate action described above can be illustrated by considering the famous American jack-of-all trades, Benjamin Franklin, who set a goal to become a better writer by trying to emulate some of the best British writers of his day (Bigelow, 1868).

To illustrate the other two actions above, I provide an example from my own research (Graham et al., 2005), of third-grade children who identified something they learned through instruction that could potentially be applied in another setting. They then set a goal to apply it in the new setting, determined how it needed to be modified for the new setting, and evaluated whether it worked or did not work and why. This occurred multiple times over the course of the study. This deliberate articulation, externalization, and application of what was learned resulted in improved writing in instructed and uninstructed genres.

The fifth catalyst for development is learning as a result of accumulated writing capital. In essence, development as a writer serves as stimulus for further development. As writers acquire more knowledge about writing, develop new strategic approaches to writing, or become more motivated, any of these outcomes may spur further development (Graham, 2006). For example, as writers become more knowledgeable about the craft of writing, they are more likely to become intrinsically motivated to write, value writing, view themselves as competent writers, and develop a positive image of themselves as writers. Likewise, more motivated writers are likely to be more invested in writing, devoting greater effort, persistence, and cognitive resources to composing, including creating strategic solutions to solve new writing problems (Alexander, Graham, & Harris, 1998).

Final Comments

This chapter proposes that writers differ in cognitive capabilities, resources, and functioning. It further proposes that where writing communities acquire their competence varies widely, and that these communities are dynamic and evolving structures. Thus, variations in contexts and individuals are the catalysts for differences in writing development within a writer and between writers. I would like to end this chapter by considering a contextual and an individual factor not specifically addressed in the model. Both play important roles in shaping writing.

First, family wealth predicts children's skills as writers, at least on writing tasks emphasized in schools (Graham, 2006). As a group, children from poorer families do not perform as well on measures of writing as children from more affluent families (Walberg & Ethington, 1991). This is not to say that children from poor families are destined to become weaker writers (see Pressley, Raphael, Gallagher, & DiBella, 2004, for instance). Rather, poverty increases the risk that young writers will not reach their full potential.

Second, I did not address the role of the brain, genes, and the interplay between gene, brain, and environment in writing or its development. This does not mean that these factors are unimportant. Research in behavioral genetics demonstrates that in a variety of educational domains nature and nurture contribute almost equally to development, interacting with environmental factors (Haworth & Plomin, 2012). Moreover, the development of the brain "supporting writing undergoes continual change, in part, because of genes that regulate neural migration, neural development and function that supports writing" (p. 118), and such change is further influenced by interactions between the brain and the environment (James, Jao, & Berninger, 2016). As more insight into the interactions among writers' genes, brains, and environments is obtained, it should be possible to build a broader and more complete model of writing and the factors that contribute to its development.

Notes

1. This chapter is dedicated to Arthur Applebee and the Lifespan Writing Development Group that authored this book. I especially wish to thank Deborah Rowe, Chuck Bazerman, Deborah Brandt, Xinghua Liu, Clarence Ng, Paul Matsuda, and Mary Schleppegrell, who provided critical, but helpful, comments about the model. I also thank students in my 2016 Writing Research Seminar for their feedback, especially Angelique Aitken.

2. Written text can include pictures, drawings, verbal narration, and videos. Neither film nor an oral speech alone is considered writing in this chapter, but any text used to create them would count as writing, such as a screenplay. There are instances where writing may not involve print, however, as when very young children produce marks, scribbles, lines, or pictures with the intent to construct meaning through writing (see Rowe, 2008).

3. An exception to this definition is a community that includes a single person who acts as both author and reader. A writer composing a diary for personal consumption provides an example of a one-person writing community, as this person acts as both writer and reader.

4. The functions involved in writing can be and often are distributed across members in a writing community (see Klein & Leacock, 2012).

5. Mature writers, however, can and do use writing strategies similar to those applied by beginners at times, as when they apply the knowledge-telling strategy to write an entry on a social media site detailing the events of the last hour, with little or no reflection on these events.

References

Alexander, P. A., Graham, S., & Harris, K. R. (1998). A perspective on strategy research: Progress and prospects. *Educational Psychology Review, 10*(2), 129–54.

Allodi, M. W. (2007). Assessing the quality of learning environments in Swedish schools: Development and analysis of a theory-based instrument. *Learning Environments Research, 10*(3), 157–75. doi:10.1007/s10984-007-9029-9

Ansberry, C. (2016, January 26). The power of daily writing in a journal: Keeping a journal for 52 years has helped Charley Kempthorne to be happier, healthier. *Wall Street Journal*, D1–D2.

Baddeley, A. (2000). The episodic buffer: A new component of working memory? Review article. *Trends in Cognitive Sciences, 4*(11), 417–23. doi:10.1016/S1364-6613(00)01538-2

Bandura, A. (1986). *Social foundations of thought and action: A social cognitive theory*. Englewood Cliffs, NJ: Prentice Hall.

Barton, D. (1991). The social nature of writing. In D. Barton & R. Ivanič (Eds.), *Writing in the community* (pp. 1–13). Newbury Park, CA: SAGE.

Bazerman, C. (1994). Systems of genres and the enactment of social intentions. In A. Freedman & P. Medway (Eds.), *Genre and the new rhetoric* (pp. 67–86). London, UK: Taylor & Francis.

Bazerman, C. (2016). What do sociocultural studies of writing tell us about learning to write? In C. A. MacArthur, S. Graham, & J. Fitzgerald (Eds.), *Handbook of writing research* (2nd ed., pp. 11–23). New York: Guilford Press.

Bazerman, C., Applebee, A. N., Berninger, V. W., Brandt, D., Graham, S., Matsuda, P. K., Murphy, S., Rowe, D. W., Schleppegrell, M. (2017). Taking the long view on writing development. *Research in the Teaching of English 51*(3), 351–60.

Bazerman, C., & Prior, P. (2005). Participating in emergent socio-literate worlds: Genre, disciplinarity, interdisciplinarity. In J. Green, R. Beach, M. Kamil, & T. Shanahan (Eds.), *Multidisciplinary perspectives on literacy research* (2nd ed., pp. 133–78). Cresskill, NJ: Hampton Press.

Bereiter, C., & Scardamalia, M. (1984). Learning about writing from reading. *Written Communication, 1*(2), 163–88. doi:10.1177/0741088384001002001

Bigelow, J. (Ed.). (1868). *Autobiography of Benjamin Franklin.* Philadelphia, PA: J. P. Lippincott.

Boekaerts, M. (2007). Understanding students' affective processes in the classroom. In P. A. Schutz & R. Pekrun (Eds.), *Emotion in education* (pp. 37–56). San Diego: Academic Press.

Boekaerts, M. (2011). Emotions, emotion regulation, and self-regulation of learning. In B. J. Zimmerman & D. H. Schunk (Eds.), *Handbook of self-regulation of learning and performance* (pp. 408–25). New York: Routledge.

Brandt, D. (2001). *Literacy in American lives.* New York: Cambridge University Press.

Brown, S., & Attardo, S. (2009). *Understanding language structure, interaction, and variation: An introduction to applied linguistics and sociolinguistics for nonspecialists* (2nd ed.). Ann Arbor: University of Michigan Press.

Cameron, C. A., Hunt, A. K, & Linton, M. J. (1996). Written expression as recontextualization: Children write in social time. *Educational Psychology Review, 8*(2), 125–50.

Chenoweth, N. A., & Hayes, J. R. (2001). Fluency in writing: Generating text in L1 and L2. *Written Communication, 18*(1), 80–98. doi:10.1177/0741088301018001004

Coffman, W. E. (1966). On the validity of essay tests of achievement. *Journal of Educational Measurement, 3*(2), 151–56.

Conway, M. A. (2005). Memory and the self. *Journal of Memory and Language, 53*(4), 594–628. doi:10.1016/j.jml.2005.08.005

Cook, M. (2003). *A brief history of the human race.* New York: Norton.

Costa, P. T., Jr., & McCrae, R. R. (1992). Four ways five factors are basic. *Personality & Individual Differences, 13*(6), 653–55. doi:10.1016/0191-8869(92)90236-I

Couzijn, M. (1999). Learning to write by observation of writing and reading processes: Effects on learning and transfer. *Learning and Instruction, 9*(2), 109–42. doi:10.1016/S0959-4752(98)00040-1

Cumming, A. (2016). Writing development and instruction for English language learners. In C. A. MacArthur, S. Graham, & J. Fitzgerald (Eds.), *Handbook of writing research* (2nd ed., pp. 364–76). New York: Guilford Press.

Curcio, G., Ferrara, M., & De Gennaro, L. (2006). Sleep loss, learning capacity and academic performance. *Sleep Medicine Reviews, 10*(5), 323–37. doi:10.1016/j.smrv.2005.11.001

Daly, J. A. (1985). Writing apprehension. In M. Rose (Ed.), *When a writer can't write: Studies in writer's block and other composing-process problems* (pp. 42–82). New York: Guilford Press.

Deci, E. L., & Ryan, R. M. (2000). The "what" and "why" of goal pursuits: Human needs and the self-determination of behavior. *Psychological Inquiry, 11*(4), 227–68.

Diamond, A. (2006). The early development of executive functions. In E. Bialystok & F. I. M. Craik (Eds.), *Lifespan cognition: Mechanisms of change* (pp. 70–96). New York: Oxford University Press.

diSessa, A. A. (2014). A history of conceptual change research: Threads and fault lines. In R. K. Sawyer (Ed.), *The Cambridge handbook of the learning sciences* (2nd ed., pp. 88–108). Cambridge, UK: Cambridge University Press.

Driskell, J. E., & Salas, E. (1996). *Stress and human performance.* Mahwah, NJ: Erlbaum.

Duckworth, A. L., & Yeager, D. S. (2015). Measurement matters: Assessing personal qualities other than cognitive abilities for educational purposes. *Educational Researcher, 44*(4), 237–51. doi:10.3102/0013189X15584327

Dweck, C. S. (1999). *Self-theories: Their role in motivation, personality, and development.* Philadelphia, PA: Psychology Press.

Dweck, C. S., & Leggett, E. L. (1988). A social-cognitive approach to motivation and personality. *Psychological Review, 95*(2), 256–73. doi:10.1037/0033-295X.95.2.256

Dyson, A. (1999). Coach Bombay's kids learn to write: "Children's appropriation of media material for school literacy." *Research in the Teaching of English, 33*(4), 367–402.

Eccles, J. S. (2005). Subjective task value and the Eccles et al. model of achievement-related choices. In A. J. Elliot & C. S. Dweck (Eds.), *Handbook of competence and motivation* (pp. 105–21). New York: Guilford Press.

Elliott, A. J. (1999). Approach and avoidance motivation and achievement goals. *Educational Psychologist, 34(3),* 169–89.

Elliott, E. S., & Dweck, C. S. (1988). Goals: An approach to motivation and achievement. *Journal of Personality and Social Psychology, 54*(1), 5–12. doi:10.1037/0022-3514.54.1.5

Fitzgerald, J. (2006). Multilingual writing in preschool through 12th grade: The last 15 years. In C. A. MacArthur, S. Graham, & J. Fitzgerald (Eds.), *Handbook of writing research* (pp. 337–54). New York: Guilford Press.

Freedman, S. W., Hull, G. A., Higgs, J. M., & Booten, K. P. (2016). Teaching writing in a digital and global age: Toward access, learning, and development for all. In D. H. Gitomer & C. A. Bell (Eds.), *Handbook of research on teaching* (5th ed., pp. 1389–1450). Washington, DC: American Educational Research Association.

Fridja, N. H. (1988). The laws of emotion. *American Psychologist, 43*(5), 349–58.

Gabrial, B. (2008). History of writing technologies. In C. Bazerman (Ed.), *Handbook of research on writing: History, society, school, individual, text* (pp. 23–34). New York: Erlbaum.

Galbraith, D. (1999). Writing as a knowledge-constituting process. In M. Torrance & D. Galbraith (Eds.), *Knowing what to write: Conceptual processes in text production* (pp. 139–59). Amsterdam: Amsterdam University Press.

Geary, D. (2008). An evolutionarily informed education science. *Educational Psychologist, 43*(4), 179–95. doi:10.1080/00461520802392 133

Graham, S. (2000). Should the natural learning approach replace traditional spelling instruction? *Journal of Educational Psychology, 92*(2), 235–47. doi:10.1037/0022-0663.92.2.235

Graham, S. (2006). Writing. In P. A. Alexander & P. H. Winne (Eds.), *Handbook of educational psychology* (pp. 457–78). Mahwah, NJ: Erlbaum.

Graham, S., & Harris, K. R. (1994). The role and development of self-regulation in the writing process. In D. H. Schunk & B. J. Zimmerman (Eds.), *Self-regulation of learning and performance: Issues and educational applications* (pp. 203–28). Mahwah, NJ: Erlbaum.

Graham, S., & Harris, K. R. (2000). The role of self-regulation and transcription skills in writing and writing development. *Educational Psychologist, 35*(1), 3–12.

Graham, S., Harris, K. R., & Chambers, A. B. (2016). Evidence-based practice and writing instruction: A review of reviews. In C. A. MacArthur, S. Graham, & J. Fitzgerald (Eds.), *Handbook of writing research* (Vol. 2; pp. 211–26). New York: Guilford Press.

Graham, S., Harris, K., & Hebert, M. (2011). *Informing writing: The benefits of formative assessment: A report from Carnegie Corporation of New York.* Washington, DC: Alliance for Excellent Education.

Graham, S., Harris, K. R., & Mason, L. (2005). Improving the writing performance, knowledge, and self-efficacy of struggling young writers: The effects of self-regulated strategy development. *Contemporary Educational Psychology, 30*(2), 207–41. doi:10.1016/j.cedpsych.2004.08.001

Graham, S., Harris, K. R., & Santangelo, T. (2015). Research-based writing practices and the Common Core: Meta-analysis and meta-synthesis. *Elementary School Journal, 115*(4), 498–522.

Graham, S., & Hebert, M. (2011). Writing to read: A meta-analysis of the impact of writing and writing instruction on reading. *Harvard Educational Review, 81*(4), 710–44, 784–85.

Graham, S., Hebert, M., & Harris, K. R. (2011). Throw 'em out or make 'em better? State and district high-stakes writing assessments. *Focus on Exceptional Children, 44*(1), 1–12.

Graham, S., Hebert, M., & Harris, K. R. (2015). Formative assessment and writing: A meta-analysis. *Elementary School Journal, 115*(4), 524–47.

Graham, S., Hebert, M., Sandbank, M. P., & Harris, K. R. (2016). Assessing the writing achievement of young struggling writers: Application of generalizability theory. *Learning Disability Quarterly, 39*(2), 72–82. doi:10.1177/0731948714555019

Graham, S., McKeown, D., Kiuhara, S., & Harris, K. R. (2012). A meta-analysis of writing instruction for students in the elementary grades. *Journal of Educational Psychology, 104*(4), 879–96. doi: 0.1037/a0029185

Graham, S., & Santangelo, T. (2014). Does spelling instruction make students better spellers, readers, and writers? A meta-analytic review. *Reading and Writing: An Interdisciplinary Journal, 27*(9), 1703–43. doi:10.1007/s11145-014-9517-0

Graham, S., & Weiner, B. (2012). Motivation: Past, present, and future. In K. R. Harris, S. Graham, & T. C. Urdan (Eds.), *APA educational psychology handbook: Vol. 1. Theories, constructs, and critical issues* (pp. 367–97). Washington, DC: American Psychological Association.

Greeno, J. G., & Engeström, Y. (2014). Learning in activity. In Sawyer, R. K. (Ed.), *The Cambridge handbook of the learning sciences* (2nd ed., pp. 128–47). Cambridge, UK: Cambridge University Press.

Hacker, D. J., Keener, M. C., & Kircher, J. C. (2009). Writing is applied metacognition. In D. J. Hacker, J. Dunlosky, & A. C. Graesser (Eds.), *Handbook of metacognition in education* (pp. 154–72). New York: Routledge.

Haworth, C. M. A., & Plomin, R. (2012). Genetics and education: Toward a genetically sensitive classroom. In K. R. Harris, S. Graham, & T. C. Urdan (Eds.), *APA educational psychology handbook: Vol. 1. Theories, constructs, and critical issues* (pp. 529–59). Washington, DC: American Psychological Association.

Hayes, J. R. (1996). A new framework for understanding cognition and affect in writing. In C. M. Levy & S. Ransdell (Eds.), *The science of writing: Theories, methods, individual differences, and applications* (pp. 1–27). Mahwah, NJ: Erlbaum.

Hayes, J. R. (2012). Modeling and remodeling writing. *Written Communication, 29*(3), 369–88. doi:10.1177/0741088312451260

Hendrickson, R. (1994). *The literary life and other curiosities* (rev. ed.). San Diego: Harvest Books.

Hendrix, S. H. (2016). *Martin Luther: Visionary reformer*. New Haven, CT: Yale University Press.

Hillocks, G. (2002). *The testing trap: How state writing assessments control learning*. New York: Teachers College Press.

History of Wikipedia (n.d.). In *Wikipedia*. Retrieved 12 November 2017 from https://en.wikipedia.org/wiki/History_of_Wikipedia

Hodgson, G. M., & Knudsen, T. (2010). *Darwin's conjecture: The search for general principles of social and economic evolution.* Chicago: University of Chicago Press.

Hsiang, T. P., & Graham, S. (2016). Teaching writing in grades 4–6 in urban schools in the Greater China Region. *Reading and Writing: An Interdisciplinary Journal, 29*(5), 869–902. doi:10.1007/s11145-015-9597-5

Hull, G., & Schultz, K. (2001). Literacy and learning out of school: A review of theory and research. *Review of Educational Research, 71*(4), 575–611.

Jacob, R., & Parkinson, J. (2015). The potential for school-based interventions that target executive function to improve academic achievement: A review. *Review of Educational Research, 85*(4), 512–52.

James, K. H., Jao, R. J., & Berninger, V. (2016). The development of multileveled writing systems of the brain: Brain lessons for writing instruction. In C. A. MacArthur, S. Graham, & J. Fitzgerald (Eds.), *Handbook of writing research* (2nd ed., pp. 116–29). New York: Guilford Press.

Jones, I. (1998). Peer relationships and writing development: A microgenetic analysis. *British Journal of Educational Psychology, 68*(2), 229–41. doi:10.1111/j.2044-8279.1998.tb01286.x

Kalman, J. (1996). Joint composition: The collaborative letter writing of a scribe and his client in Mexico. *Written Communication, 13*(2), 190–220. doi:10.1177/0741088396013002002

Kaufer, D., Hayes, J., & Flower, L. (1986). Composing written sentences. *Research in the Teaching of English, 20*(2), 121–40.

Kellogg, R. T. (1994). *The psychology of writing.* New York: Oxford University Press.

Kellogg, R. T., & Whiteford, A. P. (2009). Training advanced writing skills: The case for deliberate practice. *Educational Psychologist, 44*(4), 250–66. doi:10.1080/00461520903213600

Klein, P. D., & Leacock, T. L. (2012). Distributed cognition as a framework for understanding writing. In V. W. Berninger (Ed.), *Past, present, and future contributions of cognitive writing research to cognitive psychology* (pp. 133–52). New York: Psychology Press.

Kleinman, R. E., Hall, S., Green, H., Korzec-Ramirez, D., Patton, K., Pagano, M. E., & Murphy, J. M. (2002). Diet, breakfast, and academic performance in children. *Annals of Nutrition & Metabolism, 46*(supplement), 24–30. doi:10.1159/000066399

Knobel, M. (1999). *Everyday literacies: Students, discourse, and social practices.* New York: Peter Lang.

Knudson, R. E. (1989). Effects of instructional strategies on children's informational writing. *Journal of Educational Research 83*(2), 91–96.

Kwok, M. N., Ganding, E., Hull, G., & Moje, E. B. (2016). Sociocultural approaches to high school writing instruction: Examining the roles of context, positionality, and power. In C. A. MacArthur, S. Graham, & J. Fitzgerald (Eds.), *Handbook of writing research* (2nd ed., pp. 257–71). New York: Guilford Press.

Lave, J., & Wenger, E. (1991). *Situated learning: Legitimate peripheral participation.* Cambridge, UK: Cambridge University Press.

Locke, E. A., Shaw, K. N., Saari, L. M., & Latham, G. P. (1981). Goal setting and task performance: 1969–80. *Psychological Bulletin, 90*(1), 125–52. doi:10.1037/0033-2909.90.1.125

MacArthur, C. A., & Graham, S. (1987). Learning disabled students' composing under three methods of text production: Handwriting, word processing, and dictation. *Journal of Special Education, 21*(3), 22–42. doi:10.1177/002246698702100304

Madigan, R., Linton, P., & Johnson, S. (2006). The paradox of writing apprehension. In C. M. Levy & S. Ransdell (Eds.), *The science of writing: Theories, methods, individual differences, and applications* (pp. 295–308). Mahwah, NJ: Erlbaum.

Many, J. E., Fyfe, R., Lewis, G., & Mitchell, E. (1996). Traversing the topical landscape: Exploring students' self-directed reading-writing-research processes. *Reading Research Quarterly, 31*(1), 12–35.

Mayer, R. E. (2012). Information processing. In K. R. Harris, S. Graham, & T. C. Urdan (Eds.), *APA educational psychology handbook: Vol. 1. Theories, constructs, and critical issues* (pp. 85–100). Washington, DC: American Psychological Association.

McCarthy, S. J. (1994). Authors, text, and talk: The internalization of dialogue from social interaction during writing. *Reading Research Quarterly, 29*(3), 201–31.

McCutchen, D. (1988). "Functional automaticity" in children's writing: A problem of metacognitive control. *Written Communication, 5*(3), 306–24. doi:10.1177/0741088388005003003

Mitchell, S. D. (2003). *Biological complexity and integrative pluralism.* Cambridge, UK: Cambridge University Press.

Moje, E. (2009). Standpoints: A call for new research on new and multiliteracies. *Research in the Teaching of English, 43,* 348–62.

Moje, E. B., & Lewis, C. (2007). Examining opportunities to learn literacy: The role of critical sociocultural research. In C. Lewis, P. Enciso, & E. B. Moje (Eds.), *Reframing sociocultural research on literacy: Identity, agency, and power* (pp. 15–48). Mahwah, NJ: Erlbaum.

Moll, L. C. (1990). *Vygotsky and education: Instructional implications and applications of sociohistorical psychology.* Cambridge, UK: Cambridge University Press.

Morphy, P., & Graham, S. (2012). Word processing programs and weaker writers/readers: A meta-analysis of research findings. *Reading and Writing: An Interdisciplinary Journal, 25*(3), 641–78. doi:10.1007/s11145-015-9588-6

Morrow, L. M., & Young, J. (1997). A family literacy program connecting school and home: Effects on attitude, motivation, and literacy achievement. *Journal of Educational Psychology, 89*(4), 736–42. doi:10.1037/0022-0663.89.4.736

Mulderig, J. (Ed.) (2015). *Philip Sparrow tells all: Lost essays by Samuel Steward, writer, professor, tattoo artist.* Chicago: University of Chicago Press.

Olinghouse, N. G., Graham, S., & Gillespie, A. (2015). The relationship of discourse and topic knowledge to fifth graders' writing performance. *Journal of Educational Psychology, 107*(2), 391–406. doi:10.1037/a0037549

Paas, F., & Sweller, J. (2014). Implications of cognitive load theory for multimedia learning. In R. E. Mayer (Ed.), *The Cambridge handbook of multimedia learning* (2nd ed., pp. 27–42). Cambridge, UK: Cambridge University Press.

Pajares, F., Johnson, M., & Usher, E. (2007). Sources of writing self-efficacy beliefs of elementary, middle, and high school students. *Research in the Teaching of English, 42*(1), 104–20.

Pekrun, R., Frenzel, A. C., Goetz, T., & Perry, R. P. (2007). The control-value theory of achievement emotions: An integrative approach to emotions in education. In P. A. Schutz & R. Pekrun (Eds.), *Emotion in education* (pp. 13–27). San Diego: Academic Press.

Perry, K. (2012). What is literacy? A critical overview of sociocultural perspectives. *Journal of Language and Literacy Education, 8*(1), 50–71.

Pressley, M., Raphael, L., Gallagher, J. D., & DiBella, J. (2004). Providence–St. Mel School: How a school that works for African American students works. *Journal of Educational Psychology, 96*(2), 216–35. doi:10.1037/0022-0663.96.2.216

Rowe, D. (2008). The social construction of intentionality: Two-year-olds' and adults' participation at a preschool writing center. *Research in the Teaching of English, 42*(4), 387–434.

Russell, D. R. (1997). Rethinking genre in school and society: An activity theory analysis. *Written Communication, 14*(4), 504–54. doi:10.1177/0741088397014004004

Scardamalia, M., & Bereiter, C. (1986). Research on written composition. In M. C. Wittrock (Ed.), *Handbook of research on teaching* (3rd ed., pp. 778–803). New York: Macmillan.

Schultz, K., & Fecho, B. (2000). Society's child: Social context and writing development. *Educational Psychologist, 35*(1), 51–62.

Schunk, D. H. (2012). Social cognitive theory. In K. R. Harris, S. Graham, & T. C. Urdan (Eds.), *APA educational psychology handbook: Vol. 1. Theories, constructs, and critical issues* (pp. 101–23). Washington, DC: American Psychological Association.

Scribner, S., & Cole, M. (1981). *The psychology of literacy.* Cambridge, MA: Harvard University Press.

Shanahan, C., Shanahan, T., & Misischia, C. (2011). Analysis of expert readers in three disciplines: History, mathematics, and chemistry. *Journal of Literacy Research, 43*(4), 393–429. doi:10.1177/1086296X11424071

Shanahan, T. (2006). Relations among oral language, reading, and writing development. In C. A. MacArthur, S. Graham, & J. Fitzgerald (Eds.), *Handbook of writing research* (pp. 171–83). New York: Guilford Press.

Smagorinsky, P., & Mayer, R. E. (2014). Learning to be literate. In R. K. Sawyer (Ed.), *The Cambridge handbook of the learning sciences* (2nd ed., pp. 605–25). Cambridge, UK: Cambridge University Press.

Sperling, M., & DiPardo, A. (2008). English education research and classroom practice: New directions for new times. *Review of Research in Education, 32*, 62–108.

Stedman, R. C. (2003). Is it really just a social construction? The contribution of physical environment to sense of place. *Society and Natural Resources, 16*(8), 671–85. doi:10.1080/08941920309189

Swales, J. M. (1990). *Genre analysis: English in academic and research settings.* Cambridge, UK: Cambridge University Press.

Swerdlow, J. (1999). The power of writing. *National Geographic, 196*(2), 110–32.

Tierney, R. J., & Shanahan, T. (1991). Research on the reading-writing relationship: Interactions, transactions, and outcomes. In R. Barr, M. L. Kamil, P. B. Mosenthal, & P. D. Pearson (Eds.), *The handbook of reading research* (Vol. 2, pp. 246–80). New York: Longman.

Torrance, M., Thomas, G. V., & Robinson, E. J. (1996). Finding something to write about: Strategic and automatic processes in idea generation. In C. M. Levy & S. Ransdell (Eds.), *The science of writing: Theories, methods, individual differences, and applications* (pp. 189–206). Mahwah, NJ: Erlbaum.

Walberg, H. J., & Ethington, C. A. (1991). Correlates of writing performance and interest: A US National Assessment study. *Journal of Educational Research, 84*(4), 198–203.

Weiner, B. (1985). An attributional theory of achievement motivation and emotion. *Psychological Review, 92*(4), 548–73.

Wigfield, A., Tonks, S., & Klauda, S. L. (2009). Expectancy-value theory. In K. R. Wentzel & A. Wigfield (Eds.), *Handbook of motivation at school* (pp. 55–75). New York: Routledge.

Yancey, K. B. (2009). *Writing in the 21st century: A report from the National Council of Teachers of English.* Urbana, IL, National Council of Teachers of English.

Zeidner, M., & Matthews, G. (2012). Personality. In K. R. Harris, S. Graham, & T. C. Urdan (Eds.), *APA educational psychology handbook: Vol. 2. Individual differences and cultural and contextual factors* (pp. 111–37). Washington, DC: American Psychological Association.

Zimmerman, B. J., & Campillo, M. (2003). Motivating self-regulated problem solvers. In J. E. Davidson & R. J. Sternberg (Eds.), *The psychology of problem solving* (pp. 233–62). Cambridge, UK: Cambridge University Press.

Zimmerman, B. J., & Risemberg, R. (1997). Becoming a self-regulated writer: A social cognitive perspective. *Contemporary Educational Psychology, 22*(1), 73–101. doi:10.1006/ceps.1997.0919

Lifespan Longitudinal Studies of Writing Development: A Heuristic for an Impossible Dream

CHARLES BAZERMAN

University of California, Santa Barbara

Writing is not only a school subject, it is a medium of ex-change, communication, and action throughout life—and we need to understand how use and skill in writing develop across the lifespan.

Writing is a medium that has grown in its importance, variety, and pervasiveness since its multiple inventions in the Fertile Crescent, China, South Asia, and Meso-America a few millennia ago. As it has grown it has become an ever-richer resource for participation in a wider set of activities that have themselves come to depend on writing. Full participation in these activities has required ever-greater skills and ever-more-subtle understanding of the many refined resources available within writing.

Accordingly, apprenticeship in writing has become an in-creasingly long and complex one, requiring decades for advanced flexible expertise, with skill potentially increasing throughout one's life. Further, expertise itself has become more variable, with people skilled in one domain and not others, and each person's path and repertoire distinctive, even within the same domain. Being a skilled poet does not necessarily coincide with being a skilled novelist, and neither necessarily with being a great drafter of legislation, writer of scientific papers, or effective contributor to collaborative workplace reports. Yet even as writing has presented more challenges, it has become imperative for every person to learn to gain place and voice in the world, to gain the benefits of participation, and to avoid the costs of exclusion. In this context of growing demands and growing rewards for writing, schooling has developed to meet social needs for literates, starting with the early schools for scribes in the ancient Middle East and leading to current norms of universal education through adolescence, within which writing is taking an increasing role.

Understanding the varied pathways to competence and expertise in writing can help educators provide support to writers at every stage from early childhood through adulthood, and further it can help people self-monitor and guide their own development in realistic terms. But how can we understand people's varied pathways into writing and their varied pathways to achievement? Or how can we understand the complexity of even one individual's idiosyncratic pathway to the mature competence that provides a confident, strong, and unique written presence within the individual's lifeworld? These concerns form the basic problematic of this volume and the Lifespan Writing Development Project.

An obvious contribution to answering these questions would be a rich body of longitudinal studies of the writing development across the entire lifespan of many people of varied backgrounds and experience. Lifespan longitudinal data can break down the silos we now have of writing being researched only within age groups or levels of schooling. They can reveal how writing takes on different roles, purposes, and meanings at different moments in life as well as when and how different forms of development emerge at different times in life. This knowledge will give us insight into how writing developments can be supported in a timely, appropriate way, suggesting how curriculum and instruction might be varied to be developmentally appropriate throughout the course of education. It will highlight the individuality of developmental accomplishment and pathways in writing.

Such a project may seem quixotic and perhaps impossible in its magnitude, expense, and logistical complexity, as well as in terms of simple data collection and records maintenance. Yet it is worth contemplating as a thought experiment to help us conceive of writing development, reframe and synthesize existing research, and plan other less ambitious projects with more modest goals.

Adopting a lifespan longitudinal perspective helps put the focus on the uniqueness, creativity, and meaning of writing development for individuals, within the complexity of their separate lives. Longitudinal studies offer the possibility of understanding individuals following unique pathways leading to unique skills, orientations, and responses in situations rather than being normalized through cross-sectional groups of age, educational level, or other category, with individuals being characterized as either typical or atypical. Rather, a long-term longitudinal view perceives the individual in relation to access to resources and experiences, sequences of events, learning opportunities and challenges, orientations to those opportunities, developmental sequences, formation of writing processes, and emerging identities. That is, we can see how the writer at each moment draws on unique prior experiences and resources to identify, understand, and act in each new event, thereby further developing through the solving of new writing problems. If we collect adequate situational data, we can see writing growth taking place as a response to social situations and demands, and formative of social relations and identities, which in turn provide further opportunities for challenge and development. In this way we can come to better understand the interaction between the intraindividual and the interindividual within writing development.

These processes continue throughout life with the potential for increased and varied competence as the years go on, as the most skilled may not reach the highest levels of achievement and individual distinctiveness until their later years. Further, transitions of life conditions and writing needs, stagnation, disruptions, redirections, or deterioration of writing also are important to understand, and can occur in different ways at different points in life. Thus longitudinal studies ideally should extend across the entire lifespan to see the total picture and to understand how early experiences and growth affect later opportunities, resources, and challenges, as well as how future goals may motivate earlier learning.

Drawing such a large picture, lifespan longitudinal studies of writing development will need to collect rich linguistic, textual, social, interactional, psychological, economic, cultural, and even neurological data in order to look at all dimensions potentially relevant to writing development. The contextual and developmental data themselves will need to be dynamic, as writing, society, and people are ever creative, ever changing. Yet such a project will provide us the materials to see the variety of experiences, and perhaps give us understanding of some underlying processes that are engaged broadly. At the very least we will see how long and complex the journey is for each individual and how far the different journeys take people in different directions within the contingencies of society, politics, economy, and personal life. This larger picture will extend beyond schooling to include all of literate life, though schooling is likely to be an important part at least of the early development, providing resources and orientations for later challenges. Indeed, part of the goal of such research would be to highlight writing development as something distinct from passage through particular curricula or school experiences. Finally, collection of such rich data can provide a resource for future researchers to draw on, reanalyze, or compare to newly collected data. Even a few lifetime cases collected in rich detail can support many kinds of after-the-fact research. A wider scope of cases will further increase the potential usefulness, widening our vision and questioning our assumptions.

The remainder of this essay will project the potential scope of such a project in the most ambitious terms as a prod to future investigators. As part of considering what a lifespan study might look like, and its challenges, I will first examine some of the principles and practices of longitudinal studies in other domains, and particularly multidecade or lifespan longitudinal studies, to see how they are organized and how similar and different they are to what would be needed in studying lifespan development of writing. While some aspects of longitudinal studies in other fields may seem more distant from the needs of writing studies than others, it is useful for clarity to consider the full range of thinking about longitudinal studies. In this early section, comments on writing studies will appear sporadically as they seem appropriate. After examining the broad scope of long-term longitudinal studies, I will propose more systematically some key features of the design of a longitudinal study of writing development. The strategy in that design will be heuristically to draw as broad an investigative scope as possible, making few narrowing choices, while being transparent about the theoretical standpoint and the practical difficulties involved. Of course, actual studies to follow will need to make narrowing choices as they focus their inquiries into doable projects.

Longitudinal Studies in Other Fields

Longitudinal studies have been used as far back as the eighteenth century (Tetens, 1777; Carus, 1808), in biological development, health and medicine, epidemiology, well-being studies, developmental psychology, demography, sociology, and other fields. In each field they have had somewhat different designs, different kinds of data, and different data sources, pursuing the interests of those disciplines and professions. What they have in common is the periodic collection of data from a designated population of specific individuals in a time-ordered study for description and explanation. What counts as appropriate and adequate description and explanation, of course, also depends on disciplinary interests, standards, and states of theory and knowledge. The disciplinary issues for the study of writing will be discussed below. However, more generally, description might include trajectories of consistencies and changes, and explanation might include patterns across individuals (Robins et al., 2002), identification of characteristics that remain consistent within individuals (for example, Roberts & DelVecchio, 2000; Roberts, Walton, & Viechtbauer, 2006), sequences of development or developments associated with life epochs, variables of individual characteristics that correlate with later outcomes to indicate causes (Nesselroade & Baltes, 1979; Orth, Robins, & Widaman, 2012; Sarkadi, Kristiansson, Oberklaid, & Bremberg, 2008), or models of development (Reitzle & Vondracek, 2000).

For a study to be considered longitudinal it must follow its subjects over sufficient time to make visible earlier differences and later changes, typically a number of years, though in periods of rapid change, such as the first months of life, shorter periods may be appropriate. To allow comparisons over time, typically some measures and instruments are repeated, but because of life changes some data collections may vary at different times (Lynn, 2009). For example, while measures of social connection at the youngest ages may rely on observations or parent surveys, in school years data about neighborhood and schooling may be added along with child oral self-reports and interviews, to be displaced in adulthood by periodic subject self-reports through digital surveys.

Different from prospective longitudinal lifespan studies are retrospective longitudinal studies that collect existing data and records (such as health or schooling records) to see how earlier records predict current outcomes. These have the benefit of not requiring such extensive institutional apparatus and being doable within a compact period of time, but they are dependent on the quality and continuity not only of records but also of the particular interests that motivated the data collection. These studies cannot gather additional or different historical data that might be of interest for the research questions, but which were not the concern of earlier recordkeepers. A longitudinal perspective on development can also be obtained by retrospective interviews, such as has been pursued in writing studies by Deborah Brandt (2001, 2015, and this volume). These have the benefits and limitations of drawing on memories of individuals, offering the continuous presence and perspective of the individual, but subject to the vagaries of memory, the selectivity of self-presentation, and the absence of real-time external data and confirmation.

In longitudinal research the focus is on individuals, but longitudinal studies can also reveal how interindividual interactions may influence intraindividual change and how intraindividual change may in turn influence interindividual interactions (Nesselroade & Baltes, 1979). In this respect longitudinal research differs from age-stratified cross-sectional methods that treat subjects as part of categories rather than as individuals (Rajulton, 2001). Robinson, Schmidt, & Teti (2005) suggest that though cross-sectional studies are easier and cheaper, and may be useful for proposing hypotheses and identifying age group differences and subgroups within cohorts, they cannot indicate the causes or trajectories of change within individuals. The longitudinal focus on individuals over time, and the potential for considering the relation between the individual and others are of obvious value for studying writing development, which can be highly individualized but takes place within social orientations, perceptions, behavior, imitation, typifications, and effects, that themselves may be idiosyncratically experienced and perceived by individuals.

In longitudinal research, groups of individuals are usually tracked in parallel to support comparison, with a common starting point, whether defined by birth, entering a school, or suffering a trauma or other initiating event. These historical events may identify a small group, such as via entrance to an educational institution or diagnosis with a specific medical or psychiatric condition, or they may be shared across a large group, such as via the initiation of a war. A variation is to seek developmental epochs or developmental sequences and to match subjects engaged in such sequences. Whatever the starting point, usually the longitudinal groups are chosen to share that initiation point. However, sequences of cohorts may also be chosen to provide for comparisons across historical change or for other reasons.

Another characteristic of longitudinal studies is an intentional periodicity in measures and data collection, as well as a consistency of measures over time as opposed to life histories constructed from whatever records, data, and reports are available or otherwise loosely structured narratives (Janson, 1981.) Data may be collected from many kinds of sources including institutional records such as hospital, school, or justice systems; surveys; interviews; medical or psychiatric examinations; observations; or repeated task performance or psychological instruments. Variables collected for correlation tend to be focused and limited (e.g., diet, income, geographic mobility) and are usually readily associated as characteristics of individuals. Thus health studies look at how behavioral, environmental, and biological variables correlate with morbidity or health problems. Even social issues (such as attendance at different schools, number of social contacts, or kinds of family arrangements) can be characterized as variables of individuals.

Although some studies use qualitative data, the larger number of studies rely largely on quantitative data that are then statistically analyzed, and much of the methodological literature on longitudinal studies is devoted to statistical issues (for example, Cook & Ware, 1983; Helms, 1992), modeling issues (for example, Petersen, 1993; Hertzog & Nesselroade, 2003), or computational tools (Brandmaier, von Oertzen, Ghisletta, Hertzog, & Lindenberger, 2015). Such studies can be useful in writing studies to see if there are patterns in family and social situations, schooling characteristics, and the amount of writing or use of writing that might predict later engagement with writing, or to uncover other patterns to be investigated by other means, but such studies do not seek out the meanings embodied in texts, writing strategies or repertoires, writing practices or processes, the quality or efficacy of the texts, complex processes and practices, or the orientations and meanings for the authors engaged in specific situations. So while some statistical measures may be of use for studying writing development, they would likely need to be used in conjunction with more qualitative, individualized studies.

Multidecade and Lifespan Longitudinal Studies

While longitudinal studies typically track subjects over a number of years, full lifespan or even multiple-decade studies are less common. The costs and logistical challenges of all longitudinal studies tend to be high, including keeping track of subjects, keeping attrition to a minimum, keeping records, and maintaining a research team over years. At the same time the payoff in results and publications is slow. So the anticipated benefit of long-term longitudinal study over stratified samples must be apparent, and significant enough to offset the difficulties and costs. To that is added the need to recruit new researchers and to account for changing theories, research interests, and data-collection methods. Initial interests may define the data-collection regime, which then constrain later studies. For example the longest-standing continuous lifespan study, the Terman study of gifted individuals started in 1921, relied on the Stanford-Binet intelligence test to identify the study population (Terman, 1925). The value and meaning of such tests have since been called into question, definitions of giftedness have changed and remain contended, and the outcome variables and data-collection methods have now been long outdated. Further, since IQ was thought to be a fixed individual genetic characteristic, fewer social data were collected about opportunities and experiences that might serve to allow talents to flourish or enhance capacities. The only systematic collection of data was periodic mail-in self-report surveys of accomplishments and life conditions. Despite the limitations of the study (and the substantial critiques of the underlying theory, the subject selection, and the data collection) the study did have a number of direct and indirect findings, one of which was in fact to disconfirm the underlying hypothesis that high scores in intelligence tests would result in better career, economic, and health outcomes than matched peers (Terman & Oden, 1959). Less directly, since the study added subjects over a period of seven years and the cohorts experienced both the Great Depression and the World War II military draft, the effect of these events could be compared across matched cohorts of different generations (Elder, Shanahan, & Clipp, 1997).

Another long-term longitudinal study, the Harvard Study of Adult Development, initiated in 1937 and based on similar genetic beliefs about talented individuals, tells an even more complex story about how with sufficient flexibility studies may be maintained over long periods and data remain useful despite changes in theories, directors, institutional arrangements, historical conditions, technologies, measurement interests, and measurement instruments. Over the years research questions changed, new measurements and data-collection methods were added, and many different kinds of findings were drawn from the research data (see Vaillant, 2002 and 2012, for further details). The 268 study subjects were selected from Harvard students in the classes from 1939 to 1945. The selection of students and the initial measures were intended to elaborate now-outdated theories of biological superiority and success in life. Reflecting the Harvard population at the time, the subjects were all male and overwhelmingly Protestant, from well-off, even affluent backgrounds. However, 10 percent of the sample was Jewish and 10 percent Catholic. Also included were scholarship students from working-class backgrounds who were judged as highly talented. The men were chosen, in the terms of the time, for "soundness." Other potential subjects were eliminated for signs of weakness of character, deviance, lack of psychological fitness, weak body type, and similar reasons. Early measures included interviews but focused on physical condition, body measures, physical dexterity, psychiatric and intelligence measures, family background, even the primitive EEGs available at the time and handwriting samples for character analysis. Early data did not support the initial hypotheses, as a number of the subjects had less happy or less successful lives than expected. But the data turned out to be useful for other questions, such as what factors may have contributed to leadership as indicated by rise in the officers' ranks in

World War II. Interestingly, the only positive correlation for career advancement came from a personality predisposition to politics and the only negative correlation from creative and imaginative personalities (Valliant, 2012, Chapter 2). Another analysis used the carefully matched sample to show that medical doctors turned out to abuse prescription medication at twice the rate as did others of similar background but following different professions (Vaillant, Brighton, & McArthur, 1970). Over the years funders and funding levels changed, dominant theories changed, study directors changed, and technological means changed. Some data collection was dropped, new data collection was added, and the data were analyzed for different purposes. But periodic surveys and interviews continued, maintaining some continuity. For example, as theories of social relations became more important, the effect of personal relations on life measures was added as a research focus. Interviews with wives, siblings, and children were added as the men matured, and new assessments were made of work, love, and play adjustments. Then as the men grew older, questions of successful aging became the central research focus— with new questions added to the interviews. The effects of aging and new biological knowledge led also to a return in later years to health and physical data as well as genetic DNA analysis, but within new theoretical contexts.

One important element of study success was the development of personal relationships between the researchers and the subjects over the years and repeated cycles of data gathering. The trust and intimacy (along with the extensiveness of knowledge of each subject aggregated in files) helped maintain the engagement of the subjects and led to depth in the interviews (Vaillant, 2012, Chapter 3; see also Thomson & Holland, 2003). The return of a staff member who had temporarily retired even helped bring back subjects who had stopped communicating with the study. On the other hand, this importance of relationships highlights how repeated contact and data collection in longitudinal studies can influence the behavior and thinking of subjects, resulting in panel conditioning (Rajulton, 2001; Lynn, 2009).

An important lesson of the Harvard Study of Adult Development is that even though researchers cannot control or foresee the future, and even though hindsight would lead to regrets about limitations of prior data collection, the overall continuous record remains of value if flexibly and creatively used, and could answer many questions beyond the initial scope of the study. Despite the ideal of consistent data collection over the years built into the initial plan, data collection can be modified to fit new perspectives.

Lessons from Long-Term Longitudinal Studies in Psychological Development

The principles of understanding writing development proposed by the Lifespan Writing Development Group in this volume point to multiple dimensions of writing developing simultaneously and through engagement with a variety of learning and problem-solving experiences. While focused longitudinal studies that attempt to examine one dimension of writing development might call for only a limited data set, a more multidimensional picture would require a richer, more multidimensional data set, which will consider individual pathways through varied experiences, both in school and out as well as before the school years and beyond—through career, life experiences, and ultimately old age. This essay will spell out some of the possible data needs and gathering techniques below, but it is evident that the amount of potentially relevant data is massive, and that analysis will be even more challenging, as suggested by the two substantial data sets collected of just the undergraduate years in two particular institutions, Stanford and Harvard, as discussed below.

The dilemma faced by writing studies bears some similarity to those faced by the study of psychological development. Within both there is a desire to map out the particularity of individual experience and to trace changes and pathways over time, seeing the responses, performances, and understandings of the older person as a result of the experiences, orientations, resources, and skills amassed previously. Further, in both areas development has been understood to be a function not only of biological development but also of situation, context, and experience; engagement with others; and learning from them by explicit, implicit, and mediated means. This complexity widens the need for multiple kinds of data that extend beyond the individual. Thus as the person develops the potential dimensions of data expand, and the developmental story becomes potentially more complex. In both domains longitudinal studies have a great attraction, but meet many challenges. In this volume, Brandt also considers the lessons from developmental psychology for understanding writing development; but here I will focus on the methodological lessons to be drawn from developmental psychology, as the field has a substantial history of puzzling through the designs of longitudinal studies and then carrying them out, with successes and shortcomings.

Kagan (1981) suggests that rather than searching for simple patterns of development, within the complexity of multivariate data one should look for questions of how structures maintain and preserve themselves, which ones change, what the mechanisms of change are, what elicits growth, and how growth rates might differ. The implication is that we not seek immediate comparison across individuals, but that we analyze first the nature of each individual's development, what structures we can find within the individuals, what patterns and mechanisms of structural maintenance and change appear, and what variables or conditions or events initiate change and affect the rate of change. These processes and variables may then be more fruitfully compared across individuals. Robinson, Schmidt, & Teti (2005) similarly suggest that rather than comparing across age, cohorts, life periods, or events we match comparisons across the actual developments of interest to us. Thus in writing studies we might compare all individuals who are able to handle a particular syntactic pattern or all those who show a spontaneous tendency to reflect on larger text structure or all those who are aware of the stance their text takes toward an audience. Further, Reitzle and Vondracek (2000, p. 446) suggest that timing is more informative than accumulated time; that is, more important than chronological age or period of time is the point at which an individual is able to make complex decisions of a particular sort, and how that change might appear within a sequence of prior events and the individual's awareness of the relevant considerations. Peterson also focuses attention on event histories, sequencing, time in state, and timing of change within individuals.

Schooler (1984), in reviewing a number of studies, finds strong evidence for a hypothesis that might have important implications for writing development. The hypothesis posits that diversity of stimuli and complexity of environment leads to effective cognitive functioning and nonconformist orientations. That is, the richer the environment, the more novel are the decisions made by the individual. The implications for writing development may be both that complex environments may generate more distinctive individualized writing, and that writing activities can provide rewards for cognitive originality. Consequently, the further an individual is drawn into the complexity of writing situations and the potentials of decision making on multiple dimensions, the more the individual may be further drawn to uniqueness of expression and production. The writing work then itself becomes a complex problem-solving environment.

Baltes (1987) makes a related methodological suggestion that the way to study cognitive flexibility and developmental plasticity—that is, the ability to adapt and grow rapidly (as well as to measure periods of decline)—is to test the limits of individuals' responses to situations. This may in fact suggest a mechanism for development in that those who grow are those who are in positions and have dispositions that test their limits and put them at risk with challenging tasks. On the other hand, Baltes & Nesselroade (1979) point to the possibilities that development may be discontinuous, open to attrition, and multidirectional rather than unidirectional. This is important to point out for writing development, where growth is unequally distributed. Only part of the population finds itself addressing challenging situations, whereas others may avoid challenges or find that their lives do not require writing challenges of them. Attrition may occur for many reasons, or writing development where it does occur may be multidirectional, with directions developing at different paces and some directions advancing at the cost of others.

Longitudinal Studies in Writing

Prior shorter-term longitudinal studies in writing can also provide us some guidance in how we might design a lifespan study, even though they have been of shorter duration and have not faced the problems of studying development across multiple stages of life. Prior studies usually have been contained within students' attendance in an institution, most commonly an undergraduate university program, or their entry into a professional position (see Rogers, 2010, for a review). These have tended to rely on qualitative analysis of texts combined with periodic interviews and perhaps observations in order to understand individual pathways, interests of students, and sometimes disciplinary enculturation. The analyses have been individualized and interpretive. The most detailed and in-depth of these have been of a small number of subjects (between one and four), revealing how skills, orientation toward writing, and identity have developed interactively as students' educational and life situations have evolved (for example, Herrington & Curtis, 2000; McCarthy, 1987; Beaufort, 2004; Haas, 1994; Spack, 1997; Chiseri-Strater, 1991; Artemeva, 2009). There have been a few similar studies for graduate students (for example, Berkenkotter, Huckin, & Ackerman, 1991; Blakeslee, 1997; Prior, 1998).

Longitudinal studies of a somewhat larger size have typically led to generalization in the analysis and reporting and a loss of detail. Carroll (2002), with 46 subjects, reports only generalized trends, using individual cases as examples or exceptions to the trends rather than understanding individual pathways. As the driving purpose of the study was program design, there is substantial justification for the strategies that seek common threads, but from the point of view of understanding developmental pathways such studies contribute only some general themes. Larger samples have produced even greater challenges to analyses; in particular the Harvard Study of Writing (n=422) and the Stanford Study of Writing (n=189) have yet to produce any overall aggregative or contrastive analyses, rather presenting only a single-subject case study (Fishman, Lunsford, McGregor, & Otuteye, 2005) or interpretive thematic essays using anecdotal examples from the corpus (Sommers & Saltz, 2004). Rogers (2008), however, has attempted trait-based analyses of a subset of the Stanford corpus (n=40) to examine variations in growth in different dimensions, along with a grounded thematic analysis of a subset of the annual student interviews concerning their perceptions of their changing writing experiences.

Sternglass's (1997) midsize cohort (n=53) attends both to individuals and to larger thematic findings, supported systematically by the data. Through qualitative analyses of texts and interviews, Sternglass found certain developmental pathways for students of similar background and challenges as open admissions students, but also found individual differences in how these pathways developed for different students.

A different strategy for gaining more focused longitudinal studies has been to limit the data to language production. Within higher education Haswell (2000) used detailed linguistic and trait-based scoring of two writing samples from the same students (n=64) two years apart to identify changes in the texts between the first and third years. Loban (1967) used a wide range of spoken and written samples of student language from 211 subjects from kindergarten to grade 12, to identify changes in spoken and written language use. While the collection was longitudinal for the 211 subjects, and some sociocultural demographic data was gathered and used for correlations, the analysis is aggregative, revealing typical patterns across all users, and then compared across sociocultural groups.

Hunt (1965) examined changes in syntactic structures of eighteen students at each of three grade levels (4, 8, and 12) using stratified samples, with aggregated results and analysis to indicate general patterns of change. More recently and in greater detail Christie (2012) and Christie and Derewianka (2008) mapped grammatical development across grade levels, differentiated by discipline and genre, using extensive stratified data from numerous studies and piecing together investigations at different levels. That research is further analyzed in this volume by Schleppegrell and Christie.

Most longitudinal studies of writing development in the early years and early grades have viewed writing within the context of overall emergent literacy, tending to focus more on reading than writing, with a few notable exceptions (see Tierney & Sheehy, 2003, for a review). Emergent-literacy studies of individual young children have described early productive behavior in the context of total literacy awareness. Some of these have included writing as indicating print awareness and alphabetic knowledge

(MacIntyre & Freppon, 1994), letter formation and spelling, including invented spelling (e.g., Cochran-Smith, 1984; Beers & Henderson, 1977; Goodman, 1986; Bloodgood, 1999; Treiman, 1993), and phonological awareness (Chapman, 1996). Rowe (1987) found literacy events developing within social interactions as 3- and 4-year-olds learned from one another, incorporating meanings and communicative tools shared in interaction in order to construct their own texts and respond to the texts of others.

A few longitudinal studies of emergent literacy based on parent journals have focused more centrally on writing (Hildreth, 1932, 1934, 1936; Butler, 1979; Bissex, 1980). In early school years, as students progress through the first four grades, King and Rentel have found an increase in coherence through the use of identity and similarity markers, and the use of narrative structures as early as the second grade (King & Rentel, 1982; Rentel & King, 1983). Sipe (1998) also found in the first grade a movement toward conventionality. A team study of third- and fourth-grade students (Goodman & Wilde, 1992) looked at a number of different aspects of writing development within the longitudinal group. Wilde (1992), Wilde et al. (1992), and Kasten (1992) found both narrative and conventionality increasing with increasing use of human and inanimate resources and invented spelling moving toward conventional. Berninger, Abbott, Nagy, and Carlisle (2010) show variable growth rates for phonological, orthographic, and morphological awareness across the elementary grades. Vaughan (1992) found increasing genre and audience awareness, growing writers' identities, and increasing syntactic complexity and length. Wilde et al. (1992) found that while progress was not linear, overall there was long-term growth in audience awareness, conventions, and genres. In a different series of studies, Abbott, Berninger, and Fayol (2010) found relations among development of word reading, comprehension, spelling, and composing in grades 1 to 7. Dyson (1993, 1997, 2003) found children developing written meanings within their social interactional environment using resources they had found from their entire cultural experiences. Digital changes in process and activity have opened up new kinds of studies, with some in informal settings, tracking the influence of engagement in new technology (for example, Tierney & Sheehy, 2003), and also the benefits and costs of handwriting versus keyboarding for various populations.

Only a few studies have been able to track students in their transition from one educational setting to another. Beaufort (1999), Dias, Freedman, Medway, and Paré (1999), and Winsor (1996) have followed students from the university to the workplace, highlighting the difference of conditions and writing goals and the requirements for new orientations and developmental paths. Tremain (2015) examined how efficacy and dispositions toward writing of high school students influenced how well they were able to transfer their prior writing knowledge to writing at the university.

Overall, prior longitudinal studies in writing have presented the challenge of tradeoffs between, on one hand, individual and text-sensitive measures that highlight the particulars of individual pathways of development, and that are attentive to the meanings developed and the sophistication of text production, and, on the other hand, the aggregation of larger corpora that are amenable to quantitative analysis but that wash out variability and developmental pathways along with individuality of accomplishment and repertoire. These challenges are both in the collection of sufficient data of appropriate kinds and in the analysis of the rich data that might be collected. The greatest successes have been when the literacy experiences and accomplishments have been most contained within the family and early schooling. As the child gets older and engages in more activities and more complex productions with more resources, within more varied situations, the potential data and dimensions of development expand rapidly, making comprehensive collection and analysis more difficult.

Study Design

Based on what we have learned from prior longitudinal studies in writing and other fields, this essay will now project how a writing development study could be designed. Issues to be considered include selection of the study population, kinds of data that would be useful, data-gathering techniques, periodicity of data gathering, recordkeeping, study management, and other logistics. Many possibilities will be presented here, but of course any real study would necessarily need to make choices.

But first, given the history of longitudinal studies, we should consider the underlying theory that drives the design I offer, even though data collected can be reused and reanalyzed as theories are discredited or found less useful and new theoretical ideas come to the fore. Further, also given the lessons of the value of flexibility, we might consider how some of the data collection might extend beyond our current interests to other possible orientations, even if the theories, measurements, and analytical tools may not yet be well developed.

The design features proposed here rest on an understanding of the social nature of writing; the importance of the individual's perception of the situations and attitudinal and emotional orientation to the situation; the available language resources for choice making; the intertextual resources drawn on and intertextual position adopted; the available technologies and materialities of production and communication; genres and other typifications of meaning and situation; and activity systems mediated by and participated in through writing. Development in this view is achieved through a history of engaged and motivated experiences that extend the writer's perception of situations, resources, and possible decisions. These experiences may be supported by instruction, models, and other forms of explicit information and advice, but development can also occur though implicit and spontaneous improvisatory responses to perceived situations and the implicit rewards and costs for the choices made. Writing and writing development follow unique individual tracks based on those histories of experiences and engagements within activity systems, and on the pursuit of one's own stances, interests, and meanings within those systems. Overall, while writing has psychological, rhetorical, linguistic, intertextual, graphic, material, cultural, and social elements, it is ultimately a form of social participation and social meaning making, with development being part of the process of increasing one's engagement with social groups, forming identities within them, and carrying out activities through the sharing of meanings. These views I believe are consistent with the overall principles developed by the Lifespan Writing Development Group presented in Chapter 2. I believe they are also consistent with my more extended theoretical statements in *A Rhetoric of Literate Action* and *A Theory of Literate Action* (Bazerman, 2013a, 2013b).

Other theories of writing development might of course point to other kinds of data. Some of these theories might be consistent with the picture presented here, supplementing it, while others might lead to basically different explanatory systems. For example, although at the moment neurological and brain studies are limited in their applicability to writing, they might provide another dimension, as we are able to track how the brain and neurological system respond during writing processes and how brain architecture might constrain and direct writing development, or might itself develop in response to writing experiences, making more enduring structures out of what might otherwise be contingent and fleeting assemblages. It might even turn out that there are neurobiologically determined elements to meaning, meaning making, and sign use that cannot be influenced by experience, but rather shape experience and thus writing development. While it is likely that neuroscience will develop theories that bear on writing in the coming decades it is hard to predict where they will go and whether they might obviate some or all of the ideas that are built into this design of the study. This would suggest that we collect at least some baseline brain and neurological data for the research subjects using current technology, even though they will likely be superseded by new forms of data and data gathering.

Similarly, given that technologies of communication are likely to change rapidly, we might include more data than would be suggested by our existing theories on how flexibly and creatively our subjects respond to new technologies and how creatively they explore the opportunities provided, as well as how new technologies serve to disrupt prior established writing practices and modes of development. Recent studies, for example, of the response to and effect of learning keyboarding without handwriting are the leading edge of much broader technological studies. As technology may also take over more of the functions of production (as spellchecking, keyboarding, and templates have already done) or facilitate processes (such as revision, collaboration, intertextual access and incorporation, and graphic design), different dimensions of the composition process may come to the fore, even to the point of overtaking features we had previously thought of as central.

While it is easy to see that developments in neuroscience and technology may lead to new issues to explore and perhaps major theoretical reorientations, other developments may lead in other directions, such as our understanding of the role of written communication in social cooperation, division, and attitude formation, or the formation of larger-group knowledge and beliefs. The multiple variables potentially of importance to writing performance and development both contained within the current theoretical perspectives and within possible future ones suggest that a study be as broad-ranging in its data collection as possible in the initial collection and be flexible in expanding or adding dimensions of data as changing theoretical perspectives come to the fore and new technologies allow enhanced data gathering. Of course, as we will explore below, some relevant data would be difficult and resource-intensive to collect, and the data are of different sorts, so collecting them would require multiple methods. Every extension of data would require further resources and difficulties, so ultimately choices and tradeoffs will have to be made. Yet the broader the initial picture is, the more informed the tradeoff decisions and focused choices may be.

Subject Population and Study Maintenance

This study should have multiple cohorts, representing many different life situations. One possibility would be cohorts of closely matched individuals large enough to show interindividual differences among people of similar socioeconomic and linguistic background as well as initial schooling. For this purpose, choosing each cohort from a single neighborhood that feeds into a single school system would be a reasonable strategy. With perhaps ten to twenty in each cohort cluster, the study could explore both how individual and family variables might have an impact, as well as how individual experiences, dispositions, and interests lead in different directions. But then there should be multiple cohorts from rather different circumstances (such as different socioeconomic situations, different linguistic situations, or different educational backgrounds). Further, it would be useful to have cohorts from different countries with different national languages and educational systems. Immigration would create further challenges in tracking, but would also be an opportunity to study the impact of mobility. While it would be best to have a high degree of coordination of the research and data collection at these many sites, it is also possible that independently formed and maintained projects can provide useful data for comparison. For example, Vaillant (2002, 2012) was able to make comparisons between the privileged subjects of his Harvard Study of Adult Development and a less privileged set of subjects in the Inner-City Cohort of youth who had gotten into legal troubles (Glueck & Glueck, 1950), even though the designs and purposes of the studies were substantially different.

The usual uncertainties of attrition in such a lifetime study would be compounded by a number of factors. Those with most divergent and expansive writing development may be most difficult to keep track of and may be most geographically mobile. The amount of participation required to get the wide-ranging data of multiple sorts that might be deemed important may get tiresome or inconvenient for participants. Further, as participants get older they may become ashamed or anxious about writing or have some other personal reasons for nondisclosure. While personal contact with researchers who come to be known and trusted, as well as the potential benefits of reflective understanding of writing and the sense of specialness that might come from being part of the study, may help maintain participant loyalty to the research over the years, writing at least currently is viewed as so tied to personal worth and socioeconomic position that there may be much self-selection in and out of the study. That self-selection may be based on what participants view as positive outcomes, so the study might lose sight of trajectories that the participants are not proud of.

In addition to all the difficulties of locating, keeping track of, and maintaining engagement of diverse subjects, and of gathering, maintaining, and analyzing the massive and multidimensional data collected, there will also be practical problems of maintaining research teams in multiple locations with continuity and coordination across multiple generations of researchers. Then there are problems of getting enough initial funding to get such a large project or even a piece of it off the ground and enough commitments going forward to take the risk. Finally, a research strategy that produces research publications from early on, using only partial data, may be important to demonstrate the value of the study and maintain the commitment of the stakeholders.

Age of Initiation

Since emergent writing behaviors may appear very early in the form of the infant observing and interacting with older sibs and parents and engaging in early play with writing implements, surfaces, and electronic devices, it would be useful to identify subjects as early as possible, possibly even within the first year. While such early interactions may not be considered to be distinctive, there may be substantial differences in the amount of literate behavior around the infant subjects, how they attend to it, and what interactive play and imitative behaviors they engage in. These differences may provide beginning links in the various trajectories people develop as writers and how deeply literacy and writing enter into their formation of communicative consciousness and identity. While we have some broad-stroke understanding of how general exposure to reading and literacy in the family facilitates reading and educational achievement, we really have no detailed understanding of individual formations and how earlier experiences are enacted later, particularly with respect to writing. Early exposure may also have impacts that are not directly expressed in school performance, but may influence other domains of writing outside or beyond schooling. Think, for example, of the child who early on enters into a text-messaging world, perhaps facilitated by touch icons or videos prior to mastery of spelling.

While enlisting infants and their families may present special difficulties and may lead to sociocultural biases in the sampling, children by ages three or four entering daycare and prekindergarten settings might be easier to locate. A careful selection of sites may also overcome sampling bias. Starting data collection at that age would reasonably catch most of the early struggle with writing conventions and discovery of the communicative power of writing, but subjects would best be observed from the first day to establish starting baselines, which should be supplemented by family visits, observations, and caregiver interviews to gain at least some idea of the child's engagement with language, literacy, and writing prior to organized educational settings.

Consistency and Variation of Data Collection

We should also consider the consistency of data across the life-span. This study suggests something other than the simple repetition of data collection across all subjects and across all years, as you might have in a health study where the same medical indicators are recorded periodically. At least four considerations suggest a more complex and varying set of data.

First there is difference that comes from different regions. Different samples may present different opportunities, constraints, and strategies for data collection. For example, early childhood facilities and arrangements vary across regions and classes. National curricula and national assessments may also structure educational activities differently. Extracurricular opportunities for writing may vary, such as student journalism or youth organizations. Differently available technologies and popular uses may also influence what can be observed and collected. During adult years, structures of economies and careers, including credentialing and the relation of local to international business, may affect the data to be gathered. Different cultures of personal disclosure may also facilitate or inhibit some kinds of inquiry. Further, the research team within each national research culture and funding regime may have special interests that would supplement the collection for that region. But within these and other considerations, insofar as possible, comparable data should be collected from each of the sites and cohorts.

Second is the influence of age. Interviewing the youngest children might look only for responses and behaviors, perhaps combined with observations of engagement in tasks. These might be supplemented with interviews with parents and siblings. Observations would be in home settings or in interaction with the parents. If there are any documents to be collected, they would be brief, and there will be little self-reporting of processes. As children develop, more information can be gleaned from them directly through self-reports, though interviews would have to take into account the age, reflectiveness, and experience of subjects. School documents, personal writing, and extracurricular productions could start to be collected. However, since these will be guided by school curricula and standards the relevant institutional documents would need to be collected along with perhaps observations of lessons. Only in later adolescence, the college years, and beyond are written self-reports likely to be informative. As subjects' writing reaches out into complex worlds either in advanced education or the workplace, collection of relevant intertexts that help define the writing situation, the issues at stake, and the available knowledge resources might also be increasingly useful. On the other hand, as writers develop into adulthood, greater self-awareness and experience may allow greater depth and accuracy of self-reporting, including of context. The ability to describe and characterize contexts and strategies for different texts may itself be an indicator of development.

Similarly, the timing of collections would need to be sensitive to age. In the earliest years change is rapid and continuing, so some kind of continuous monitoring by parents, caregivers, or teachers, perhaps through journals, would be useful. Certainly data-collection intervals should be measured in units no larger than months. As children advance through schooling, semiannual collection corresponding to terms might be adequate. And for adults, an intermittent sample of every five years supplemented by self-identified unusual writing and major changes in writing demands might be adequate. While it is hard to calibrate in the abstract what the frequency should be to give a sense of redundant saturation, the production of a few days every five years would generate perhaps 0.1 percent of the overall total, which would nonetheless be a massive amount of data.

Third, as writing lives differentiate so must collection practices. An adult whose writing consists of household records, family notes, text-messaging and social media among friends and family, and routinized job tasks, such as filling out order and inventory forms (all of which might be initiated and completed within a few minutes) might only require limited data collection. On the other hand, someone who has become a prominent blogger, spending several hours every day reading the blogs of others and other informational sources, and composing and responding to the responses of others, all the while spending all his or her free time thinking about potential themes and ideas, would require a much more extensive collection of data. This in turn would be different from a high-level government worker preparing a single report over several months, consulting many resources in collaboration with others and incorporating much field data collected by both the worker and his or her colleagues. While self-reports in interviews or surveys might capture some of the variety and the extensiveness of people's writing at any life stage, more intense and individualized probes would be needed for more complex cases.

Finally, social and technological changes are likely to mean that writing will be carried out in different ways for different situations over the near century of a lifespan longitudinal study. A study over the last century would have needed to be flexible to accommodate the growing role of typing and then word processing, with its ancillary tools of spell- and grammar-checking, along with the ease of cutting and pasting. The increasing access to knowledge culminating in the World Wide Web would have required greater attention to search and its interaction with memory. Wider access to higher education and graduate professional education would have required new kinds of contextual as well as textual collection, as would the expansion of corporate paperwork, government reporting, and other workplace writing, along with the invention of new forms of personal and leisure communication including the most recent social media. Changing technology also brings new tools of research, which will open up new domains of useful data—in the last century from audio and video to eye-tracking, screen-capture, and network analysis. In the coming century, as technology makes possible new sociocommunicative relations, expands the possibilities of texts, changes the kind of work that goes into text production, and provides new research tools, it will be hard to predict all the kinds of data that will be useful to understand the writing trajectories of the possible subjects of this study.

General Categories of Data

Whatever accommodations are made for age, region, individual activity, and historical change, some basic categories of data are worth considering.

Socioeconomic Position and Uses of Writing. Periodic interviews and self-reports can provide a picture of the socioeconomic position and well-being of the writers and how that might affect opportunities and constraints for writing development. These data might also include the oral and written linguistic environment at home and at school or work. Particularly for children, but also possibly adults, this might include data gathered from family, friends, teachers, or coworkers. The data might indicate perceptions about the kinds of actions, powers, and purposes of writing the socioeconomic position affords, as well as the subject's sense of efficacy. These data could be combined with periodic use of standard psychological instruments measuring efficacy, motivation, perceived value of writing activities, resilience, and the like. Regular self-report surveys can also provide an overall picture of current writing activity including the kinds of writing demands made on the subject in school, workplace, and community. Further, these self-reports could be used to identify moments of change or special uses of writing that might be further investigated by interviews or other more in-depth means. Technology may afford more convenient, quick, and regular self-reporting.

Texts. A sample of texts recently completed and being worked on can be used to evaluate current challenges and the nature of writing being done. As the product of writing processes and the actual accomplishments of writers, they could be analyzed from many directions including language, rhetoric, theme, genre, organization, intertext, format, multimedia, information, self-representation, and interaction. The sample should include texts of all sizes and ambitions, from major projects to daily notes and lists. The samples might be collected in conjunction with periodic surveys or interviews, but more effective might be periodic emails or other communications asking for a list of texts worked on in the previous day or week, plus digital or paper copies. It may also be possible to ask participants to keep a portfolio of their major productions and samples of their more quotidian ones over a fixed period of months around the periodic data collections, or even a full portfolio of all the most extensive productions across the lifetime. Electronic submission (such as a one-click dropbox) could facilitate the process. With technology already available we could even imagine seamless automated collection of everything produced on personal devices and then some form of automated mining to notice patterns and moments of change. This lifetime file could then be available for later recovery of specific documents.

Situations. For each text collected (or a selection thereof) we could also use reports of the situation within which it arose, the regulations and constraints of the situation, the surrounding texts, and the audience, as well as the affordances and opportunities, the writer's role and authority within the situation, the intended goals and activities, and the strategies and genres perceived as appropriate. The time spent on each of these tasks and the total time of each day or week spent on various writing tasks would also give a sense of the extent of writing in the subject's life at this point. Much of this information can be gained by the writer's self-report through a questionnaire accompanying each submission. As the subjects persist in the study over years the standard self-reports should become routine and easier to accomplish. On the other hand, more complex tasks embedded in complex social activity systems within schooling and outside might gain from some ethnographic study and observation—though this should be reserved for only the most interesting of cases as it is costly in time, effort, and finances. Also, as mentioned earlier for younger subjects, starting in family and prekindergarten and extending perhaps to middle school the collection and context would have to be gathered by ethnographic observation and interviews with caregivers.

Success Measures. In analyzing these texts we need to be careful to be descriptive and not evaluative based on school testing criteria. It is, however, worth gathering information on the texts' success for their intended purposes. For school texts that might well include how they were evaluated in the school context, but also looking to other purposes from the student's or teacher's point of view. Outside schooling the natural success criteria are whether the texts are effective for the tasks at hand, whether the authors feel the forms have expressed their desired meanings, and whether the texts have resulted in the desired consequences among relevant audiences. Writer self-perception of text success may be especially important for development of internal criteria, goals, strategies, and efficacy. Given the different natures of different texts we might need different data to measure success in addition to author perceptions. Much of this can be gained by writers' self-reports and some general psychometric instruments, though interviewing might allow the probes to fit the nature of the tasks more precisely. Interviews could also elicit data on perceived challenges and problems to be solved for each task. Additionally, external measures of success might be useful, such as whether the sale was made from the correspondence, the report accepted and incorporated into the town's plan, or how many responses a comment got on social media.

Processes. Some probe of changing processes would also be useful to understand development. Think-alouds of standard tasks, or delayed think-alouds through keystroke or screen-capture replay, can be useful. On the other hand, processes activated by motivated, consequential, authentic tasks may be substantially different from the processes used for assigned experimental tasks. Self-reports of actual current tasks, particularly of the more ambitious sort, explored in interviews, may be even more informative of how processes, strategies, and self-monitoring are developing. Self-reports of work habits and spaces might be useful. Drawings of workspaces and cartoon storyboards of the process of a recent task have turned out to be useful heuristic devices and prompts for interviews. The extensiveness of these process inquiries would in part depend on how ambitious the current writing world is for each of the participants.

Human Collaborative Interactions. Major aspects of writing development seem to be fostered by learning in interaction with others, including dispositions, relationships, and imitated strategies. Further, since so much writing is produced in collaborative interactions, developing the skills to contribute to effective collaboration is itself part of writing. Yet, even within collaborations, some processes occur primarily within the individual to produce the ideas, wording, or critical perspectives then shared with others. We have little idea of the balance or dynamics of individual and collaborative work in group composition, but it seems evident that some people have learned to make more fundamental and consequential contributions than others and seem to be better at formulating and aligning with group goals, in order to harness personal resources. There may be many other kinds of skills and dispositions for group productions. While observation of experimental tasks with groups might present some data about processes so robust they could survive the decontextualization and loss of authentic motivations of experiments, collaborative processes may well also rely on trust and other relationship variables developed with specific partners. Therefore some form of naturalistic observation of work teams on the job or in schools during both earlier conceptual stages and later text-production and review stages would be useful. Follow-up interviews using text drafts or videotape prompts can then elicit what the subjects were thinking, their strategies of participation, and their evaluations of their own and others' participation. Further, as collaboration is increasingly electronically mediated, the data collecting needs to be cognizant of the varying platforms and tools employed.

Use of Electronic Media and Technologies of Text Production. The now-familiar technological affordances of spelling and grammar assistants are being supplemented by increasingly sophisticated template support, word and phrase completion, and even complete message production including current data insertion. Further, information search and text borrowing is being integrated into text production. It takes little stretching of the imagination to see more complete cyborgian integration of human beings, technology, and information access, such that what roles and decisions will be left to the human being are changing and thus too is what it means to write (Bazerman, forthcoming). Any longitudinal study will have to gather data on what technological supports are being used, what the human role is within the technological system, and what strategies human beings develop to make most effective use of the technology. These data can include self-reports of technology use and personal response, strategies, and processes, but may also include full keyboard and screen capture, which can then be used as interview prompts.

Educational and Mentoring Supports. In studying development it is also useful to understand the educational, mentoring, and other supports that guide learning and production, and thus development. In the earliest ages this might come from observation of play and learning interactions, along with interviews of the mentoring adults. As children enter organized schooling, curricular documents, lessons, and assignments, as well as possible interviews with instructors to understand their goals, philosophies, and interactions, may provide some understanding—along with information about the technologies used to teach, produce, and support writing. Self-reports may take more of a role as the subjects age and enter the more complex worlds of universities and work. Follow-up with the mentors identified in the interviews or other reports, nonetheless, may also help clarify the mentors' goals and strategies and what they see as the paths of development they are trying to foster.

Reading Data. The virtual world of reading is also important to an understanding of the general literate environment the writer lives in, the resources he or she might draw on, and the specific literate contexts he or she addresses in writing. This information can be gathered as part of the general questionnaires sent periodically and in the specific questionnaires that accompany submission of texts. With younger children, however, this information could be gathered from caregivers, teachers, and curricula.

Neurological and Brain Data. As writing development will likely be realized in development of neurological resources, getting some baseline of neurological measures could potentially be useful as our technologies for measurement and our knowledge of the relation of neurological architecture to thought and emotion become more refined. Writing processes are hard to capture in current devices such as FMRI, which require subjects to remain still; however, even with current technologies we can get FMRI scans of subjects as they are asked to imagine writing tasks, engage in organizing or other planning tasks, and adopt strategies for various texts or engage in other imaginative tasks. Stationary subjects may also be asked to mentally edit displayed texts. Contrastive scans of subjects more highly engaged with complex writing activities and those less so may also provide clues about the interaction of writing and brain development. Additionally, general measures of short- and long-term memory and executive control may provide insight into the effect of individual difference on writing development. Even more simply, chemical blood assays can determine the elevated presence of anxiety- or euphoria-associated endogenous substances during writing activities. As technology develops and we get a better idea of the relevant processes and associated architectures we are looking for, we will be able to design more relevant and refined ways of gathering data.

Health, Social, Career, Economic, Psychological, and Intellectual Engagement Data. These are all potential input and output data, so it would be useful to capture them in some form. Health may affect one's ability to write, not only as potential impediment, but also positively, as limited mobility or other disability may increase the written channel as the medium of social communication. Health and psychological well-being may also be fostered by writing (see for example, Pennebaker, 1997).

Since writing itself is a form of social and economic engagement, data about the emerging social roles, identities, and career paths that people develop will provide important context to understand the demands, opportunities, and meanings of writing in their lives. Writing also can engage one in the world of ideas, knowledge, and the arts, developing forms of consciousness and stances toward the world.

Conclusion

This review has exposed the difficulties of a comprehensive lifespan longitudinal study of writing development, even as it has also helped identify the parameters of choices to be made. This review has highlighted, nonetheless, how such research, or whatever smaller pieces of it we can manage, will add to our understanding of writing development, and the consequences of that development for lives. It highlights how much people's writing lives are intertwined with the other aspects of their lives, personally and socially, and how those in turn are functions of the time and place in which individuals live and the positions they adopt within that space. This review, in identifying data that might be collected, has helped clarify, at least to this author, a vision of what an understanding of development of writing across the lifespan might look like, and why we might want it. In heuristics begin responsibilities.

References

Abbott, R. A., Berninger, V. W., & Fayol, M. (2010). Longitudinal relationships of levels of language in writing and between writing and reading in grades 1 to 7. *Journal of Educational Psychology 102*(2), 281–98. doi:10.1037/a0019318

Artemeva, N. (2009). Stories of becoming: A study of novice engineers learning genres of their profession. In C. Bazerman, A. Bonini, & D. Figueiredo (Eds.), *Genre in a changing world* (pp. 158–78). Fort Collins, CO: WAC Clearinghouse.

Baltes, P. B. (1987). Theoretical propositions of life-span developmental psychology: On the dynamics between growth and decline.

Developmental Psychology, 23(5), 611–26. doi:10.1037/0012-1649.23.5.611

Baltes, P. B., & Nesselroade, J. R. (1979). History and rationale of longitudinal research. In J. R. Nesselroade & P. B. Baltes (Eds.), *Longitudinal research in the study of behavior and development* (pp. 1–39). New York: Academic Press.

Bazerman, C. (2013a). *Literate Action: Vol. 1. A rhetoric of literate action.* Fort Collins, CO: WAC Clearinghouse. Available at http://wac.colostate.edu/books/literateaction/v1

Bazerman, C. (2013b). *Literate Action: Vol. 2. A theory of literate action.* Fort Collins, CO: WAC Clearinghouse. Available at http://wac.colostate.edu/books/literateaction/v2

Bazerman, C. (forthcoming). What do humans do best? Developing communicative humans in the changing socio-cyborgian landscape. In S. Logan & W. Slater (Eds.), *Perspectives on academic and professional writing in an age of accountability.* Carbondale: Southern Illinois University Press.

Beaufort, A. (1999). *Writing in the real world: Making the transition from school to work.* New York: Teachers College Press.

Beaufort, A. (2004). Developmental gains of a history major: A case for building a theory of disciplinary writing expertise. *Research in the Teaching of English, 39*(2), 136–85.

Beers, J. W., & Henderson, E. H. (1977). A study of developing orthographic concepts among first graders. *Research in the Teaching of English 11*(2), 133–48.

Berkenkotter, C., Huckin, T. N., & Ackerman, J. (1991). Social context and socially constructed texts: The initiation of a graduate student into a writing research community. In C. Bazerman & J. Paradis (Eds.), *Textual dynamics of the professions: Historical and contemporary studies of writing in professional communities* (pp. 191–215). Madison: University of Wisconsin Press.

Berninger, V. W., Abbott, R. D., Nagy, W., & Carlisle, J. (2010). Growth in phonological, orthographic, and morphological awareness in grades 1 to 6. *Journal of Psycholinguistic Research, 39*(2), 141–63. doi:10.1007/s10936-009-9130-6

Bissex, G. L. (1980). *Gnys at wrk: A child learns to write and read.* Cambridge, MA: Harvard University Press.

Blakeslee, A. M. (1997). Activity, context, interaction, and authority: Learning to write scientific papers in situ. *Journal of Business and Technical Communication, 11*(2), 125–69. doi:10.1177/1050651997011002001

Bloodgood, J. W. (1999). What's in a name? Children's name writing and literacy acquisition. *Reading Research Quarterly, 34*(3), 342–67. doi:10.1598/RRQ.34.3.5

Brandmaier, A. M., von Oertzen, T., Ghisletta, P., Hertzog, C., & Lindenberger, U. (2015). LIFESPAN: A tool for the computer-aided design of longitudinal studies. *Frontiers in Psychology, 6*, 272–81. doi:10.3389/fpsyg.2015.00272

Brandt, D. (2001). *Literacy in American lives.* New York: Cambridge University Press.

Brandt D. (2015). *The rise of writing: Redefining mass literacy.* New York: Cambridge University Press.

Butler, D. (1979). *Cushla and her books.* London, UK: Hodder & Stoughton.

Carroll, L. A. (2002). *Rehearsing new roles: How college students develop as writers.* Carbondale: Southern Illinois University Press.

Carus, F. A. (1808). *Geschichte der psychologie.* Leipzig, Germany: Barth & Kummer.

Chapman, M. L. (1996). The development of phonemic awareness in young children: Some insights from a case study of a first-grade writer. *Young Children, 51*(2), 31–37.

Chiseri-Strater, E. (1991). *Academic literacies: The public and private discourse of university students.* Portsmouth, NH: Heinemann.

Christie, F. (2012). *Language education throughout the school years: A functional perspective.* Malden, MA: Wiley-Blackwell.

Christie, F., & Derewianka, B. (2008). *School discourse: Learning to write across the years of schooling.* London, UK: Continuum.

Cochran-Smith, M. (1984). *The making of a reader.* Norwood, NJ: Ablex.

Cook, N. R., & Ware, J. H. (1983). Design and analysis methods for longitudinal research. *Annual Review of Public Health, 4*, 1–23.

Dias, P., Freedman, A., Medway, P., & Paré, A. (1999). *Worlds apart: Acting and writing in academic and workplace contexts*. Mahwah, NJ: Erlbaum.

Dyson, A. H. (1993). *Social worlds of children learning to write in an urban primary school*. New York: Teachers College Press.

Dyson, A. H. (1997). *Writing superheroes: Contemporary childhood, popular culture, and classroom literacy*. New York: Teachers College Press.

Dyson, A. H. (2003). *The brothers and sisters learn to write: Popular literacies in childhood and school cultures*. New York: Teachers College Press.

Elder, G. H., Jr., Shanahan, M. J., & Clipp, E. C. (1997). Linking combat and physical health: The legacy of World War II in men's lives. *American Journal of Psychiatry, 154*(3): 330–36.

Fishman, J., Lunsford, A., McGregor, B., & Otuteye, M. (2005). Performing writing, performing literacy. *College Composition and Communication, 57*(2), 224–52.

Glueck, S., & Glueck, E. T. (1950). *Unraveling juvenile delinquency*. New York: Commonwealth Fund.

Goodman, Y. M. (1986). Children coming to know literacy. In W. H. Teale & E. Sulzby (Eds.), *Emergent literacy: Writing and reading* (pp. 1–14). Norwood, NJ: Ablex.

Goodman, Y. M., & Wilde, S. (Eds.). (1992). *Literacy events in a community of young writers*. New York: Teachers College Press.

Haas, C. (1994). Learning to read biology: One student's rhetorical development in college. *Written Communication, 11*(1), 43–84. doi:10.1177/0741088394011001004

Haswell, R. H. (1991). *Gaining ground in college writing: Tales of development and interpretation*. Dallas: Southern Methodist University Press.

Haswell, R. H. (2000). Documenting improvement in college writing: A longitudinal approach. *Written Communication, 17*(3), 307–52. doi:10.1177/0741088300017003001

Helms, R. W. (1992). Intentionally incomplete longitudinal designs: I. Methodology and comparison of some full span designs. *Statistics in Medicine, 11*(14–15), 1889–1913. doi:10.1002/sim.4780111411

Herrington, A. J., & Curtis, M. (2000). *Persons in process: Four stories of writing and personal development in college.* Urbana, IL: National Council of Teachers of English.

Hertzog, C., & Nesselroade, J. R. (2003). Assessing psychological change in adulthood: An overview of methodological issues. *Psychology and Aging, 18*(4), 639–57. doi:10.1037/0882-7974.18.4.639

Hildreth, G. (1932). The success of young children in number and letter construction. *Child Development, 3*(1), 1–14.

Hildreth, G. (1934). Reversals in reading and writing. *Journal of Educational Psychology, 25*(1), 1–20. doi:10.1037/h0074907

Hildreth, G. (1936). Developmental sequences in name writing. *Child Development, 7*(4), 291–303.

Hunt, K. W. (1965). *Grammatical structures written at three grade levels.* Champaign, IL: National Council of Teachers of English.

Janson, C.-G. (1981). Some problems of longitudinal research in the social sciences. In F. Schulsinger, S. A. Mednick, & J. Knop (Eds.), *Longitudinal research: Methods and uses in behavioral science* (pp. 19–55). Boston: Martinus Nijhoff.

Kagan, J. (1981). Issues in psychological development. In F. Schulsinger, S. A. Mednick, & J. Knop (Eds.), *Longitudinal research: Methods and uses in behavioral science* (pp. 66–92). Boston: Martinus Nijhoff.

Kasten, W. C. (1992). Speaking, searching, and sharing in the community of writers. In Y. M. Goodman & S. Wilde (Eds.), *Literacy events in a community of young writers* (pp. 87–103). New York: Teachers College Press.

King, M. L., & Rentel, V. M. (1982). *Transition to writing.* Columbus: Ohio State University Research Foundation.

Loban, W. (1967). *Language development: Kindergarten through grade twelve.* NCTE Research Report No. 18. Urbana, IL: National Council of Teachers of English.

Lynn, P. (2009). Methods for longitudinal surveys. In P. Lynn (Ed.), *Methodology of longitudinal surveys* (pp. 1–20). Chichester, UK: Wiley.

MacIntyre, E., & Freppon, P. A. (1994). A comparison of children's development of alphabetic knowledge in a skills-based and a whole language classroom. *Research in the Teaching of English*, *28*(4), 391–417.

McCarthy, L. (1987). A stranger in strange lands: A college student writing across the curriculum. *Research in the Teaching of English*, *21*(3), 233–65.

Nesselroade, J. R., & Baltes, P. B. (Eds.). (1979). *Longitudinal research in the study of behavior and development*. New York: Academic Press.

Orth, U., Robins, R. W., & Widaman, K. F. (2012). Life-span development of self-esteem and its effects on important life outcomes. *Journal of Personality and Social Psychology*, *102*(6), 1271–88. doi:10.1037/a0025558

Pennebaker, J. W. (1997). Writing about emotional experiences as a therapeutic process. *Psychological Science, 8*(3), 162–66.

Petersen, T. (1993). Recent advances in longitudinal methodology. *Annual Review of Sociology, 19*, 425–54.

Prior, P. A. (1998). *Writing/disciplinarity: A sociohistoric account of literate activity in the academy*. Mahwah, NJ: Erlbaum.

Rajulton, F. (2001). The fundamentals of longitudinal research: An overview. *Canadian Studies in Population*, *28*(2), 169–85.

Reitzle, M., & Vondracek, F. W. (2000). Methodological avenues for the study of career pathways. *Journal of Vocational Behavior, 57*(3), 445–67. doi:10.1006/jvbe.2000.1751

Rentel, V., & King, M. L. (1983). *A longitudinal study of coherence in children's written narratives*. Retrieved from http://files.eric.ed.gov/fulltext/ED237989.pdf

Roberts, B. W., & DelVecchio, W. F. (2000). The rank-order consistency of personality traits from childhood to old age: A quantitative review of longitudinal studies. *Psychological Bulletin*, *126*(1), 3–25. doi:10.1037/0033-2909.126.1.3

Roberts, B. W., Walton, K. E., & Viechtbauer, W. (2006). Patterns of mean-level change in personality traits across the life course: A meta-analysis of longitudinal studies. *Psychological Bulletin, 132*(1), 1–25. doi:10.1037/0033-2909.132.1.1

Robins, R. W., Trzesniewski, K. H., Tracy, J. L., Gosling, S. D., & Potter, J. (2002). Global self-esteem across the life span. *Psychology and Aging, 17*(3), 423–34. doi:10.1037//0882-7974.17.3.423

Robinson, K., Schmidt, T., & Teti, D. M. (2005). Issues in the use of longitudinal and cross-sectional designs. In D. M. Teti (Ed.), *Handbook of research methods in developmental science* (pp. 3–20). Malden, MA: Wiley-Blackwell.

Rogers, P. M. (2008). *The development of writers and writing abilities: A longitudinal study across and beyond the college-span* (Doctoral dissertation). Available from ProQuest Dissertations and Theses Global. (Order No. 3319795)

Rogers, P. M. (2010). The contributions of North American longitudinal studies of writing in higher education to our understanding of writing development. In C. Bazerman, R. Krut, K. Lunsford, S. McLeod, S. Null, P. Rogers, & A. Stansell (Eds.), *Traditions of writing research* (pp. 365–77). New York: Routledge.

Rowe, D. W. (1987). Literacy learning as an intertextual process. In J. E. Readence & R. S. Baldwin (Eds.), *Research in literacy: Merging perspectives* (pp. 101–120). Rochester, NY: National Reading Conference.

Sarkadi, A., Kristiansson, R., Oberklaid, F., & Bremberg, S. (2008). Fathers' involvement and children's developmental outcomes: a systematic review of longitudinal studies. *Acta Pædiatrica, 97*(2), 153–58. doi:10.1111/j.1651-2227.2007.00572.x

Schooler, C. (1984). Psychological effects of complex environments during the life span: A review and theory. *Intelligence, 8*(4), 259–81.

Sipe, L. R. (1998). Transitions to the conventional. *Journal of Literacy Research, 30*(3), 357–88. doi:10.1080/10862969809548004

Sommers, N., & Saltz, L. (2004). The novice as expert: Writing the freshman year. *College Composition and Communication, 56*(1), 124–49.

Spack, R. (1997). The acquisition of academic literacy in a second language: A longitudinal case study. *Written Communication, 14*(1), 3–62. doi:10.1177/0741088397014001001

Sternglass, M. S. (1997). *Time to know them: A longitudinal study of writing and learning at the college level.* Mahwah, NJ: Erlbaum.

Terman, L. M. (1925). *Mental and physical traits of a thousand gifted children. Genetic Studies of Genius: Vol. 1.* Stanford, CA: Stanford University Press.

Terman, L. M., & Oden, M. H. (1959). *The gifted group at mid-life: Thirty-five years' follow-up of the superior child. Genetic Studies of Genius: Vol. 5.* Stanford, CA: Stanford University Press.

Tetens, J. N. (1777). *Philosophische versuche über die menschliche Natur und ihre Entwicklung.* Leipzig, Germany: M. G. Weidmanns Erben und Reich.

Thomson, R., & Holland, J. (2003). Hindsight, foresight and insight: The challenges of longitudinal qualitative research. *International Journal of Social Research Methodology, 6*(3), 233–44. doi:10.1080/1364557032000091833

Tierney, R. J., & Sheehy, M. (2003). What longitudinal studies say about literacy development, what literacy development says about longitudinal studies. In J. Flood, D. Lapp, J. R. Squire, & J. M. Jensen (Eds.), *Handbook of research on teaching the English language arts* (2nd ed., pp. 171–91). Mahwah, NJ: Erlbaum.

Treiman, R. (1993). *Beginning to spell: A study of first-grade children.* New York: Oxford University Press.

Tremain, L. D. (2015). *"I feel confident most of the time": A study of the relationships between writing transfer, dispositions toward learning and writing, and perceptions of classroom contexts.* (Doctoral dissertation). Available from ProQuest Dissertations and Theses Global. (Order No. 3700214)

Vaillant, G. E. (2002). *Aging well: Surprising guideposts to a happier life from the landmark Harvard Study of Adult Development.* Boston: Little Brown.

Vaillant, G. E. (2012). *Triumphs of experience: The men of the Harvard Grant Study.* Cambridge, MA: Belknap Press of Harvard University Press.

Vaillant, G. E., Brighton, J. R., & McArthur, C. (1970). Physicians' use of mood-altering drugs: A 20-year follow-up report. *New England Journal of Medicine, 282*(7), 365–70.

Vaughan, S. (1992). Bringing it all together: Anna writing in a community of young writers. In Y. M. Goodman & S. Wilde (Eds.), *Literacy events in a community of young writers* (pp. 148–74). New York: Teachers College Press.

Wilde, S. (1992). Spelling in third and fourth grade: Focus on growth. In Y. M. Goodman & S. Wilde (Eds.), *Literacy events in a community of young writers* (pp. 125–47). New York: Teachers College Press.

Wilde, S., Goodman, Y. M., Bridges Bird, L., Gespass, S., Kasten, W. C., Vaughan, S., & Wetherill, D. (1992). The research story: Context, methodology and findings. In Y. M. Goodman & S. Wilde (Eds.), *Literacy events in a community of young writers* (pp. 17–63). New York: Teachers College Press.

Winsor, D. A. (1996). *Writing like an engineer: A rhetorical education.* Mahwah, NJ: Erlbaum.

III

FINAL THOUGHTS

The Challenges of Understanding Developmental Trajectories and of Designing Developmentally Appropriate Policy, Curricula, Instruction, and Assessments

Acts of writing are individual responses to socially available opportunities and challenges, using socially available tools to achieve personal and group ends (see Graham's chapter, this volume). Each person's engagement with writing and trajectory of development is different, even people who are born into the same family, share genes, attend the same schools, and adopt similar adult roles. The most direct evidence of this is that on the same occasion they write different things, expressed in different terms, and adopting different positions. Dispositions, particular experiences, contact with different resources, emerging interests, different reading, different peers, and all the things that make siblings different people will differentiate their writing as their literacy lives unfold. People born into different social and cultural environments with different neurobiological inheritances, family and peer relations, languages or multiple languages, literacy resources, life opportunities, and careers may have even more varied experiences with writing and consequent development (see Bazerman's chapter, this volume). At the same time, this individuality is operating in contexts of strong compulsion, conformity, and convention, as our writing development is shaped by the schooling process, the reactions of our readers, and the writing norms of the particular communities or social groups with whom we interact.

Writing is essential to writing development; that is, writers develop by solving writing problems as they occur and by building repertoires, strategies, and understanding through repeated encounters with writing. At some moments a writer's development is significantly directed and supported by formal and informal mentoring and education, but at other moments development is largely self-sponsored and self-directed. While writing development relies on the neurological and physical resources of the individual as well as on technological extensions of the self, there is nothing in our biology or technology that predetermines writing development. Even when individuals have the same socially available resources, opportunities, or constraints, they perceive and experience them differently because of their own interests, abilities, and vantage points. The individual's purposeful engagement with writing mobilizes these resources and potentials of writing, and through the mobilization and responses to the writing, the individual learns what can be accomplished through the resources and how to make use of them (see Brandt's chapter, this volume).

The discussions of the Lifespan Writing Development Group and the statements emerging from them presented in this volume have highlighted how complex and various the process of writing development is. The group has noted that each individual's biological, neurological, cognitive, and affective diversity interacts with that individual's experiences, situations, opportunities, motivations, language repertoire, and other resources. Each writer finds his or her own writing path through the literate world he or she experiences. All come to their own voices and talents to create individual forms of participation and self-representation as they engage in social contexts that shape, constrain, motivate, and support them.

To put it another way, writing is a human invention of immense complexity and possibility, constantly transformed by the actions of each writer within the changing situations, opportunities, and resources available to that writer. This is as true of eighteenth-century political pamphleteers and ancient Mesopotamian scribes as it is of contemporary bloggers and bestselling novelists. There is no biologically directed path of growth as there would be of a plant under optimum conditions of light, soil, climate, and water. Nor is there even a standard path of learning.

The world of literacy is an ever-changing, extensive virtual world of representations interpreted and responded to by an evolving individual who is situated in and making sense of a small part of that world, encountered from the perspective of personal and communal interests and purposes. Further, writers are repeatedly inventing new moves, new positions, new objects of attention, new interactions with readers—changing who they are and the communicative landscape they emerge from and participate in constructing.

Dimensions of Writing Development

The discussions, statements, and syntheses of the Lifespan Writing Development Group highlight three aspects of the research agenda that will contribute to our understanding of this issue: dimensions along which development occurs, related forms of development that interact with writing development, and some of the relevant environmental variables that facilitate and constrain writing development.

Some of the dimensions along which development occurs include:

♦ interest and confidence in writing as a tool for accomplishing specific social and/or personal goals

♦ awareness of the emotions and purposes that motivate writing and ability to discipline these to communicate effectively

♦ ability to perceive, distinguish, and manipulate material technologies of inscription

♦ ability to draw on the symbolic elements of the inscription system (both linguistic and literate knowledge), recognizing the value of respecting normative standards as well as the occasions for innovation and transgression

♦ ability to construe meanings by means of the material and symbolic inscription system

♦ ability to share those meanings with others, both through conventional usage and by creating novelty that is nonetheless interpretable

- awareness of the interests, needs, and perceptions of readers so as to make messages significant, engaging, and congruently interpretable by readers (audience awareness) and to form relationships with them (social understanding), and carry out significant actions with them

- ability to increasingly regulate and orchestrate the writing environment, social situations involved in writing, and one's beliefs and knowledge about writing, the intended audience, and the context in which the message is created and delivered

- ability to select, define, respond to, and influence social events where writing may have an effect (rhetorical situation)

- recognition of and ability to produce messages that enact different purposes, situations, and actions (genre knowledge)

- sense of one's ability to carry out specific writing tasks (efficacy)

- awareness of the processes and resources of writing one draws on, ability to seek and orchestrate processes and resources, and ability to make strategic decisions about them (metacognition)

- ability to work with others in completing a joint writing task (collaboration).

The Lifespan Writing Development Group has also identified several forms of development that may interact with writing development, including:

- Vision, hearing, and motor skills

- Neurology

- Cognition

- Linguistic capacity

- Society, culture, and community

- Emotion

- Character, dispositions, and values

- Experience of the world

- Education

- Reading

♦ Economic and work life

♦ Technology

Finally, we have described several environmental variables that provide occasions, opportunities, resources, activities, and situations with and within which writing development can occur, and which, therefore, influence writing development:

♦ linguistic, cultural, social, and literate environments of the family and community and the changing roles of the child and adult within them

♦ curricula, pedagogies, and classroom activities of the school, both in their particulars and sequencing within institutions and across transitions to different institutions

♦ the role of literate activities in peer relations during school years and after

♦ economic situations of the family within the larger economic structures and opportunities of the time and place, and the economic, work, and social possibilities for the maturing writer

♦ the historical repertoire of writing, texts, writing strategies, writing forms, and literate activity systems available to the writer and how these are perceived by the relevant audiences for the developing writer

These lists do not present a comprehensive or exhaustive picture, but rather are starting points for thinking about what can influence writing development and the dimensions along which that development unfolds. Identifying processes and patterns that emerge as individual writers create their trajectories of writing development within these dimensions of learning, related developments, and environments, is a more uncertain and more hubristic task at this moment for researchers, because processes and patterns suggest commonalities rather than variability and variations. Nonetheless, some regularities have been established within areas of developmental writing studies.

Emergent-literacy studies, for example, have through numerous case studies identified some patterns in the discovery and making sense of writing systems, realized differently given the nature of the phonetic systems and the writing systems available (both in their phonetic and graphological components), neurobiological diversity (such as deafness), multilinguality, and available writing technologies, as well as by simple variability among individuals (see Rowe's chapter, this volume). These processes include a coming to terms with and making sense of the basics of the system and the technology, in part by idiosyncratic reinvention, but moving toward communally shared practices in the presence of peers and more skilled users. While there is some debate as to whether a fixed sequence of events in this movement toward conventionality exists, many of the recurrent moments and activities have been identified, such as distinction of scribbles the child identifies as writing and drawing, adapting scribbles toward the letter strokes, and then moving toward the representational logic of the graphological system the child is making sense of. Sequences of writing events seem to arise within interaction among motor, neurological, visual, and graphological systems. Not all children under all conditions and in all language environments will necessarily share these trajectories (for example, children without access to ambient literate practices or writing tools) or the pace and sequence at which these learning events will unfold, but if children do engage with writing early on, these events seem to provide pathways toward basic inscription ability.

Linguists as well (see Schleppegrell and Christie's chapter, this volume) have found patterns of transformation of linguistic resources available as individuals engage with writing over time and move from congruent "commonsense" structures that are close to experience toward the linguistic resources associated with abstraction and "uncommon sense." Here the chief variable for change is not chronological age but support for and time engaged with writing and reading, typically in relation to school tasks and curricular demands. Some of these findings seem to cut across cultural and curricular systems, and may be shaped by the complexity of language and the subtlety of the resources of language that are only gradually incorporated and made sense of over time and with experience.

Variations in family and social life and schooling within any region and population mean that each child and developing writer will orient differently to form identity and individuality and meet individually perceived needs within these social arrangements (see chapter by Wilcox and Jeffery). Nonetheless, commonalities in the social environment create shared opportunities, limits, incentives, and resources that frame the development likely under those situations. For example, in most circumstances children spend their earlier years within families, either nuclear or extended, which influence the experienced literacy environment and early literate engagement. At the same time, in contemporary societies there is likely to be an extensive media environment that reaches both into the home (whether by print or electronic entertainment media) and into community and institutional spaces, as well as a general expectation of schooling between certain years (depending on national policy). Many countries have national or state curricula, regulated with various force and mechanisms, with variable impact on different socioeconomic strata. In these different contexts, there are patterned junctures for school assessment, transition, and leaving, with different access to the work and job market at different ages, and some populations to which these conditions might not apply. These distinctions then help define conditions that influence the trajectories of large numbers of people and therefore allow more focused studies of processes, practices, and trajectories in the relevant populations.

The processes and patterns that lend themselves to different developmental trajectories suggested here may not be directly observable in the characteristics of written productions, but may lie somewhere underneath, in how writers move through their own development and learn from their unique sets of experiences with their particular resources and motivations. Our attempt to understand these is at a very early moment. In any event we should not confuse these underlying processes and patterns with normative expectations created through a set of curricular expectations or assessment measures. As we have suggested, curricula can influence development by setting opportunities and organizing writing experiences within schools, but they do not fully describe the actual developmental trajectories of individuals.

While it is tempting at this point to turn to synthesizing the research on writing at different ages to form a composite view about what we have learned about how writing might unfold across the lifespan, we resist that temptation. The research on writing has been so tied to success within educational institutions and the literate professions or academic careers, despite some remarkable counterexamples, that such a synthesis will have strong tendencies to harden the conflation between educational goals and ideals and the actual human processes of development. Such just-so stories of movement toward socially valued and rewarded writing or specialized skills or practices of writing that have intrigued researchers may obscure the processes experienced by most people and may not even form the underlying reality for those who are successful by traditional measures. That is, students successful at school writing tasks may be developing in ways different from or beyond the pathways imagined in the curriculum (see Berninger, Geselowitz, and Wallis's chapter, this volume). From the viewpoint of the educational enterprise, and particularly writing education, the teleological ideology or goal-directedness of curriculum is understandable and even warranted; further, this logic of stepwise success through school with formation of distinct and unique communicative identities within academic and professional worlds presents a socialization pressure and opportunity for those who manage to succeed. Yet at this stage in our understanding of writing development we need to be cautious about the possibilities of conflating development with conventional or recognizable success in writing-based careers, occupations, or avocations, and viewing all others not captured in this pyramid as somehow falling away or incomplete in their development or developmental potential. So while a synthesis might provide some recognizable story frameworks for us to imagine what lifespan development might look like, until we have more empirically grounded views of a range of individuals, in a variety of circumstances, it is wisest to forego the just-so stories of continuing accomplishment and distinctiveness of writing.

NONETHELESS: Implications for Policy, Assessment, and School Curricula

So, where does this leave us for policy, assessment, and school curricula? While we can define no one "natural pathway" into what is in fact an artifice, a skillful and complex mobilization of human inventions in artful and purposeful ways, does this mean we cannot identify any particular sequences for teaching and learning? Since any person at any age may work on any of the dimensions of writing, and may approach it from a unique perspective, does this mean we cannot define appropriate expectations for each grade level, sequences of lessons, and series of tasks that provide appropriate challenges for students? Despite the complexity of writing development the members of the Lifespan Writing Development Group believe that research can guide policy, assessment, and curricula in creating capacious, flexible, and situationally meaningful writing education that will be developmentally appropriate (see Murphy and Smith's chapter, this volume).

Teachers, schools, and districts, as well as state and national policymakers, have a responsibility to provide some guidance with regard to effective pathways for writing development. Curricula reflect societal values and goals, facilitating beliefs, skills, understandings, and uses of writing relevant to the local time, place, community, and economy. Curricula also reflect the historical embedding of the wisdom of repeated experiences informally transmitted in educational practices and codified in educational policies. Yet as those responsible for guiding education reflect on received practice and policy directions to improve teaching and learning, they should also be informed by the complexity of development that each child is working through in order to understand the multiple challenges developing writers face; recognize what is meaningful and accessible within the cognitive, linguistic, and social conditions of their lives; form plausible sequences and activities for overcoming and learning from those challenges; engage writers in the difficult task of expanding their writing repertoires and deepening their choices; and provide appropriate supports to facilitate development.

While current curricula, standards, and assessments must necessarily be formed from the best wisdom of the moment, ongoing engagement with research can provide constant reevaluation of traditional choices and search for deeper patterns and issues that can inform educational innovation. This research should have its eye not just on the immediate success of a lesson or the short-term improvement of scores through a particular curriculum, intervention, or practice—for such studies do not look beyond the current standards or curricula to see whether the learned curriculum best serves the long-term development of writers. For that purpose we need also to get a better understanding of the pathways by which writers develop competence over the long term and continue to engage with writing, making it part of their personal, professional, and civic lives.

If there is one overriding message to come from the research that has informed this group and its project, it is that writing takes a long time to develop, resting on growth in many dimensions—some obviously part of writing (such as expanding linguistic and genre repertoires) but some less obviously so (such as social maturity). One consequence of this fact is that in guiding and assessing writing development we should not expect rapid, linear growth. Writing needs time to mature, in fact decades, though at various moments motivated writers may make rapid progress on some dimensions. When and where those moments occur, however, may be hard to predict. Thus demands and expectations of curriculum need to be realistic and flexible, responding to both the variations of development and the long haul. No short courses, whether for a month or a year, no matter how helpful, can solve all problems, make up for prior lack of practice and education, or move students from basic to advanced levels of competence. Only long and consistent support and practice over many years within meaningful, motivating writing situations are likely to make success possible. Further, that long educational support must be flexible to meet the variability and needs of the students and provide recognition and rewards for the differing ambitions and goals for their writing, even while curriculum and assessment may provide guidance on how those goals may be better accomplished. All of this needs to be done with an eye toward the future, where writers are likely to engage in writing in multiple languages and via a variety of technologies that inevitably will transform the way they write and for whom.

A direct corollary of this long apprenticeship is that writing education is an intensive project, requiring students to engage in many kinds of tasks within communicative environments that provide multiple kinds of feedback, so students can learn from their various choices and understand the necessity of addressing dimensions of writing they may not have previously considered. While not all writing needs to be responded to by teachers at every moment (indeed, peer or external audiences can play important and necessary roles in writing development), teacher engagement with students' writing processes and response to written products is important and cannot be bypassed.

An essential component of that teacher engagement is the recognition of the individuality of each writer and of each message. The teacher must be receptive to and supportive of what the student is trying to communicate in the writing even when pointing out work that still needs to be done to make the text intelligible and forceful in fulfilling its purpose within the shared language. Audiences confer the social value of the meaning conveyed by the writer, and the teacher inevitably is a major audience and facilitator of the writing. As a mentor the teacher can guide the student writer to more effective writing and more effective processes, but only when the teacher listens carefully to the student and is attentive to student's productions. In staying attuned to the student writer's struggles, the teacher can then provide more focused and useful guidance. When feedback facilitates what writers are trying to accomplish, they are more likely to engage with it, use it, and learn from it. The feedback and dialogue can then encourage students' reflection on what they are doing, and support the development of metacognition that will enable students to become aware of and make more informed choices about their writing situations, processes, and textual productions. This metacognition then helps the writers become more independent and able to take on greater challenges.

This work of attentiveness, listening, and providing feedback is time- and energy-consuming. It requires social contexts in classrooms where students' points of view are heard, respected, and engaged with, even when those points of view are not the ones the teacher expects to hear. We need changes in the social contexts of classrooms to enable individuality and creativity to flourish for all students.

The teacher also needs some degree of comfort, competence, and reflective understanding of writing. If teachers themselves do not have sufficient practical and reflective knowledge about writing they will have difficulty in leading students into the complexities of the craft. Rather they will be tempted to focus solely on easily noticed issues of mechanical correctness, which provide little sense of why one would write and what one can accomplish by writing. We would expect a tennis or a piano instructor to know how to play, to be a reasonably competent player, and to understand the pleasures and rewards of playing in order to lead a student into engagement and skilled performance. We would also expect the instructor to understand, articulate, and put into practice principles of good play and to be able to convey these principles and practices to the student while activating love of the game or love of music. The expectations of writing teachers and all teachers who assign and guide writing should be at least as high, especially since the teacher is an influential audience and validator for so much of student writing.

An even deeper reason for teacher sensitivity and flexibility in curriculum and assessment is that writing development leads to individuation of voice, identity, and message and is representative of and contributor to higher-order thinking. The school situation must not only accommodate this individuation and higher-order thinking, it must make it the core of writing instruction. Writing competence requires identifying what one needs to communicate in a situation and finding the most effective form in which to express it, whether it is a practical work email, a business report, a critique of sociological theory, or a work of imaginative fiction. We do not want one student's piece of writing to be exactly like the work of another. The most highly developed writer in whatever field, whether law or journalism or management, is most recognizable as presenting a highly developed perspective and contribution, accomplishing the work of the field in distinctive and relevant ways. So the teacher, curriculum, policy, and assessment must recognize and support this individuation and help the student express it.

This development toward individuation creates a tension, if not a paradox, within standards that all students should meet. Further, curricula and assessments should seek to articulate the most efficient pathways and benchmarks to get the students to meet those standards. The most convenient way to do this, unfortunately, is to make each student's work most like another's, so the work can be readily compared and rated. Moreover, since writing conveys meanings within situations, assessments usually position students within common testing situations, which are not necessarily meaningful or inspiring to writers. These issues challenge policymakers to articulate standards and assessments that are capacious, flexible, and situationally meaningful enough to motivate and give focus to student writing, and then evaluate that writing appropriately, consistent with the writer's goals.

SO

While, at least in this moment, writing research cannot provide standardized benchmarks for writing development that are appropriate for all students or define a "natural" sequence of events the developing writing will pass through, it can raise our curricular vision beyond the easily measurable to recognize that writing development is far more than the accretion of easy testable skills, and that successful writing development cannot be defined as movement toward a standard. Future research on writing development across the lifespan can help sort out what is developmentally appropriate, in two senses. First, research can help identify the kinds of challenges students in different situations and with different experiences and from different language backgrounds may be able to address productively and learn from. Second, research can help identify what practices, challenges, and activities may foster development over longer periods. Because writing is so complex, with many dimensions to work on, writing education needs to look beyond immediate success in locally defined activities to foster long trajectories of development that will expand students' abilities to participate as powerful voices in our literate society. By understanding pathways to success, research can iteratively improve the educational support, guidance, and challenges we offer developing writers, enabling them to realize their potential to create and contribute through writing.

INDEX

Clay, M. M., 63
Clifford, G. J., 212–13
Cochran-Smith, M., 237
Cognitive overload, 287
Cognitive processes
 attention, 295
 beliefs, 292–94
 components of, 288–303, 289f
 conceptualization, 300
 control mechanisms, 294–99
 emotions, 302
 executive control, 296–99
 "hijacking" of, into writing
  processes, 14–15, 33–35
 ideation, 300
 knowledge, 290–92
 limitations of, 285–88
 long-term memory, 289–94
 modulators, 301–3
 personality traits, 303
 physiological states, 303
 production processes, 299–301
 reconceptualization, 301
 as shaping written products,
  284–85
 transcription, 301
 translation, 300–301
 working memory, 295–96
Cole, M., 27, 309
Collaboration. *See also*
  Relationality; Writing
  community
 cross-generational, 168–69
 in early childhood writing, 57,
  61
 and longitudinal studies, 354
 in workplace writing, 252
 and writers' identities, 23–24
 and writing curriculum,
  217–18
 in writing development, 9–10
Complexity, 24–27, 104
Conceptualization, 300
Congruence
 defined, 114–15

vs. noncongruence, 124, 128
Content, of writing, in early
  childhood, 76–77, 78–79t,
  85–87, 86t
Contexts, 22–24, 103–4
Control mechanisms, 294–99
Crossley, S. A., 140
Curriculum. *See also* Teachers
 and assessments, 43–44
 and childhood writing development, 103–4
 customizing, 219–25
 defined, 210
 effective, 142–43
 implications of research for,
  376–81
 instructional time for writing
  in, 213–15
 and multilingual writers,
  222–25
 multiplicity of, 215–16
 operational vs. official, 210
 and participatory writing,
  217–18
 and positive deviance, 239–40
 of reading vs. writing, 212–13
 role of, in writing development, 39–41
 students as focus of, 225–28
 and technology, 218–19

Darling-Hammond, L., 228, 229,
  232
Darwin, Charles, 308
Deaf writers, 13, 144n2
Derewianka, B., 40, 340
Development. *See* Writing
  development
Dias, P., 342
Directionality categories, 71–73,
  72t, 73f, 82–84, 83t
Disability, 30–31, 154–56, 166–
  68, 170
Dispositions, 262–67
Domain knowledge, 142–43, 291

Ideation, 300
Identity
  and collaborative writing,
    23–24
  and efficacy, 292–93
  and multilingual writers, 184
  role of, in writing develop-
    ment, 152, 294
  and variability, 29
Infection control, 238–39
Intentionality, 56–57, 61, 74–76,
  75t, 84–85, 84t
Interpersonal meaning, 141
Intrinsic motivation, 293
Inverness Research study, 230

Jago, Carol, 235
James, K. H., 25
Jao, R. J., 25

Kagan, J., 337
Kasten, W. C., 341
Kellogg, R. T., 286
Kempthorne, Charley, 308
Kennedy, Judy, 218–19, 226
Kind, Stella, 260–61
King, M. L., 341
Kiuhara, S. A., 213, 214–15
Knobel, M., 294

Labaree, D. F., 231
Lachicotte, W., 184
Langer, J. A., 213, 214
Language development, 8–9,
  37–38. See also Speech
Leadership, 234–36
Learning
  through accumulated capital,
    313
  and agency, 312
  experiential, 310–11
  observational, 311
  from others, 311–12
  reciprocal relationship of,
    with writing development,
    35–36

Left-to-right directional patterns.
  See Directionality
    categories
Lewis-Murphy, Zack, 220
Lexicogrammar, 144n1
LGBTQIA issues, 260–61
Lieberman, Ann, 231, 234
Life-course development. See
  Human development
Linearity, 63–64
Listening skills, 290
Loban, W., 340
Longitudinal studies
  age of initiation, 347–48
  attrition in, 346
  benefits of, 327–29
  data categories, 351–57
  data collection, 348–50
  design of, 342–45
  Harvard Study of Adult Devel-
    opment, 334–35
  multidecade and lifespan,
    333–36
  and neurology, 344, 356
  overview of, 330–33
  in psychological development,
    336–38
  relationships between subjects
    and researchers, 335, 346
  subject population and study
    maintenance, 345–47
  and technology, 344–45,
    349–50, 354–55
  Terman study, 333–34
  of writing, 338–43
Long-term memory, 289–94
Luria, A. R., 64
Lytle, S. L., 237

MacLean, Marion, 236–37
Maday, Corine, 227
Matsuda, P. K., 186
Matthews, G., 303
Mayer, K. U., 247
McCarthy, P. M., 140
McIntosh, A., 144n3

Authors

Arthur N. Applebee was Distinguished Professor in the School of Education of the University at Albany, State University of New York; chair of the Department of Educational Theory and Practice; and director of the Center on English Learning and Achievement until his death in 2015. He was a frequent advisor at international, national, state, and local levels on effective approaches to language and literacy education. Applebee was a past president of the National Conference on Research in Language and Literacy and was recognized for the cumulative contribution of his work by election to the Reading Hall of Fame and by the David H. Russell Award for Distinguished Research in the Teaching of English.

Charles Bazerman, Distinguished Professor of Education at the University of California, Santa Barbara, inquires into academic writing, the role of writing in society, and how writing forms and transforms people and societies. He is founder and former chair of the International Society for the Advancement of Writing Research and former chair of the Conference on College Composition and Communication. His books include *A Rhetoric of Literate Action; A Theory of Literate Action; The Languages of Edison's Light; Constructing Experience; Shaping Written Knowledge: The Genre and Activity of the Experimental Article in Science; The Informed Writer: Using Sources in the Disciplines;* the *Handbook of Research on Writing: History, Society, School, Individual, Text; Traditions of Writing Research; Genre in a Changing World;* and *What Writing Does and How It Does It: An Introduction to Analyzing Texts and Textual Practices.* He also has published more than 100 articles and chapters.

Virginia W. Berninger (PhD, psychology, Johns Hopkins University; licensed clinical psychologist) is a professor emeritus at the University of Washington, where she taught courses and advised doctoral and masters' students for 30 years in educational psychology, was a principal investigator on NICHD-funded research (1989–2008, 2011–2016) on assessing and teaching writers with and without specific learning disabilities in writing and a key investigator on other projects, and was active in service and outreach. Her career has been interdisciplinary (including Harvard Medical School and Tufts New England Medical

Center faculty positions and collaborations with geneticists, neuroimagers, educators, speech and language scientists, and computer scientists). Her research on writing has included the role of writing in creating hands-on engagement, developmental stepping-stones in writing, assessment and writing instruction for specific grade levels and populations (dysgraphia, dyslexia, OWL LD, cerebral palsy, spinal-cord injury), the writing path to reading, and the use of computers in writing assessment and writing instruction.

Deborah Brandt is a professor emeritus of English at the University of Wisconsin–Madison. Her research has focused on the changing conditions for literacy and literacy learning in the late twentieth- and early twenty-first-century United States. She has held fellowships from the Guggenheim Foundation, the National Endowment for the Humanities, the American Council of Learned Societies, and the US Department of Education, among others. Her most recent book is *The Rise of Writing: Redefining Mass Literacy* (2015), winner of the 2016 Mina P. Shaughnessy Prize from the Modern Language Association.

Steve Graham is a Mary Emily Warner Professor in the Division of Educational Leadership and Innovation in the Mary Lou Fulton Teachers College at Arizona State University. For more than 30 years he has studied how writing develops, how to teach it effectively, and how writing can be used to support reading and learning. In recent years, he has been involved in the development and testing of digital tools for supporting writing and reading. His research involves typically developing writers and students with special needs in both elementary and secondary schools, with much of it occurring in classrooms in urban schools. He is coeditor of the *Handbook of Writing Research*, the *Handbook of Learning Disabilities*, and the *APA Educational Psychology Handbook,* and coauthor of *Writing Better: Effective Strategies for Teaching Students with Learning Difficulties, Powerful Writing Strategies for all Students,* and *Making the Writing Process Work: Strategies for Composition and Self-Regulation.* He is also coauthor of three influential Carnegie Corporation reports: *Writing Next: Effective Strategies to Improve Writing of Adolescents in Middle and High Schools, Writing to Read: Evidence for How Writing Can Improve Reading,* and *Informing Writing: The Benefits of Formative Assessment.*

Jill V. Jeffery examines how competent writing is conceptualized in instruction and assessment in secondary and postsecondary settings. Her research on writing instruction, assessment, and development has been published in *Research in the Teaching of English;* the *Journal of Literacy Research; Writing and Pedagogy; Assessing Writing;* and *Reading and Writing.* In her current position at the Centre for Linguistics at Leiden

University in the Netherlands, Jeffery is analyzing how frameworks for writing development compare cross-nationally.

Paul Kei Matsuda is a professor of English and director of second language writing at Arizona State University. He has published widely on the teaching and learning of writers who are actively developing language proficiency along with literacy. He is founding chair of the Symposium on Second Language Writing and editor of a book series on second language writing, and has served as the president of the American Association for Applied Linguistics. His recent publications include the *Handbook of Second and Foreign Language Writing* and *Professionalizing Second Language Writing.*

Sandra Murphy, professor emeritus at the University of California, Davis, has coauthored several books on writing and writing assessment, including *Designing Writing Tasks for the Assessment of Writing* (with Leo Ruth), *Writing Portfolios: A Bridge from Teaching to Assessment* and *Uncommonly Good Ideas: Teaching Writing in the Common Core Era* (with Mary Ann Smith), *Portfolio Practices: Lessons from Schools, Districts and States* (with Terry Underwood), and a book series, *Assessment for Learning: Using Rubrics to Improve Student Writing* (with Sally Hampton and Margaret Lowry). She has served as a consultant for a range of educational and assessment programs, including the National Assessment of Educational Progress, the New Standards Project, the Common Core State Standards Initiative, the Smarter Balanced Assessment Consortium, and the National Writing Project.

Deborah Wells Rowe is a professor of early childhood education at Peabody College, Vanderbilt University. Her research focuses on how preschool and primary-grade children learn to write. Recently, she has developed a descriptive measure of preschool writing and conducted research exploring young emergent bilinguals' use of tablet computers and digital cameras for multimodal, multilingual composing. She is the author of a book, *Preschoolers as Authors: Literacy Learning in the Social World of the Classroom,* and numerous research articles.

Mary Schleppegrell is a professor of education at the University of Michigan. Her research studies language development and the role of language in learning, with particular attention to second language learners of English. With her colleague Dr. Chauncey Monte-Sano, she is currently studying the ways middle school teachers support writing development in history/social studies. Her books include *The Language of Schooling: A Functional Linguistics Perspective* (2004*), Developing Advanced Literacy in First and Second Languages: Meaning with Power* (coedited with Cecilia Colombi, 2002), *Reading in Secondary Content Areas: A*

Language-based Pedagogy (with Zhihui Fang, 2008*)*, and *Focus on Grammar and Meaning* (with Luciana de Oliveira, 2015). Her research is published in journals including *Learning and Instruction, Linguistics and Education, TESOL Quarterly,* the *Journal of Writing Research, Language Learning, Research in the Teaching of English, Reading and Writing Quarterly,* the *Annual Review of Applied Linguistics, Assessing Writing,* and *Written Communication.*

Kristen Campbell Wilcox is an assistant professor in the Educational Theory and Practice Department of the University at Albany, State University of New York. A former ESL and EFL teacher at the elementary, secondary, and postsecondary levels in the United States, Puerto Rico, and Brazil, she has focused her research on the intersections of language, culture, and achievement in different disciplinary contexts. She conducted a yearlong ethnography, as well as embedded state and national data analyses in the National Study of Writing Instruction (NSWI), from which she has published articles in journals such as *Writing and Pedagogy, Research in the Teaching of English,* and *English for Specific Purposes.* She also contributed a chapter to the Applebee and Langer book based on NSWI, *Writing Instruction That Works: Proven Methods for Middle and High School Classrooms.*

CONTRIBUTORS

Frances Christie trained as a secondary school teacher of English and history. After some years working in schools she moved into university life, and became involved in the education of teachers of the English language, both as a mother tongue and as a secondary language. She is an emeritus professor of language and literacy education at the University of Melbourne. Her major research and teaching interests are functional grammar, classroom discourse analysis, and writing development. Her publications have included *Language, Knowledge and Pedagogy: Functional Linguistics and Sociological Perspectives* (with J. R. Martin, 2007); *School Discourse: Writing Development across the Years of Schooling* (with B. Derewianka, 2008); *Disciplinarity: Functional Linguistic and Sociological Perspectives* (with K. Maton, 2011); and *Language Education throughout the School Years: A Functional Perspective* (2012).

Kira Geselowitz is currently the learning support specialist for a neuropsychology clinic in Bellevue, Washington, while working toward certification as a school counselor. She discovered her passion for understanding how people learn during undergraduate courses and research in cognitive psychology and Spanish at Northwestern University. In 2013, Geselowitz earned her MEd in curriculum and instruction at the University of Washington and then continued there with three more years of doctoral studies and research in teacher education. She has held various teaching and tutoring roles for students and educators of all ages, ranging from designing and teaching a seventh-grade personal development course to creating and leading multiple teacher professional development and teaching preservice courses focusing on developmental psychology and social-emotional learning. She recently taught a professional development course on integrating a STEAM curriculum in Beijing, and she looks forward to continuing to work with and learn from people around the world.

Mary Ann Smith directed the Bay Area and California Writing Projects and served as director of government relations and public affairs for the National Writing Project. She has coauthored several books on writing and writing assessment, including *Writing Portfolios:*

A Bridge from Teaching to Assessment and *Uncommonly Good Ideas: Teaching Writing in the Common Core Era* (with Sandra Murphy) and *Assessing Writing, Teaching Writers: Putting the Analytic Writing Continuum to Work in Your Classroom* (with Sherry Seale Swain). She served as a consultant to the Department of Defense Dependents' Schools and as a teacher of teachers through the writing project.

Peter Wallis is the director of learning systems and assessment for the University of Washington's Continuum College and a doctoral candidate in the University of Washington College of Education. His work and research most often focus on how adults formulate complex skills. He works with teams to use design-based and quantitative methods to study the learning of complex skills in technology-supported environments. Working at the university provides the opportunity to practice theories of learning in a rich organizational context, with real-world impact on learners around the country. Wallis earned his MEd from the University of Washington with a thesis about poetry as a set of educational technologies. He is currently exploring mycology and dance. He seeks holistic lessons through various life pursuits. Currently he is working on stories and poetry about humans learning in science fiction, using his mycological hobbies to think about ecosystems of learning, and developing talks about the relationship between dancing and leadership.

This book was typeset in Sabon by Barbara Frazier.
The typeface used on the cover is Proxima Nova.
The book was printed on 50-lb. White Offset paper
by King Printing Company, Inc.